BLACK LITERARY MARK
—— 2012 ——

BAPWD

BLACK AUTHORS
&
PUBLISHED WRITERS DIRECTORY

6ᵗʰ Edition

Edited by Grace Adams

A Grace Company Publication

BAPWD

BLACK AUTHORS
&
PUBLISHED WRITERS DIRECTORY

Published by The Grace Publishing Company (USA)

6th Edition. Copyright © 1993, 1995, 2005, 2006, 2007, 2008, 2009, 2010, 2012, The Grace Publishing Company

International Standard Book Number 1-877807-38-9

International Standard Serial Number 1060-9148

Photo Credit: Molefi by Chester Higgins May 19, 2008

Cover Design: Jeff Chen

BLACK LITERARY MARKETPLACE
2012

BAPWD

BLACK AUTHORS
&
PUBLISHED WRITERS DIRECTORY

6th Edition

Edited by Grace Adams

A Grace Company Publication

Carol, McConnell, Jr., Christopher, Aaron, Cache, April, Che'lyn

Introduction

The purpose of the **Black Authors & Published Writers Directory** is to save you from long hours of literary research in your marketing and publishing efforts. All the resources for identifying and reaching Black authors, publishers, producers, agents, services, suppliers and speakers you are likely to ever need are listed here! During the process of compiling and verifying information for this directory, notices and questionnaires were mailed to over 15,000 Black professionals in the literary industry. The tremendous response and completion of the questionnaires by the *Black Literary Marketplace* serves as the basis for the successful completion of this directory. If an author, or literary firm is not listed, it may be due to insufficient information for a complete directory listing, or they may have requested deletion from the directory. Literary professionals currently listed in this directory are encouraged to keep us up-to-date with any change in information appearing in the directory. All additions, changes, or deletions should be sent to the address indicated below.

The world needs to know who you are! We invite all Black literary professionals interested in being listed in future editions of this very resourceful directory to send us their name, address, telephone and fax numbers, e-mail and website addresses. Send all literary information to BAPWD c/o The Grace Publishing Company, 829 Langdon Court, Suite 45, Rochester Hills, Michigan 48307 E-mail: **info@bapwd.com** Website: **www.bapwd.com**

Submitting Your Book or Work

A listing in this directory should not be interpreted as an indication that the publisher, producer or agent accepts unsolicited material. If you are seeking a publisher, producer, or agent, you should first investigate the type of material the agent handles or that the company publishes before submitting your material. Send a query letter. If your material is accepted you may be requested to send additional material which may include sample chapters, or articles previously written about your work. If you are seeking publicity for your book or work e-mail, phone, fax, or postal mail your news/press release, press kit, sales letter, available for interview/tip sheet with teaser questions, mock-up review, and your book to the appropriate media contacts.

Media Coverage

Don't waste your time and money trying to get interviews on a show, or in a newspaper section where your book or work does not fit. To capture media coverage most effectively, you must first understand that newspapers, magazines, newsletters, radio programs, and television news are all driven by common needs to attract advertisers. They have a need to fill time and space, to stand out, to be special, to be first, as well as provide information of value to their readers, viewers, and listeners. Newspaper and magazine editors look for stories that inform, educate, or entertain their viewers. Demonstrate to magazine and newspaper editors, and radio and TV talk show hosts that yours would be a good interview subject, and they will interview you!

"The Ability To Read Awoke In Me A Long Dormant Craving To Be Mentally Alive."

-Malcolm X

About The Editor

Grace Adams
Editor * Publisher * Signatory Agent

In 1990-92, Adams impressed with the vast pool of Black talent in the media, began to compile a listing for her publication, <u>Black Authors and Published Writers Directory.</u> Over 1,000 Black authors, publishers, producers, distributors, song, film, and playwrights, agents, librarians, talk show hosts, consultants, advertising agents and other marketing resources were listed in the book. In 2003, Adams created and founded BAPWD.com the official website of the <u>Black Authors & Published Writers Directory</u>. Like the book, the website is a "must" for anyone interested in networking with major Black media professionals and services. In 2011, Adams founded the first annual <u>Black Literary Marketplace Expo</u>.

Native Greenville, Mississippian, Adams is the first Black signatory agent (*Writers Guild of America*). She has assisted and represented several major talents with book publishing projects, and is editor and publisher of <u>Black Literary Players *(BLP)*</u>, an on-line newsletter update for the <u>Black Authors and Published Writers Directory</u>. Published monthly, the *BL P* newsletter update features Black authors and published writers, profiles and literary and media professional services. Her Rochester, Michigan firm, **The Grace Company,** also acts as a distribution agent for several publishing entities that provide material that meet the needs of business.

What others are saying about . . .

BLACK AUTHORS
&
PUBLISHED WRITERS DIRECTORY

". . . A book that should be on the shelf of any person who is interested in African-American literature and arts."

Lenard D. Moore, author, <u>Desert Storm: A Brief History</u>, Staff Reviewer For Library Journal

"This ground-breaking publication is <u>"the doorway"</u> to the extraordinary world of African creativity. Along with its contents, the book's easy-to-read and well organized format makes it a must resource for anyone interested in the Black writers' market."

Steven Whitehurst, author, <u>Words From An Unchained Mind</u>

"A major resource directory for years to come. . . unleashes the hidden treasure chest of the finest African-American writers, publishers and griots the world over..."

Deborah Ray-Sims, president, Diasporic Communications

Contents

Contents

Profiles

This book is dedicated to Black authors and the thousands of published writers working to effect a change in the world by eliminating illiteracy. May your wonderful works and deeds – as captured on these pages – help others to learn faster and enjoy "the journey" more . .

- Grace Adams

Agents

Barrett Books Agency In 1999, Audra Barrett established Barrett Books, a Maryland-based literary agency, to support a growing population of talented African-American authors who were underrepresented in the publishing industry. Submit original query, book proposal, and resume. Barrett Books Agency, 12138 Central Avenue, Suite 183, Mitchellville, Maryland 20721 E-mail: **audra@barrettbooksagency.com** Website: **www.barrettbooksagency.com**

Marie Brown & Associates Agent, Marie Brown. Literary agent. 40-year veteran of the book business. Since 1984, her agency has represented over 100 authors. Contact Ms. Marie Brown, Marie Brown & Associates, 412 West 154th Street, New York, New York 10032 Phone: (212) 939-9725 Fax: (212) 939-9728 E-mail: **mbrownlit@aol.com**

Connor Literary Agency Agent, Marlene Connor Lynch. Literary agent for books; also handles TV and film rights, general and non-fiction books - popular audience, mystery, thrillers, romance, self-help, how-to, cookbooks and general. Special ability to work with illustrated books. We do some packaging and book producing; negotiates the terms of the publishing agreement, and handles all subsidiary rights retained by the author including first serial, movie/TV rights, and foreign rights. "Query with SASE, Outline." Marlene Connor Lynch, Connor Literary Agency, 2911 West 71st Street, Minneapolis, Minnesota 55423 Phone: (612) 866-1486 E-mail: **connoragency@aol.com**

Crichton & Associates, Inc., Literary Agency Agent, Sha-Shana N.L. Crichton. Crichton & Associates represents writers of fiction and non-fiction works, including materials with African, African-American, Caribbean and Latin American themes. Seeking non-fiction by expert authors, contemporary fiction, commercial fiction, chick-lit, and romance novels (contemporary, inspirational, African-American and multicultural). Contact Crichton & Associates, Inc., 6940 Carroll Avenue, Takoma Park, Maryland 20912 Phone: (301) 495-9663 Fax: (202) 318-0050 E-mail: **cricht1@aol.com** Website: **www.crichton-associates.com**

The Grace Company Literary Agency Agent, Grace Adams. Founder and Editor of the highly acclaimed 'Black Authors & Published Writers Directory,' Also founder and editor of the annual Black Literary Marketplace Expo, since 2011. She is the First Black Signatory Agent (Writers Guild of America). Email queries accepted. Contact Ms. Grace Adams, The Grace Company, 829 Langdon Court, Suite 45, Rochester Hills, Michigan 48307 Phone: (248) 651-6775. E-mail: **graccointern@msn.com** Website: **www.bapwd.com**

Milligan Literary Agency Agent, Dr. Rosie Milligan. Editorial consultant and book agent; ghost writing, book evaluation, book rewriting services for mainstream publishing submission. Milligan Literary Agency, 1425 West Manchester Avenue, Suite C, Los Angeles, California 90047 Phone: (323) 750-3592 E-mail: **DrRosie@aol.com** Website: **www.drrosie.com**

Victoria Sanders & Associates LLC Victoria Sanders, agent. Founded in 1992, represents writers of both fiction and non-fiction. She has been an agent for over a decade, worked in-house at Simon & Schuster, Legal & Contracts and has a law degree. Also has a background in film and television. E-mail us a query letter. Victoria Sanders & Associates LLC, 241 Avenues of Americas, Suite 11H, New York, New York 10014 Phone: (212) 633-8811 Fax: (212) 633-0525 E-mail: **queriesvsa@hotmail.com**

Serendipity Literary Agency LLC Agent, Regina Brooks. A boutique literary agency representing a select list of authors and illustrators. Founded by Regina Brooks in 2000, Serendipity has established a diverse base of award-winning clients in adult and young adult fiction, non-fiction, and children's literature. Our agencies focus is to find and support authors who respect and understand the true craft of writing and are willing to aggressively promote their work. Serendipity Literary Agency LLC., 732 Fulton Street, Suite 3, Brooklyn, New York 11238 E-mail: **rbrooks@serendipitylit.com** Website: **www.serendipitylit.com**

Tracy Sherrod Literary Services Agent, Tracy Sherrod. Formerly in marketing at Holt, Sherrod offers clients everything from marketing to author career counseling, typing, editing, and inputting services. Accept e-mail queries. Tracy Sherrod, Tracy Sherrod Literary Services, Inc., 2034 5th Avenue, Suite 2A, New York, New York 10035 Phone: (212) 369-6785

Nichole L. Shields Associate Agent. Connor Literary Agency is a full service agency dedicated to advising and guiding writers in every aspect of their literary career, as well as advising writers of the best way to develop their book idea for the successful presentation to publishers. Nichole L. Shields, Connor Literary Agency, 1645 West Ogden Avenue, Suite 309, Chicago, Illinois 60612 E-mail: **nicholelshields@yahoo.com**

Maxine Thompson's Literary Services and Literary Agency Agent, Maxine E. Thompson. Literary services, and literary agency works with ebooks, fiction, non-fictional books, short story collections, memoirs or autobiographies. Contact Ms. Maxine E. Thompson, Black Butterfly Press, Post Office Box 25279, Philadelphia Pennsylvania, 19119 E-mail: **maxtho@aol.com** Website: **www.maxinethompson.com**

Artists/Illustrators

James Eugene Albert Digital Artist. Exhibitions: Permanent Gallery Artist at World Fine Art, Inc., 2002 - 2004, New York; Permanent Gallery Artist at ARTWorks Gallery, 1997- 2004. Honors and Awards: "First runner up to First Place" Encyclopedia of Living Artists, 9th Edition, 1995; Academic Associate Art Institute, Verbano, Italy, 2001. Juried Shows: "The Best Contemporary Art Juried Collection" CD, Art Communications International, 1996, New York; "Out of the Internet," Sharon Arts Center, Peterborough, New Hampshire, 1995. Education: 1971 - 1985, University of California at Los Angeles and Berkeley. Contact Mr. James Eugene Albert, 601 Van Ness, Suite E 3518, San Francisco, California 94102 Phone: (415) 776-6632 E-mail: jamesealbert@email.msn.com Website: www.jameseugenealbert.com

Paul Alleyne Visual artist, poetry and fiction author of two books, Whatever It Takes, and the book, These Are Our Stories. Paul Alleyne, 2643 Bridgewater Drive, Grand Prairie, Texas 75054 E-mail: paul.alleyne@gmail.com Website: www.redbubble.com/people/bambooo

Ron Anderson Visual Artist and art consultant, Mr. Anderson is an oil painter and an art educator and has been a successful working artist for more than 20 years. He has earned many awards for his oil paintings and was a nominee for the 2005 Governor's Awards for the Arts in Ohio, in the Individual Artist category. Ron's biographical information/photograph was included in the 2004 edition, the 2006 edition, and the 2007 edition of Who's Who in Black Columbus. Mrs. Robin Anderson, Ron Anderson Studio, LLC, Post Office Box 340241, Columbus, Ohio 43234 E-mail: admin@ronandersonstudio.com Website: www.ronandersonstudio.com

Michael Billups Artist. Paintings, watercolors, graphite drawings, giclee's and poems. My paintings pay homage to the diverse beauty of the Black Woman. Michael Billups, 702 15th Street South East, Washington, DC 20003 Phone: (202) 544-7285 Fax: (630) 214-2225 E-mail: michaelbillups@hotmail.com Website: www.billupsstudio.com

Deborah Branch Artist/Illustrator. B.A. Fine Arts. Drawings done in chalk pastels, pen & ink, pencil, watercolor. Portraits done from photos. Oil paintings on canvas, collage, digital photography. Jewelry. Contact Ms. Deborah Branch, 402 Lake Havasu Drive, Virginia Beach, Virginia 23454 Phone: (757) 831-2256 E-mail: drawu@juno.com

Kimberly Cheri Brown Author/illustrator of "Beautiful Like ME!", the multicultural coloring activity book that focuses on building positive self-esteem. Ms. Brown is a much sought after illustrator and writer (grants, children's books, niche audiences). Certificate in Graphic Arts, Madison County Career Academy, Huntsville, Alabama, 1999. Concentration: Graphic Design. Clients include: Tennessee State University, YWCA, Arvie Personnel Services, Professionally Speaking, Inc., Lawson State Community College, and many others. Kimberly Cheri Brown, Post Office Box 331971, Nashville, Tennessee 37203 Phone: (615) 474-1487 E-mail: kim@kimberlycbrown.com Website: www.kimberlycbrown.com

Vonetta Booker-Brown   Accomplished journalist and writer, editor, virtual assistant, web designer and graphic artist, Ms. Brown's client roster includes CB Commercial, UBS Warburg, Pitney Bowes, Weekly Reader Corporation, Essence Communications, Daymon Worldwide and PH Factor Productions. She is also designer, creator and editor of Triscene.com, an online magazine that covers the New York and Connecticut area. Ms. Vonetta Booker-Brown, Right Hand Concepts, 2020 Pennsylvania Avenue, North West, #341, Washington, DC 20006 E-mail: chiefelement@gmail.com Website: www.righthandconcepts.com

Cliff Chandler   Professional Photographer - German School of Photography, Jazz Musician - The New Muse, Brooklyn, New York, and an editorial writer for a local newspaper. His education includes: Fine Art Major, Pratt Institute, Brooklyn, New York, Masters Writing courses at New York University, and Editing classes at The New School. His photographs hang in private collections all over the world and in museums here in America. An award winning author he has written a book of poetry, Chants, Rants, and Raves, and ten novels, four of which are published, The Paragons, Vengeance Is Mine, and Devastated. Devastated was selected as Mystery Novel of the Year, 2004, by JADA PRESS. Motherless Child is his fourth novel. Cliff Chandler, 2492 Tredway Drive, Macon, Georgia 31211 E-mail: CDuke23@aol.com Website: www.authorsden.com/cliffchandler

Ron Clowney Design   Design company offers both traditional art services in addition to computer graphics design work in the areas of print and animation. The traditional art services are pencil or painted portraits, pencil drawings. We also design and construct websites. Contact Ron Clowney, 5027 Brighton Avenue, San Diego, California 92107 Phone: (619) 459-8805 E-mail: rclowney@cox.net Website: www.ronclowney.net

Maurice Copeland Artist, author and poet, Maurice Copelands' poems have appeared in National publications, Frontier Report and The Secular Humanist. Contact Mr. Maurice Copeland, 8415 East 56th Street, Kansas City, Missouri 64129 Phone: (816) 550-9563

Jerry Craft   Worked with cartoonist Barbara Slate on comic books such as New Kids On The Block for Harvey Comics, and Sweet 16 and Yuppies From Hell, two series that she developed for Marvel Comics. In 1987, I sold my first comic strip, The Outside View, to a couple of local newspapers in New York. In September of 1990, I began self-syndicating this retooled strip (which I renamed Mama's Boyz) to The City Sun in New York and 10 other weekly papers across the country. In 1995, Mama's Boyz was picked up by the King Features Weekly Service-- a collection of cartoons and columns that is distributed to more than 1,500 newspapers around the world! The New York Daily News then used Mama's Boyz as part of their special Harlem Week supplement in August of 1995. My comics have appeared in The Village Voice and The New York Daily News, to name a few. Also drawn or written gags for a couple of syndicated features such as Laff-A-Day, and Tar Pit. Jerry Craft, 304 Main Avenue, PMB #114, Norwalk, Connecticut 06851 E-mail: JerryCraft@aol.com Website: www.mamasboyz.com

Ronald Davis Award winning visual artist and graphic designer providing full artistic services, quality web backgrounds, book and CD covers, posters/fliers/handbrochures, fine art, etc. Ronald Davis, Upfromsumdirt, Post Office Box 3861, Midway, Kentucky 40347 Phone: (859) 433-1503 E-mail: upfromsumdirt@yahoo.com Website: www.mythiumlitmag.com

Anna W. Edwards Fine Artist. Open Thursday from 1pm-5pm. Contact Ms. Anna W. Edwards, 237 East 14th Street, San Leandro, California 94577 Phone: (510) 636-1721 E-mail: **annawedwards@gmail.coms.com** Website: **www.annawedwards.com**

Conrad E. Gardner A self taught artist who grew up in Bronx, New York. His work is inspired by his love of history and predominantly depicts African/African Americans in roles in which they are not traditionally seen. Mr. Conrad E. Gardner, Hotep Creations, 2776 Parkview Terrace, Suite 1L, Bronx, New York 10468 E-mail: **hotepcreations@yahoo.com** Website: **www.hotepcreations.com**

J. Lee Cooper-Giles Author of The Hypocrites. A lifelong political and social activist, Cooper-Giles has three under-graduate college degrees from the Ohio State University, a BA in Black Studies and English, BA in Journalism, BFA in Painting and Drawing. J. Lee Cooper-Giles, 1761 Clifton Avenue #10, Columbus, Ohio 43203 E-mail: **leegiles78@hotmail.com**

Cassandra Gillens A self-taught artist, Cassandra's art can be found from all parts of the Low country, and various states throughout America and featured in dozens of newspapers and magazines such as Southern Living Magazine. Benjamin Gillens, Studio Manager. Cassandra Gillens Studio, Post Office Box 884 Beaufort, South Carolina 29901 Phone: (843) 592-0944 E-mail: **gillensart@hargray.com** Website: **www.cassandragillens.com**

Tania Guerrera Artist: Fine Art Originals, Glicee reproductions, posters, greeting cards, t-shirts, books, and more by this artists. Also, author of the book Thoughts and Transformations, thoughts, art, and revolutionary essays. Tania Guerrera, 311 North Avenue #11, New Rochelle, New York 10801 Phone: (917) 578-4264 E-mail: **TheArtist@taniaGuerrera.com** Website: **www.TaniaGuerrera.com**

Akua Lezli Hope Poet, Writer, Artist. Ms. Akua Lezli Hope won two Artists Fellowships from the New York Foundation for the Arts (1987, 2003), a Ragdale U.S.-Africa Fellowship (1993), and a Creative Writing Fellowship from The National Endowment for The Arts (1990). She received an Artists Crossroads Grant (2003) from The Arts of the Southern Finger Lakes for her project, Words on Motion. She is a founding section leader in the Poetry Forum on CompuServe. Her manuscript, The Prize is the Journey was a finalist in the 1983 Walt Whitman contest. Also, a founding member of the Black Writers Union and the New Renaissance Writers. Contact Ms. Akua Lezli Hope, Post Office Box 33, Corning, New York 14830 E-mail: **akua@artfarm.com** Website: **www.artfarm.com**

Adin Kachisi Visionary, social critic, writer and an artist, his writings deal with societal issues like values, development, politics, economics, education, identity, spirituality and societal transformation. Mr. Adin Kachisi, 4049 Broadway, Box #190, New York, New York 10032 Fax: (360) 406-9287 E-mail: **akachisi@yahoo.com**

Roxann Latimer Writer, poet, journalist, artist, and entrepreneur, Roxann works as a television producer with her company WIM Media and as Publisher and Editor in Chief of Women In Motion magazine. Roxann Latimer, 3900 West 22nd Lane #10G, Yuma, Arizona 85364 Phone: (928) 257-5974 E-mail: **roxann@roxannlatimer.com** Website: **www.roxannlatimer.com**

Mythium The brain child of award-winning author, Crystal E. Wilkinson and visual artist/poet, Ronald Davis (upfromsumdirt). Wilkinson is a visiting professor, Morehead State University, 2002 recipient of the Chaffin Award for Appalachian Literature. Contact Ms. Crystal Wilkinson, Mythium Literary Journal, 1439 Leestown Road, Lexington, Kentucky 40511 Phone: (859) 381-8133 E-mail: **wilkinsoncrystal@aol.com** Website: **www.mythiumlitmag.com**

Leo D. Sullivan Artist/Animator, writer, publisher and producer of videos and books. Contact Vignette Multimedia, 1800 South Robertson Boulevard, #286, Los Angeles, California 90035 Phone: (323) 939-4174 Fax: (323) 939-2762 E-mail: **vignmulti@aol.com** Website: **www.afrokids.com**

Nicole Tadgell Illustrator. Nicole Tadgell, 14 Sampson Street, Spencer, Massachusetts 01562 Phone: (508) 885-7723 E-mail: **nickietart@yahoo.com** Website: **www.nicoletadgell.com**

George Edward Tait Multi-talented artist, musician, educator, and activist. Editor/ Publisher: Cosmic Colors (A Black Music Magazine) 1974. Curator and featured artist for The Black Solar Art Gallery (1973). Chairman, Pan-Alkebu-Lan Rhythm. Composer, sound editor, and actor for film Oh! My God! (1972). Faculty Member, Queens College S.E.E.K. Program. Contact Mr. George Edward Tait, Post Office Box 1305, New York, New York 10035 E-mail: **georgeedwardtait@msn.com** Website: **www.georgeedwardtait.org**

Monroe S. Tarver Attended Savannah College of Art. Monroe S. Tarver, 8926 North Greenwood Avenue, 133, Niles, Illinois 60714 Phone: (847) 398-5060 Fax: (847) 398-1156 E-mail: **worldoftarver@msn.com** Website: **www.talesfromthemapmaker.com**

Michele Treesong New Jersy-born artist. Prints and commissioned works. Contact Ms. Michele Treesong, Post Office Box 135, Cochran, Georgia 31014 Phone: (404) 665-7199 E-mail: **micheletreesong@artuncommon.com** Website: **www.artuncommon.com**

Charlotte Riley-Webb Earned her B.F.A. degree from The Cleveland Institute of Art. Began her M.F.A. at Georgia State University, screen printing at The Atlanta College of Art, mono-printing and abstract art at Tougaloo College, Mississippi. Webb's work is included in numerous, private, business and corporate collections. She received a September 2005 fellowship to The Hambidge Art Center and the Women's Studio Workshop, New York in January 2006. Ms. Charlotte Riley-Webb, 120 Sandy Drive, Stockbridge, Georgia 30281 Phone: (678) 284-1770 E-mail: **cwebbart@bellsouth.net** Website: **www.charlotterileywebb.com**

Fredrick Woodard Visual artist and poet. Professor at the University of Iowa. Contact Mr. Fredrick Woodard, 2905 Prairie du Chien Road, North East, Iowa City, Iowa 52240 E-mail: **fredrick-woodard@uiowa.edu**

Associations

Association For The Study Of African-American Life And History Committed to education, research, and publishing African American history and culture. Ms. Sylvia Cyrus, Executive Director, ASALH, 2225 Georgia Avenue, NW, Suite 331, Washington, DC 20059 Phone: (202) 238-5910 Fax: (202) 986-1506 E-mail: info@asalh.net Website: www.asalh.net

Association Of African American Web Designers (AAWDD) Online index of black professional web developers located through out the United States. In our listing, you will find web and graphic designers, programmers, writers, system administrators, marketers, e-commerce, flash and network specialist, and other web professionals. Contact AAWDD, Post Office Box 146, Malone, New York 12953 Website: www.africanamericanwebdesigners.com

Bay Area Black Journalists Association (BABJA) Formed in 1982 the BABJA exists to serve as an advocate and beneficial network of journalists, students and media-related professionals. Bob Butler, President. BABJA, 1714 Franklin #100-260, Oakland, California 94612 Phone: (510) 464-1000 E-mail: sfbabja@gmail.com Website: www.babja.org

Black Caucus Of The American Library Association (BCALA) National association of Black librarians serves as an advocate for the development, promotion, and improvement of library services and resources to the nation's African American community. The BCALA publishes a monthly newsletter and librarians list on labels. Wanda Brown, President. Contact BCALA, Jos N. Holman, County Librarian, Tippecanoe County Public Library, 627 South Street, Lafayette, Indiana 47901 E-mail: webeditor@bcala.org Website: www.bcala.org

Black Entertainment & Music Association Bob Lott, President. Black Entertainment & Music Association, 1501 Christian Street, Suite 200, Philadelphia, Pennsylvania 19146 Phone: (215) 545-5850 Fax: (215) 609-4425 E-mail: blott@bemanow.org Website: www.bemanow.org

Black Entertainment & Sports Lawyers Association (BESLA) Members represent leading celebrities and professionals in the entertainment and sports industries. Denis E. Kellman, Esq. President. BESLA, Post Office Box 441485, Fort Washington, Maryland 20749 Phone: (301) 248-1818 Fax: (301) 248-0700 E-mail: BESLAmailbox@aol.com Website: www.besla.org

Black Journalists Association of Southern California A chapter of the National Association of Black Journalists. Lois Pitter Bruce, President. BJASC, Post Office Box 75129, Los Angeles, California 90075 Phone: (213) 427-8246 E-mail: info@bjasc.org Website: www.bjasc.org

Black Storytellers Association National association promotes and perpetuates the art of Black storytelling-an art form which embodies the history, heritage, and culture of African Americans. Linda Goss NABS, Post Office Box 67722, Baltimore, Maryland 21215 Phone: (410) 947-1117 Fax: (410) 947-1117 E-mail: questions@nabsinc.org Website: www.nabsinc.org

Historical Black Press Foundation Founded in late 1999, HBPF fosters dialogue between mainstream media and minority news organizations, executives, and professionals. Operates Black Press Radio and the Black Press Career Diversity Center. Held on the third Friday of September HBPF established the Black Press All Stars Awards to honor the Leaders in the Black press. Also publishes the Black Press Yearbook, a national directory with complete listings of the Black and minority media. Contact Black Press Foundation, 1629 K Street, North West 3rd Floor, Washington, DC 20006 Phone: (646) 322-3047 Fax: (203) 738-3047 E-mail: **blackpressmagazine@yahoo.com** Website: **www.blackpress.org**

Motown Alumni Association, Inc. The Association helps artists, performers, and or musicians to move forward as professional entertainers. Most of our consulting services are free. We deal with amateurs, semi-professionals and professional entertainers. Billy J. Wilson, Founder, Motown Alumni Association, Inc. 621 Orleans # 65, Detroit, Michigan 48207 Phone: (734) 972-7582 E-mail: **Billy_j_Wilson@Yahoo.com** Website: **www.motownalumniassociation.com**

National Association For Multi-Ethnicity in Cable NAMIC educates the industry on marketing approaches, programming interests and operations strategies for our nation's ever-changing population, and guides industry understanding of these complex issues. Our leadership development programs give the tools for professional growth directly to employees, ensuring people of color will be a major part of the power base in the new millennium. Kathy Johnson, President. NAMIC, Inc., 336 West 37th Street, Suite 302, New York, New York 10018 Phone: (212) 594-5985 E-mail: **info@namic.com** Website: **www.namic.com**

National Association For The Study and Performance Of African American Music (NASPAAM) Newsletter/Professional Organization. Organized in 1972, in Atlanta, Georgia as the National Black Music Caucus. Two-hundred black musicians attending the biennial meeting of the Music Educators National Conference gathered at Morehouse College to protest their exclusion from MENC divisional and national Planning sessions and programs. NASPAAM now exists as a non-profit professional organization whose members are dedicated to promoting, performing, and preserving all facets of African American music. The organization serves by increasing the awareness of Black Music and its contribution to the arts, culture, and society. Frank Suggs, President. NASPAAM, 1201 Mary Jane, Memphis, Tennessee 38116 Phone: (901) 396-2913 E-mail: **f.suggs@naspaam.org** Website: **www.naspaam.org**

National Association Of African American Studies & Affiliates Seeks to further research and promote interest in African American studies. The association provides a forum for research and artistic endeavors; provides information and contact resources for its members, and conducts educational programs. Host a national conference. Contact NAAAS & Affiliates, Post Office Box 6670, Scarborough, Maine 04070 Phone: (207) 839-8004 Fax: (207) 839-3776 E-mail: **natlaffiliates@earthlink.net** Website: **www.naaas.org**

National Association Of Black Accountants (NABA) Represents the interests of over 100,000 African-Americans and other minorities participating in the fields of accounting, auditing, business, consulting, finance, and information technology. Annual convention. Calvin Harris Jr., NABA, 7474 Greenway Center Drive, Suite 1120 Greenbelt, Maryland 20770 Phone: (301) 474-6222 Fax: (301) 474-3114 E-mail: **media@nabainc.org** Website: **www.nabainc.org**

National Association of Black Female Executives in Music & Entertainment, Inc. A 501 (c) (6) nonprofit professional organization led by volunteer entertainment executives, NABFEME was launched in February 1999 with a mission to raise the profile and elevate the awareness of Black women in music and entertainment. Former DreamWorks Records Head of Urban Promotion, Johnnie Walker, founded NABFEME in 1998. Before taking the reins at DreamWorks, Walker had previously served as Senior Vice President of R&B Promotion at the Island Def Jam Music Group, having joined the staff of Def Jam Recordings in 1990 at the personal invitation of label founder Russell Simmons. During her 14-year tenure at the Island Def Jam Music Group, Walker was instrumental in developing the careers of some of the biggest names in recorded music including Jay-Z, Ja Rule, Ashanti, Ludacris, DMX, LL Cool J, Musiq, Dru Hill, Foxy Brown, Method Man, Case, Onyx and Montell Jordan, as well as fostering the success of the "Rush Hour" and "The Nutty Professor" soundtracks, among numerous other projects. The organization's COO and annual Women's Leadership Summit Executive Director is Elektra Entertainment Vice President, Michelle Madison. Contact Ms. Johnnie Walker, President, NABFEME, 111 South Highland, Suite 388, Memphis, Tennessee 38111 Phone: (901) 236-8439 E-mail: **mailto:johnnie_walker1@msn.com nabfeme@gmail.com** Website: **www.nabfeme.org**

National Association of Black Journalist (NABJ) Organization of journalists, students and media-related professionals that provide quality programs and services to and advocates on behalf of black journalists worldwide. National Association of Black Journalists, 1100 Knight Hall, Suite 3100, College Park, Maryland 20742 Phone: (301) 405-0248 Fax: (301) 314-1714 E-mail: **mfoster@nabj.org** Website: **www.nabj.org**

National Association Of Black Owned Broadcasters (NABOB) The first and largest trade organization representing the interests of African-American owners of radio and television stations across the country. The association was organized in 1976 by a small group of African-American broadcasters who desired to establish a voice and a viable presence in the industry and to address specific concerns facing African-American broadcasters. James Winston, Executive Director. NABOB, 1201 Connecticut Avenue, North West, Suite 200, Washington, DC 20036 Phone: (202) 463-8970 Fax: (202) 429-0657 E-mail: **nabobinfo@nabob.org** Website: **www.nabob.org**

National Association of Negro Musicians, Inc. Founded in Chicago, Illinois on May 3, 1919, NANM is the country's oldest organization dedicated to the preservation, encouragement and advocacy of all music of African Americans. NANM provides assistance, performance opportunities and black cultural awareness to serious music students and awards scholarships to scores of talented young musicians throughout the country. NANM holds a national convention in a different city each year, offering a chance to participate in workshops, seminars, lectures and performances. NANM, Post Office Box 43053, Chicago, Illinois 60643 Phone: (773) 568-3818 Fax: (773) 568-5388 E-mail: **organdiva@earthlink.net** Website: **www.nanm.org**

National Black MBA Association (NBMBA) Professional organization. Members. Publishes a monthly magazine and a newsletter. Contact Robin Melton, NBMBA, 180 North Michigan Avenue, #1400, Chicago, Illinois 60601 Phone: (312) 236-2622 Fax: (312) 236-0390 E-mail: **mail@nbmbaa.org** Website: **www.nbmbaa.org**

National Newspaper Publishers Association (NNPA)   Also known as the Black Press of America, The NNPA is a 62-year-old federation of more than 200 Black community newspapers from across the United States.   Since World War II, it has also served as the industry's news service, a position that it has held without peer or competitor since the Associated Negro Press dissolved by 1970.   NNPA, 3200 13th Street, North, Washington, DC 20010 Phone: (202) 319-1291 E-mail: **news@nnpa.org** Website: **www.nnpa.org**

Unity: Journalists of Color, Inc.   A strategic alliance advocating news coverage about people of color, and aggressively challenging its organizations at all levels to reflect the nation's diversity. Unity represents more than 10,000 journalists of color comprised of four national associations: Asian-American Journalists Association, National Association of Black Journalists, National Association of Hispanic Journalists, and the Native American Journalists Association. Newsletter. Executive Director, Onica Makwakwa. Contact Unity, 1601 North Kent Street, Suite 1003, Arlington, Virginia 22209 Phone: (703) 854-3585 E-mail: **info@unityjournalists.org** Website: **www.unityjournalists.org**

The Warwick Valley Writers' Association   Founder and Director L. Guy Burton, through this local writers' group has been able to polish, complete and promote several Works in various genres, as well as help others to do the same. L. Guy Burton, The Warwick Valley Writers' Association, 12 Burton Lane, Warwick, New York 10990 E-mail: **el_guybur@hotmail.com** Website: **www.warwickinfo.net**

Attorneys

Abdul-Jalil al-Hakim President/CEO of Superstar Management world renowned for unprecedented services for Muhammed Ali, Brian Taylor, U.S. Rep. J.C. Watts, Warner Bros. Records, Deion Sanders, Delvin Williams, Giant Records, Kareem Abdul-Jabbar, Capitol Records, Lyman Bostock, Evander Holyfield, EMI Records, to name a few. We negotiate and draft all agreements for all publishing, merchandising and licensing; commercial advertisements and product endorsements; corporate sponsorships and affiliations; motion picture, television, radio and personal appearances; electronic multimedia, literary, publishing, merchandising, and licensing, He was the first African-American in the field and has taught and lectured Entertainment Law for 30 years. Mr. Abdul-Jalil al-Hakim, Superstar Management, 7633 Sunkist Drive, Oakland California 94605 E-mail: (510) 638-0808 Fax: (510) 638-8889 E-mail: jalil@superstarmanagement.com Website: www.superstarmanagement.com

Corey D. Boddie Entertainment attorney specializing in copyright/trademark litigation in the areas of music, fashion, and film, Mr. Boddie is a summa cum laude graduate of the University of Virginia, and a graduate of Southern University Law Center. His client roster includes: the clothing company Meoshe, KING and RIDE Magazine, Todd 1 and Visionary Media, LLC, Nokio of R&B group, Dru Hill, Lady Bug Mecca, formerly of Grammy Award Winning group, Digable Planets, musical icon, KOOL & THE GANG, chart-topping reggae artists Wayne Wonder, Bad Boy recording artists Black Rob and MTV's "Da Band" E. Ness, songwriter "Taj" Jackson, and many other stars in the entertainment world. Corey D. Boddie, Esq., Boddie & Associates, 2040 Exchange Place, Suite 1800, New York, New York 10005 Phone: (212) 480-7652 Fax: (212) 480-6581 E-mail: **C.Boddie@earthlink.net** Website: **www.boddieassoc.com**

John L. Burris An author and an attorney Burris earned a law degree from UC Berkeley School of Law - Boalt Hall and MBA from UC Berkeley Graduate School of Business. He is best known for his work in the area of plaintiff's civil rights over the last 25 plus years and as a legal analyst on Fox, MSNBC, Court TV, CNN and many local television and radio stations. He is the author of the book BLUE vs. BLACK: Let's End the Conflict between Police and Minorities. He has represented Barry Bonds, Tupac Shakur, Delroy Lindo, Dwayne Wiggins, Keyshawn Johnson, Gary Payton, Jason Kidd, and numerous public officials. He was selected as a member of the top 100 trial lawyers in California in 2007, by the American Trial Lawyers Association. John L. Burris, Esq. Airport Corporate Centre, 7677 Oakport Street, Suite 1120, Oakland, California 94621 Phone: (510) 379-7215 Fax: (510) 839-3882 Website: **www.johnburrislaw.com**

Robert A. Celestin, Esq. A multi-faceted law firm which provides hands-on legal advice and counsels the careers of recording artists, record producers, publishers, songwriters, record company executives, managers and production companies. Our firm drafts, negotiates and renegotiates entertainment-related publishing, producer, management, touring, and copyright license agreements. Robert A. Celestin, Esq., 250 West 57th Street, Suite 2331, New York, New York 10107 Phone: (212) 262-1103 Website: **www.raclawfirm.com**

Sha-Shana N.L. Crichton, Esq.   Author and entertainment attorney, Crichton frequently lectures on negotiating publishing contracts and author-editor-agent relationships. She counsels artists, authors, musicians, photographers, and other creative entities regarding drafting, and negotiating contracts, copyrights, wills, small business management, permits and employment issues relating to intellectual property, Sha-Shana N.L. Crichton, Esq. Crichton & Associates, Inc., 6940 Carroll Avenue, Takoma Park, Maryland 20912 Phone: (301) 495-9663 Fax: (202) 318-0050 E-mail: cricht1@aol.com Website: www.crichton-associates.com

Crystal Clear Music Company provides independent record labels with copyright and royalty administration and accounting for their albums they distribute. Also provides royalty collections, royalty accounting & audits, music/sample clearance and music publishing administration for recording artists, producers, songwriters, music publishers, entertainment attorneys and more. Also provides music/sample clearance, royalty collections and royalty audits on behalf of its clients. Founder Cheryl M. Potts was selected as one of the Top 50 Black Women in Entertainment by Black Noir Magazine. Cheryl Potts, NABFEME, 59 Maiden Lane, 27th Floor, New York, New York 10038 Fax: (201) 313-1192 E-mail: emailus@crystalclearmusic.com Website: www.crystalclearmusic.com

Dedra S. Davis One of the most highly sought after speakers in the nation on entertainment law issues, Davis represents platinum, gold, as well as uncertified artists, producers, writers, record labels, managers and publishing companies from all over the world. In addition to reading, writing, and negotiating entertainment contracts, placing tracks, and placing music in movies and TV, she provides worldwide entertainment business consulting services, and has strong relationships with major records labels, publishing, production, movie, and television companies all over the world. The world took notice when she began independently representing Saregama India Limited, against Dr. Dre, Aftermath, Interscope, and Universal Records in a copyright infringement case. Dedra S. Davis, Esq., 26 Broadway, Suite 400, New York, New York 10004 Texas: 7322 Southwest Freeway, Suite 1100, Houston, Texas, 77242 Phone: (713) 981-3861 Fax: (713) 981-3862 E-mail: DEDRADAVIS@musiclw.com Website: www.musiclw.com

Andrea Hence Evans, Esq.   Intellectual Property, Patent, Trademark, and Copyright Law. Working as a former Patent Examiner and Trademark Examining Attorney at the United States Patent and Trademark Office (USPTO), Evans provides intellectual property counseling services, international intellectual property consulting, and intellectual property litigation and licensing services. Currently servicing solo inventors, entrepreneurs, small, medium and Fortune 100 clients. Andrea Hense Evans, Esq., 1425 K Street NW, Suite 350, Washington, DC 20005 Phone: (202) 461-3254 Fax: (888) 799-0847 E-mail: **Andrea.Evans@evansiplaw.com** Website: **www.evansiplaw.com**

Alicia D. Ferriabough An Associate attorney, who focuses her practice on transactional entertainment law counseling and advising clients in a wide range of matters in the music and film industry, including drafting and negotiating recording, producer, and personal management agreements to advising clients regarding film financing, development and licensing. She has represented artists, such as Mobb Deep, Darryl McDaniels (DMC of Run DMC), and Japanese recording artist Toshi, to name a few. Alicia D. Ferriabough, Esq., 250 West 57th Street, Suite 2331, New York, New York 10107 Phone: (212) 262-1103 Website: **www.raclawfirm.com**

Willie Gary, Esq. Featured in Ebony magazine as one of the "100 Most Influential Black Americans," and Forbes magazine has him listed as one of the "Top 50 Attorneys in the U.S," Mr. Willie Gary's is in great demand as a motivational speaker. In addition, he is committed to enhancing the lives of young people through education and drug prevention. In 1991, Mr. Gary donated $10.1 million to his alma mater Shaw University, and in 1994, he and his wife, Gloria, formed The Gary Foundation which provides scholarships and other resources to youth, so they can realize their dreams of achieving a higher education. Mr. Willie Gary, Esq., The Gary Law Group, 320 South Indian River Drive, Ft. Pierce, Florida 34948 Phone: (772) 464-2352 Fax: (772) 464-4226 Website: **www.garylawgroup.com**

Richard B. Jefferson, Esq. Began his career working in-house at Virgin Records America, Inc. where he routinely interacted with the high profile artists and companies that were part of the Virgin family, such as Janet Jackson, Lenny Kravitz, Tina Turner, Blackground Records (Aaliyah, Tank), Smashing Pumpkins, Beanie Man, John Lee Hooker, N.E.R.D. (The Neptunes), Guru, D'Angelo, Rap-A-Lot Records (Scarface, Ghetto Boys). Thereafter, he worked with an Entertainment Law firm that represented a wide range of high profile company and talent clients in music, film, television, fashion, and new media including the conglomeration of companies owned by hip hop pioneer Master P. His client list covers music, motion picture, home video, television, print, new media, fashion, Internet, mobile, and video gaming. Richard B. Jefferson, Esq., Fagerholm & Jefferson, 3500 West Olive Avenue, 3rd Floor, Burbank, California 91505 Phone: (818) 973-2731 Fax: (818) 973-2781 E-mail: **rbjefferson@fjlawcorp.com** Website: **www.fjlawcorp.com**

Richard Manson, Esq. Manson, Johnson, Stewart & Associates is a full service law firm with a diverse practice encompassing broad areas of the law. Areas of Experience: Entertainment Law, Contract Drafting, Review and Negotiations, Corporate Formation and Litigation, Intellectual Property. Attorney Manson formed Millennium Entertainment Group (MEG) a wholly integrated entertainment and sports management company specializing in Personal Management, Intellectual Property Development, Alternative Marketing and Special Event Production. (MEG) is the management company behind successful career directions of Eight Time Grammy Winner - CeCe Winans, Creator & Host of BET's #1 Program - Bobby Jones Gospel and Video Gospel. MEG was instrumental in acquiring multi-platinum recording artist, Two Time Grammy Winner - Kurumt for Death Row's "Dogg Pound", Roscoe - a young rapper signed to Priority Records, and MTV's-The Cut Winner, Silk-E, and others. Richard Manson, Esq., 1223 5th Avenue, North Germantown, Nashville, Tennessee 37208 Phone: (615) 254-1600 Fax: (615) 891-2407 E-mail: **richard.manson@themansongroup.com** Website: **www.themansongroup.com**

Darrell D. Miller, Esq. Film, Motion Picture, Television. A prominent entertainment lawyer with more than 19 years experience in entertainment law, Miller focuses his practice on transactional law with an emphasis on the motion picture, television, music and multimedia industries. Prior to joining Fox Rothschild as a partner, he was a partner and co-founder of Mason Miller LLP, where he has been consistently named among the Top 50 Showbiz Players by Black Enterprise magazine. Mr. Miller was also inducted into the Black Entertainment & Sports Lawyers Association Hall of Fame in, 2007. Contact Darrell D. Miller, Esq., Fox Rothchild LLP, 2000 Market Street, Philadelphia, Pennsylvania 19103 Phone: (310) 598-4174 Fax: (310) 556-9828 E-mail: **dmiller@foxrothschild.com** Website: **www.foxrothschild.com**

Gregory J. Reed, Esq. Author, agent, entertainment attorney and producer, Reed's experiences are diverse and he is the only attorney to represent six (6) world champion boxers: Thomas Hearns, Hilmer Kenty, Leon Spinks, Pipino Cuvas, and Tony Tucker. He was instrumental in negotiating one of the largest contracts in boxing history in excess of 30 million dollars involving Thomas Hearns and Sugar Ray Leonard. Reed negotiated the unification of all boxing titles involving Mike Tyson and Tony Tucker. He was the chief lead counsel involving the first historical multi-million dollar lawsuit case, Miss Carole Gist (first black Miss USA 1990) v. Miss Universe, Inc., Pageant, settled (Jan. 1992). Reed was selected to be the legal counsel for Nelson Mandela's tour committee of Michigan. Civil Rights Legend, Ms. Rosa Parks' attorney for the last 15 years, he represented her in her case against rappers OutKast/BMI Records. Contract areas include The Statue of Liberty restoration projects; radio announcers; movie contracts; TV project syndication; corporate clients; and attorneys. Education: B.S., Michigan State University (Engineering); M.S., Michigan State University (Management Science); J.D., Wayne State University; L.L.M., Wayne State University (Master Of Taxation Law). Gregory J. Reed, Esq., Gregory J. Reed & Associates, 1201 Bagley, Detroit, Michigan 48226 Phone: (313) 961-3580 Fax: (313) 961-3582 E-mail: gjrassoc@aol.com Website: www.gjreedlaw.com

Jock Smith, Esq. An original founder of The Cochran Firm; of the late, famed attorney Johnnie L. Cochran, Jr., Jock Smith upholds Johnnie's legacy as the Firm's National President. Sports Agent/Principal Stockholder, Cochran Sports Management (Certified via National Football Players Association and National Basketball Players Association as a players agent). Represented along with partner Johnnie L. Cochran, Jr., professional athletes with contract negotiations with professional teams as well as promotional appearances; provide investment opportunities. A Senior Partner Jock Smith has obtained numerous record setting verdicts and settlements including an $80 million verdict and a $1.6 billion verdict, the largest verdict in America for the year 2004, as well as the top verdict in the history of the nation by an African American lawyer as lead counsel. Jock M. Smith, Esq., Cochran, Cherry, Givens & Smith, P.C., 306 North Main Street, Tuskegee, Alabama 36083 Phone: (334) 727-0060 (334) 727-7197 E-mail: karla@jocksmith.com Website: www.jocksmith.com

Darcell Walker With over 20 years of experience in the field of Intellectual Property law attorney and author Darcell Walker specializes in matters related to Intellectual Property (i.e., patents, trademarks, trade secrets, copyrights and product licensing). His book Godly Ideas: Perceiving and Pursuing God-Given Ideas is a resource designed to help people manifest their ideas. The book contains a spiritual section that discusses how our ideas relate to building of God's kingdom. His second book is Turn on Your Power, a companion book to Godly Ideas. It provides information about the steps in the product development process enabling an individual to take their idea from conception through commercialization. He received his B.S. in Electrical Engineering from Prairie View A & M University. His practice includes the preparation and prosecution of patent applications and trademark applications, negotiation and preparation of technology licenses and other agreements related to technology development and preparing patent validity and infringement opinions. He conducts an Intellectual Property workshop for the University of Houston Small Business Development Center titled "Protecting Your Ideas. Darcell Walker, Esq., Post Office Box 25048, Houston, Texas 77265 Phone: (713) 772-1255 Fax: (877) 523-2178 E-mail: dw0914@sbcglobal.net Website: www.dwalkerlaw.net

Tonya M. Evans-Walls Author, performance poet, Visiting Professor of Law at Widener University School of Law (Harrisburg campus) and an attorney specializing in the areas of entertainment law (literary, music and film), intellectual property (copyright and trademark), estate planning, and municipal finance. Ms. Evans-Walls will be joining the tenure track faculty as Assistant Professor of Law at Widener beginning July 2008. She is the Chair of the Pennsylvania Bar Association Sports, Entertainment and Art Law Committee, and has served as an adjunct professor of copyright, publishing and licensing at York College of Pennsylvania. Tonya, known affectionately as "Lawyer by Day, Poet by Night" is also a performance poet and writer, and the author of numerous books, including Contracts Companion for Writers, Copyright Companion for Writers, Literary Law Guide for Authors: Copyright, Trademark, and Contracts in Plain Language, Seasons of Her and SHINE! Forthcoming titles include Contracts Companion for Writers (Spring 2007). Tonya M. Evans-Walls, Esq., TME Law, LLC, 6703 Germantown Avenue, Suite 200, Philadelphia, Pennsylvania 19119 Phone: (215) 438-0468 Fax: (215) 438-0469 E-mail: tme@tmelaw.net Website: www.tmelaw.net

Gary A. Watson Film. Entertainment attorney, Gary has served as lead attorney for Universal Pictures on "The Guardian," a film by the director of "The Exorcist" William Friedkin; two pictures by Spike Lee, "Mo' Better Blues" and "Jungle Fever;" "Childs Play 3;" Wes Craven's and Shep Gordon's "People Under The Stairs;" the John Goodman starrer, "The Babe;" the film featuring Goldie Hawn, Bruce Willis and Meryl Streep, directed by Robert Zemekis, entitled "Death Becomes Her;" and the Oscar Award winning picture starring Al Pacino titled "Scent of a Woman." He is Chair Elect and a Governing Committee Member of the American Bar Association's Forum on Entertainment and Sports Industries. He served as Division Chair of the Motion Pictures, Television, Cable and Radio Division and as Celebration of Black Cinema Committee Member for The 35th Chicago International Film Festival. Gary Watson, Esq., Gary A. Watson & Associates, 1875 Century Park East, Suite 1000, Los Angeles, California 90067 Phone: (310) 203-8022 Fax: (310) 203-8028 E-mail: gwatson@garywatsonlaw.com Website: www.garywatsonlaw.com

Gary A. Watson, Esq.
Attorney * Lecturer

Gary A. Watson was an attorney in the Law Department of Universal Pictures at MCA, Inc., in Universal City, California, before establishing his own law firm. He handled a broad range of legal matters for clients. Specifically he negotiated, arranged and prepared contracts for the financing, development, production and exploitation of motion pictures, television programs, books, plays and musical recordings. He served as lead attorney for Universal Pictures on "The Guardian," a film by the director of "The Exorcist" and "The French Connection," William Friedkin; two pictures by Spike Lee, "Mo' Better Blues" and "Jungle Fever;" "Childs Play 3;" Wes Craven's and Shep Gordon's "People Under The Stairs;" the John Goodman starrer, "The Babe;" the film featuring Goldie Hawn, Bruce Willis and Meryl Streep, directed by Robert Zemekis, entitled "Death Becomes Her;" and the Oscar Award winning picture starring Al Pacino titled "Scent of a Woman." His music industry clients have included Motown Records, Def Jam Records, Tommy Boy Records, and Dr. Dre. In the motion picture industry he represented BET Pictures, II and the producers of the feature film, "Get On The Bus," which was executive produced by Spike Lee and starred Ossie Davis and Charles Dutton. Television industry clients included BET, actresses Lisa Gay Hamilton from "The Practice" and Suzzanne Douglas from the series, "The Parenthood," consulting producer, Kathleen McGhee Anderson on the series, "Soul Food" and "Any Day Now" and the producer of the movie "Free of Eden," which stars Sidney Poitier.

Before joining Universal Pictures' Law Department, Gary was an associate with the law firm of Dern, Mason and Floum located in Century City, California. There he was responsible for drafting, commenting on and negotiating rights acquisition, writers, producers, directors, actors, composers, distribution and sales agency agreements and completion bonds for a wide range of clients in the television and motion picture industries. He handled matters for clients who are well established in their respective fields, such as Dustin Hoffman, Warren Beatty, Nicole Kidman, Michael Jackson, Oliver Stone, Gene Hackman and others. Mr. Watson is Chair Elect and a Governing Committee Member of the American Bar Association's Forum on Entertainment and Sports Industries and served as the Division Chair of the Motion Pictures, Television, Cable and Radio Division. He also serves on the Board of Trustees of the American Cinematheque, and is a member of the Beverly Hills and Los Angeles County Bar Associations, as well as, the State Bar of California.

Mr. Gary A. Watson is an active member of the Black Entertainment and Sports Lawyers Association (BESLA) and has served as a member of the Board of Directors as well as Chair of the Public Relations Committee and has been inducted into the BESLA Hall of Fame.

Authors

Stacy Hawkins Adams Stacy has been putting pen to paper for as long as she can remember. Her debut novel, Speak To My Heart, was voted 2004 Best New Multicultural Christian Fiction, and Stacy was named 2004 Best New Multicultural Christian Fiction Author by Shades of Romance Magazine. Stacy has penned five inspirational fiction novels, including her fourth, THE SOMEDAY LIST (Jan. 2009), and fifth, Worth A Thousand Words (June 2009). Stacy Hawkins Adams, Post Office Box 25985 Richmond, Virginia 23260 Phone: (804) 768-1292 E-mail: stacy@stacyhawkinsadams.com Website: www.stacyhawkinsadams.com

Darlene Aiken Author of How to Be A Young Lady: Your Total Guide for Being the Best Possible You! Aikens is also President/CEO of Inner Beauty Solutions which provides self-esteem services to youth across the country. Darlene Aiken, MPS, Post Office Box 313, Central Islip, New York 11722 Phone: (631) 561-8006 E-mail: innerbeautysolutions@hotmail.com Website: www.innerbeautysolutions.net

Curtis L Alcutt Author of the novel, "Dyme Hit List," an erotic, urban love story based in Oakland, California. Other books by the author include, Bullets & Ballads, Sins of a Siren, and Eyes of a Player. Mr. Curtis L. Alcutt, Post Office Box 5534, Sacramento, California 95817 Phone: (916) 775-3780 E-mail: blackauthor@yahoo.com Website: www.curtisalcutt.com

Vincent R. Alexandria Author, actor, producer, director, composer, lyricist, screenwriter, vocalist, and musician, Vincent has completed a book of poetry, From the Bottom of My Heart, and three murder detective mystery novels, "Postal Blues," "Black Rain," and his first novel, "If Walls Could Talk. He holds a Masters degree in literature from Baker University and holds a Bachelor's degree in Psychology from Rockhurst College. He is the founder of the Brother 2 Brother African-American Male Literary Symposium. Mr. Vincent R. Alexandria, Post Office Box 752481, Houston, Texas 77275 Phone: (816) 914-1560 E-mail: raychone1@yahoo.com Website: www.vincentalexandria.com

Humza al-Hafeez Author of Some Things To Think About (2003), a collection of speeches and letters concerning the state of the black men and woman experience in America. Mr. al-Hafeez has lectured at universities and correctional institutes through out the country. In 1959, Mr. Hafeez entered the New York Police Department (NYPD) where he worked as Narcotic Bureau Investigator, and as: Special Investigator (Undercover) U.S. DEA, NAAP Commission Investigator. He also worked as a consultant for the U.S. Justice Department, and as Personal Security to Minister Louis Farrakhan. Minister Humza al-Hafeez, 1211 Atlantic Avenue, Brooklyn, New York 11216 Phone: (718) 638-2403 E-mail: alhafeez@earthlink.net

Y. Jamal Ali Author of Heartfire Rendezvous adventure trilogy: Book I - Destiny, Book II - The Crossing, Book III - Culmination. Y. Jamal Ali, Post Office Box 332, San Pedro, California 90733 Phone: (310) 876-9332 E-mail: PtahOgun@yahoo.com

David E. Alston Author of books: (Release Your Glory), (Know Pain......Know Gain), (The Rough Road to Destiny), and (The Ten Commandments for Surviving Children with Behavioral Problems). Pastor of Progressive Harvest Fellowship Church in Henderson, South Carolina. Bishop David Alston, 66 Mt. Pleasant Church Road, Manson, North Carolina 27553 Phone: (252) 915-7339 Fax: (252) 456-9977 E-mail: bishop@strengtheningthebody.org Website: www.strengtheningthebody.org

Karima Amin Performing storyteller and a children's author who provides programming for adults and children in a variety of venues. She is the author of The Adventures of Brer Rabbit and Friends and several of her stories have appeared in publications produced by Publications International of Lincolnwood, Illinois. Karima is also author of You Can Say That Again! which includes six of her favorite stories plus commentary on CD. Karima Amin, Do Tell Productions, Post Office Box 273, Buffalo, New York 14212 E-mail: karimatells@yahoo.com

Adrienne Anderson Freelance writer and music journalist with credentials in academic journals, magazines and online journalism, Adrienne skillfully incorporated the burgeoning rap movement with academics and was one of the first writers to use rap in the context of social movement and historical reference. She has also written the book WORD: RAP, POLITICS + FEMINISM. Contact Adrienne Anderson Fax: (415) 680-2413 (no unrelated faxes, please). E-mail: me@adrienneanderson.com Website: www.adrienneanderson.com

Claud Anderson Author of the books, Black Labor, White Wealth: A Search for Power and Economic Justice and PowerNomics: The National Plan to Empower Black America. Founder of The Harvest Institute, a research educational, policy and advocacy organization. Claud Anderson, 623 Florida Avenue, North West, Washington, DC 20001 Phone: (202) 518-2465 Fax: (301) 564-1997 E-mail: harvest623@aol.com Website: www.harvestinstitute.org

Kimberly Griffith Anderson Author of Good Girl, 2008, and, Single Dad 19, 2009. Kimberly Griffith Anderson, 286 Notable Lane, Rock Hill, South Carolina 29732 Phone: (803) 448-3548 E-mail: kanderson576@yahoo.com Website: www.goodgirlonline.com

Monica Anderson Motivational speaker, dentist, and author of, I Stand Accused. Her debut novel, "When A Sistah's FED UP," was an Essence, Dallas Morning News, and Booking Matters Best Seller for paperback fiction, 2006. She has also authored two non-fiction books: Black English Vernacular and Mom, Are We There Yet? Her short stories and poetry are included in several anthologies. Earned Bachelor of Arts degree from Baylor University, and her doctorate from the University of Minnesota School of Dentistry. In 1996, she became the first African-American columnist for the Arlington Star-Telegram. Monica Anderson, Post Office Box 14115, Arlington, Texas 76094 Phone: (817) 446-6636 E-mail: drmoeanderson@sbcglobal.net Website: www.drmoeanderson.com

Stanice Anderson Inspirational Speaker, playwright and freelance writer. Author of, I Say A Prayer For Me: One Woman's Life of Faith and Triumph (Walk Worthy Press/Warner Books) and 12-Step Programs: A Resource Guide. Her latest book is Walking On Water When The Ground Ain't Enuf. Stanice Anderson, Shout Glory, LLC, 9605 Muirkirk Road, Suite D-160, Laurel, Maryland 20708 E-mail: stanice@stanice.com Website: www.stanice.com

Vinton R. Anderson Retired Bishop in the African Methodist Episcopal Church. Author of My Soul Shouts! (Judson Press). Bishop Vinton R. Anderson, 22 West Sherwood Drive, Overland, Missouri 63114 Fax: (314) 427-2794 E-mail: vander2201@aol.com

Lena Arnold Author of For This Child We Prayed: Living with the Secret Shame of Infertility, For This Dream We Prayed Companion Journal, Strong Black Coffee: Poetry and Prose to Encourage, Enlighten, and Entertain Americans of African Descent, and In the Absence of My Father. Her work has been featured in numerous periodicals. Mrs. Lena Arnold, Post Office Box 13215, Dayton, Ohio 45414 Phone: (937) 546-6298 E-mail: lena@infertilitypress.com Website: www.infertilitypress.com

Molefi Kete Asante Professor, Department of African American Studies at Temple University. Considered by his peers to be one of the most distinguished contemporary scholars, Asante has written 70 books, among the most recent are Maulana Karenga: An Intellectual Portrait, (2010); Erasing Racism, 2nd edition, (2009); Encyclopedia of African Religion, (2009), co-edited with Ama Mazama; The History of Africa, (2008); and Ancient Egyptian Philosophers (2003). Contact Ana Yenenga, Post Office Box 30004, Elkins Park, Pennsylvania 19027 Phone: (215) 782-3214 E-Mail: Yenenga2@aol.com Website: www.asante.net

Jabari Asim Author of Not Guilty: Twelve Black Men Speak Out on Life, Justice and the Law and The Road to Freedom: A Novel of the Reconstruction. Deputy Editor, Washington Post Book World. Columnist, washingtonpost.com. Mr. Jabari Asim, 1150 15th Street, North West, Washington, DC 20071 E-mail: asimj@washpost.com Website: www.washingtonpost.com

Keidi Awadu Author of 18 published books including the latest "The Road to Power: Seven Steps to an African Global Order." Host of a daily talk radio show, The Conscious Rasta Report on LIBRadio.com and LIBtv.com. Keidi Obi Awadu, 664 West Arbor Vitae Street, Suite 5, Inglewood, California 90301 Phone: (661) 526-4787 E-mail: keidi@libradio.net Website: www.Keidi.biz

Azarel A native of North Carolina, her first novel, A Life to Remember provides the opportunity to show her readers everyone can change. Her other books include Bruised, Bruised 2, Daddy's House, and Carbon Copy Azarel, Post Office Box 423, Brandywine, Maryland 20613 E-mail: Tressa428@cs.com Website: www.lifechangingbooks.net

Shonell Bacon Co-author of Luv Alwayz and Draw Me with Your Love. Currently working on her MFA in Creative Writing at McNeese University, as well as teaching English courses at McNeese. Shonell Bacon, 605 Division Street, Lake Charles, Louisiana 70601 Phone: (337) 433-9728 E-mail: sdb6812@hotmail.com Website: www.shonellbacon.com

Michael Baisden A Chicago native Michael self-published his first book, Never Satisfied: How and Why Men Cheat, and his novel, "Gods Gift to Women" was released on October 1, 2002. His second and third books, The Maintenance Man, and Men Cry in the Dark, were adapted into stage plays by I'm Ready Productions. Contact Ms. Pamela Yvette Exum, Business Manager, 1844 North Nob Hill Road, #610, Plantation, Florida 33322 Phone: (877) 622-3269 E-mail: hotnews@minglecity.com Website: www.michaelbaisden.com

Sharonda Baker Ghostwriter, radio personality and mentor, Sharonda "Mecca" Baker is author of Heat: Code of the Streets Book Series Part 1, 2, 3. She is CEO of S. Baker Publishing and S. Baker Media Group. Sharonda "Mecca" Baker, S. Baker Media Group, Post Office Box 7537, Newark New Jersey 07107 Phone: (718) 650-7798 E-mail: sbakerpublishing@gmail.com Website: www.sbakermediagroup.com

Michele Barkley Artist, writer, and poet, Michele Barkley lives in Seattle, Washington. She is author of Wayfaring Stranger-Poems, producer of the video poem - In View Of A Cup Half-Full, and author of a recently completed novel manuscript, Still A Blue Sky. Michele Barkley, PMB 88, 3703 South Edmunds Street, Seattle, Washington 98118 Phone: (206) 818-1091 E-mail: michelebarkley@artuncommon.com Website: www.artuncommon.com

Lindamichelle Baron Drawing on 20 years of hands-on literacy instruction, Dr. Baron creates fun, educationally sound, literacy-based books that encourage critical thinking through strategies based on Best Practice and State Standards. Her publishing company Harlin Jacque Publications has sold more than a quarter million books to school systems, libraries, churches, and literacy organizations across the nation. She is currently an Assistant Professor in the Teacher Education Department of York College (CUNY) in New York City. Dr. Lindamichelle Baron, Post Office Box 336, Garden City, New York 11530 Phone: (516) 489-0120 Fax: (516) 292-9120 E-mail: harlinjacquepub@aol.com Website: www.lindamichellebaron.com

Cheryl Beasley Native of Orange, Texas, Cheryl is the author of three books. Piano Paradise: My Piano Has a Big Secret is the first book of a series explores the life a little girl who stumbles upon a piano that challenges and changes her life forever. The next book in the series, is One Step Higher: Piano Paradise Book II, and a third book of poetry book titled, So Far, Yet So Near. The name in which the books are authored under is, Elerya. Cheryl Beasley, 7810 East Douglas Avenue, #204, Wichita, Kansas 67206 E-mail: msbeasley@mail.com

Rose Jackson-Beavers Author, of four books, Rose received her Bachelor and Master degrees from Illinois State and Southern Illinois Universities. Her first book is Summin to Say is a book of poems, Her second book, Quilt Designs, and her book Poetry Rhymes was co-written with nationally known fabric artist, Edna Patterson-Petty. Rose Jackson-Beavers, Post Office Box 2535, Florissant, Missouri 63032 Phone: (314) 741-6789 E-mail: rosbeav03@yahoo.com

Wayne Beckles Baltimore based divorced father of three, college professor and author of Crossing the Desert, part autobiography, part instruction manual, and all of a riveting tale of one mans transformation to compassion. Mr. Wayne Beckles, Post Office Box 3633, Baltimore, Maryland 21214 E-mail: musicforwayne@yahoo.com

Cassandra Darden Bell As a graduate of East Carolina University in 1992, Cassandra took her first job with WNCT-TV9 as a part-time Production Assistant and went on to be a News Reporter and News Anchor. In May 2002 she self-published her first book The Color of Love and completed her second manuscript, Mississippi Blues, a few months later, which landed her a two-book deal with BET/ Kensington Publishing Company. She is a member of the Southeast Black Writers Group. Contact Ms. Cassandra Darden Bell, Post Office Box 1395, Winterville, North Carolina 28590 E-mail: cdbell@cassandrabell.com Website: www.cassandrabell.com

Kenda Bell Author and motivational speaker, Kenda's two books are My Soul Craves A Touch and a new book titled, For Every Love There Is a Reason. Contact Ms. Kenda Bell, 2360 Eutaw Place, Unit #2, Baltimore, Maryland 21217 Phone: (410) 900-7601 E-mail: kb621@aol.com Website: www.kendabell.com

LaVerne A. Smith-Bell Author of The Newlyweds' Promises To Keep Manual, LaVerne A. Smith-Bell holds a Masters of Science in Education, Guidance and Counseling Degree, and a Bachelors of Science Degree in Psychology. Mrs. LaVerne A. Smith-Bell, 9043 South Greenwood Avenue, Chicago, Illinois 60619 Phone: (773) 731-0118 Fax: (773) 731-3162 E-mail: Lavernsmithbell@aol.com Website: www.laverneasmithbell.com

Kendra Norman-Bellamy Full-time writer and part-time fitness instructor, Kendra is a native of West Palm Beach, Florida. She has authored several poems, short stories and novels highlighting love for family and for Christ. Graduated with honors from Valdosta Technical College with an Associates in Applied Science, Valdosta, Georgia. Kendra Norman-Bellamy, KNB Publications, LLC, Post Office Box 54491, Atlanta, Georgia 30308 Phone: (937) 304-9473 E-mail: kendra_bellamy@hotmail.com Website: www.knb-publications.com

T. Garrott Benjamin Jr. Author, and senior pastor of the historic 3,000 member Light of the World Christian Church in Indianapolis, Indiana. Contact Pastor T. Garrott Benjamin Jr., Heaven on Earth Publishing, Post Office Box 18088, Indianapolis, Indiana 46218 Phone: (317) 254-5922 E-mail: ahord@lightoftheworld.org Website: www.lightoftheworld.org

Carolyn Ladelle Bennett Author. Listed in: Who's Who in the South and Southwest, 1997-98; Who's Who of American Women, 1979-80; Phi Kappa Phi Honor Society, MSU, 1976. Memberships: Association for Education in Journalism and Mass Communication, American Journalism Historians Association, Society of Professional Journalists, Association for the Study of African American Life and History, and others. Founding Editor and Publisher: Network of North Carolina Women Newspaper [501(c)(3)], Fayetteville, North Carolina. Ms. Carolyn L. Bennett, 221 Greystone Lane-16, Rochester, New York 14618

Bertice Berry Best-selling author of an inspirational memoir, I'm On My Way, But Your Foot Is On My Head, and the hilarious bestsellers Sckraight From the Ghetto, You Might Be Ghetto If, and the sequel, You STILL Ghetto. Her first work of fiction, Redemption Song, published by Double Day in 2000, is also a Best Seller and has been praised by critics for it's ability to entertain, inspire and educate. Berry followed with another bestseller, The Haunting of Hip Hop. In August 2002, she released Jim & Louella Homemade Heart-fix Remedy. Dr. Berry graduated magna cum laude from Jacksonville where she was awarded the President's Cup for leadership and subsequently earned a Ph.D. in sociology from Kent State University at the age of 26. Dr. Bertice Berry, Abercorn Street, Savannah, Georgia 31401 Website: www.berticeberry.com

S. Torriano Berry An associate professor in Film at Howard University, he co-authored with Venise Berry two books, The Historical Dictionary of African American Cinema (Scarecrow Press, 2007) and The 50 Most Influential Black Films (Citadel 2001). Contact S. Torriano Berry, BerryBooks, Post Office Box 5411, Coralville, Iowa 52241 Phone: (319) 335-3361 Fax: (319) 335-3502 E-mail: sogood@mchsi.com Website: www.veniseberry.com

Wanda Shiryl Miller-Berry Author of the novel, BUCK, and a graduate of Oklahoma Baptist University, and a graduate student at the University of Central Oklahoma. Miller-Berry is also a Cushcity.com 2007 Best New Author Award Nominee. Wanda Shiryl Miller-Berry, 1000 North East 14th Street, Oklahoma City, Oklahoma 73117 Phone: (405) 525-9249 Fax: (405) 601-0774 E-mail: wandasb2002@cox.net

Venise Berry Associate professor of Journalism and Mass Communication at the University of Iowa in Iowa City. She is the author of three national bestselling novels; So Good, An African American Love Story (1996), All of Me, A Voluptuous Tale (2000) and Colored Sugar Water (2002). In 2003, she received the "Creative Contribution to Literature" award from the Zora Neale Hurston Society. Her book All of Me received a 2001 Honor Book Award from the Black Caucus of the American Library Association. Venise Berry, Post Office Box 5411, Coralville, Iowa 52241 Phone: (319) 335-3361 Fax: (319) 335-3502 E-mail: sogood@mchsi.com Website: www.veniseberry.com

Janie P. Bess Author, her first book a memoir is titled VISIONS. Janie also founded a non-profit writing organization Writers Resource Center. She is listed in the 2000 edition of Who's Who Among American Teachers. Janie initiated a Fairfield, California chapter for the International Women's Writers Guild (WWG). Contact Ms. Jamie P. Bess, Writers Resource Center, 1500 Oliver Road, Suite K, PMB 265, Fairfield, California 94534 Phone: (707) 399-9169 E-mail: janie@Janiepbess.com Website: www.janiepbess.com

ReShonda Tate Billingsley The author of My Brother's Keeper (#1 Essence Magazine Bestselling Book), Let the Church Say Amen, and the bestseller, I Know I've Been Changed, Everybody Say Amen, and her teen inspirational novels, Nothing But Drama, Blessings in Disguise (which was voted a #1 pick by Ebony Magazine) and With Friends Like These, and non-fiction title, Help! I've Turned into my Mother. She is a general assignment reporter for KRIV-TV, the Fox affliate in Houston, Texas, and a 1991 graduate of The University of Texas at Austin, where she majored in Broadcast Journalism. Contact Ms. ReShonda Billingsley E-mail: ReShondaT@aol.com Website: www.reshondatatebillingsley.com

Sabrina D. Black National and international speaker Sabrina is contributing author to the Soul Care Bible (Thomas Nelson, 2001). She is co-author of Prone to Wander: A Woman's Struggle with Sexual Sin and Addiction, (Infinity 2002, rev. PriorityONE 2003); co-editor of Counseling in African American Communities, (Zondervan, 2002); the author of Can Two Walk Together? Encouragement for Spiritually Unbalanced Marriages (Moody Press 2002), and co-author of HELP! For Your Leadership, (PriorityONE Publications 2003). Dr. Sabrina D. Black, Abundant Life Counseling Center, 20700 Civic Center Drive #170, Southfield, Michigan 48076 Phone: (313) 201-6286 E-mail: jadebooks@aol.com Website: www.sabrinablack.com

Andrea Blackstone Author of the novel Schemin, Confessions of a Gold Digger. Andrea majored in English and minored in Spanish at Morgan State University where she was recipient of The Zora Neale Hurston Scholarship. She earned an M.A. from St. John's College in Annapolis, Maryland. Contact Ms. Andrea Blackstone, Dream Weaver Press, Post Office Box 3402, Annapolis, Maryland 21403 E-mail: Andrea@dreamweaverpress.net Website: www.dreamweaverpress.net

Gwyneth Bolton   The author was born and raised in Paterson, New Jersey. She currently lives in Syracuse, New York with her husband Cedric. She has a BA and an MA in creative writing and a Ph.D. in English. She teaches classes in writing and women's studies at the college level. Gwyneth Bolton, Post Office Box 9388, Carousel Center, Syracuse, New York 13290 E-mail: **Gwyneth@gwynethbolton.com** Website: **www.gwynethbolton.com**

Kola Boof   In 2004, three of her best books were released, Nile River, a collection of her best and most controversial poems, Train to the Redeeming Sin, her acclaimed bestselling short story collection and the English translation (by Said Musa) of her provocatively erotic Black American historical romance, Flesh and the Devil. Contact Ms. Kola Boof c/o Door of Kush, 324 South Diamond Bar Boulevard, Suite 504, Diamond Bar, California 91765 E-mail: **kolaboof_email@yahoo.com** Website: **www.kolaboof.com**

Angela Boone   Author and successful business owner of her own construction management and interior design firm for more than twenty years, Angela's first book "Faith Cometh By Hearing." is primarily nonfiction in the areas of business, education, personal development and relationships. Her children's books are We Are All Gods Children Let Us Pray, and Faith Cometh By Hearing. Angela Boone, Boone International, Post Office Box 211144, Detroit, Michigan 48221 E-mail: **aboone@angelaboone.com** Website: **www.angelaboone.com**

Kenneth Bowens   Born in Paris, Texas, Kenneth (Kanko) Bowens is author of the book Dirtied Brown Leaves, the story of African American rage personified through its main character, Baby. Mr. Kenneth Bowens, 1208 North West 106th Street, Oklahoma City, Oklahoma 73114 E-mail: **kennethbowens1@kennethbowens.com** Website: **www.kennethbowens.com**

Sheritha Bowman   New, up and coming writer who is staking her claim in the Christian fiction and non-fiction writing field with her debut book, Soul Inspiration For Women Married To Unbelievers, (1998). Contact Ms. Sheritha Bowman, Post Office Box 817, Germantown, Maryland 20875 E-mail: **godlytheatre@aol.com** Website: **www.sherithabowman.com**

Nicole Rouse Bradley   "Contradictions" is Ms. Bradley's first novel, about relationships. She is a graduate of Indiana University, where she was a member and president of the theater group, SWAV which performed her original play entitled; "Unforgotten Memories." She is a member of Zeta Phi Beta Sorority Inc, and Authors For Charity. She currently teaches high school in Gary, Indiana and is currently working on her second novel. Contact Ms. Nicole Bradley, Post Office Box 2916, Gary, Indiana 46403 E-mail: **n-bradley@sbcglobal.net** Website: **www.nicolebradley.com**

LaTonya Branham   Author and editor of CultureSeek (1st and 2nd edition) and Spirit Seek (2007). She is also a contributing writer to Chicken Soup for the Soul: Devotional Stories for Women (2009). LaTonya earned a Master of Arts degree from Antioch University McGregor and a Bachelor of Science degree from Wilberforce University. She is a founding member of the Soul of the Pen literary group. Currently, she serves as a college administrator and as an adjunct professor teaching multicultural education. She co-founded the 2010 Dayton Book Expo. LaTonya Branham, Post Office Box 1271, Dayton, Ohio 45401 Phone: (513) 265-9412 E-mail: **Latonyabranham@hotmail.com** Website: **www.LaTonyaBranham.com**

Donna L. Brazile   Author of the book Cooking with Grease (June 2004, Simon & Schuster), an intimate account of Donna Brazile's thirty years in politics, following her rise to greater and greater political and personal accomplishments to working on the Jesse Jackson, Dick Gephardt, Michael Dukakis and Bill Clinton presidential campaigns, and leading Al Gore's 2000 campaign, making her the first African American to lead a major presidential campaign.   Donna L. Brazile, Post Office Box 15369, Washington, DC 20003 Phone: (202) 783-0300 E-mail: info@brazileassociates.com Website: www.brazileassociates.com

Alice Talbert Breaux Completed her first novel titled, "I'll Make Them All Pay!" in 2003. Alice Talbert Breaux, 1410 Sumner Street, New Orleans, Louisiana 70114 Phone: (504) 368-0543 E-mail: bigmamaal1@aol.com

Kim Marshella Brewer Author of the newly released book Grief: The REAL Deal: A Realist Perspective was released in January, 2006 (PriorityOne Publications). Kim M. Brewer, Real Life Ministries, 18452 Washburn, Detroit, Michigan 48221 Phone: (313) 477-2529 E-mail: kbrewer20@gmail.com   Website: www.kimmbrewer.com

Regina Brooks Literary agent and published author, Brooks penned the how-to-book Writing Great Books For Young Adults. Regina Brooks, Serendipity Literary Agency LLC., 732 Fulton Street, Suite 3, Brooklyn, New York 11238 E-mail: rbrooks@serendipitylit.com Website: www.serendipitylit.com

Wilbur Lee Brower Educational consultant and trainer, Dr. Brower is also a certified teacher high school and founder and president of the Institute for Youth Development & Educational Resources (IYDER), Inc. He is author of A Little Book Big Principles—Values and Virtues for a More Successful Life (1998) and Me Teacher, Me…Please! (2002). Wilbur Lee Brower, Ph.D., Post Office Box 1719, Fayettevile, North Carolina 28302 E-mail: brower311@aol.com

Brian Christopher Brown Author of the book Think About It: A Write and Reflect Book, is about major issues that young people have to face on a day to day basis. Brian Christopher Brown, RAP Publishing, Inc., 19785 West 12 Mile Road, Suite #303, Southfield, Michigan 49076 E-mail: Blackprince006@aol.com

Bertrand E. Brown Author of The Heart is a Lonely Hunter. A former elementary and middle school teacher, social worker, program director, and sports editor for The Challenger newspaper. Mr. Brown Bertrand E. Brown, 1706 Kay Street, Greensboro, North Carolina 27405 E-mail: berttheveran@yahoo.com

Clayton F. Brown   Author, Under The Green Tree. Founder, Charlotte African-American Writers Group (CAAW). Clayton F. Brown, Post Office Box 29155, Charlotte, North Carolina 28229 E-mail: claytonfbrown@msn.com

Crystal C. Brown Author of Caramel and Cream. She is also CEO and President of Crystal Clear Communications an award winning public relations and marketing firm. Contact Ms. Crystal C. Brown, Crystal Clearn Communications, 2470 South Dairy Ashford #252, Houston, Texas 77077 E-mail: cbrown5530@aol.com Website: www.crystalcommunicates.com

Delores Tyler Brown Author, visionary, Ms. Brown is the author of Manifestation of God Glory, which will help you go deeper into the Word of God. Also a Gospel Artist and Founder of Inspirations of Hope Global Ministries, she is host of a weekly online radio talk show, Fresh Hope on blogtalkradiocom. Contact Apostle Delores Tyler Brown, Inspirations of Hope Global Ministries, Post Office Box 330806, Houston, Texas 77233 Phone: (713) 504-3092 E-mail: info@dtylerministries.com Website: www.dtylerbrownministries.com

Kimberly Cheri Brown Author/illustrator of Beautiful Like ME!, a multicultural coloring activity book. Also a much sought after illustrator and writer (grants, children's books, niche audiences). Kimberly Cheri Brown, Post Office Box 331971, Nashville, Tennessee 37203 E-mail: kim@kimberlycbrown.com

Kimberly R. Brown I am a new author who has just written a book called Spiritual Advisor that has been published by Publish America. Spiritual Advisor, is a phenomenal book about Christianity and one's purpose in life. I am a Christian who resides in Sanford, Florida with my husband and son. Kimberly R. Brown, 128 Sterling Pine Street, Sanford, Florida 32773 Phone: (407) 461-1333 E-mail: kimrbrown@bellsouth.net

Les Brown Internationally recognized speaker, author and television personality, Les is author of Live Your Dreams, and the book, It's Not Over Until You Win. Former host of The Les Brown Show, a nationally syndicated daily television talk show he is one of the nation's leading authorities in understanding and stimulating human potential. Les Brown, Les Brown Enterprises, Inc., 233 North Michigan Avenue, Suite 2800, Chicago, Illinois 60601 Phone: (800) 733-4226   E-mail: lesbrown777@aol.com Website: www.lesbrown.com

Lillian Ojetta Brown Author, poet, and photographer, Brown is the author of, Remembering My Father (Rochester Hills Michigan Public Library, 2005).   She is a Psychotherapist, Ordained Minister, and Reiki Practioner. Education: Bachelor of Science Degree in Psychology from South Carolina State College, Master of Social Work Degree, Occupational Psychology and Mental Health, Wayne State University, Detroit, Michigan in 1993. L. Ojetta Brown, 34 Village Circle Drive, Rochester Hills, Michigan 48307 Phone: (248) 703-3990 E-mail: center4peace@aol.com

Luther Brown, Jr. B.S. in English from North Carolina A&T State University (1969) where he became the school's first Woodrow Wilson Fellow, and a juris doctorate degree from Georgetown University (1988). He attended graduate school in English at Rutgers University before going to work for CBS News in 1972. Later he moved to NBC News, where he was an editor, reporter and producer during a 14-year tenure. A divorced single-father of two, Brown published his memoir about the experience in 2006, titled "Raising My Best Friends: Meeting the Challenge of Being a Single Parent." He is contributor to Harvard University's African American National Biography and he also has written for many other magazines. Luther Brown, Jr., 918 14th Street, South East, Washington, DC 20003 E-mail: nikmar@pacbell.net

Misherald L Brown Author, CEO/Publisher, Reality Press. Contact Misherald L. Brown, Reality Press LLC, 2684 Ranger Drive, North Charleston, South Carolina 29405 E-mail: missy@realitypressllc.com Website: www.realitypressllc.com

Tony Brown TV Journalist/Commentator, radio talk show host, keynote speaker, self-empowerment advocate and bestselling author. Contact Tony Brown, Producer, Tony Brown Productions, Inc., 2214 Frederick Douglass Boulevard, Suite 124, New York, New York Phone: (718) 264-2226 E-mail: mail@tbol.net Website: www.tonybrown.com

Beverly A. Browning Award winning grant writer, CEO of BBA, Inc., and author of nearly two dozen grants-related publications, including audio and video products. Her books include Fundraising with the Corporate Letter, Grant Writing For Dummies™ (2001 and 2005, Wiley) and Grant Writing for Educators (2004, NES). Dr. Beverly A. Browning, BBA, Inc., 25650 West Northern Lights Way, Buckeye, Arizona 85326 Phone: (480) 768-7400 E-mail: grantsconsulting@aol.com Website: www.bevbrowning.com

Monique Miles Bruner BA and MA degrees in Public Administration and a Masters of Human Relations, University of Oklahoma. Monique has also completed the requirements for her doctoral degree in Adult Education from Oklahoma State University. She has several publications including a textbook, Strategies that Empower People for Success in College and Life (Houghton Mifflin). Monique Miles Bruner, 6409 Braniff Drive, Oklahoma City, Oklahoma 73105 Phone: (405) 615-6711 E-mail: n2delta@yahoo.com

Troy Buckner A playwright, songwriter/lyricist and literary writer, Buckner released her first 300 page novel, entitled "A Bird In Flight" in July 2007. Her NAACP endorsed novel is based on the power of self-expression with truth, integrity and character on display. Her latest novel entitled, "A Season Beyond Nightfall." Producer and playwright for the hit theatrical production, 'A Passion For Justice. She produced the theatrical play, 'Tell Hell I Aint Comin', starring Tommy Ford from the Grammy nominated R & B Group, 'Az Yet' on the La Face Record label. Troy Buckner, 1639 Parkchester Drive, Las Vegas, Nevada 89108 Phone: (714) 227-5000 E-mail: birdinflight@aol.com Website: www.abirdinflight.com

Ed Bullins Author, playwright, Ed Bullins's latest book is ED BULLINS: 12 Plays and Selected Writings (University of Michigan Press, 2006). Distinguished Artist-in-Residence, at Northeastern University, Mr. Bullins is the author of seven books, including Five Plays By Ed Bullins, The Duplex, The Hungered One, Four Dynamite Plays, The Theme is Blackness, The Reluctant Rapist, and The Ed Bullins Reader (Michigan University Press). Contact Mr. Ed Bullins, 37 Vine Street #1, Roxbury, Massachusetts 02119 Phone: (617) 442-6627 E-mail: rct9@verizon.net Website: www.edbullins.com

A'Lelia Bundles Author of On Her Own Ground: The Life and Times of Madam C. J. Walker (Lisa Drew Books/Scribner). Author and journalist A'Lelia writes biographies about the amazing women in her family: entrepreneur Madam C. J. Walker and Harlem Renaissance icon A'Lelia Walker. She also speaks at conferences, colleges, corporations and other venues about entrepreneurship, philanthropy, financial literacy, women's and African American history. After a 30-year career as an executive and Emmy award winning producer with ABC News and NBC News, she now serves on several non-profit boards and is president of the Madam Walker/A'Lelia Walker Family Archives. Contact Ms. A'Lelia Bundles, 4109 Garrison Street NW, Washington, DC 20016 Phone: (202) 363-4191 E-mail: ABundles@gmail.com Website: www.aleliabundles.com

Anita Bunkley Multi-published author of African American women's fiction, writing coach, and inventor. Author of nine book-length works of fiction, two novellas, and one work of non-fiction. Anita's latest releases include: Relative Interest (Dafina, 2004); Mirrired Life (Dafina 2003), Black Expressions Book Club Main selection and You Only Get Better (Mira, July 2006). Contact Ms. Anita Bunkley, Post Office Box 821248, Houston, Texas 77282 E-mail: arbun@sbcglobal.net Website: www.anitabunkley.com

Luther Burch, Jr. Author of "Black American (Amreekie Aswad) in the Desert Kingdom," an adventure story (fiction) based on my personal experiences and discoveries in Saudi Arabia. Luther Burch, Jr., Post Office Box 7956, Woodbridge, Virginia 22195 Phone: (703) 498-7171 E-mail: info@blackamericanindesert.com Website: www.blackamericanindesert.com

John L. Burris Author of the book BLUE vs. BLACK: Let's End the Conflict between Police and Minorities. He was selected as a member of the top 100 trial lawyers in California in 2007, by the American Trial Lawyers Association. He was named one of the top 100 most influential Attorneys in the State of California by the Los Angeles and San Francisco Daily Journal in 2005. John L. Burris, Esq., Airport Corporate Centre, 7677 Oakport Street, Suite 1120, Oakland, California 94621 Phone: (510) 379-7215 Fax: (510) 839-3882 E-mail: Website: www.johnburrislaw.com

L. Guy Burton Published writer of Follow The Right Leader (Quill,1991), novels Jack In The Pulpit, (Xlibris, 2004), and Come Die With Me, (PublishAmerica, 2006), magazine articles, poetry, and a movie script. My articles and poetry have appeared in Interrace magazine, and my screenplay Latent Blood won honorable mention in a Writer's Digest contest. L. Guy Burton, The Warwick Valley Writers' Association, 12 Burton Lane, Warwick, New York 10990 E-mail: el_guybur@hotmail.com Website: www.warwickinfo.net

Nickcole Byrd Co-author with LaTrice Martin of the book Girls From The Hood, The Delivery. Nickcole and LaTrice are the founders of Hebrew Women Ministries, a spiritually inspired quest to reach those who have been abused and are desperately seeking a way back through holy biblical teachings and continued growth in faith. She is program administrator at Rice University. Contact Ms. Nickey Byrd, 4605 West Columbary, Rosenberg, Texas 77471 E-mail: nickcolebyrd@aol.com

Ivette Cambridge Author of the new book "Hanging Without A Noose" a real life book of poems (June 1, 2006, Semaj Publications of Denver). Ivette poetically speaks on child abuse, domestic violence and the drug abuse. Ivette Cambridge, 13918 East Mississippi Avenue, #506, Aurora, Colorado 80012 Phone: (303) 325-5155 E-mail: poetivette@yahoo.com

Emory S. Campbell Executive Director Emeritus of Penn Center, a National Historic Landmark District on Saint Helena Island, South Carolina. President of Gullah Heritage Consulting where he conducts an institute on the Gullah culture through lectures, short courses, and the Gullah Heritage Trail Tours on Hilton Head Island. He is author and self-publisher of the guidebooks, Gullah Cultural (2002), and Gullah Cultural Legacies (2005). Contact Mr. Emory S. Campbell, Post Office Box 22136, Hilton Head Island, South Carolina 29925 Phone: (843) 681-3069 E-mail: esc@gullaheritage.com Website: www.gullaheritage.com

Deondriea Cantrice Author. The book Rhythm Can't Keep Time is the first in a series of recent pursuits for Deondriea Cantrice, with work progressing quickly on the horizon. Contact Ms. Deondriea Cantrice, Post Office Box 470036, Aurora, Colorado 80047 Phone: (303) 694-7482 E-mail: info@deondriea.com Website: www.deondriea.com

Carla Rowser Canty Author, air personality and producer and host of "Sayword" an entertainment television show. Interviews authors, artists. author of 'Diary of A Blackgurl.' Carla Rowser Canty, WQTQ, Post Office Box 843, Hartford, Connecticut 06143 Phone: (860) 695-1899 E-mail: wqtqfm@yahoo.com Website: www.wqtqfm.com/wqtq

Bil Carpenter In 2005, Carpenter's first book Uncloudy Days: The Gospel Music Encyclopedia (Backbeat Books) was published and the companion compilation CD Uncloudy Days (Artemis Gospel) was released. He resides in Washington, D.C. where he runs Capital Entertainment, a small public relations company that has worked extensively with gospel artists. Bil Carpenter, Capital Entertainment, 217 Seaton Place North East, Washington, D.C. 20002 Phone: (202) 506-5051 E-mail: carpbil@aol.com Website: www.bilcarpenter.com

Monica P. Carter Freelance corporate writer, motivational speaker and author of three books, As If Nothing Happened, Sacrifice the One (2004) and Scandalous Truth (Christian fiction). She has traveled across the United States speaking at colleges and events on goal achievement and success. In addition to being an author and president of RootSky Books, she also is a screenwriter. She has a degree in journalism from the University of Southern Mississippi. Monica Carter Tagore, Post Office Box 32585, Los Angeles, California 90032 Phone: (323) 825-4494 E-mail: monica@monicacarter.com Website: www.monicacarter.com

Cliff Chandler Award winning author of three mystery novels: "The Paragons", "Vengeance Is Mine," and "Devastated." Devastated was chosen as "Mystery Novel of the Year" by JADA Press. Former host of "Art With A Capital" WGNM TV64, Macon, Georgia. Poetry Awards, Short Story Awards, Marquis Who's Who In The East, and the JADA Award Mystery Novel Of The Year 2004. Education: BFA, Pratt Institute, Brooklyn, New York, Masters Writing courses at New York University, and editing classes at The New School. Contact Mr.Cliff Chandler, 2492 Tredway Drive, Macon, Georgia 31211 E-mail: CDuke23@aol.com

Frank Chase Jr. Author of False Roads to Manhood: What Women Need To Know, What Men Need to Understand. Served as a teacher, counselor, mentor and lay minister for twenty years. Earned a Bachelor of Arts Degree in Communications and a minor in Sociology from Washington State University. Currently works as a writer for an Army Magazine on Redstone Arsenal at LOGSA. Frank Chase Jr., FC Publishing, LLC, Post Office Box 5675, Huntsville, Alabama 35814 E-mail: fchase@fcpublishing.com Website: www.fcpublishing.com

Orean D. Chatman The Time is Wright is his first novel. Mr. Chatman grew up in Houston, Texas. He received a B.S. in Business Services from the University of Houston Downtown and a Masters of Public Administration from Long Island University, Brooklyn, New York. He has worked in the Health Care Support Services industry for eight years. Contact Orean D. Chatman, 7903 Indian Head Hwy, #406, Oxon Hill, Maryland 20745 E-mail: odc@oreandchatman.com Website: www.oreandchatman.com

Bernice Gorham Cherry Author of "The Onion You Are Eating Is Someone Else's Water Lily," Cherry, is currently working on her second book, as well as assisting others in achieving their dream of becoming published. Ms. Bernice Cherry, 2110 Sir Raleigh Court, Greenville, North Carolina 27858 Phone: (252) 355-8970 E-mail: zoe4u2c@suddenlink.net

Charles W. Cherry II Author, attorney, principal shareholder of the largest black owned media company in the Southeast, and publisher of his family-owned weekly newspaper. He earned his undergraduate degree in Journalism from Morehouse College in 1978, and the Master of Business Administration and Juris Doctor degrees from the University of Florida, 1982. He is the author of Excellence Without Excuse: The Black Student's Guide to Academic Excellence (1994). Charles Cherry II, Florida Courier, 5207 Washington Boulevard., Tampa, Florida 33619 Phone: (877) 352-4455 E-mail: news@flcourier.com Website: www.flcourier.com

Anna Christian Author of four books, Meet it, Greet it, and Defeat It!, The Biography of Frances E. Williams, Actress/Activist, 1999, Milligan Books; Mrs. Griffin is Missing and Other Stories, a Bobby & Sonny Mystery for preteens, 2005, iUniverse; The Big Table, tale of a family ritual, children's book, 2008, newest release, Daniel's Wife adult contemporary fiction, 2010. Anna Christian, 12910 Fontainebleau Drive, Moreno Valley, California 92555 Phone: (951) 966-8943 Fax: (951) 247-2519 E-mail: anadoodlin@dadielte.net Website: www.dadielte.net

Hope C. Clarke Author of five best selling books: Vengeance Is Mine, Carrying Mama's Baggage, Not With My Son, April 2003, Best Seller, 2003, and Shadow Lover, 2004. Hope is a full-time mom, employee of JP Morgan Chase and a devoted entrepreneur. Contact Ms. Hope C. Clarke, A New Hope Publishing, Post Office Box 1746, New York, New York 10017 Phone: (718) 498-2408 E-mail: hopeclarke@aol.com Website: www.anewhopepublishing.com

Stanley Bennett Clay Author of 3 novels, "Diva" (Holloway House), "In Search of Pretty Young Black Men" (Atria Books), and "Looker" (Atria books). His novella "House of John" was published in "Visible Lives: A Tribute to E. Lynn Harris" along with novellas by Terrance Dean and James Earl Hardy (2010, Kensington Books). Contact Mr. Stanley Bennett Clay, 1155 4th Avenue, Los Angeles, California 90019 E-mail: sbcpublishers@earthlink.net Website: http://www.myspace.com/stanleybennettclay

Blondie L. Clayton My writing began to take on a life of its own after I was faced with a husband who had two days to live. At that moment I began to seek the meaning of life and ended up receiving a spiritual revelation which altered the course of my life. The three books I authored: There in the Midst The Mysterious Exposed; Why Money Isn't Your Problem- Making the Right Connection; You Write You Publish. Blondie L.Clayton, Post Office Box 132, Sharpes, Florida 32959 Phone: (321) 637-1128 E-mail: blondie48@bellsouth.net

Nanci Clayton Miami based performance poet. Ms. Clayton is the author of I'm Every Woman (February 2000), a motivational speaker, educator, performing artist and model. Her studies in broadcast journalism were completed at the University of Miami, Florida. Contact Ms. Nanci Clayton, Nu-B Du-B Expressions, Post Office Box 531134, Miami Shores, Florida 33153 E-mail: nubdub@aol.com Website: www.nanciclayton.com

Ben Clement Author of Giants On My Shoulders, a playwright, journalist, and screenwriter, his credits include three independent films, a musical stage production also produced on DVD, newspaper and magazine articles, scripts for five television programs, award winning poetry, and a rap song entitled, "Hit Man." Ben Clement, 2929 West 24th Place, Gary, Indiana 46404 Phone: (219) 944-1201 Fax: (219) 944-1202 E-mail: ben_clement_99@yahoo.com

D. L. Cleveland Authored the book entitled, The Deterioration of Black Romance which was published by Cobs Web Angelic Press. D. L. Cleveland, Post Office Box 741124, Riverdale, Georgia 30274 Phone: (770) 472-0527 E-mail: ohiodlc@yahoo.com

Bernadene High Coleman Born in rural Louisiana the author grew up in Los Angeles. She received her MS from Loyola-Marymount, and her BA from California State University. She has also attended UCLA School of Writing. She has been presented at The Library of Congress and has appeared at many universities, colleges and high schools with her historical-factional-literary work. She is the author three novels, Mama Rose, I leave You My Dreams, and Beyond Color. She has also written a fourth book, Listen My Children, a collection of poetry. Coleman is a retired school teacher who taught in the Los Angeles Unified School District and the Pasadena School System for nearly 30 years. Bernadene High Coleman, Post Office Box 4372, Culver City, California 90231 Phone: (310) 641-0106 E-mail: bernhicole@sbcglobal.net Website: www.mamarose.com

Monica A. Coleman Author of the book The Dinah Project: A Handbook For Congregational Response To Sexual Violence, Coleman is an ordained elder of the African Methodist Episcopal Church (AMEC). She earned her undergraduate degree in Afro-American Studies at Harvard University. he obtained the master's of divinity degree and Certificate in the Study of Religion, Gender and Sexuality. Doctorate in Philosophy of Religion and Theology at Claremont Graduate University, Claremont, California. Currently the Director of Womanist Religious Studies and Assistant Professor of Religion at Bennett College for Women in Greensboro, North Carolina. Monica A. Coleman, Ph.D., Director, Womanist Religious Studies, Assistant Professor of Religion, Bennett College for Women, 900 Eeast Washington Street, Box 104, Greensboro, North Carolina 27401 Phone: (336) 517-1534 E-mail: revmonica@worldnet.att.net

Patricia A. Coleman Lived abroad for a number of years before settling near West Palm Beach, Florida. My work has been published in The International Library of Poetry, Collected Whispers. My most recent book What Mama Never Told Me is a relevant narration that guide parents toward open and effective communication. Ms. Patricia A. Coleman, 4461 Rende Lane, Lake Worth, Florida 33461 Phone: (561) 642-8605 E-mail: trishcol@comcast.net Website: www.mamatellme.com

Valerie L. Coleman Author and publisher, contributor, editor and compiler of Blended Families An Anthology and Tainted Mirror An Anthology. A real account of life in a stepfamily because we are not the Brady Bunch! There's a blessing in the blending! And Tainted Mirror An Anthology. Contributor to KNB Publications' The Midnight Clear, a Christian fiction anthology. Contact Ms. Valerie L. Coleman, Pen Of The Writer, LLC, 893 South Main Street - PMB 175, Englewood, Ohio 45322 Phone: (937) 307-0760 E-mail: info@penofthewriter.com Website: www.penofthewriter.com

Eddie Connor Author, Educator, Speaker, and TV Host, his three book are Purposefully Prepared to Persevere, E.Con the Icon, and Collections of Reflections, designed to inspire and empower. Contact Mr. Eddie Connor, 29488 Woodward Avenue, Suite 215, Royal Oak, Michigan 48073 Phone: (248) 245-0370 E-mail: **eddieconnor@eddieconnor.com** Website: **www.eddieconnor.com**

Marlene Kim Connor Author of Welcome To The Family: Memories of the Past for a Bright Future (2006) and What Is Cool? Understanding Black Manhood in America (AGATE and Crown). Marlene Connor Lynch, 2911 West 71st Street, Minneapolis, Minnesota 55423 Phone: (612) 866-1486 Fax: (612) 866-1486 E-mail: **connoragency@aol.com**

John Walton Cotman Associate Professor in the Department of Political Science at Howard University. Dr. Cotman received his Ph.D. in Political Science from Boston University in 1992. Specializations are Comparative Politics and International Relations, with a regional focus on the Caribbean. Some of his scholarly works include The Impact of Globalization on Democracy and Sovereignty in the Third World: Critical Perspectives, in Government and Politics Journal (2002), and Grenada: The New JEWEL Revolution in the Encyclopedia of Political Revolutions (1998). Dr. John Walton Cotman, Howard University Political Science Department, Douglass Hall Room 142, MSC 590536, 2400 Sixth Street, NorthWest, Washington, DC 20059 Phone: (202) 806-6848 Fax: (202) 265-3527 E-mail: **jcotman@howard.edu**

William Richard Craft Author/Editor, and publisher of two books by The Booker T. Washington, Chronicles and Character Building. Coming Soon: The Black Man's Burden, and The Liberia Chronicles. Contact Mr. William Richard Craft, Publisher, Phoenix Publications, Post Office Box 683, Bronx, New York 10475 E-mail: **phoenixpublications@yahoo.com** Website: **www.phoenixpublications.net**

Sha-Shana Crichton A licensed attorney and literary agent, Crichton lectures frequently on publishing matters. She also teaches legal writing and research. She is a graduate of Howard University School of Law (J.D. cum laude) and the University of the West Indies (B.A. Hons.). Sha-Shana is the author of *Distinguishing Between Direct and Consequential Damages Under New York Law in Breach of Service Contract Cases*, Howard Law Journal 2002. Crichton & Associates, Inc., 6940 Carroll Avenue, Takoma Park, Maryland 20912 Phone: (301) 495-9663 Fax: (202) 318-0050 E-mail: **cricht1@aol.com** Website: **www.crichton-associates.com**

Alice T. Crowe New York Attorney and author of the new book Real Dads Stand Up! A legal guide to help single fathers in family court. She is a partner in the law firm of Crowe & Crowe with her identical twin sister and author Alicia Crowe. Contact Ms. Alice T. Crowe, Crowe & Crowe, 99 Main Street, Suite 321, Nyack, New York 10960 Phone: (845) 348-1160 E-mail: **theurbanevoice@yahoo.com**

Alicia M. Crowe Attorney/Author of the new book, Real Dads Stand Up! What Every Single Father Should Know About Child Support. Rights and Custody (Blue Peacock Press). A guide for fathers about how to navigate the legal system and maintain access to their children. Alicia M. Crowe, Post Office Box 1011, Nyack, New York 10960 Phone: (845) 348-1160 Fax: (845) 348-1964 E-mail: **acrowe@yahoo.com** Website: **www.realdadsstandup.com**

Matthew Cruise Author the novel Bloodbath: In Jasper County Mississippi, a documented vivid account of the struggle that the Cruise family had to endure in rural Mississippi. It started in the Blue Ridge Mountains of Picken Country Georgia and takes us through the most difficult period of enslavement. It also tells about the murder and intimidation of the decedents of ex slaves. Matthew Cruise, 11403 Darlington Avenue, Bakersfield, California 93312 Phone: (661) 829-3500 E-mail: **cru1935@sbcglobal.net** Website: **www.pullupfrompoverty.com**

George Curry Author, journalist and nationally acclaimed columnist, and radio commentary host, Mr. Curry is former editor-in-chief of the National Newspaper Publishers Association News Service and BlackPressUSA. Author/editor of three books, Best of Emerge Magazine Edited by George E. Curry, The Affirmative Action Debate edited by George Curry, and Jake Gaither: America's Most Famous Black Coach. George E. Curry, 3200 13th Street, North West, Washington, DC 20010 E-mail: **george@georgecurry.com** Website: **www.georgecurry.com**

Karen E. Dabney Author of a novel, The Magic Pencil. Karen E. Dabney, 19703 Steel, Detroit, Michigan 48235 E-mail: **dabsandco@att.net** Website: **www.dabsandcompany.com**

Natalie L. Darden Voted Best New Self-Published Author 2003, Mahogany Book Club and Awarded Afro-American Author of Excellence 2003 by Dare 2 Dream Book Club, for her book All about Me. Also author of a novel "Single as a Dollar Bill: Love Yourself First, the Rest Is Easy," (2004). Natalie is a graduate of Rutgers University, where she obtained a BA in English and Communications. Natalie L. Darden, Post Office Box 1501, Bloomfield, New Jersey 07003 Phone: (973) 454-1214 E-mail: **naldarpub@yahoo.com**

Brooklyn Darkchild Author of This Ain't No Hearts and Flowers Love Story. Owner of Brooklyn Dreams Publishing (through Lulu.com). Brooklyn Darkchild,1886 Windmill Way, Cincinnati, Ohio 45240 Phone: (513) 238-6898 E-mail: **BKDarkchild@yahoo.com**

E-K. Daufin A visionary activist performance artist (musician, vocalist, actor), poet, author, consultant, college professor and public speaker, Dr. Daufin is a national expert on issues of weight discrimination, cited by CNN. She has published book chapters, news stories, magazine features, editorials and poetry usually related to issues of race, gender, and class equity. A member of the Central Alabama Storytellers' Guild. Rev. Dr. E-K. Daufin, 3705 Oak Shadow Lane, Montgomery, Alabama 36116 Phone: (334) 229-6885 E-mail: **ekdaufin@alasu.edu**

Floyd B. Davis "1896" is his first work of fiction taken from the history of struggle against oppression that defined the lives of Africans during colonial times and African Americans during post-Reconstruction in America. Floyd B. Davis, 324 West 84th Street, #72, New York, New York 10024 Phone: (212) 501-9187 E-mail: **fbdav@earthlink.net**

Wayne Dawkins Author, "Black Journalists: The NABJ Story," Rugged Waters: Black Journalists Swim the Mainstream," (August Press, 2003). Editor and contributing author, "Black Voices in Commentary: The Trotter Group," August Press, 2006. Editor and founder, Black Alumni Network newsletter, Columbia University Journalism, 1980-present. Wayne Dawkins, August Press, Post Office Box 6693, Newport News, Virginia 23606 Phone: (757) 727-5437 **wdawkins4bj@aol.com** Website: **www.augustpress.net**

Deborah Day President of Ashay by the Bay, a publishing and marketing company that she founded in 1997. Poet, author and publisher of the book (s) Mindful Messages. In 2002 she wrote and published Mindful Messages and the Mindful Messages Mentoring Workbook. Currently she is working on the Mindful Messages Teachers Guide. Deborah Day, Ashay by the Bay, Post Office Box 9388, Vallejo, California 94591 Phone: (510) 520-2742 Fax: (510) 441-0498 E-mail: ashaybythebay@gmail.com Website: www.ashaybythebay.com

Cedric Lamonte Dean Author of "For The Love of the Streets," "Best Friends for What," "This Ain't Living," "Pimping in the Name of the Lord," and "How to Stop Your Children From Going to Prison." Cedric Lamonte Dean, Kreative Konsepts, Inc., 25422 Trabuco Road #105, Lake Forest, California 92630 E-mail: KreativeKonsepts@aol.com

Theresa A. Dear Author, executive, Ordained Minister, speaker, professor, leader. Her book, Already Chosen, will make you think, thank, believe, journal, act and change. It takes us on a personal journey with Hannah and Peninnah, in the Old Testament, and allows us to see ourselves and God in each woman. Ms. Dear's second book, Inconceivable Seasons. Contact Ms. Theresa A. Dear, 868 Prairie Avenue, Bartlett, Illinois 60103 Fax: (630) 830-4445 E-mail: tdear@alreadychosen.com Website: www.alreadychosen.com

Montez DeCarlo Detroit native and co-author of Our Sacred Identity: The Book of American Indian Names and Their Meanings, makes his Novel debut with Black Chameleon Memoirs. He currently mentors troubled teens by sharing his experiences and allowing them to shadow him on the job. Montez DeCarlo, Post Office Box 141, Wake Forest, North Carolina 27588 E-mail: mdecarlo@blackchameleonmemoirs.com Website: www.blackchameleonmemoirs.com

Ruby Dee Author, actor, playwright, and activist, Ms. Dee is author of children's books, Tower to Heaven and Two Ways to Count to Ten; a book of poetry and short stories, My One Good Nerve (which she has adapted into a solo performance piece); and With Ossie and Ruby: In This Life Together, a joint autobiography co-authored with her late husband. Ms. Ruby Dee, c/o Author Mail, Little, Brown and Company, 237 Park Avenue, New York, New York 10017 Website: www.hachettebookgroupusa.com

Anita Davis-DeFoe Author of the book, A Woman's Guide to Soulful Living…Seven Keys to Life and Work Success, and a variety of other publications, Dr. Defoe is an Associate Editor with the Caribbean Voice, a South Florida newspaper. In addition, she is the television host of caribbeanwomentoday, a segment on Caribbean Weekly which is an informational and community affairs program. Contact Dr. Anita Davis DeFoe, The Afia Development Corp, 10690 North West 28th Place, Sunrise, Florida 33322 Phone: (954) 213-4093 E-mail: theafiadevelopmentcorporation@yahoo.com Website: www.dranitadavisdefoe.com

Antoine Maurice Devine Author of THE CURE, a medical thriller. Mr. Devine was born in Milwaukee, Wisconsin, raised in Arizona, and was educated at Jackson State University and the University of Texas at Austin School of Law. He maintains a securities law consulting practice, and resides in Phoenix, Arizona near the Ahwatukee Foothills. Antoine Maurice Devine, BluQuill Publishing, LLC., 2155 East Liberty Lane, Suite 381, Phoenix, Arizona 85048 Phone: (480) 772-1782 E-mail: thebluquill@yahoo.com

Christina Dixon Contributing writer in the Wisdom and Grace Devotional Bible for Young Women of Color (Nia Publishing) and HELP! for Your Leadership (PriorityONE Publications) and she has written articles for WOW! Women's Magazine by Joy2BHizz.com, Just for You Ministries, and TRUTH magazine. Active member of the Writer's Resources and Accountability in Publishing (WRAP). Contact Ms. Christina Dixon, PriorityONE Ministries, Post Office Box 725, Farmington, Michigan 48332 Phone: (313) 283-3596 E-mail: info@christinadixon.net Website: www.christinadixon.net

Shaneisha Dodson The author of Cheating On My Mistress and A Diamond For A Diva, Shaneisha is currently pursing her doctorate degree in Education specializing in Adult Learning and Higher Education. She has a Masters degree in Counseling from Dallas Baptist University and a Bachelor degree in Psychology from Grambling State University. She is a member of the Alpha Kappa Alpha Sorority Incorporated. Shaneisha Dodson, 11108 Gainsborough Court 3, Fairfax, Virginia 22030 Phone: (571) 232-0392 E-mail: st_dodson@yahoo.com

Norris Dorsey Author of the book, The Art of Inclusion: Success Stories of African American in the Nonprofit Sector (2006), Dr. Dorsey is a college professor currently at California State University and Los Angeles Mission College. Doctoral degree in Education from the University of La Verne. Consultant, also teaches various business classes such as: accounting, business, management, marketing, and supervision. Norris Dorsey, 11024 Balboa Boulevard, Suite #328, Granada Hills, California 91344 Phone: (818) 402-5050 E-mail: ndorsey@socal.rr.com

Shani Greene-Dowdell Founder of Nayberry Publications and author of Keepin-Tight, Secrets of a Kept Woman, Mocha Chocolate: Taste A Piece., and Mocha-Chocolate-Escapades-Passion-ebook. Shani Greene-Dowdell, Shanibooks, Post Office Box 1001, Opelika, Alabama 36803 E-mail: info@nayberrypublications.com Website: www.nayberrypublications.com

Celise Downs The author's young adult fiction books are Secrets and Kisses, and Dance Jam Productions. Celise Downs, Gemini Mojo Press, 2343 West Claremont Street, Phoenix, Arizona 85015 E-mail: celise@geminimojopress.com Website: www.GeminiMojoPress.com

Janet Carr-Dudley Author of Mama's Last Chance, a fiction novel that deals with domestic violence. Contact Ms. Janet Carr-Dudley, 960 Ellis Mill Road, Glassboro, New Jersey 08028 E-mail: janetdud_57@yahoo.com

Karen Dumas President of her own PR firm, Images & Ideas, Inc., and currently working on her Masters in PR/Organizational Communication at Wayne State University. She just completed her first book, In Other Words. Contact Ms. Karen Dumas, Post Office Box 14724, Detroit, Michigan 48214 Phone: (866) 330-4585 E-mail: karendumas2@aol.com Website: www.KarenDumas.com

Kia DuPree Author of the book Robbing Peter, and a novel Like Holding A Butterfly, native of Washington, DC., Ms. DuPree is a public relations specialist, college English instructor and a freelance copy writer. She is a graduate of Hampton University and Old Dominion University. Contact Kia DuPree, Prism Pages, Post Office Box 7189, Hampton, Virginia 23666 E-mail: info@prismpages.com Website: www.prismpages.com

Sherry Sherrod Dupree Teacher, historian, research specialist, and former librarian, Sherry Dupree is the author of two books, Displays for Schools, and The African-American Holiness Pentecostal Movement, an annotated bibliography guide to the Afro-American Pentecostal churches in the U.S. Contact Mrs. Sherry Sherrod Dupree, Santa Fe Community College, 3000 North West 83rd Street, Building S-212, Gainesville, Florida 32606 Phone: (800) 250-4645 E-mail: rosewood@displaysforschools.com Website: www.displaysforschools.com

Michelle Dunn In 1998, Dunn opened M.A.D Collection Agency and published her first book, How to Make Money Collecting Money - Starting a Collection Agency, in 2002. She is now publishing Become the Squeaky Wheel, A Credit and Collections Guide for everyone and a book of 7 short stories. Michelle Dunn, Never Dunn Publishing, Post Office Box 40, Plymouth, New Hampshire 03264 E-mail: michelle@michelledunn.com Website: www.michelledunn.com

Michael Eric Dyson Scholar, author, cultural critic and media personality, Dyson is hailed as one of the nation's most inspiring African Americans. His seventeen books provide some of the most significant commentary on modern social and intellectual thought. His works such as Making Malcolm; I May Not Get There With You; Holler If You Hear Me; Mercy, Mercy Me: The Art, Loves and Demons of Marvin Gaye; Is Bill Cosby Right? Or Has the Black Middle Class Lost Its Mind?; and more recently, Come Hell or High Water: Hurricane Katrina and the Color of Disaster, deeply probe social themes and cultural politics. Mr. Michael Eric Dyson, c/o WEAA-FM 89.9, 1700 East Cold Spring Lane, Baltimore, Maryland 21251 Phone: (443) 885-3564 E-mail: staff@dysonshow.org Website: www.dysonshow.org

Amanda Easton Author of The Last Love Letter, the raw, provocative and humbling story of a heartbreaking relationship involving a young African-American couple that begins with a one-night stand. Additionally, she is launching Dirty Laundry Ink, an independent publishing company. Amanda Easton, c/o Dirty Laundry Ink, Post Office Box 65862, West Des Moines, Iowa 50265 Phone: (515) 314-0812 E-mail: amanda@thelastloveletter.com

Bill Jong-Ebot Writer (fiction and nonfiction). Nonfiction subjects include press freedom, communication, self-help (college), media and society, media and minority. Fiction subjects include race relations. Publications include Press Freedom and Communication in Africa. Contact Mr. Bill Jong-Ebot, Alpha Marketing & Management Group, Inc, 612 SW 168 Lane, Pembroke Pines, Florida 33027 Phone: (954) 392 4016 E-mail: wjongebot@bellsouth.net

Gloria Taylor Edwards Mystery writer/women's issues, inspirational speaker, and radio talk show host, Edwards is the author of The Proclamation, 1992, Stories From Ancient Africa, 1995, Death Will Pay The Debt, 2000, and, Sins Of The Parents, 2004. Contact Ms. Gloria Taylor Edwards, Voices from the Drum, Post Office Box 27504, Richmond, Virginia 23261 Phone: (804) 323-6441 E-mail: vftdgte@aol.com Website: www.gloriatayloredwards.com

Jefferson D. Edwards, Jr. Author of 6 books including: "Where Are All the Fathers," "Purging Racism From Christianity," "Gifted - Discovering Your Hidden Greatness," and "The Call of God," subtitled (Since I've Been Called to Preach - Now What?). Dr. Jefferson D. Edwards, Jr., Jeff Edwards Ministries International, Post Office Box 300873, Kansas City, Missouri 64130 E-mail: jemikcmo@aol.com Website: www.jeffedwards.org

Dorothy G. Elliott   An author, writer, Afro-American children books. Contact Ms. Dorothy G. Elliott, Hosanna Productions, Post Office Box 3011, Petersburg, Virginia 23805 E-mail: elliottoge2003@yahoo.com

K. Elliott   A native of Charlotte, North Carolina, K. Elliott attended Central Piedmont Community College in the early nineties. Elliott placed in a competition and later earned a scholarship to the North Carolina Writer's Conference in 2001 the same year in which he began working on his first Novel entitled "Entangled." Contact K. Elliott, Urban Lifestyle Press, Post Office. Box 12714, Charlotte, North Carolina 28205 E-mail: kelliott11@carolina.rr.com

Marvie Ellis Received her Bachelor of Science degree in Communicative Disorders from Jackson State University, Jackson, Mississippi and her Master of Science degree from the University of North Carolina, Chapel Hill (1996). Owns a private pediatric speech-language and occupational therapy practice, Marvie has specialized training in working with the birth to five population, children with autism spectrum disorders. Mrs. Marvie Ellis, Speech Kids Texas Press, Inc., 3802 Beaconsdale Drive, Austin, Texas 78727 Phone: (512) 426-0163 E-mail: marvie_ellis@yahoo.com Website: www.speechkidstexaspress.com

Nishawnda Ellis Author of the new book Snowed, A Lesson In Love. After, graduating from Boston Latin Academy with honors, Nishawnda attended Hampton University in Hampton Virginia where, she earned a Bachelors of Science degree and went on to practice as a Registered Nurse. She is also founder of the Boston Book Bazaar. Ms. Nishawnda Ellis, Post Office Box 692092, Quincy, Massachusetts 02269 E-mail: nishawnda@kindleeyesbooks.com Website: www.kindleeyesbooks.com

CC Fann Last year she released Part one of "Can't Let Go." Part two of "Can't Let Go: The Hidden Agenda" was released in November. Her latest release is "Common Sense Do Not Play The Game With An Inmate." She has been featured in Booking Matter Magazine for Black Authors. She also conducts workshops at the Corrections Academy for the Georgia Department of Corrections. She is a member of Buckeye Baptist Church of Dublin GA, and Southern States Correction Association, Peace Officers Association. She is retired from the Department of Corrections with 14 years. CC Fann, Post Office Box 81, Wrightsville, Georgia 31096 mail: jabspub@yahoo.com Website: www.ccfanncommonsense.com

Holly K. Ferguson Author of "Getting Deep with God", "Spring Cleaning", "Encouragements from the Heart," and "Where Is The Church." Holly K. Ferguson, Now U No Publishing Company, Post Office Box 9501, Cincinnati Ohio 45209 Phone: (513) 226-6450 E-mail: carla.sams@nowuno-enterprises.com Website: www.nowunopublishingco.com

Peggy M Fisher   Author of "Lifting Voices:Voices of the Collective Struggle." Her poems have appeared in several anthologies. Her lastest book, "Search Lights for My Soul," just received the Readers View 2007 Award in the category of Self Help. Featured author in an anthology of essays, "The Story That Must Be Told," published by Loving Healing Press in June 2007. Peggy M Fisher, Pyramid Collections, Post Office Box 2775, Camden, New Jersey 08101 Phone: (856) 964-4284 E-mail: pyramidcl@cs.com Website: www.pmmfisher.com

Valdez V. Fisher, Jr. His book, I Ain't Bitin' My Tongue is one of the most unconventional books of its genre. Although pregnant with truth and delivering vital points, it manages to remain absolutely hilarious all throughout. Valdez Vincent Fisher, Jr., Post Office Box 23951, Baltimore, Maryland 21203 Phone: (410) 456-3660 E-mail: booksbyvaldez@aol.com

Barry Fletcher Author/ Poet, and expert who has studied hair for the last 25 years, Barry is the most informed and sought after cosmetological entrepreneur in the business. A professional trichologist (someone who scientifically studies the hair and scalp), is author of the book, WHY ARE BLACK WOMEN LOSING THEIR HAIR? It is a must read for every family, with 10 chapters written by various experts. Fletcher's second book, HAIR IS SEXUAL, examines the relationship between a woman's hair and her sensuality. Barry Fletcher, 6304 Marlboro Pike, District Heights, Maryland 20747 Phone: (301) 710-5566 E-mail: fletchpro@aol.com

Pansie Hart Flood Children's author and educator her first book was Sylvia & Miz Lula Maye. Two sequels followed. Secret Holes was released in 2003 and September Smiles was released in 2004 and a young readers series called Tiger Turcotte is forthcoming. She earned her bachelor's degree from East Carolina University in Greenville, North Carolina. She teaches at E. B. Aycock Middle School. Member of the Society of Children's Book Writers and Illustrators, North Carolina Writer's Network and North Carolina Association of Educators. Pansie H. Flood, Post Office Box 20614, Greenville, North Carolina 27858 E-mail: floodpan@earthlink.net

Nancey Flowers Editor-In-Chief of Game Sports Magazine and publisher of Flowers In Bloom Publishing, Inc., Nancey attended Morgan State University in Baltimore, Maryland, where she received her bachelor's degree in mass communications with a minor in journalism. She is author of A Fool's Paradise, and Shattered Vessels, and No Strings Attached. Contributing author in Twilight Moods, and the anthology Proverbs For The People. Contact Ms. Nancey Flowers, Flowers In Bloom Publishing, Inc., Post Office Box 473106, Brooklyn, New York 11247 E-mail: nanceyflowers@msn.com Website: www.flowersinbloompublishing.com

Penelope Flynn Author and Screenwriter of Erotica, Science Fiction, Fantasy, Sensual Romance, Paranormal Romance, Legal comedy and drama and Horror. Penelope Flynn, 824 North Marsalis Avenue, Suite C, Dallas, Texas 75203 Phone: (214) 371-7366 Fax: (214) 942-0980 E-mail: penelope@penelopeflynn.com Website: www.penelopeflynn.com

Dawn Fobbs Born September 24, 1972 in Houston Texas. Writer, Creative Publisher of Stand Magazine since 2004. Entrepreneur, Mentor, Author of 7-Days of Networking, a book for the serious networkers taking the initiative to take their business and branding to the next level. Contact Ms. Dawn Fobbs, Stand Magazine, Post Office Box 6667, Katy, Texas 77491 E-mail: msdawwn@sbcglobal.net Website: www.standmagazine.biz

Gyasi A. Foluke Author of The Real-Holocaust (1995), The Old Time Religion (1997), The Crisis and Challenge of Black Mis-education in America (2001), The Scoundrel Syndrome, Revisiting The Real-Holocaust (2004) and A Wholistic Freedom Agenda (2007). Contact Dr. Gyasi A. Foluke, The Kushite Institute for Wholistic Development, 4215 Colonial Drive, Columbia, South Carolina 29203 Phone: (803) 754-8317 E-mail: gflack1@bellsouth.net Website: http://tkifwd.tripod.com

Michael Fontaine Writer and author, his mainstream fiction novel titled: "Yesterday I Could Sing", was inspired by society's incredible failure at juvenile delinquent rehabilitation. He served as a juvenile probation officer with the Lake County Superior Court System, in Gary, Indiana from 1973 through 1978 where he had an active caseload of more than 200 delinquents involved in crimes against person and property. Michael Fontaine, #34 Queensbrook Place, Saint Louis, Missouri 63132 Phone: (314) 994-9927 E-mail: drfontaine303@sbcglobal.net

Darnella Ford Author of the novel Rising (St. Martin's Press, Jan. 2003), a raw tale of incest and redemption hailed by Ebony Magazine as the "Survival anthem of the year." She is author of four other novels: Crave (March 2004); Choke (2005); 19 Floors (2006); Naked (2007). Upcoming projects include the screenplay adaptation of Rising, Salvaged, a non-fiction book 2007, Skin (Kensington) 2008, Crack'd (Feature Film), and Intercept (Feature Film). Darnella Ford Phone: (818) 458-2062 E-mail: dapoet@aol.com Website: www.darnella.com

Roger A. Forsyth Author of Black Flight, the story of the three flights of Albert Forsythe and Al Anderson (later the chief instructor for the Tuskegee Airmen). Mr. Forsyth details their three exciting flights. Contact Mr. Roger Forsyth, Allcourt Publishing, Post Office Box 491122, Los Angeles, California 90049 E-mail: allcourtpublishing@yahoo.com

Gwendoline Y. Fortune Author of three novels, Growing Up Nigger Rich, Family Lines, and Weaving the Journey, Gwen has been a classical soprano and has traveled on five continents. She holds degrees in education and social science. A former elementary school teacher and professor of history and social science, Ms. Fortune is active in the alumni associations of Bennett College, J. C. Smith, Roosevelt, and Nova Southeastern Universities. Gwendoline Y. Fortune, Ed. D., 8620 North West 13th, Suite #71, Gainesville, Florida 32653 Phone: (352) 372-0021 E-mail: gyfort@earthlink.net Website: www.zenarts.com

Rebera Elliott Foston Author, poet, Dr. Foston was the valedictorian of Gary Roosevelt High School in 1966. She was a Phi Beta Kappa, Magna Cum Laude 1970 graduate of Fisk University, and a 1974 graduate of Meharry Medical College, Nashville, Tennessee. In 1981, she received her masters' degree in Public Health from the University of North Carolina, Chapel Hill, where she was elected to Delta Omega, the honor society for Public Health. She completed a Post Doctoral fellowship in teaching Family Medicine at Michigan State University in East Lansing, Michigan, her residency in Family Practice and became Board Certified in 1984. She has published an inspirational journal entitled Peace on Earth, and 20 books of poetry. Her signature poems are You Don't Live On My Street, Annie's Baby and Not My Chile. Dr. Rebera Elliott Foston, M.D., DMin, Post Office Box 726, Clarksville, Tennessee 37041 Phone: (800) 418-0374 Fax: (931) 645-3500 E-mail: minfoston@aol.com Website: www.drfoston.com

Antoinette V. Franklin An author, poet and educator, Antoinette Franklin has written six chap books of poetry, These Rainy Days, An Untouched Song, My Rock And My Salvation, A New Beginning, Going Home, Sisterly Love, and In The Mist Of Struggle. Ms. Franklin has been published in over 100 anthologies including Violets and Delta Girl Stories and Poets Along The River, her book, Hot Woman Needing a Man (2007), a play and other stories. Ms. Antoinette V. Franklin, Author House, 550 Crestway Drive, San Antonio, Texas Phone: (210) 264-1518 E-mail: antoinettevfranklin@gmail.com Website: www.antoinettefranklin.com

Mike Frazier Author of Surviving the Storm: Finding life after death, about a torrential storm ravaged Dallas, Texas, on May 5, 1995, devastating the life of Mike Frazier forever. Using his talent as a bass guitarist and drummer, Mike Frazier has toured with artist such as Kirk Franklin, R. Kelly, Stevie Wonder, La Shun Pace and Ann Nesby. He has appeared on live recordings of Bishop T.D. Jakes and gospel great James Moore, and has been touring the country with Tyler Perry Gospel Stage plays. Mike Frazier, Post Office Box 201571, Arlington, Texas 76006 E-mail: mike@survivingthestorm.com Website: www.survivingthestorm.com

Walter Fredericks Jr. Author and Entrepreneur. Walter Fredericks writes under the pen name T.F. Walters. He is the author of the critically acclaimed urban literary work, My Brothers Keeper. He vividly tells the story of two brothers growing up in poverty as they face death and betrayal as each ascends to fame and fortune in two opposites manners. Founder and CEO of Walter Fredericks Enterprises, Inc., a multimedia company that specializes in the production and marketing of urban literature (also known as Street Lit). Walter Fredericks Jr., Post Office Box 1204, Dallas, Georgia 30132 E-mail: wenterprisesinc@yahoo.com

Harrine Freeman Author of How to Get out of Debt: Get an "A" Credit Rating for Free Using the System I've Used Successfully with Thousands of Clients (2006). She has a B.S. degree in Computer Science and is pursuing a Master's degree in Information Technology. She writes frequently and has written technical documentation for several ezine on personal finance. Harrine Freeman, H.E. Freeman Enterprsies, 3 Bethesda Metro Center, Suite 700, Bethesda, Maryland 20814 Phone: (301) 280-5923 E-mail: hfreeman@hefreemanenterprises.com Website: www.hefreemanenterprises.com

Charlotte A. Clark-Frieson Owner of a mortuary company and the CEO of Wilkie Clark's Daughter Enterprises, LLC, Charlotte is author of a biography of her late father, entitled Chief Cook & Bottle-Washer, The Unconquerable Soul of Wilkie Clark, who during the 20th century, rose to the occasion of racism and economic oppression in Alabama. Charlotte A. Clark-Frieson, Wilkie Clark's Daughter Enterprises, LLC, 322 Wilkie Clark Drive, Roanoke, Alabama 36274 Phone: (334) 863-4885 Fax: (334) 863-6062 E-mail: caclarkfrieson@msn.com Website: www.wilkieclarksdaughter.net

Lisa H. Fuller Practicing psychiatrist, Community Chaplain, and author of the book, "You Already Have All of the Tools that You Need" tells us how one can transform their life based on Biblical truth and 'God is Love' (children's book). She obtained her medical degree from the West Virginia School of Osteopathic Medicine and is the executive director of LRHF Mental Health Consultants and president of Learn Realistic Habits for the Future Publishing. Lisa H. Fuller, 15565 Northland Drive, Suite 206E, Southfield, Michigan 48075 Phone: (313) 645-1596 E-mail: lf917@aol.com Website: www.drlisafuller.com

Ethel M. Gardner Author, writer, founder of my own Publishing Company! I have written 4 books, A Mother's Cry can good come from a brokenheart" and Families in crisis, The Makings Of You! Somewhere In My Lifetime, and Journaling your Journey on a road less traveled. I write for healing the heart, after the loss of a child, dealing with the dynamics of single Mother's who have no one too help them. Kennedy Austin Wellness Foundation, Post Office Box 1991, Corona, California 92878 Phone: (714) 471-2300 E-mail: ethelgardner2000@yahoo.com

Kyra Gaunt Author of The Games Black Girls Play: Learning the Ropes from Double-Dutch to Hip-hop (NYU Press, 2006), Kyra a.k.a. "Professor G" is a singer-songwriter and an associate professor of ethnomusicology at New York University who lectures nationally and internationally. Kyra Gaunt, 1 Washington Square Village, #5-H, New York, New York 10012 Phone: (646) 831-0615 E-mail: **kyraocity@yahoo.com**

Carol Gee Author, Carol Gee has been an educator for over twenty years. Carol Gee, Post Office Box 832004, Stone Mountain, Georgia 30083 E-mail: **VenusChronicles@aol.com**

Carolyn Gibson A native of Boston, Massachusetts, and a Simmons College graduate, Gibson is author of a novel, "Repairman Jones" and a collection of 60 poems titled "Urban Poetry." Contact Ms. Carolyn Gibson, Carolyn's Corner, 7 Verrill Street, Boston, Massachusetts 02126 Phone: (617) 298-7484 Fax: (617) 298-1018 E-mail: **Carolynscorner@aol.com** Website: **www.Carolynscorner.com**

Richard Charles Gibson The author's first book of short stories Life Lessons was published in 2003. Mr. Richard C. Gibson, 2517 West Harrison Street, Chicago, Illinois 60612 Phone: (312) 243-5343 E-mail: **gibsonsnoopy@aol.com**

Gladys "Nyagus" Gikiri Creator of a new children's book series called My Malaika. Nyagus has a BBA and an MBA and for many years she worked as a Finance Professional. When she quit her job to spend more time with her young children she discovered her true calling: writing children's books. Nyagus enjoys visiting schools and motivating children to read. Ms. Gladys Nyagus Gikiri, 5413 Whistler Drive, Tallahassee, Florida 32317 Phone: (850) 878-7741 E-mail: **gladys@mymalaika.com** Website: **www.mymalaika.com**

J. Lee Cooper-Giles Author of The Hypocrites. Lifelong political and social activist, he has three under-graduate college degrees from the Ohio State University, a BA in Black Studies and English, BA in Journalism, BFA in Painting and Drawing. J. Lee Cooper-Giles, 1761 Clifton Avenue #10, Columbus, Ohio 43203 E-mail: **leegiles78@hotmail.com**

Nancy Gilliam Her work has been published in Chicken Soup for the African American Soul, Chicken Soup for the African American Woman's Soul, Chicken Soup for the Soul: Teens Talk Middle School, The Hustler's Ten Commandments. She authored the companion study guide to BJ Robinson's LeBron James: King of the Court, and was the lyricist behind the Billboard #1 Dance hit, Take a Chance. Ms. Nancy Gilliam, 5525 West Girard Avenue, Philadelphia, Pennsylvania 10131 E-mail: **melodicg2003@hotmail.com**

Thomas Gist Author of You Too, Can Have, The Fruits of Life! Without "White Folks" BS (Business Suck-ins). Thomas Gist, 112 South Lavergne Avenue, Chicago, Illinois 60644 Phone: (312) 857-4531 E-mail: **thomas@hannibalisatthegates.com**

Sheronde Glover Business consultant, speaker and co-author of Sipping Tea and Doing Business: A Holistic Journey to Business Success. Ms. Sheronde Glover, Glover Enterprise, Attn: Sipping Tea and Doing Business, Post Office Box 870354, Morrow, Georgia 30287 E-mail: **sheronde@sippingteaonline.com** Website: **www.sippingteaonline.com**

Beverly T. Gooden Author of Confessions of a Church Girl. Ms. Beverly T. Gooden, 1754 Woodruff Road, #121, Greenville, South Carolina 29607 E-mail: info@beverlyt.com Website: www.BeverlyT.com

Walter L. Gordon, III A criminal and appeals lawyer in Los Angeles, California since 1974. Attorney Gordon has both a law degree and a PHD from UCLA. He has taught and written about the law and other issues. Mr. Gordon's current book is The Nat Turner Insurrection Trials, A Mystic Chord Resonates Today. Walter L. Gordon, III, 2658 Griffith Park Blvd., #176, Los Angeles, California 90039 Phone: (323) 732-7170 E-mail: w.l.Gordon@att.net Website: www.natturnertours.com

Theresa E. Grant Writer of contemporary romance for twelve years, Ms. Grant has published A Faithful Choice, All My Bright Tomorrows and Hope and Desire. She has lived in Rockville, Maryland for the past thirty-six years, is married to Dr. Warren H. Grant, and has one daughter and one son. Theresa E. Grant, 4917 Morning Glory Court, Rockville Maryland 20853 Phone: (301) 929-1154 Fax: (301) 929-1154 E-mail: Grant_Theresa@msn.com

Maurice M. Gray, Jr. Author and owner of Write The Vision, Inc., a Christian publishing company, Maurice is the author of To Whom Much Is Given, I Really Didn't Mean To Get HIV by Livingston N. Lee, Jr. as told to Maurice M. Gray, Jr., and All Things Work Together. Mr.Maurice M. Gray, Write The Vision, Inc., Box 12926, Wilmington, Delaware 19850 Phone: (302) 778-2407 E-mail: writevision2000@yahoo.com Website: www.writethevision.biz

Carmen Green Author of more than twenty novels and novellas. Her most recent novel is FLIRT, a romance novel (Kensington/Dafina). Her first collaboration novel with Victor McGlothlin and Tracey Price Thompson is entitled Indecent Exposure (February, 2006). Her next comedy What A Fool Believes (August, 2006). Carmen Green, 325 Wildcat Lake Drive, Lawrenceville, Georgia 30043 E-mail: carmengreen1201@yahoo.com

Kisha Green Author of "And Even If I Did," "If It Ain't One Thing, It's Another," "Dear Mommy" and "Mental Seduction." Divabook, Inc., 2 Evergreen Drive, Wayside, New Jersey 07712 E-mail: kisha@divabooksinconline.com Website: www.divabooksinconline.com

Thomas Green, Jr. Ex athlete and ex sports reporter, Thomas has self published four such novels, Courting Miss Thang, Love's Home Run, Player No More, When It Hurts So Bad and Ice Thug Blues (October 2004). Contact Mr. Thomas Green Jr., 3371 Adkins Road, Atlanta, Georgia 30331 E-mail: tjverde05@yahoo.com Website: www.CourtingMissThang.com

Thomas J. Greene Children's book author and publisher. Thomas J. Greene, Greene Bark Press Inc, Post Office Box 1108, Bridgeport, Connecticut 06601 Phone: (610) 434-2802 Fax: (610) 434-2803 E-mail: greenebark@aol.com Website: www.greenebarkpress.com

Evelyn Gresham Author of Brown Little Babies, a children's picture book of poetry honoring African American babies. Contact Evelyn Gresham, Elg Books and Collectibles, Otter Branch Drive, Apt. #8, Magnolia, New Jersey 08049 E-mail: contactus@elgbooksanddolls.com Website: www.elgbooksanddolls.com

Neisha Brown Grice   Author of the book, F.A.M.I.L.Y - Fathers And Mothers In Loving Youth group. Contact Ms. Neisha Brown Grice, 700 West Center Street, Suite #297, Duncanville, Texas 75116 E-mail: **neishabrown31@yahoo.com**

Vanessa Davis Griggs   Author of three novels: Destiny Unlimited, The Rose of Jericho and the latest books: Promises Beyond Jordan published by BET Books/New Spirit, Wings of Grace published by BET Books in 2005. She is the recipient of numerous recognitions including finalist for the BWA 2002 Gold Pen Award for Christian Fiction, named 2002 Self-published African American Author Book of the Year. Ms. Vanessa Davis Griggs, Post Office Box 101328, Birmingham, Alabama 35210 E-mail: **Vanessa@VanessaDavisGriggs.com** Website: **www.vanessaDavisGriggs.com**

Tania Guerrera   Artist. Author of the book Thoughts and Transformations. The book contains poetry, art and essays all dealing with love, social issues, justice and spirituality. Tania Guerrera, 311 North Avenue #11, New Rochelle, New York 10801 Phone: (917) 578-4264 E-mail: **TheArtist@taniaGuerrera.com** Website: **www.TaniaGuerrera.com**

Shirley Hailstock   An award-winning novelist, Shirley Hailstock holds a bachelors degree in Chemistry from Howard University in Washington, DC, and an MBA in Chemical Marketing from Fairleigh Dickinson University in Teaneck, New Jersey. Whispers of Love, Shirley's debut novel, was published in September, 1994, won the Holt Medallion from the Virginia Romance Writers, is now in its 4th printing and recently was optioned for a television movie of the week. She has been an Adjunct Professor of Accounting at Rutgers University, New Brunswick campus and taught Novel Writing at Middlesex County College. Shirley T. Hailstock, Post Office 513, Plainsboro, New Jersey 08536 Phone: (609) 275-8323 E-mail: **shirley.hailstock@comcast.net** Website: **www.shirleyhailstock.net**

Alex Hairston   An Essence best-selling author and nurse originally from Baltimore. Alex Hairston now resides in Randallstown, Maryland with his wife and three kids. He is the author of two books, "If Only You Knew" and Love Don't Come Easy, A Novel. Alex Hairston, Post Office Box 1138, Randallstown, Maryland 21133 E-mail: **alexhairston@yahoo.com** Website: **www.alexhairston.com**

Forest Hairston   Author of the book "Spirit Ran Free", Forest Hairston is a Detroit, Michigan, native. His successful career as a songwriter-music producer, screenwriter and poet, extends his talents a step further as a great author with a definite voice. Mr. Forest Hairston, ForGen Productions, 3654 Barham Boulevard, Suite Q301, Los Angeles, California   E-mail: **theater@forgen.com** Website: **www.forgen.com**

William Hairston   Author, playwright and poet Mr. Hairston's books include: "The World of Carlos" (novel) "Sex and Conflict" (novel) "History of The National Capital Area Council/Boy Scouts of America" "Spaced Out" (space adventure) "Showdown At Sundown" (western novel)" Ira Frederick Aldridge" (The London Conflict) (Play, non-fiction), "Swan Song" (novel), "It's Human Nature" (short story collection), "Passion And Politics" (novel) and "Poetry And Prose Of Passion And Compassion" (poetry). William Hairston, 5501 Seminary Road, #511-S, Falls Church, Virginia 22041 Phone: (703) 845-1281 E-mail: **WilliamRHairston1@msn.com**

Patricia Haley   Author and motivational speaker.   National bestselling author of Nobody's Perfect, Blind Faith, and No Regrets is a trailblazer.   She self-published Nobody's Perfect in 1998 and her faith-based debut novel was the first of its kind to repeatedly make numerous bestselling lists, including #1 on the Essence list.   With her engineering degree from Stanford University and M.B.A. in marketing and finance from the University of Chicago, she works part-time as a project manager.   Patricia is also a member of Delta Sigma Theta Sorority.   Ms. Patricia Haley, Anointed Vision, Post Office Box 80735 Valley Forge, Pennsylvania 19484   E-mail: **publicity@patriciahaley.com**   Website: **www.patriciahaley.com**

Evelyn D. Hall   Self-published author, residing in, Atlanta, Georgia.   The author has published three books, Enter Eve's Poetic Paradise, Dontay's Poetic Playground and Dontay's Alphabet Book of Color.   Contact Evelyn D. Hall, Post Office Box 1775, Mableton, Georgia 30126   E-mail: **lilpoet2you@aol.com**   Website: **www.poeticparadise.ipfox.com**

Hallema   Author of two books, Mass Deceptions (2003) and a novel, True Intentions (2004).   She holds dual Bachelor of Science degrees in Criminology and Political Science from Florida State University.   Upon graduating from FSU, she was awarded a full scholarship to Stetson University College of Law, where she continued to nurture her writer's voice.   Following law school, Hallema returned to her roots in Miami. Hallema, Mahogany Publishing, Post Office Box 170952, Hialeah, Florida 33017   E-mail: **Hallemawrites@aol.com** Website: **www.hallema.net**

Sandra Hamer   A native of Grand Junction, Tennessee, Sandra is author of the book Glory...the Hair.   Sandra Hamer, 1779 Kirby Parkway #1-PMB161, Memphis, Tennessee 38138   Phone: (901) 272-2031   E-mail: **glorythehair@yahoo.com**   Website: **www.glorythehair.com**

John Hamilton   Educator, consultant and author of two books, The Elevator is Broken and Vainglorious: How Today's Black Men Graduate, Dr. Hamilton founded Hamilton and Associates Consulting, a Los Angeles based consulting firm, since 2004.   Contact Mr. John P. Hamilton, Hamilton & Associates Consulting, Post Office Box 2627, Gardena, California 90247   Phone: (323) 309-2502   Fax: (310) 538-0760   E-mail: **Johnphamilton@aol.com**   Website: **www.hamiltonandassociatesconsulting.org**

Robyn Maria Hamlin   Author and Screenwriter.   Novels, "The Zone of Danger Test" is my breakout novel.   "Shades of Gray" and "Zone of Danger" are my only two registered screenplays to date.   Poetry, "The Red Flag," "Bread Crumbs," "The Teamplayer," "A Hand for ME," and "There Is A River" are a few of my poems. My writings have also been featured in both EBONY and ESSENCE.   Robyn Maria Hamlin, 1900 Wesleyan Drive, #2807, Macon, Georgia 31210   Phone: (478) 476-8776   E-mail: **weeda5weeda@aol.com**

Julian Vaughan Hampton   An author of adult and children's fiction, poetry, commentary, and an award winning songwriter.   His first published book, a crime drama titled, The Contradiction, was an underground hit.   Julian's second book, a thriller titled, Limbus received rave reviews, setting the stage for the release of a book of spoken word poetry titled Love, Life and Kingdom. He is the founder and CEO of Vaughanworks, a literary empowerment and publishing company. Julian Vaughan Hampton, Vaughanworks, Post Office Box 18511-0511, Milwaukee, Wisconsin 53218   Phone: (877) 829-6757   E-mail: **Vaughanworks1@mfire.com**

Daniel D. Hardman Christian writer and author of the book titled Essays from Church: Volume One. Writes a column, The Other Side at theblackmarketcom. Daniel D Hardman, Post Office Box 1886, Cedar Hill, Texas 75106 E-mail: **essaysfromchurch@edincorporated.com**

P. Stephen Hardy Co-author with Sheila Jackson Hardy, M.Ed., of Extraordinary People of the Harlem Renaissance (Scholastic). P. Stephen Hardy, 6125 South LaCienega Boulevard, Los Angeles, California 90056 E-mail: **thenewnegro@hotmail.com**

Sheila Jackson Hardy Co-author with P. Stephen Hardy, of Extraordinary People of the Harlem Renaissance, winner of 2001 New York Public Library Best Books for the Teen Age 2001 and the Children's Book Council/National Council for Social Studies Notable Social Studies Trade Book for Young People - published by Scholastic Inc. Their recently completed Extraordinary People of the Civil Rights Movement, was released in September 2006. Sheila Jackson Hardy, M.Ed., 6125 South LaCienega Boulevard, Los Angeles, California 90056 E-mail: **thenewnegro@hotmail.com**

Julia Hare Nationally acclaimed speaker and master teacher, Dr. Julia Hare was named Educator of The Year by American University, World Book Encyclopedia, and the Junior Chamber Of Commerce. Contact Dr. Julia Hare, 1801 Bush Street, Suite 118, San Francisco, California 94109 Phone: (415) 474-1707 Fax: (415) 771-3485

Nathan Hare Born: 04-09-33. First person hired to coordinate a Black studies program in the United States, Dr. Hare coined the term "Ethnic Studies," which initially was being called "Minority Studies." Co-winner with Harold Cruse, of the National Award for Distinguished Scholarly Contributions to Black studies, National Council for Black Studies; 1990 winner of the Marcus and Amy Garvey Award from the Institute of Pan-African Studies. Dr. Nathan Hare, The Black Think Tank, 1801 Bush Street, Suite 118, San Francisco, California 94109 Phone: (415) 474-1707 Fax: (415) 771-3485 E-mail: **nhare@pacbell.net**

CaNon Harper Writer. I'm the CEO of Grown Man Publishing, LLC, and author of When Your Associates R More Dangerous Than U. Orginally from Detroit, I now reside in Southern Indiana. Grown Man Publishing, LLC, Post Office Box 205, Jeffersonville, Indiana 47131 Phone: (502) 994-9344

Keith Harrell Dynamic coach and highly acclaimed and innovative professional speaker, Keith is the author of Attitude is Everything: Ten Life Changing Steps to Turning Attitude into Action. Contact Mr. Keith Harrell, Harrell Performance Systems, Inc., 8374 Market Street, #504, Lakewood Ranch, Florida 34202 Phone: (703) 757-1204 E-mail: **info@keithharrell.com** Website: **www.keithharrell.com**

A. C. Jones-Harris Author of Which Road Should I Take? Learning To Live With AIDS (PublishAmerica). He is the president and founder of Greater Deliverance Ministries, Inc., a keynote speaker about AIDS prevention, paralegal and peer counselor. Received significant education from Troy State University, Darton College, Georgia State University, and University of Georgia. Contact Apostle A.C. Jones-Harris, Greater Deliverance Ministries, Inc., Post Office Box 911, Blakely, Georgia 39823 Phone: (229) 309-0083 E-mail: **greater@alltel.net**

Ardara Harris His first novel is titled Foolish Men and a second novel, Whoa-Man (Because Men Just Don't Give a Damn!), was birthed due to his personal experience of marriage and the struggles of life and being able to gain an understanding of the another side of the coin. After the tragic loss of his brother, Harris pushed through a place where no one should have to go and through his pain, his passion was once again rekindled which produced yet a third book titled, Skin Games (Is Success Measured by Tint?). An active member of the Alpha Phi Alpha Fraternity and a self-proclaimed idealist. Ardara Harris, 7422 Gatecraft Drive, Missouri City, Texas 77489 Phone: (281) 437-0434 E-mail: **thetalentedharris@sbcglobal.net**

Kathy Harris Author, motivational speaker, publisher & CEO, Angels Press, Post Office Box 870849, Stone Mountain, Georgia 30087 Phone: (770) 873-2072 Fax: (678) 254-5018 E-mail: **info@angelspress.com** Website: **www.angelspress.com**

Latasha S. Harris Editor and publisher of non fiction. Latasha S. Harris, 805 Anvil Road, Fredericksburg, Virginia 22405 E-mail: **tasha.harris@sbcglobal.net**

Saundra E. Harris Born in Maryland, Saundra is author of the book, THE PARTY (2003). Her company Saphari books re-released the book in 2006. She holds a Bachelors Degree in Business Management, from the University of Phoenix. Contact Ms. Saundra E. Harris, Saphari Books, Inc., Post Office Box 232, Pasadena, Maryland 21123 Phone: (443) 517-7196 E-mail: **sapharibooks@yahoo.com** Website: **www.sapharibooks.com**

Sonya Harris Resides in Boston, Massachusetts where she is an educator, a licensed General Securities Representative (Series 7 & 63), a State Examination Proctor, a Promising Pen Pal, and an organizer of Emerging-Authors Writers' Group. She has published two novels: Guilty Pleasures which received the 2004 Phenomenal & Outstanding African American Fiction Award from the Woman in ME 2002 Book Club. Her book My Body Is Calling was penned to promote and encourage health awareness for women's health issues. Sonya graduated from Boston Technical High School, and graduated with honors from Emmanuel College with a BS degree in Business Administration. Ms. Sonya Harris, Soya Pub, Post Office Box 260274, Boston, Massachusetts 02126 E-mail: **sh@sonyaharris.com** Website: **www.sonyaharris.com**

Natasha Brooks-Harris Author of Panache, a contemporary romance novel, Ms. Harris' two latest projects are novellas published in the books, Summer of Love, and Can I Get An Amen? She is a full-service copy editor, line editor, and proofreader of novel and short fiction manuscripts. Nathasha is the editor of Black Romance and Bronze Thrills magazines. And co-owner of Write On! Literary Consortium. Natasha Brooks-Harris, 297 7th Street, Brooklyn, New York 11215 E-mail: **nabrooks@aol.com**

Shelia Dansby Harvey A native Houstonian, Mrs. Shelia Dansby Harvey was inspired to write Illegal Affairs when she returned to her alma mater, Thurgood Marshall School of Law at Texas Southern University, as an adjunct professor. She received her law degree from Texas Southern University, a HBCU. She is a practicing attorney and has taught at Texas Southern's law school and at Rice University's graduate school. Mrs. Shelia Dansby Harvey, S & H Productions, LLC, Post Office Box 42257, Houston, Texas 77242 E-mail: **shelia@sheliadansbyharvey.com** Website: **www.sheliadansbyharvey.com**

Cynthia L. Hatcher Author of the following books: The Abuser's Daughter, Bewitched in the Local Church, Choosing to Dream, and A Man and His Wife. Cynthia L. Hatcher, Dare to Dream Ministries Inc., Post Office Box 494, Genesee, Michigan 48437 Phone: (810) 394-8612 E-mail: clynn@truevine.net

Lorenzo L. Heard Author of the book Stuck In A Storm and Missing Your Calm: Discovering God's Purpose for Your Life. A native of Leesburg, Lee County, Georgia, Pastor Heard began preaching at the age of seventeen and after three years began his first pastorate at the Macedonia Baptist Church in Patterson, Georgia. In 1987, he became the pastor of the Saint Galilee Baptist Church in Sparta, Georgia. In 1993, he became pastor of the Greater 2nd Mt. Olive Baptist Church in Albany, Georgia where he is presently pastoring. He is a 1981 Graduate of the Lee County High School. After high school, he attended the formerly known FVSC, which is now known as Fort Valley State University and after two years transferred to Morehouse College in Atlanta. He received a Bachelor's Degree in Business Management from Albany State University. Contact Lorenzo L. Heard, Senior Pastor, Greater Second Mount Olive Missionary Baptist Church, 302 Adkins Street, Albany, Georgia 31701 Phone: (229) 435-9961 E-mail: Pastor.Heard@theolivexperience.org Website: www.theolivexperience.org

Michelle Heath Author of the book 7 Principles to Become Your Own Superhero. In her twenty years as a nurse, Michelle Heath witnessed an incredible amount of pain and suffering. Overweight, with uncontrolled high blood pressure and unhappy the book was written as part of Heath's own healing and as a means to help others on their own path to inner freedom and peace. Contact Ms. Michelle L. Heath, 167 Benziger Avenue, Staten Island, New York 10301 E-mail: Msouli7@yahoo.com

Janet Marlene Henderson Author of LUNCH WITH CASSIE (2005), about a preacher's daughter-in-law who has an affair with a billionaire when her marriage hits the skids, will be releasing another book soon. THE ASSASSIN WHO LOVED HER, a romance novel about a journalist who is stalked by a serial killer she once wrote about, will be released in Summer 2008. Dr. Janet M. Henderson lives in Chicago and teaches English at Malcolm X College. She has a Ph.D. in Biblical Studies, an M.A. in English Composition and an M.A. in Education. Contact Janet Marlene Henderson, 7837 South Ada Street, Chicago, Illinois 60620 Phone: (773) 620-2778 E-mail: jhendalert2@yahoo.com Website: www.janethenderson.net

Kenneth R. Henry Jr. Owner of Real Ink Publishing and author of a poetry book entitled Tears That Grip A Whole Nation. Real Ink specializes in poetry, self help, and youth centered books. Kenneth R. Henry Jr., Real Ink Publishing, Post Office Box 496, League City, Texas 77574 Phone: (409) 641-2320 E-mail: realinkpub@yahoo.com

Shawn Hicks C.E.O and President of Brok'n English Publications, with the goal of providing a medium for telling his literary works. He received an Associates Degree in Video Arts from the Borough of Manhattan Community College. His first book is SCREAM, An Anthology of Sacred Thoughts, which is a collection of poetry, opinions, and anecdotes that described a provocative view of the world and Product Of The Enviornment, a gripping story of four seniors. Contact Shawn Hicks, 2152 Ralph Avenue, #519, Brooklyn, New York 11234 E-mail: shawn@broknenglishpublications.com Website: www.broknenglishpublications.com

Ida Byrd-Hill Author of the book, Breakin' Out of Your Financial Funk! Ida Byrd-Hill is also the President of Uplift, Inc., a 501(c)3 Idea Incubator. She has spent 15 years as a financial advisor and mortgage lender attempting to educate people to view their mortgage as a part of an integrated financial plan and not the plan alone. Ms. Ida Byrd-Hill, Post Office Box 241488, Detroit, Michigan 48224 Phone: (313) 483-2126 E-mail: **breakinout@upliftinc.org** Website: **www.upliftinc.org**

Askhari Johnson Hodari A practitioner of Black/Africana Studies. She regularly studies and travels the African diaspora. She received her bachelor of arts degree from Spelman College and her doctorate from Howard University. She is the author of The African Book of Names (2009) co-author of Lifelines: The Black Book of Proverbs (Broadway Books, October 2009); and the author of the Black Facts Calendars. Askhari Johnson Hodari, Ph.D., Post Office Box 110637, Birmingham, Alabama 35211 Phone: (205) 910-7952 E-mail: **writedrhodari@gmail.com**

Jessica Holter Founder of The Punany Poets, of HBO notoriety, Ms. Holter self-published 6 titles before signing to Zane's Strebor Books in 2006. Simon & Schuster will publish her controversial book of erotic poetry and HIV/AIDS awareness entitled Verbal Penetration, April 17th, 2007. Ms. Jessica Holter, 3133 Maxwell Avenue, Oakland, California 94619 E-mail: **ghettogirlblue@yahoo.com** Website: **www.JessicaHolter.com**

Joe C. Hopkins Attorney, since 1982, and publisher of The Pasadena/San Gabriel Valley Journal News since 1989, serving Altadena, Pasadena, Monrovia and Duarte and surrounding cities in the west San Gabriel Valley, California area. Author of "I WILL NOT APOLOGIZE - Uncompromising Solutions to Black America's Dilemma in the 21st Century." Mr. Joe C. Hopkins, 1541 North Lake Avenue, Suite A, Pasadena, California 91104 Phone: (626) 398-1194 Fax: (626) 798-3972 E-mail: **pasjour@pacbell.net**

Renda Horne Best-selling author of Seven Years in Egypt: Recognizing Your Setbacks as Set-Ups for Your comeback! She is a highly sought-after conference speaker and founder president of Woman at the Wail Ministries, Renda Horne Ministries, and Wailing Enterprises. Renda Horne, Post Office Box 401479, Redford, Michigan 48240 E-mail: **renda@rendahorne.com** Website: **www.rendahorne.com**

Marlin L. Houser Author of the award winning series The Adventures of Little Fox Book One: "Generations" (two awards) Book Two: The Secret of Squirrel Meadow (two awards). Winner of the USABOOKNEWS Best Book Award 2005 for The Adventures of Little Fox, Book One Generations. I'm also a two time winner of the FPA President Children's Fiction Award 2006 & 2007. Martin L. Houser, Post Office Box 150605, Altamonte Springs, Florida. 32714 Phone: (407) 599-5307 E-mail: **marlin@adventurefox.com** Website: **www.adventurefox.com**

Elbert Howard One of the 6 original members of the Black Panther Party. Author of "Panther on the Prowl (self-published, 2003); College Peer Counseling Handbook (Merritt College, Oakland, California, 1967); Each One Teach One (Merritt College, Oakland, California, 1967). He recently wrote the foreword for the book Up Against the Wall by Curtis J. Austin (2006). Elbert "Big Man" Howard, Post Office Box 130, Forestville, California 95436 Phone: (901) 921-0493 E-mail: **bigman0138@aol.com** Website: **www.bigmanbpp.com**

Sylvia Hubbard Published author of 10 novels. Also lectures on writing, internet marketing and journalism. Chairperson of The Essence of Motown Literary Jam & Conference. Founder of Motown Writers Network, Michigan Literary Network and The African American Electronic Literary Network. Sylvia Hubbard, Post Office Box 27310, Detroit, Michigan 48227 Phone: (313) 289-8614 E-mail: **motownwriters@yahoo.com** Website: **www.SylviaHubbard.com**

Cheryl Willis Hudson Publisher and co-founder of Just Us Books. Began career in publishing in 1970 with Houghton Mifflin; worked for Macmillan Publishing Company, as design manager and Arete Publishing Company as assistant art director. Free-lance consultant; has designed or art directed projects for Waldenbooks' Longmeadow Press, Angel Entertainment, Hayden Company, Grosset & Dunlap, Grolier and Three Continents Press. Cheryl Willis Hudson, Just Us Books, 356 Glenwood Avenue, 3rd Floor, East Orange, New Jersey 07017 Phone: (973) 676-4345 E-mail: **justusbooks@mindspring.com** Website: **www.justusbooks.com**

Pamela Jane Hudson Co-Author of HELP for Your Leadership book and Workbook. Contact Pamela Jane Hudson, 0110 Trinity, Detroit, Michigan 48219 Phone: (313) 205-7300 E-mail: **pamela5673@att.net**

Wade Hudson President and CEO, of Just Us Books, Mr. Wade Hudson is the author of nearly 20 books for young people including the picture books Jamal's Busy Day, Pass It On: African American Poetry for Children and his latest title for young adults, Powerful Words. An advocate of diversity in literature, he conducts workshops and presentations and serves on the board of many organizations, including the Langston Hughes Library. Wade Hudson, Just Us Books, 356 Glenwood Avenue, East Orange, New Jersey 07017 Phone: (973) 676-4345 Fax: (973) 677-7701 E-mail: **justusbooks@mindspring.com** Website: **www.justusbooks.com**

Wanda D. Hudson Author of Wait for Love: A Black Girl's Story; LuvMe - Because Everybody Needs A Little Luv. Coming Soon – A Sheltered Life. Contributing Author - Succulent - Chocolate Flava 2 Purple Panties - An Eroticanoir.com Anthology. Comedian - Miss WandaLuv. Wanda D. Hudson, 2284 Grand Avenue 1J, Bronx, New York 10468 Phone: (347) 589-5857 E-mail: **wanda_d_hudson@yahoo.com** Website: **www.wandadhudson.com**

Gloria P. Humes Author of the book Divorced: Marriage Over!...But God! (2002) and two short stories, "A Gift of Faith" (2004), and "The Christmas Daddy Moved" (2007). Certified in Family and Consumer Sciences, Certified Christian Counselor, Certified Behavioral Consultant, Newsletter Editor for FEFACS (Florida Educators of Family and Consumer Sciences), 2003-present. Gloria P. Humes, 18865 North West 54th Court, Miami Gardens, Florida 33055 Phone: (305) 625-6371 E-mail: **gloriahumes@bellsouth.net**

Earl Ofari Hutchinson Author of nine books about the African-American experience in America and his numerous published articles appear in newspapers and magazines across the country. Host of a weekly talk show, On Target With Earl Ofari Hutchinson. Holds a Bachelor's degree in Humanities from California State University, Dominguez Hills, and a Doctorate in Social Sciences from Pacific Western University. Earl Ofari Hutchinson, 614 East Manchester Boulevard, Suite 204, Inglewood, California 90301 Phone: (323) 296-6331 Fax: (323) 291-6324 E-mail: **ehutchinson@thehutchinsonreport.com** Website: **www.thehutchinsonreport.com**

Rene Robinson-Ikeola Author of the new book Determined: Suceeding Against The Odds. Rene Robinson-Ikeola, 2102 Silent River Court, Richmond, Texas 77406 Phone: (713) 894-0527 E-mail: robinson@sbcglobal.net Website: www.reneikeola.net

C.F. Jackson Author of the book Won't Be Denied, C.F. Jackson is a poet, and mentor. She has been featured on one Atlanta's largest radio station, WVEE 103.3 FM, and spotlighted on Atlanta's UPN69 Community Calendar. She obtained a B.S. degree in Criminal Justice from Georgia Southern University. Ms. C.F. Jackson, Post Office Box 920622, Norcross, Georgia 30010 Phone: (678) 492-7644 E-mail: info@cfjackson.us Website: www.cfjackson.us

Edwardo Jackson An author, actor and screenwriter, Jackson is a graduate of Morehouse College ('97; B.A. Drama/English) in Atlanta, Georgia, and the University of Phoenix ('02, M.B.A.) in Gardena, California. Previously published in the anthologies Proverbs for the People (Kensington, 2003) and Intimacy (Plume, 2004). He is author of several screenplays, as well as the prequels to I Do? (February 2006), Ever After and Neva Hafta (Random House/Villard). Contact Mr. Edwardo Jackson, JCM Books, 15228-B Hawthorne Boulevard, Suite 203, Lawndale, California 90260 Phone: (310) 349-3309 Fax: (310) 370-6098 E-mail: EverAfterANovel@aol.com

Sibyl Avery Jackson Author of the book Degree of Caution (2003 Books and Authors.net Award for Literary Excellence; 2002 Sistah Circle Book Club Self-Publishing Award for Best Mystery). She is has a B.A. degree in English from Spellman College in Atlanta, Georgia. Sibyl Contact Ms. Avery Jackson, 1101 Heights Boulevard, Houston, Texas, 77008 E-mail: SibylAJackson@aol.com Website: www.sibylaveryjackson.net

Jahzara Author of the novel Luv Don't Live Here Anymore. Jahzara, Tranquil Moments LLC, Post Office Box 2916, Gary, Indiana 46403 E-mail: jahzara2007-books@yahoo.com

Roland S. Jefferson Award winning author and a graduate of Howard University Medical College, Mr. Jefferson has been writing literary fiction since the early 70's. His first novel, The School On 103rd Street was self published and released to critical acclaim. Twenty five years later it was republished by mainstream publisher WW Norton & Co and ultimately was listed in The Guide To Literary Los Angeles 2000 by the Los Angeles Times Book Review. This first work was followed by novels: A Card For The Players and 559 To Damascus. In 2004 under the banner of Simon & Schus-ter's imprint Atria Books, he published the exciting heist thriller Damaged Goods and in 2006 the current sensual crime noir mystery One Night Stand. His latest book is White Coat Fever (Author House, 2009). Contact Mr. Roland S. Jefferson, 3870 Crenshaw Blvd. #215, Los Angeles, California 90008 Phone: (310) 281-6023 E-mail: rsjeff@hotmail.com Website: www.rolandsjefferson.com

Jovita Jenkins Author of the highly acclaimed book, Get Out Of Your Own Way – Create The Next Chapter Of Your Life, Jovita brings a wealth of experience from her 30-year career in aerospace where she rose through the ranks from software engineer to the executive level before creating her own next chapter as an author, leadership coach, lecturer, and business owner. Jovita Jenkins, 5875 Doverwood Drive, Suite 211, Culver City, California 90230 Phone: (310) 337-7343 E-mail: Jovita@jovitajenkins.com Website: www.jovitajenkins.com

K.B. Jenkins Author of four books An Epidemic of Singleness, Royal Moments of A King's Daughter, Pacifying The Flesh: Sexual Alternatives?, and Collegebound on Higher Ground. K.B. is a graduate of the State University of New Jersey, and currently in pursuit of her Masters of Divinity. She is founder/president of S.O.L.O. 4 Christ c/o The King's Daughters Ministries, Inc., and Messianic Music, as well as the RestPress Publishing Company. Minister K.B. Jenkins, RestPress Publishing, Post Office Box 244086 Atlanta, Georgia 30324 Phone: (800) 630-4813 E-mail: info@restpresspublishing.org Website: www.restpresspublishing.org

Tony Jenkins Author of "Exposing Racism & Sexism in the American Arts." (How the Federal Courts covered up racism & sexism for the Metropolitan Opera). He attended Duquense University, The University of Pittsburg, USC Opera Workshop, and he holds a BA and MS from City College in New York City. Contact Tony Jenkins, Walls Tumbling Down Publishing, Manhattanville Station, Post Office Box 871, New York, New York 10027 Phone: (212) 865-6008 E-mail: Antonioj365@aol.com

King Jewel Author of the book, Thirteen and a half, a gripping story about friendship, trust and taking responsibility for one's action. Co-owner of New World Publishing. King Jewel, New World Publishing, Submission Department, Post Office Box 660, Randallstown, Maryland 21133 Phone: (410) 948-8088 E-mail: Newworldpublishing@hotmail.com

Siddeeq Jihad Accomplished author and lecturer, Qur'aanic Arabic Teacher, Imam Jihad is also the publisher of The Good New Journal. Siddeeq Jihad, Good News Journal, Post Office Box 43474, Detroit Michigan 48243 Fax: (313) 532-5246 E-mail: siddeeq@msn.com

Yolanda Joe Prolific writer and author, journalist, former producer and writer for CBS news, Chicago, Yolanda Joe is author of nine best selling books, Falling Leaves of Ivy, The Hatwearer's Lesson, He Say, She Say, Bebe's By Golly Wow, This Just In, Details at Ten, Hit Time and My Fine Lady. Yolanda earned her B.A. in English literature from Yale University; and her M.A., Journalism, Columbia University. E-mail: yolandajoe416@aol.com Website: www.yolandajoe.com

Beverly Black Johnson The first in our series of publications is Gumbo For The Soul: the Recipe for Literacy in the Black Community. Gumbo For The Soul is a savory blend of anthologies that focus on humanitarian issues effecting communities worldwide! From education to adoption and everything in between, we will bring inspirational and informative publications that promise to spark change, heighten awareness and offer resources and resolutions to the issues we outline. Beverly Black Johnson, GFTS, Post Office Box 5193, San Jose, California 95150 Phone: (209) 947-4743 E-mail: gumboforthesoul@yahoo.com

Charlotte Russell Johnson Writer, motivational speaker, and Christian evangelist, Johnson gained national fame following the release of her first novel A Journey to Hell and Back. In the past four years, she has penned four additional books: Daddy's Hugs, Grace Under Fire: The Journey Never Ends, The Flipside: A Journey to Hell and Back, and Mama May I. Gifted, she delivers a message that is both timely and challenging. Ms. Charlotte Johnson, Reaching Beyond, Inc., Post Office Box 12364, Columbus, Georgia 31917 Phone: (706) 573-5942 E-mail: admin@reachingbeyond.net Website: www.reachingbeyond.net

Keith Lee Johnson A native of Toledo, Ohio, Keith has written four books and is currently working on his fifth. Author of two books; Sugar and Spice, November 2003 and Pretenses, June 2004. He is currently working on SCARECROW another Phoenix Perry novel. Coming soon, The Whirlwind and Mama Said. Mr. Keith Lee Johnson, 1013 Marmion Avenue, Toledo, Ohio 43607 E-mail: keithleejohnson1@aol.com Website: www.keithleejohnson.com

Kevin Wayne Johnson Author of the book series, Give God the Glory! Kevin graduated from Virginia Commonwealth University earning a BS degree in Business Administration. He is a 2002 graduate of the True Disciple Ministries Bible Institute, Somerville, New Jersey. Kevin Wayne Johnson, Writing For The Lord Ministries, 6400 Shannon Court, Clarksville, Maryland 21029 Phone: (443) 535-0475 Fax: (443) 535-0476 E-mail: kevin@writingforthelord.com Website: www.writingforthelord.com

Rayford L. Johnson Author of Thug Mentality Exposed: Journal of a Correctional Counselor & Photojournalist. Contact Mr. Rayford Johnson, 7119 Elk Grove Boulevard, Suite 121, Elk Grove, California 95758 Phone: (916) 714-5840 E-mail: rayfordjohnson@mac.com Website: www.thugexposed.com

Tenita C. Johnson Author of 100 Words of Encouragement: Tidbits of Inspiration. Tenita C. Johnson, Post Office Box 39095, Redford, Michigan 48240 Phone: (313) 999-6942 E-mail: soitiswritten@msn.com Website: www.soitiswritten.net

Vanessa Alexander Johnson Author of This Far by Faith: Stories of Hope and Victory Through Jesus Christ (Butterfly Press, 2008), Gumbo for the Soul Anthology: The Recipe For Literacy In The Black Community, by Beverly Black Johnson, (iUniverse, 2007), Songs of Hope by Sachel, Timeless (Avatar Press, 2006), Help, I've Turned Into My Mother, by ReShonda Tate-Billingsley (Strebor Books, 2005), An Essay in Divine Appointment: A Caregiver's Guide by Delores Thornton, (iUniverse, 2004), and others. Vanessa Alexander Johnson, Post Office Box 9, Ama, Louisiana 70031 Phone: (504) 377-7380 E-mail: vjohns1@bellsouth.net Website: www.vanessaajohnson.com

Yolanda M. Johnson Author of the novel My Daughter's Keeper (2004). She is currently obtaining her IT degree at the University of Phoenix and will be transferring to the University of North Texas to major in Literary Sciences. Yolanda M. Johnson, Prosperity Enterprises, Post Office Box 821473, Dallas, Texas 75382 E-mail: yolanda@awarenessmagazine.net

Patricia Jonea Author of the book, Healing Hurts, a fascinating account of the healing process from any hurt. Patricia Jonea, Post Office Box 13756, Oklahoma City, Oklahoma 73113 E-mail: imblessed4@cox.net Website: www.healinghurtsbook.com

Frank A. Jones Author of What Have We Done To Our Children? He has written several books: poetry, a novel, collections of social essays and some religious discussions. Educated at San Francisco City College, University of California, Berkeley, University of San Francisco, and The Union Institute and University, Cincinnati, Ohio, he earned his BA, MA, and PhD degrees. Frank A. Jones, Mirror-Gibbs Publication, Post Office Box 6573, Oakland, California 94603 Phone: (510) 409-9571 E-mail: pinoquit@hotmail.com Website: www.gibbsmagazine.com

Franklin Jones Author / Self-Publisher of the book entitled: The Black Matrix: The Modern Mental and Social Suppression of African American Under National Interest (2006, 2008). Franklin G. Jones, 2045 Mount Zion Road, No 233, Morrow, Georgia 30260 Phone: (678) 895-5216 E-mail: **thanubian2@yahoomail.com**

Jusbee Jones Author of Confessions of the Twelfth Man: A Different Game Played Off The Field. Under the pseudonym of Jusbee Jones, sports publicist LaShirl Smith has been associated with sports most of her life. She has worked with professional athletes for over fifteen years in the capacity of sports public relations and marketing. Contact Ms. Jusbee Jones, 15030 Ventura Boulevard, Suite 525, Sherman Oaks, California 91403 E-mail: **JusbeeJones@aol.com** Website: **www.confessionsofthe12thman.com**

Marsha Jones In 2005, her debut novel, Love Begins With Truth, and Slices of Soul, a compilation book of celebrity interviews, was published by St. Vincent's Press. Currently, Marsha is working on two novels, Win-Win and Shorts. Her short stories have been published in the books, Visions and Viewpoints: Voices of The Genesee Valley and COMPEER's The Healing Power of Friends and she has edited three books, Shadow of Dreams and Who's Who in Black Rochester, Volumes One and Two. Contact Ms. Marsha Jones, 411 Communications, 97 Culver Parkway, Rochester, New York 14609 E-mail: **defdefyingmj@yahoo.com**

Rashun Jones Author of Healthy Attitudes Smart Choices: Living the Life You Choose, Power of Life: Use It or Lose It You Decide, and Blueprints A Way of Life. Owns a publishing company that provides books and speaker services. Rashun Jones, Nushape Publication, Post Office Box 36651, Oklahoma City, Oklahoma 73136 Phone: (405) 424-5445 Fax: (800) 550-9718 E-mail: **rashun@nushapepublication.com** Website: **www.nushapepublication.com**

Sophie Jones Author of the novels Twisted Lies, A Mother's Love, and Twisted Lies 2: The Lies Untwisted. Sophie Jones, 19703 B Eastex Freeway #126, Humble, Texas 77338 Phone: (713) 560-5708 E-mail: **sophie@sophieswords.com** Website: **www.sophieswords.com**

Twana Bond-Jones Author of When It's Right, It's Right, Twana has published a volume of poetry Treasures from the Deep and a children's book, The Big Big Waterfall. She founded the S.T.A.Y Coalition (Supporting Teens and Youth) and the Po'Art Literary Foundation to help promote literacy in school age children through poetic art. She is also Editor in Chief of the Po'Art Press. Twana Bond-Jones, Po'Art Press, Post Office Box 611510, Birmingham, Alabama 35261 E-mail: **tbondjones@poartpress.com** Website: **www.poartpress.com**

Joylynn M. Jossel A Graduate of Columbus State Community College's Associates Degree program and Capital University's Bachelor Degree program. Joy completed her first self-published novel The Root of All Evil, which St. Martin's Press picked up and re-released in June 2004. In addition, they have signed Joy to a three book deal, When Souls Mate, Harlem's Blues, and a novella, An All Night Man, in which Joy's contribution is titled Cream. Her street novel Dollar Bill, published by Triple Crown Publications, was on the Essence Magazine best-sellers list for April, 2004. Her latest books are Mama, I'm in Love …with a gangsta (2006, Urban Books) and Wet (2007). Joylynn M. Jossel, Post Office Box 298238, Columbus, Ohio 43229 Phone: (614) 284-7933 E-mail: **joylynnjossel@aol.com** Website: **www.joylynnjossel.com**

Ella Joyce Author of Kink Phobia, Journey Through A Black Woman's Hair, Ella Joyce is an accomplished actress of stage, TV and film, most remembered for her role as "Eleanor" on Fox TV's sitcom "Roc." She is also the author of "A Rose Among Thorns," a one-woman, one-act, dramatic tribute to Civil Rights icon Rosa Parks. She is married to actor/photographer, Dan Martin, and lives in southern California. Ella Joyce, c/o Landmark Artists Management, 4116 West Magnolia Boulevard., Suite 101, Burbank, California 91505 Phone: (818) 848 9800 Fax: (818) 848 9821 E-mail: ellajoyce@mymailstation.com Website: www.ellajoyce.com

Carmen D. Julious Fiction, short stories, some sci fi. Nonfiction, women's issues, public health, literature, entertainment. Grant writing, research and editing. Carmen D. Julious, Julious & Associates, 9 Brookmist, Columbia, South Carolina 29229 Phone: (803) 318-4707 Fax: (803) 699-0263 E-mail: cjulious@aol.com

Adin Kachisi A visionary, social critic, writer, artist, and author of three books, Beyond the Talented Tenth, Tears of Ether and Depths of Melancholy. Mr. Adin Kachisi, 4049 Broadway, Box #190, New York, New York 10032 Phone: (212) 862-5027 Fax: (360) 406-9287 E-mail: akachisi@yahoo.com

Baruti K. Kafele Author and publisher of several best seller books, A Black Parent's Handbook to Educating Your Children (Outside of the Classroom) and A Handbook for Teachers of African-American Children (May, 2004). Honor: 1998 Proclamation - Baruti K. Kafele Day, City of Dickinson, Texas. Baruti K. Kafele, Post Office Box 4088, Jersey City, New Jersey 07304 Phone: (201) 433-9484 E-mail: bkafele@earthlink.net

Djehuti wa Kamau Cultural journalist, author of the book Warrior Song, an Africentric exposition of Black music and the international music industry. Djehuti wa Kamau, First Scribe Books, Box 62, Fort Lauderdale, Florida 33302 E-mail: firstscribebooks@yahoo.com Website: www.firstscribebooks.com

Prince M. Kaywood Jr. Author of the books, Self Publish: By Starting Your Own Company, and Katrina That Bitch! The Drama Continues. Contact Mr. Prince M. Kaywood, Jr., Parallel View Publishing, Post Office Box 741353, New Orleans, Louisiana 70174 E-mail: godsight2@yahoo.com Website: www.parallelviewpublishing.com

Janis F. Kearney Former presidential diarist to President William Jefferson Clinton, Janet Kearney debuted her first book, Cotton Field of Dreams, a Memoir, about her journey from a sharecropper's environment in the south Arkansas delta, to the most revered address in America: 1600 Pennsylvania Avenue, in January 2005. Kearney's second book, Conversations: William Jefferson Clinton...from Hope to Harlem, is an oral and pictorial biography (2006). Janis F. Kearney, Writing our World Press, 1507 East 53rd Street #278, Chicago, Illinois 60615 Phone: (773) 493-2007 E-mail: janisfk@aol.com Website: www.writingourworldpress.com

Jennifer Keitt Author of the book, "The Power Of Being A Real Woman," She is host of a nationally syndicated radio show. Ms. Jennifer Kreitt, The Today's Black Woman Corporation, Post Office Box 440981, Kennesaw, Georgia 30160 Phone: (678) 569-2407 Fax: (678) 354-4334 E-mail: zakarmagazine@gmail.com Website: www.todaysblackwomanradio.com

Lewis V. Kelley Author of the novel Auslander, Lewis was born in Kansas City Missouri. He has been a Denver Firefighter for nearly 15 years. Contact Mr. Lewis Kelley, 705 South Florence Street, Denver, Colorado 80247 E-mail: lkwriter@comcast.net

Janice Kenyatta Co-Author of The Truth About Black Hairstyles: The Whole Story Revealed. Janice Kenyatta, 1471 Indian Mountain Lake, Albrightsville, Pennsylvania 18210 Phone: (215) 325-1893 Fax: (570) 643-4162 E-mail: donedeal8@earthlink.net Website: www.black-hairstyles-truth.com/black-hair-book.html

Kamau Kenyatta Co-Author of The Truth About Black Hairstyles: The Whole Story Revealed. Contact Kamau Kenyatta, 1471 Indian Mountain Lake, Albrightsville, Pennsylvania 18210 Phone: (215) 325-1893 Fax: (570) 643-4162 E-mail: donedeal8@earthlink.net Website: www.black-hairstyles-truth.com

Tanya Kersey Author of Black State of the Arts: A Guide to Developing a Successful Career as a Black Performing Artist, considered by many to be the "Bible" for blacks in the performing arts. She also authors two annual publications -- The Black Film Report, a comprehensive report on the financial performance of black films; and The Urban Hollywood Resource Directory, a "yellow pages" of urban entertainment contacts and resources. Tanya has also appeared on news and entertainment programs on countless television and cable networks including CNN, NBC, FOX-11, KTLA, BET and Reelz Channel. Her most recent endeavors are as the host and producer of "Inside Urban Hollywood" on BlogTalkRadio. Ms. Tanya Kersey, 8306 Wilshire Blvd. Suite 2057, Beverly Hills, California 90211 Phone: (310) 203-1336 E-mail: tanya@tanyakersey.com Website: www.tanyakersey.com

Dorothy Jackson-Kimble Self-published author of her debut memoir "A Mighty Long Way." Dorothy Kimble, 19200 Archer, Detroit, Michigan 48219 Phone: (313) 532-3624 E-mail: dotkimble@comcast.net

Willie J. Kimmons One of America's leading authorities on higher education, leadership, parental involvement and health related issues, Dr. Kimmons holds a Bachelor of Science Degree in Health Education and Psychology; a Master of Science Degree in Curriculum and Instruction and a Doctorate in Educational Administration and Supervision in Higher Education. His current book is, A Parenting Guidebook. Contact Dr. Willie J. Kimmons, 1653 Lawrence Circle, Daytona Beach, Florida 32117 Phone: (386) 253-4920 E-mail: wjkimmons@aol.com Website: www.savechildrensaveschools.com

Woodie King, Jr. An Obie-award winner and legend, Mr. Woodie King, Jr., is a writer, director, and producer, and the founding director of New York's landmarke New Federal Theater in New York City. He has produced Off-Broadway and on Broadway. He co-produced 'For Colored Girls Who Have Considered Suicide When the Rainbow Is Enuf', and What the Winesellars Buy.' His new book 'The Impact of Race' is an impassioned stand against racism, sexism, and classism in theatre and culture. In 'Race' he explores the politics of theatre. He is Chair, Dept of Theatre Arts, University of Mississippi. Mr. Woodie King Jr., New Federal Theatre, 292 Henry Street, New York, New York 10002 Phone: (212) 353-1176 Fax: (212) 353-1088 E-mail: info@newfederaltheatre.org Website: www.newfederaltheatre.org

Kimani Kinyua   Author of The Brotherhood of Man (Strebor International/Simon & Schuster). Kimani Kinyua has lived in the Washington, D.C. area for more than fifteen years. He graduated from Howard University in 1995 with a bachelor's degree in journalism. He is currently an independent project manager and web site contractor and consultant project manager in the Washington D.C. Metropolitan area. He has written a number of technology-related articles for trade magazines. Kimani Kinyua, 6253 Fernwood Terrace, Riverdale, Maryland 20737 Phone: (301) 326.3917 E-mail: author@kimanikinyua.com Website: www.kimanikinyua.com

Y. N. Kly Author of five books: The Invisible War: The African Anti-Slavery Resistance from the Stono Rebellion Through the Seminole Wars; International Law and the Black Minority in the US; The Anti-Social Contract: The Black Book: The True Political Philosophy of Malcolm X; Societal Development and Minority Rights and A Popular Guide to Minority Rights. Editor of: In Pursuit of the Right to Self-determination and In Pursuit of an International Civil Tribunal. Dr. Kly holds a Ph.D. in Political Science, with specialty in International Law from Laval University, an Int. LPD from the College of Law of England and Wales and the International Bar Association, a Masters degree from the University of Montreal, a D.E.S. from the University of Algiers, B.A. from the University of Iowa, and a JD from the NCBL Community College of Law and International Diplomacy Chicago Dr. Y. N. Kly, Clarity Press, Inc., 3277 Roswell Road, Suite. 469, North East, Atlanta, Georgia 30305 E-mail: yussuf.kly@uregina.ca Website: www.claritypress.com

Jawanza Kunjufu   A renowned educator, published author, and the president of African American Images, a communications company based in Chicago Illinois, Jawanza Kunjufu is constantly on the lecture circuit where he conducts over thirty different workshops/retreats, addressing students, parent, teachers, and other community members on developing positive self-images and discipline in Black children. Contact Dr. Jawanza Kunjufu, African American Images, 1909 West 95th Street, Chicago, Illinois 60643 Phone: (773) 445-0322 E-mail: aarcher@africanamericanimages.com Website: www.africanamericanimages.com

Otu Kwaku Co-founder and chief editor of Ujima Press Real Communication, Baba Otu's passion for the Black literature, the written word, and art show through his own seasoned poetry, prose and classes he teaches. He also facilitates Ujima Press RC's Soulful Writing workshop, held annually. Baba Otu a minister of the International Society of Indigneous Sovereigns is founder of Hippos Books And Things at HipposBooksAndThings.com, and published author of Hair PieceZ: The Anthology. Otu Kwaku, 59 Westview Street, Philadelphia, Pennsylvania 19119 Phone: (888) 330-8005 E-mail: UjimaPRC@aol.com

Naana Kyereboah Childrens author of Soul Name. Naana Kyereboah, Nabina Publications, An African Touch, Post Office Box 4091, Midlothian, Virginia 23112 Phone: (804) 276-0454 E-mail: nabina@comcast.net

Evangeline Lacey Self-published author and her first novel, "Imminent Darkness" published in January 2010, received a four star review on Amazon.com. Lacey is active in the writing community and a member of the National Writer's Union and the Chicago Writers Association. Contact Ms. Evangeline Lacey, 4015 North Milwaukee Avenue, Unit 202, Chicago, Illinois 60641 E-mail: writeremlacey@gmail.com

Anita Hackley Lambert Biographer, researcher, genealogist and author of the book F.H.M. MURRAY: First Biography of a Forgotten Pioneer for Civil Justice. Murray, who happens to be Ms. Lamberts' great-grandfather, left an inspiring and dynamic legacy to his African American race, to U.S. history, and to his family. Contact Anita Lambert, HLE Publishing, 13001 Jackson Drive, Fort Washington, Maryland 20744 Phone: (301) 292-7960 E-mail: author@anitahackleylambert.com Website: www.AnitaHackleyLambert.com

Rena Deloris Canady Laster Founder of Omega Sherhawabeth Associates, a business dedicated to the upbuilding of family and faith. Publisher of P. J. and Friends Christian Alphabet, an interactive coloring/Activity Book for Children. Rena Deloris Canady Laster, Omega Sherhawabeth and Associates, 300 Northfield Drive, Warner Robins, Georgia 31093 Phone: (478) 929-8585 Fax: (478) 929-0055 E-mail: renacanadylaster@aol.com

Roxann Latimer Writer, poet, journalist, and entrepreneur, Roxann has published 2 romance novels and 1 book of poetry. Murder Most Mystic, a romance mystery is her second novel in a series of mysteries written by Roxann. She works as a television producer with her company WIM Media. Roxann Latimer, WIM, 3900 West 22nd Lane #10G, Yuma, Arizona 85364 Phone: (928) 343-9729 E-mail: wimmedia@yahoo.com Website: www.roxannlatimer.com

Kristin Hunter Lattany Author of eleven books. Four of her titles are for young people; the others are for adults. Her latest books are Breaking Away (One World/Ballantine, 2003) and The Lakestown Rebellion (Coffee House Press 2003). Contact Ms. Kristin Hunter Lattany, c/o Dystel & Goderich Literary Management, One Union Square West, New York, New York 10003 E-mail: klattany@comcast.net

HB Lawrence A 23 year adult club veteran and author of the book Fast Women Fast Money, a look into four dancers lives as seen through their DJ's eyes! If you've ever wondered what goes on in adult clubs for REAL, this is the book for you! It's sex, money,and mayhem at a breathtaking pace. The author currently is the General Manager of Detroits #1 topless club. HB Lawrence, Allstar,14541 West 8 Mile Road, Detroit Michigan 48235 Phone: (313) 598-1141 E-mail: hblawrence@msn.com

Jacqueline Lawrence Christian fiction author of Single & Waiting, Prosperity Planning God's Way, The Hidden Mysteries for Hearers are TOP SECRET and Won't Somebody Come Correct?, includes real, down-to-earth poems in her works. A doctor of Christian Counseling, her writing style is inspirational, witty and humorous. Two of her books, Single & Waiting and Won't Somebody Come Correct? are published by Harlequin, formerly BET Books, and the other two are self-published (Xlibris). Dr. Jacqueline Lawrence, 212 Kittery Point Santa Rosa, California 95403 Phone: (707) 566-9778 E-mail: drjministries@yahoo.com Website: www.drjacquelinelawrence.com

Clara Baldwin Leake An active member of the NAACP and a Parish Nurse, Clara is the author of "The Love Inside" (Iuniverse, 2003), and the sequel, "A Brand New Life" (2006). Served in the United States Women's Army Corp from 1959-1961. Also worked part time as a Home Health Registered Nurse. Ms. Clara Baldwin Leake, 631 Franks Street Asheboro, North Carolina 27203 Phone: (336) 625-9174 E-mail: cleake1@triad.rr.com

Charles E. Lee, II A 1973 Graduate of Rutgers University, New Jersey, with a degree in liberal arts, Lee is an Ordained Minister, Motivational Speaker, Seer, Spiritual Advisor, Teacher, Author, Publisher, and a certified master celebrity protection specialist instructor with Executive Protection Academy International in Atlanta, Georgia. Books Authored: Know Thyself: Start to Reclaim Your Life-1998, Know Thyself: The Essence of Truth Workshop Hand Book Pamphlet-2003; Know Thyself: The Prophecy of Truth-2003, SKIF/Know Thyself: Empower Children to Think Successfully-2005, The Black descendants of General Robert E. Lee and Mary Elizabeth Lee - 2006, Bodyguarding: The Art of Personal Protection Executives, Dignitaries, Celebrities and Clergy - 2006, The Essence of Truth: The Holy Spirit Thy God, Excuses-less Handbook, 2007. Charles E. Lee, II, Post Office Box 2052, Hiram, Georgia 30141 Phone: (770) 443-9957 Fax: (770) 505-2839 E-mail: **SKIF2PPIC@aol.com**

Dante Lee The 24-year old president and CEO of Diversity City Media, a very successful multicultural marketing and public relations firm based in Columbus, Ohio, is author of the new book, How To Think Big...When You're Small. Contact Mr. Dante Lee, Diversity City Media, 750-Q Cross Pointe Road, Columbus, Ohio 43213 E-mail: **dante@diversitycity.com** Website: **www.HowToThinkBig.com**

Ramelle Lee   Poet and author of the book Step Into His Greatness. Ramelle Lee, 3605 South Electric, Detroit, Michigan 48217   Phone: (313) 383-4429 E-mail: **Ramelleskip@aol.com** Website: **http://thecalledandreadywriters.org/ramelle_lee**

Harold Leffall   Author of Brother CEO: A Business Success Guide for African-American Men which has been featured in Black Enterprise and Entrepreneur magazines. With no experience and very little money, he turned his dream of owning his own business into a multi-million dollar reality in four years. He travels all over sharing his message of perseverance and success in workshops and seminars. He has been featured in Black Enterprise, Essence, and Entrepreneur magazines. Harold Leffall, 2175 Boulder Forest Drive, Ellenwood, Georgia 30294 Phone: (404) 381-0423 E-mail: **leffall@aol.com** Website: **www.brotherceo.com**

Sylvia Willis Lett Born in the small town of Rusk, Texas, Ms. Sylvia Willis Lett is a 1982 graduate of Rusk High School and a 1984 graduate of Tyler Junior College with a Computer Science Degree, Ms. Lett has been writing romance novels since the age of 18. Her love for reading shines through in her writing. For Christina's Sake has made the Dallas Best Seller List. Ms. Lett is a member of Romance Writers of America. Ms. Sylvia Willis Lett, Letts Dream Big Publishing, Post Office Box 472172, Garland, Texas 75047 Phone: (972) 271-2072 E-mail: **smlett@comcast.net** Website: **www.lettsdreambigpublishing.com**

Clarence L. Lewis III Author of Mutual Combat/Mutual Respect (1st in series of 6 books). Clarence L. Lewis III, 5052 Wittenmeyer Court, Antioch, California 94531 Phone: (415) 290-1721 E-mail: **dunieboy@att.net** Website: **www.dunieboy.com**

Elliott Lewis Author of "Fade: My Journeys in Multiracial America," (Carroll & Graf). The book weaves his memoirs as a black-and-white biracial American with the voices of dozens of multiracial people who are challenging how we think and speak about race today. Elliott Lewis, Post Office Box 2247, Rockville, Maryland 20847 E-mail: **FadeAuthor@aol.com**

Jakeshia Monique Lewis Author/Novelist of the book, I Found One, the first in a series. Her next book, Not Work Related, is due to be released in 2008. Jakeshia Monique Lewis, 505 Cypress Station Drive, Apt. 5010, Houston, Texas 77090 Phone: (832) 882-9944 Fax: (281) 895-0446 E-mail: **jakeshialewis320@sbcglobal.net** Website: **www.jakeshialewis.com**

Natosha Gale Lewis Author of the book Only Fools Gamble Twice, Natosha Gale Lewis recently released her children's books series, entitled, The adventures of Squally Squirrel which discuss child safety issues. Natasha is a graduate of Rosemont College. She holds a Bachelor of Arts in Business Communications and is an active member of the Wilmington Delaware Alumni Chapter, Delta Sigma Theta Sorority. Ms. Natosha Gale Lewis, Post Office Box 12723, Wilmington Delaware 19850 Website: **www.natoshagalelewis.com**

Shelia E. Lipsey Christian fiction author of Into Each Life (Kensington, 2007), Sinsatiable (Kensington/Urban Christian, 2007), My Son's Wife (Kensington, 2008), and Beautiful Ugly (Kensington, 2009). Sheila Lipsey is an avid reader, inspirational speaker and a full time writer. She was awarded Conversations Book Club 2008 Author of the Year; and Dallas Morning News Bestselling Author 2007. Contact Ms. Sheila E. Lipsey, 436 Bonita Drive, Memphis, Tennessee 38109 Phone: (901) 348-2511 E-mail: **shelialipsey@yahoo.com** Website: **www.shelialipsey.com**

Anthony L. Littlefield Author of Bittersweet Journey: The Story Of The Wounding, Healing And Triumph Of A Family. The search for my African American ancestors during the period of slavery in North and South Carolina. Contact Mr. Anthony Lawrence Littlefield, 2298 Waterfall Lane, Columbus, Ohio 43209 E-mail: **email@anthonylittlefield.com** Website: **www.anthonylittlefield.com**

Catherine McGhee Livers Author, college instructor, ordained minister and lecturer, Ms. Livers translates the original Greek and Hebrew text of the Old and New Testament of the Bible. She is the author of Biblical History of Black Mankind translated from the original Hebrew and Greek text of the Bible. She is a most sought after speaker, teacher and translator and has taught these languages at several colleges. Catherine McGee Livers, Shahar Institute, 8605 Allisonville Road #283, Indianapolis, Indiana 46250 Phone: (317) 577-0392 E-mail: **shaharpublishing@hotmail.com** Website: **www.blackmankind.com**

Julius R. Lockett Author of "Urban Essentials 101: Unleashing the Academic Potential in Urban Underperforming Schools, " Julius holds a Bachelor's and Master's of Science in Public and Urban Affairs from Georgia State University, and in 1997 completed work on his California Teaching Credential at Fresno Pacific University. He was a history and language arts teacher with the Fresno County Office of Education, working at the Elkhorn Correctional (Boot Camp) facility, and he has worked as a social sciences teacher in underperforming school settings in San Diego. Julius received a Professional Clear California Teaching Credential in Social Sciences, and he obtained a Cross-Cultural, Language and Academic Development Certificate from the University of California San Diego. He is currently employed as Dean of Student Success at Samuel Gompers High School in San Diego, California. Julius R. Lockett, 5026-1/2 Field Street, San Diego, California 92110 Phone: (619) 276-4987 E-mail: **thelocketts@peoplepc.com** Website: **www.ue101.com**

Nancy Ann Long Author of "The Life and Legacy of Mary McLeod Bethune", a 128 page biography and first-hand accounts of Dr. Bethune with photos (September, 2004). Dr. Nancy Ann Long, 1967 Red Cedar Circle, South Daytona, Florida 32119 Phone: (386) 767-6163 E-mail: bethunelegacy@earthlink.net

Vicky Spring Love Author of the book Stop Robbing Peter To Pay Paul, foreword by Dr. Myles Munroe, Vicky is an associate minister at Family Victory Fellowship in Southfield, Michigan. She is founder and president of Victory Financial Corporation, a residential mortgage company. She has worked for 12 years in the mortgage field where she not only provides mortgage financing but also counsels people on how to get their finances in order. She holds a BA degree from the University of Detroit and a MBA in Finance from Oakland University. Vicky Spring Love, Post Office Box 3286, Southfield, Michigan 48037 Phone: (248) 354-3686 E-mail: service@StopRobbingPeter.com Website: www.StopRobbingPeter.com

Matthew Lynch Professional educator, grant reviewer, grant writer, and author, Mr. Lynch is currently employed as an Exceptional Education Teacher at Sykes Elementary School and is CEO of Lynch Consulting Group, LLC. He is also a Doctoral Candidate at Jackson State University majoring in Early Childhood Education, with a cognate in Educational Administration. Also author of Closing the Racial Academic Achievement Gap, and a children's book, entitled Matthew and the Money Tree. Mr. Lynch is a contributing columnist for several publications including the Mississippi Link, Emerging Minds Magazine, Renaissance Men Magazine, Bahiyah Women Magazine, etc. Also founder of Project E.P.I.P.H.A.N.Y, a research based mentoring program. Matthew Lynch, 2324 Princess Pine Drive, Jackson, Mississippi 39212 Phone: (601) 373-1552 E-mail: lynch39083@aol.com

C. Lynn Author of the new book, "The Abuser's Daughter." This gripping novel shares the story of one woman's struggle with domestic violence, sexual abuse, promiscuity and drug addiction. C. Lynn, HATCHBACK Publishing, Post Office Box 494, Genesee, Michigan 48437 Phone: (810) 394-8612 E-mail: clynn@truevine.net

Kelly Starling Lyons A children's book author and award-winning journalist. Her first book, NEATE: Eddie's Ordeal (Just Us Books), is title #4 in the middle-grade series NEATE and has won praise for exploring the relationship between a 13-year-old student athlete and his civil rights veteran father. Her picture book, One Million Men and Me (Just Us Books), debuts February 2007. Lyons is also a story contributor to Chicken Soup for the African American Woman's Soul. Contact Kelly Starling Lyons, Post Office Box 1341, Durham, North Carolina 27702 E-mail: email@kellystarlinglyons.com Website: www.kellystarlinglyons.com

Cassandra Mack Native New Yorker, Cassandra is president of Strategies for Empowered Living Inc., a company that provides corporate coaching, workplace seminars and consultation to nonprofits, private companies and governmental agencies. Author of several books including, Her Rite of Passage: How to Design and Deliver A Rites of Passage Program for Girls, also, Cool, Confident and Strong: 52 Power Moves for Girls, and Young, Gifted and Doing It: 52 Power Moves for Teens. Cassandra Mack, Strategies for Empowered Living, Inc., 333 Madison Street, New York, New York 10002 E-mail: empoweredliving4u@yahoo.com Website: www.strategiesforempoweredliving.com

Haki R. Madhubuti Best-selling author of poetry and non-fiction, Mr. Madhubui is publisher and editor of Third World Press, the nation's oldest's continually running Black owned publishing company, and the Institute of Positive Education in Chicago, Illinois. He is one of the world's bestselling authors of poetry and non-fiction with books in print in excess of 3 million. Some of his published books are Think Black: Don't Cry, Scream (1970), We Walk The Way of The New World (1970); Directionscore: Selected and New poems (1971); and To Gwen, With Love (1971). He is president of the African American Book Centers also located in Chicago and editor of Black Books Bulletin. Mr. Haki R. Madhubuti, Third World Press, 7822 South Dobson Street, Chicago, Illinois 60619 Phone: (773) 651-0700 Fax: (773) 651-7286 E-mail: twpress3@aol.com Website: www.thirdworldpressinc.com

Beverly Mahone Veteran journalist and best selling author of Whatever! A Baby Boomer's Journey Into Middle Age, about issues affecting middle-aged women. The Ohio University graduate has now put her expertise to work by establishing her own media coaching and consulting business called Soul Solutions/Talk2Bev where she teaches her clients the mechanics of preparing for media interviews. As a result of the book's success, Ms. Mahone has been featured as a baby boomer expert on MSNBC-TV and written about in the recently released book, Talk Radio for Authors by Francine Silverman. Contact Ms. Beverly Mahone, Post Office Box 11037, Durham, North Carolina 27703 Phone: (301) 356-6280 E-mail: beverly@talktobev.com Website: www.thebabyboomerdiva.com

Gloria Mallette Author, publisher and artist Ms. Mallette began her true literary journey by self-publishing her second novel Shades of Jade in April of 2000. By July, and 13,000 sold copies later, Gloria signed on with Random House who re-released Shades of Jade in 2001. Shades of Jade made several best sellers lists, including Black Board and Essence Magazine. She also has a featured novella, Come Tomorrow, on the USAToday website. Gloria now has several published titles: If There Be Pain, What's Done in the Dark, Distant Lover, The Honey Well, Promises to Keep, Weeping Willows Dance, Shades of Jade, When We Practice to Deceive and Living, Sassy and Breathing Lies. Sassy and Living, Breathing Lies, have twice won the National Best Books Award and the Indie Excellence Award. Gloria Mallette, Post Office Box 488, Bartonsville, Pennsylvania 18321 E-mail: gloriamallette@aol.com Website: www.gloriamallette.com

Julianne Malveaux Author, economist and commentator, Dr. Malveaux is the President and CEO of Last Word Productions, Inc, and her academic work is included in numerous papers, studies, and publications. She is the editor of Voices of Vision: African American Women on the Issues (1996); the co-editor of Slipping Through the Cracks: The Status of Black Women (1986), and recently co-edited The Paradox of Loyalty: An African American Response to the War on Terrorism (2002). She is the author of two column anthologies: Sex, Lies, and Stereotypes: Perspectives of a Mad Economist (1994), Wall Street, Main Street, and the Side Street: A Mad Economist Takes a Stroll (1999). She is the co-author of Unfinished Business: A Democrat and A Republican Take On the 10 Most Important Issues Women Face (2002). Her co-edited volume, The Paradox of Loyalty: An African American Response to the War on Terrorism (2002) was released in paperback in 2004. Dr. Julianne Malveaux, 1318 Corcoran Street, North West, Washington, DC 20009 Phone: (202) 462-1932 Fax: (202) 462-6612 E-mail: lastwordprod@aol.com Website: www.juliannemalveaux.com

Sechiquita Ratliff Marti Author, non-fiction writer, motivator and an inspirer of life, who is passionate about sharing God's Word and empowering believers to discover God's individual and unique plan and design for their lives. My first book is titled Wealth Comes From Within! A Guide To Your Wealth Blueprint. I am a frequent contributor to Maganue Magazine which contains numerous articles and several interviews. I also have written a tribute to my mother that appears in the book "Relationships And Other Stuff Vol. 2: Stories From Women." At the tender age of 47, I consider myself beginning a whole new life. I am on a journey to allow my gift to make room for me and to do what is pleasing unto the eyesight of The Lord. I am the tenth of ten children. Sechiquita Ratliff Marti, 5333 Sahalee Way, Raleigh, North Carolina Phone: (919) 749-4663 Fax: (919) 255-3696 E-mail: wealthcomesfromwithin@yahoo.com Website: wealthcomesfromwithin@yahoo.com

Cheryl Martin The author has worked as a reporter and producer for the NBC-owned and ABC affiliate television stations in Washington, D.C. For nine years, Cheryl was a popular News Anchor and Host on the national cable network, BET. In 1996, she became the moderator of the network's signature Sunday news analysis show, "Lead Story," interviewing some of the nation's top newsmakers, including former president Bill Clinton, General Colin Powell, and Condoleezza Rice. Cheryl is the author of 1st Class Single: Rules for Dating and Waiting God's Way. She also writes the column, "Successfully Single," in GOSPEL TODAY magazine. Ms. Cheryl Martin, Post Office Box 15285, Chevy Chase, Maryland 20825 Phone: (301) 907-8215 E-mail: info@cherylmartin.org Website: www.cherylmartin.org

Roland S. Martin Author, nationally award-winning journalist and syndicated columnist with Creators Syndicate, Mr. Martin is the founding editor of BlackAmericaweb.com. Also formerly executive editor of The Chicago Defender, and is a frequent commentator on TV-One, CNN, MSNBC, FOX, and Black Entertainment Television (BET). He is the author of Speak, Brother! A Black Man's View of America. Memberships include the National Association of Black Journalists (NABJ), and the Alpha Phi Alpha Fraternity, Inc. Roland S. Martin, NuVision Media, Inc., 1327 West Washington Boulevard #102B, Chicago, Illinois 60607 Phone: (312) 543-6000 E-mail: roland@rolandsmartin.com Website: www.rolandsmartin.com

Carolyn Mattocks A summa cum laude graduate of North Carolina Central University with a B.A. in History, Ms. Mattocks is the author of "I Can Do Anything" and "Essays of W.I.I.T.S. A professional writer she has written for various newspapers, federal agencies, and academic institutions; member Alpha Kappa Mu Honor Society and also available for educational lectures, workshops, and consulting. Carolyn R. Mattocks, Post Office Box 16852, Baltimore, Maryland 21206 Phone: (443) 326-7191 E-mail: carolynmattocks@historicalinspirations.net Website: www.historicalinspirations.net

Rych McCain Author of the book Black Afrikan Hair and The Insanity of the Black Blonde Psych! He is a international/nationally syndicated Urban Entertainment Newspaper/Magazine Columnist with 3.5 Million readers. His interviews and print features reads like a who's who of the urban film, TV, stage and recording arenas. McCain's print features and famous photo spreads include Hollywood Red Carpet Movie Premieres, Major Awards Shows, Press Junkets, Exclusive One to One interview/photo shoots. Rych McCain, Post Office Box 2272, Beverly Hills, California 90213 Phone: (213) 387-3493 E-mail: rychmccain@sbcglobal.net

Gary McCants The author of Challenges of Faith and Family & Challenges of Relationships, Gary McCants is a former contributing writer to Ebony and Jet Magazines. He is a relational & community building consultant. Gary McCants, 1398 East 20th Avenue, Columbus, Ohio 43211 Fax: (802) 609-2715 E-mail: **garymccants@excite.com**

Sylvia McClain Author of "Skipping Through Life, the Reason I Am," and the book, The Write Life: A beginning Writer's Guide to Writing, Money Management, Publishing and Marketing. BA General Studies: Communications, English, and Art History degree, University of Michigan, and Associates of Arts in Accounting from Wayne County Community College. Sylvia McClain, 6896 Lakeview Boulevard, Apt 203, Westland, Michigan 48185 Phone: (734) 326-3341 E-mail: **sylmcclain@juno.com** Website: **www.scribalpress.com**

DeWayne McCulley An ex-diabetic system engineer who survived a near-death, diabetic coma, weaned off insulin and reversed his type 2 diabetes. He used his 30 years of experience in engineering and biochemistry to beat his diabetes and write the book, Death to Diabetes. Also offers health coaching, workshops and teleseminar programs. DeWayne McCulley, Death to Diabetes, 1170 Ridge Road, Suite #190, Webster, New York 14580 Phone: (800) 813-1927 E-mail: **engineer@deathtodiabetes.com** Website: **www.deathtodiabetes.com**

Brian McClellan Co-founder and CEO of BAMSTRONG Presentations, a career consulting firm, and the author of The Real Bling: How to Get the Only Thing You Need. A graduate of Princeton University and the Columbia Business School, Brian is a powerful motivational speaker that has mentored countless fellow professionals seeking to improve their personal and professional lives. Brian McClellan, 2700 Braselton Highway, Suite 10-390, Dacula, Georgia 30019 Phone: (888) 276-6730 Fax: (888) 209-8212 E-mail: **bam@bamstrong.com** Website: **www.bamstrong.com**

Tia McCollors Author of the Essence best-seller book, A Heart of Devotion (Moody Publishers, Jan 2005). In addition to writing novels for the adult market, Tia is penning a series of children's early chapter books targeted towards girls, ages 7-9, include a novel Zora's Cry (2006), The Midnight Clear, (2006), and The Truth About Love (2008). She is a native of Greensboro, North Carolina and a graduate of the University of North Carolina at Chapel Hill. Over the years, she has built a career as a public relations professional and currently works for a private institution. Tia McCollors, 3653 Slakes Mill Road, Decatur, Georgia 30034 Phone: (770) 598-9599 E-mail: **Tia@TiaMcCollors.com** Website: **www.TiaWrites.com**

Jacquelin Salvatto McCord Author and publisher of four books, When We Get Straight, A Molehill Is A Mountain, Miss America and the Silver Medal and Fur Coats In My Closet. She graduated from Fordham University with a Bachelor of Science in Education, received a Master of Arts from Spertus College and a Doctor of Naprapathy from Chicago National College of Naprapathy. She has been written about in several books and magazines relating to health care issues such as Hands On Healing by the publisher of Prevention. She is the contributing writer for several magazines, newspapers and books. Member of Delta Sigma Theta Sorority, Inc., Delta Authors on Tour (DAOT), Black Literary Umbrella (BLU). Jacquelin S. McCord, Post Office Box 167054, Chicago, Illinois 60616 Phone: (733) 363-6613 Fax: (773) 363-6650 E-mail: **jsmc45@aol.com** Website: **www.jsmccord.com**

Trevy A. McDonald College professor, radio announcer/producer and writer. A graduate of the University of Wisconsin-Oshkosh and the University of North Carolina at Chapel Hill, she has taught courses in speech and broadcasting at North Carolina State University and North Carolina Central University. She is the co-editor of Nature of a Sistuh (1998) as well as Time Will Tell and How We Got Over edited by Trevy A. McDonald and Bettye J. Allen. She taught communication courses at North Carolina State University, North Carolina Central University and Spertus College prior to coming to the School of Journalism and Mass Communication. She was recently elected to the University of Wisconsin-Oshkosh Alumni Association Board of Directors where she received the Distinguished Alumni Award in 2008. Trevy A. McDonald, Post Office Box 43255, Chicago, Illinois 60643 Phone: (919) 962-0547 E-mail: trevy@email.unc.edu

Lurea C. McFadden Author of the Female Traits Trilogy. Born in 1960 in Harlem, New York, Lurea now lives in Trenton, New Jersey where she works for the State of New Jersey. She attended Jacksonville University where she received a Bachelors of Arts Degree in History. Laura has spent many years working in the public school system as a Social Studies Teacher. Currently working on fourth novel entitled Men Don't Leave, to be released late autumn 2009. Lurea C. McFadden, Bruce Publishing, 947 Carteret Avenue, Trenton, New Jersey E-mail: **brucepublishing@hotmail.com** Website: **www.lureamcfadden.com**

Anthony Ellis McGee His debut novel "Under the Same Roof" (2007) received the Black Excellence Award for Outstanding Achievement in Literature (Fiction) from the African American Arts Alliance. Mr. Anthony McGee, 621 East 84th Street, Suite 3W, Chicago, Illinois 60619 Phone: (773) 468-4225 E-mail: **anthony.mcgee@sbcglobal.net** Website: **www.anthonyellismcgee.com**

Valerie CJ McGee Writing since 1968 and currently learning Braille. Lived in four of NYC's boroughs. She retired after a combined 37 years with the military and Civil Service. Valerie is finishing her next book (of 36) and enjoying life. Valerie C J McGee, Post Office Box 5324, Williamsburg, Virginia 23188 E-mail: **AuthorOfINSIGHT@yahoo.com**

Victor McGlothin Essence and National best-selling author who almost lost an athletic scholarship due to poor reading skills. Ultimately, he overcame that obstacle and completed a Masters degree in Human Relations & Business. His published books are: Autumn Leaves (2003), Every Sistah Wants It (2004), What's a Woman to Do? (2003), Sinful (2007) Borrow Trouble (2006) Down on My Knees (2006), Indecent Exposure (2006), Whispers between the Sheets (2005). Victor McGlothin, Post Office Box 864198, Plano, Texas 75086 E-mail: **Thewritebrother@hotmail.com** Website: **www.victormcglothin.com**

Michelle McGriff   Publisher: Urban/Kensington. Genre: Mysteries / Suspense. Has ten grown up novels under her pen and still continues to entertain readers with fresh tales taken from the world around her. Her latest book is Last Breath (2008). Several of her books are The Legend of Morning (2004) with co-author, T.L. Gardner, a non-fiction work by Denise Rosier which she contributed three chapters, and Blood Relations (2009). MBA in Marketing. Contact Michelle McGriff, 11911 Pine Street, Portland, Oregon 97216 Phone: (650) 290-2019 E-mail: **Wetaugustbooks@aol.com** Website: **www.michellemcgriff.com**

Dorma McGruder A newspaper columnist for two years for Detroit Legacy News and the Michigan Chronicle, Dorma is a gifted, national public speaker since the age of four addressing crowds from 10 to 10,000 in political, educational, social and religious venues. At six years old she recited Lincoln's Gettysburg address for Dr. Martin Luther King, Jr., in Detroit at Cobo Hall in 1963, just before he gave the initial presentation of his "I Have A Dream" speech. Ms. McGruder is the author of 'I Had No Choice' the truthful fiction story of her life. She attended Mercy College and Wayne State University studying Business Administration. Also, hosted cable television events for the City of Detroit in several areas. Contact Ms. Dorma McGruder, Post Office Box 44615, Detroit, MI 48244 Phone: (313) 205-0600 Fax: (313) 531-9141 E-mail: **dormajm@sbcglobal.net** Website: **www.dormamcgruder.com**

Joel Eli McIver A graduate of Winston Salem State University where he earned a Bachelor of Arts degree is Mass Communications, Joel Eli McIver has worked in television production, in an art gallery, education and in the legal field. His debut novel is What Is Forever? He is currently working on his next two books, Dancing With My Shadow and Love Is. Mr. McIver lives in Winston Salem, North Carolina with his wife and three children. Contact Mr. Joel McIver, 4Unity Publishing, Post Office Box 548, Pfafftown, North Carolina 27040 E-mail: **mciverjoel@4unitypublishing.com**

Gracie C. McKeever A native New Yorker, McKeever has authored several novels, among them the Siren Top Sellers, Terms of Surrender, Guardian Seductress, and Bouncer's Folly. She has been writing since the ripe old age of seven when two younger brothers were among her earliest, captive audience for various short story readings and performances. It wasn't until 2001, however, when Gracie caught the erotic romance bug that produced an instant affinity for the genre and spawned her own first erotic romance, Beneath the Surface, published in 2006 by Siren Publishing, Inc. Gracie C. McKeever, Post Office Box 1074, New York, New York 10116 E-mail: **gwiz10@optonline.net** Website: **www.graciecmckeever.com**

Tina Brooks McKinney Best Selling author of All That Drama (Strebor Books, December, 2004). Its sequel Lawd Mo Drama was released in November, 2005. Tina is working and finalizing the finishing touches to the third and final part of the "Drama" series "Fool Stop Trippin'," scheduled to be published in 2008. Contact Tina Brooks McKinney, 425 Princeton Way, Covington, Georgia 30016 Phone: (678) 625-9261 E-mail: **tybrooks2@yahoo.com** Website: **www.tinamckinney.com**

Jacquitta A. McManus Author of two books, Labyrinth's Door -- A breathtaking new fantasy/adventure MagBook re-imagines how young people interact with their favorite genre, and Talee: The Fallen Object, illustrated by Jaquitta A. McManus and Brian Hardison. Jacquitta A. McManus, Post Office Box 5425, Douglasville, Georgia 30154 Phone: (678) 379-3878 E-mail: **JMcManus@WorldsToDiscover.com** Website: **www.worldstodiscover.com**

Delta McNeish Founder of Intercession Ministries, Pastor, counselor and singer, Ms. Mcneish's debut book is Crisis: Identity (2008, Xulon Press). Her first CD is The Spirit and The Bride. Contace Paster, Delta McNeish, Ph.D, Intercession Ministries, 424 Grey Street, London Ontario N6B 1H3 Phone: (519) 679-9402 E-mail: **h2h@intercessionministries.org** Website: **www.intercessionministries.org**

Angela Shelf Medearis Children's book author, Mrs. Medearis was noted as "one of the most influential writers of children's literature", by Texas Monthly magazine. Angela's desire to write books for children who had difficulty reading has blossomed into an award-winning career that spans over a decade includes over 90 children's books and three cookbooks, with sales exceeding 10 million copies worldwide. She founded and is host of The Kitchen Diva! cooking show that airs nationwide on public television as well as several educational video series including the popular and award-winning animated and bilingual "Storyteller's Series", narrated by Medearis. Contact Ms. Angela Shelf Medearis, Diva Productions, Inc., Post Office Box 91625, Austin, Texas 78709 Phone: (512) 444-3482 Fax: (512) 444-3399 E-mail: medearis@medearis.com Website: www.medearis.com

Cherlyn Michaels Author of Counting Raindrops through a Stained Glass Window her first writing experiences were in grade school where she wrote, produced, and starred in her first play, "Cindy: The Black Cinderella,". She attended a workshop with Terry McMillan in June of 2003 after which Ms. McMillan inscribed in her book, "Cheryl, you can write your butt off. She holds a Bachelor's in Chemical Engineering from the University of Missouri at Rolla. Cherlyn Michaels, 11220 West Florissant Avenue, #298, Florissant, Missouri 63033 E-mail: cherlyn@cherlynmichaels.com Website: www.cherlynmichaels.com

J.J. Michael Lifelong student and teacher of Metaphysics and healing principles, Ms. Michael is the author of Path to Truth: a Spiritual Guide to Higher Consciousness (iUniverse.com, 2000), Life is Never as It Seems (Genesis Press Inc.), and It's Not Over Yet. She conducts workshops, book readings and lectures. She is a founding member of the Rays of Healing Team of Falls Church, Virginia, and a Chios Master Healer and Teacher of the Chios Institute of Santa Rosa, California. A renowned numerologist, Ms. Michael appeared in CNN's segment, "A Wrinkle in Time." Her formal education includes a BA from Howard University and a MLS from the University of Maryland. She is a member of Delta Sigma Theta Sorority. Contact Ms. J.J. Michael, Post Office Box 55804, Washington, D.C. 20040 Phone: (202) 487-1165 Website: www.jjmichael.org

David C. Miller Co-founder and Chief Visionary Officer for the Urban Leadership Institute, LLC, David C. Miller is a nationally recognized speaker and program developer working with African American males. A sought after lecturer and advocate for youth of color, David has over 13 years of hands on practical experience working with African American males and is author of, Lessons I Learned From My Father: A Collection of Quotes From Men of African Descent. Miller designed the Dare To Be King Training Program for African American males, which is a 240 page life skills curriculum for boys ages 10-17. Contact David Miller, Urban Leadership Institute, 28 Allegheny Avenue, Suite 503, Towson, Maryland 21204 Phone: (877) 339-4300 E-mail: dmiller@urbanleadershipinstitute.com Website: www.urbanyouth.org

Gail P. Miller Author of True Love Has A Passion for You! book and journal. Her books are inspirational and devotional materials. Her new book is True Love has A Passion for You Study Guide. Miller holds a bachelor's degree in physical education from Central State University and an associate's degree in ministry from Liberated in Christ School of Ministry. She is a physical education teacher in the Dayton Public Schools System. Ms. Gail P. Miller, Post Office Box 3751, Dayton, Ohio 45401 Phone: (937) 269-1386 E-mail: miller-gail@sbcglobal.net

Minnie E Miller Fiction author and native of Chicago and activist and has worked in politics since the age of eighteen. Ms. Miller bravely served as secretary to an attorney for the Black Panther Party when it wasn't the safest job for a young lady, and worked as office manager in the State Appellant Defender's Chicago office. She also worked at the Mayor's office in San Francisco as a special assistant to his press secretary. While there she co-authored the San Francisco Mayor's Summit For Women (1998). Her novel, The Seduction of Mr. Bradley (2006) is another political statement as well as a spiritual view of love for humankind. Minnie E. Miller, 4700 South Lake Park Avenue, Suite 2104, Chicago, Illinois 60615 Phone: (773) 538-9902 E-mail: **minnie247@sbcglobal.net** Website: **www.millerscribs.com**

Moses Miller A journalist, motivational speaker and an award winning author for Mind Candy, LLC, which is a company focused on book publishing and the development of creative and thought provoking screenplays. A native New Yorker, Moses has contributed articles and written for various websites and publications including The Voice, Newsday and 88HIPHOP.COM, where he is currently the Editor in Chief of content. He holds a Bachelors degree in Business Management and a Masters of Science degree in Technology Management obtained from Polytechnic University. His first novel, Nan: The Trifling Times of Nathan Jones has received various awards and critical acclaim from critics, readers and book clubs around the world. After selling thousands of copies of his first novel, Mr. Miller cemented a deal with F.E.D.S. magazine resulting in a joint venture to publish his second release, Once Upon A Time in Harlem in September, 2007. His second book in the Nan series is The Game of Trife, 2008. His next book was The Barack in Me, an inspirational book written specifically for young African American males, 2009. Moses Miller, Post Office Box 2185, Garden City, New York 11531 Phone: (917) 848-3670 Fax: (516) 379-7676 E-mail: **Moses@MindCandyMedia.com**

Rosie Milligan Registered nurse, counselor/health consultant, author, and Ph.D. in Business Administration, Dr. Rosie lectures nationally on economic empowerment, managing diversity in the workplace, and male/female relationships. Author of 14 books. Owner of Milligan Books, Inc., one of the largest and fasting growing African-American female publisher in the nation. Dr. Milligan is founder of Black Writers On Tour. She has published 150 plus authors and helped to launch 10 publishing companies. She is a literary agent and has sold books to some of the most prestigous New York publishing houses. Dr. Milligan's books, Starting a Business Made Simple and Getting Out of Debt Made Simple have helped many across the country. Her most recent release, Creating A New You In Six Weeks Made Simple, is a must read. Rosie Milligan, Milligan Books, 1425 West Manchester Avenue, Suite C, Los Angeles, California 90047 Phone: (323) 750-3592 Fax: (323) 750-2886 E-mail: **DrRosie@aol.com** Website: **www.drrosie.com**

Sydney Molare A veterinarian by profession and Mississippi native, Sydney Molare is the author of over ten books, Somewhere In America: Situations of XX and XY, a collection of short stories is a comedic and controversial look at life in these United States, Changing Places, Grandmama's Mojo Still Working, Devil's Orchestra (2006), The Shattered Glass Effect (2009) and Small Packages. Her book, Somewhere In America, was chosen as a "Cream of the Crop" selection receiving 5/5. Her latest novel, is Devil's Orchestra. Dr. Sydney Molare, Post Office Box 362, Roxie, Mississippi 39661 Phone: (601) 384-0219 Fax: (601) 384-1667 E-mail: **sydney@sydneymolare.com** Website: **www.sydneymolare.com**

Baba Evans Moore   Author of five fiction novels: Choice of a Lifetime (2000), The Pastor's Letter (2001), While the Village Sleeps (2003), Just a Picture in A Frame (2006) and An Extra Ordinary Affair (2008). Baba has received awards from Disigold Publications and C&B Book Distributors, Inc. He resides in Temple Hills, Maryland and when not writing historical fiction novels, teaches adults in the Toyota Family Literacy Program. Baba is also CEO of the Ward 8 Mentoring Project, a parenting agency that conduct workshops promoting responsible fatherhood. Baba Evans Moore, Post Office Box 30311, Washington, DC 20030 Phone: (301) 275-0474 E-mail: **evansmoore@hotmail.com** Website: **www.babaevans.com**

Carman Moore   Composer, Author, Music Critic. A dedicated educator, Moore has taught at the Yale University Graduate School of Music, Queens and Brooklyn Colleges, Carnegie-Mellon University, Manhattanville College, and The New School for Social Research. He is presently creating a pop music album based in Outer Space and featuring Dante and Beatrice for the new SKYBAND. He has just completed *CONCERTO FOR ORNETTE AND ORCHESTRA* for jazz legend and 2006 Pulitzer prize winner Ornette Coleman. Particularly interested in reaching out to children, he spent several years in the 1960's, 70's and 80's as a teaching artist for Lincoln Center and Jazzmobile and at The Dalton School. In 1995 he served as consultant to Wynton Marsalis on his popular PBS-broadcast home video series for children, Marsalis On Music. Moore is also the author of two youth-oriented books: Somebody's Angel Child: The Story of Bessie Smith (Dell), and Rock-It (a music history and theory book for Alfred Music Publishers). He has served as Board member and adjudicator for several major organizations, including Composers Forum, the Society of Black Composers, the N.Y. State Council on the Arts, and the National Endowment for the Arts. In addition he has been music critic and columnist for the Village Voice and has contributed to The New York Times, The Saturday Review of Literature, Vogue, and Essence among others. Contact Mr. Carman Moore, 152 Columbus Avenue, New York, New York 10023 Phone: (212) 580-0825 E-mail: **skycarmuse@mindspring.com**

E. Joyce Moore   The authors writings is included in the Bestfriends Anthology (2003) and she is a contributor to Chicken Soup for the African American Soul. She has also expressed her creativity on film, directing a cable television show in Indiana back in 1984, creating an infomercial for AT&T products in 1988 and producing a video introducing African American Fine Artists for the 2001 National Black Fine Arts Show in Manhattan. She is also developing several television scripts, freelances and has just completed her first ghostwriting project. E. Joyce Moore, Post Office Box 88403, Indianapolis, Indiana 46208 E-mail: **jemiltd@aol.com**

Fred D. Moore   Author of The Pregnant Pulpit. Fred D. Moore, 500 West Decatur Street, Demopolis, Alabama 36732 E-mail: **moorebigbear@aol.com**

Katherine Bell Moore   A former college professor and national award winning business woman who served for fourteen years as the Mayor Pro Tem of the Wilmington, North Carolina City Council. While a member of the Council, Moore wrote and published a book entitled, "Memoirs of An Honest Politician." The book exposed many of the City's "dirty little secrets." The book alluded to political corruption, misuse of federal funds that were targeted for the poor, ongoing cases of police brutality, and law enforcement's negligence in prosecuting child molesters. Katherine Moore, 3530 Mystic Pointe Drive Tower 500, #1204, Aventura, Florida 33180 Phone: (954) 673-2709 Fax: (305) 933-8914 E-mail: **saintfrancisdes@yahoo.com**

Toi Moore   Author of the book, Unbreakable, An Understanding to Marriage and Relationships (2005). This book was written with her husband, Gregory Moore. Mind Games, the sequel to her first self-published novel Momma, Please Forgive Me! is a mystery thriller. The book has been endorsed by celebrities such as; Vivica A. Fox, James Ingram, Patrice Rushen, and TC Carson to name a few. Toi also writes for other publications such as Billboard, Upscale, The Cause and Saludos Hispanos Magazines to name a few, where she has over 200 published articles in various newspaper and magazines throughout the United States and Canada. She has written several short stories, four novels and two screenplays. She has also worn the hat of publisher, by publishing her own magazine titled "Mini Romances." She has several bylines to her credit in which she has authored and interviewed a variety of well-known celebrities such as: Oprah Winfrey, Laila Ali, James Ingram, Vivica A. Fox, Kweisi Mfume, Lisa "Left Eye" Lopez, Patti LaBelle, Boney James, B2K, Jaheim, and Patrice Rushen.   Today, she continues her writings, while realizing and accepting her gift from God. Toi Moore, Post Office Box 2099, Sun City, California 92586 Phone: (951) 231-1633 E-mail: toimoore@aol.com Website: **www.toimoore.com**

Wanda Moorman   Dynamic writer, poet, songwriter and speaker, Ms. Moorman is a native West Virginian but now resides in Washington, DC. She holds graduate and undergraduate degrees in Business Administration, and has worked in the Federal and Washington, DC, city governments as a Contracts Manager. She has written song lyrics for several Hollywood record companies and poetry for the International Library of Poetry. Her first novel, In His Ex-Wife's Shadow, was released in March 2000 and her sophomore novel, Corporate Sponsor, in Fall 2000. She is a member of the Black Writers Alliance, Romance Writers of America and the New Jersey Romance Writers. She is a contributing writer for The Washington Informer newspaper. She is currently at work on her third novel. Wanda Moorman, Story Book Productions, Post Office Box 60096, Washington, DC 20039 E-mail: **wandamoorman@storytale.com** Website: **www.storytale.com**

Gwendolyn R. Morris   Romantic of 'old world' proportions, Ms. Morris knows that African-American women can be strong, but feminine and educated at the same time. Thus were the beginning concepts for her sensual romance books, Angels, Nubian Passion, and Vampire. Gwen has also written 6 custom-made children's books. Contact Ms. Gwendolyn R. Morris, 542 Berlin-Cross Keys Road, Suite 3-255, Sicklerville, New Jersey 08081. E-mail: **kazi22@msn.com**

Mary B. Morrison   National bestselling author of "When Somebody Loves You Back," and "She Ain't the One." In 1999 Mary decided to step out on faith. She quit her six figure Government job to become a writer saying, "I'd rather die a failure, than to have lieved and never known whether I would become a success." Mary's first book of poetry Justice Just Us Just Me was self-published, August 23, 1999. Mary was born in Aurora, Illinois, reared in New Orleans, Louisiana, and currently resides in the Oakland, California. She is president and founder of Booga Bear Publishing and The RaW Advantage. Her books, Nothing Has Ever Felt like This, When Somebody Loves you Back, and Our Little Secret were published in 2005, 2006, and 2007. Ms. Mary "HoneyB" Morrison, ELR Entertainment, 2318 25th Avenue, Oakland, California 94601 Phone: (510) 205-8711 E-mail: **MaryBMorrison@aol.com** Website: **www.marymorrison.com**

Gloria Morrow Licensed Clinical Psychologist and author of the book, Too Broken to be Fixed? A Spiritual Guide to Inner Healing, Dr. Morrow specializes in treating adults and adolescents who suffer from depression, anxiety, PTSD, as well as grief and loss issues. Her other new books to be released are "Strengthening the Ties that Bind: A Guide to a Healthy Marriage" and "The Things that Make Men Cry." Contact Dr. Gloria Morrow, Ph.D., GM Psychological Services, 308 North 2nd Avenue, Suite B, Upland, California 91786 Phone: (909) 985-3773 E-mail: **Dr_Gloria_Morrow@msn.com** Website: **www.gloriamorrow.com**

Leah Yvonne Mullen Author, writer, Leah is originally from Chester County, Pennsylvania, the fictional setting for her debut novel, Again and Again. A prolific journalist, Leah has penned hundreds of essays, articles, reviews, and profiles which have appeared in over twenty publications and websites including: Mosaic and African American Literature Book Club (aalbc.com). She has a BA in print journalism from the Pennsylvania State University. Leah Mullen, Post Office Box 7047, JAF Station, New York, New York 10116 E-mail: **leahmullen@yahoo.com** Website: **www.leahmullen.com**

Micki L. Murphy Fire & Desire is the new authors debut novel based on a true story. In addition to being an author, Micki is a model, jazz singer, and songwriter. She is currently recording her third CD project. Contact Micki Murphy 112 Summit Creek Avenue North Las Vegas, Nevada 89031 Phone: (702) 561-6564 E-mail: **mickismonky@mickimurphy.com** Website: **www.mickimurphy.com**

Daphne Muse Award-winning author of four books, her most recent The Entrance Place of Wonders: Poems of the Harlem Renaissance (Abrams 2006) was selected by Black Issues in Book Reviews as one of the best collections of poetry for children. She is also a New Frontiers Radio Essayist and her social commentaries have been published in major newspapers and air on public radio and commercial stations across the country, including NPR and Radio. Daphne Muse, 2429 East 23rd Street, Oakland, California 94601 Phone: (510) 436-4716 Fax: (510) 261-6064 E-mail: **msmusewriter@gmail.com** Website: **www.oasisinthediaspora.com**

MWALIM Writer/Director/Producer. He is a published author of one book, A Mixed Medicine Bag: 7 Original Black Wampanoag Folk-tales, several poems and short stories appearing in numerous anthologies. Mwalim is a three-time recipient of the Ira Aldridge Fellowship. He is a professor of English and African/African American Studies at University of Massachusetts, Dartmouth. Mwalim (Professor MJ Peters), English Department, University of Massachusetts, Dartmouth, 285 Old Westport Road, North Dartmouth, Massachusetts 02747 Phone: (508) 999-8304 Fax: (508) 999-9235 E-mail: **mwalim@gmail.com**

LaShawn Myers CEO of A Time To Heal LLC, an initiative developed to provide faith-based seminars and literature to individuals who suffer from losses (i.e., job, death, unresolved childhood matters, etc., the authors book, A Time To Heal: Disposing of Closet Hurts Publication presents a nondenominational balance between spirituality and the natural grieving process individuals undergo after a traumatic event. Myers received her Master's of Social Work degree from Wayne State University, Detroit. Ms. LaShawn Myers, LLMSW, A Time To Heal LLC, 16232 Lamplighter Court, Suite #1212, Southfield, Michigan 48075 Phone: (313) 737-0018 E-mail: **ridclosethurts@yahoo.com** Website: **www.atimetohealhurts.com**

P. Durrell Nathan Author of 666 The New World Order and Secret Societies Of The New World Order. Contact P. Durrell Nathan, 1885 Forest Maple Lane, Apt-C, Columbus, Ohio 43229 Phone: (614) 256-3343 E-mail: **Diamondjewlz77@yahoo.com**

Charleszine Nelson Born and raised in Denver, Nelson is a special collection and community resource manager for the Blair-Caldwell African American Research Library and co-author with Bonnie F. McCune of Recruiting and Managing Volunteers in Libraries. She attended Manual High School, earned a Bachelor's degree in Sociology and Psychology from the University of Colorado, and a Master's degree in Information Technology and Library Science from Emporia State College. She has a master's degree in History and Preservation from the University of Colorado at Denver. Charleszine Nelson, Blair-Caldwell African American Research Library, 2401 Welton Street Denver, Colorado 80205 Phone: (720) 865-2401 E-mail: **tnelson@denverlibrary.org** Website: **www.aarl.denverlibrary.org**

Paula Newberry Author of the biographical novel, "Someone Noticed" (Author House Books) and Opera Singer, Ms. Newberry has toured with her own "Evening of Opera" and "Spirit Moving Spirituals" concerts throughout the United States. She has appeared at Carnegie Hall (Weill Recital Hall) and concert auditoriums such as The Germantown Performing Arts Center. Her awards and honors include The Chancellor's List, Spoleto Vocal Arts Vocal Scholarship, Bagby Musical Foundation Merit Award, and numerous others. Ms. Paula Newberry, Post Office Box 753446, Memphis, Tennessee 38175 Phone: (901) 216-6593 E-mail: **newdivaof2005@yahoo.com** Website: **www.classicalsinger.net**

Fred Newman Born in the South Bronx, New York City in 1935, Newman has written numerous books exploring performance and human development including: Performance of a Lifetime: A Practical-Philosophical Guide to the Joyous Life and Let's Develop! A Guide to Continuous Personal Growth. He is co-author with Dr. Lois Holzman of Lev Vygotsky: Revolutionary Scientist (Routledge, 1993); Unscientific Psychology: A Cultural Performatory Approach to Understanding Human Life (Praeger Press); and The End of Knowing: A New Developmental Way of Learning (Routledge, 1997). He is a frequent lecturer on social, psychological and political topics and has been featured on CNN, PBS, WNBC-TV and in the pages of the New York Times, Newsweek, and Christian Science Monitor. Fred Newman, Castillo Theatre, 543 West 42nd Street, New York, New York 10036 Phone: (212) 941-9400 Fax: E-mail: **castillo@allstars.org** Website: **www.castillo.org**

Lisa Nichols Co-author of the 2004 Black Book Award Winner, Chicken Soup for the African American Soul: Celebrating and Sharing Our Culture One Story at a Time, by Lisa Nichols, Tom Joyner, Jack Canfield and Mark Victor Hansen. Lisa Nichols has been a personal coach to CEO's, entrepreneurs, investors, principals, professionals, pastors, and parents. She is the Founder and CEO of Motivating the Teen Spirit, LLC which is recognized by many as the most comprehensive empowerment skills program available today for teen self-development. Ms. Nichols has been recognized for her work and dedication by receiving the 2003 Trail Blazers Entrepreneurs award, Lego Land Heart of Learning award, Emotional Literacy award and having November 20th proclaimed by the Mayor of Henderson Nevada as Motivating the Teen Spirit Day. Lisa Nichols, Post Office Box 943, Puunene, Hawaii 96784 Fax: (808) 879-8201 E-mail: **Lisa@AfricanAmericanSoul.com** Website: **www.africanamericansoul.com**

Gerald S. Norde Professor Cornel West of Princeton University has endorsed a monograph, Peculiar Affinity: The World the Slave Owners and Their Female Slaves Made, published by Gerald S. Norde. Professor West exclaims, 'Gerald S. Norde, Sr., has written a ground breaking work that lays bare the barbaric treatment of Black women during U.S. slavery. It is both revealing and riveting in it terrifying horror.' Dr. Norde is available for journal/news interviews, presentations, lectures, faculty colloquia, radio and television talk shows, and all related to the research endorsed by Professor West. Dr. Gerald S. Norde, 1308 Trice Meadows Circle, Denton, Maryland 21629 E-mail: dr.gsnorde@verizon.net

Nikki Nicole Freelance journalist, entrepreneur, published author. Nikki Nicole, G Dot Media, Post Office Box 152979, San Diego, California 92195 E-mail: thagstands4@yahoo.com

Fellina Nwadike I am a teacher. I have written two testbooks for my classes in Speech Communication and Inercultural Communication and diversity in the last four years. Presently, I have two articles for publications. Contact Fellina Nwadike, 1248 Cedarcroft Road, Baltimore, Maryland 21239 Phone: (410) 323-1248 Fax: (410) 951-3359 E-mail: nwadike@netscape.net

Oasis Entrepreneur by nature and author by trade he was born and raised in Cleveland, Ohio and is a writing mentor and a government-certified creative-writing instructor who has been teaching the craft for years. His novels include Push Comes To Shove, (2007) and Duplicity, (Oasis Publishing Group, (2007) Oasis, Post Office Box 19101, Cleveland, Ohio 44119 E-mail: oasisreader@oasisnovels.com Website: www.oasisnovels.com

Ron Oliphant The authors first book of poetry, is entitled A Player's Poetry which led to his most recent book, Love Bones. His other poetry books Manic Depressive, and As I Sit Alone are scheduled for release in the Spring of 2009, and also a novel, The South Side Of Dallas (2009). Ron Oliphant, Post Office Box 1301, Waco, Texas 76703 Phone: (254) 498-7826 E-mail: contact@ronaldoliphant.com Website: www.ronaldoliphant.com

Omowale Self-published author of several books, including A Taste of Africa, Aisha, Expect A Miracle, A Lack of Knowledge, Sun People of the Nile and I Sing Because I'm Happy, several poems and songs. Contact Omowale, Omowale's Herb Garden, Livonia Mall, 29522 West 7 Mile Road, Livonia, Michigan 48152 Phone: (248) 474-8806 Fax: (248) 474-8836 E-mail: mz_omowale@yahoo.com Website: www.A1StopOnlineShop.com

Chika Onyeani Author of the explosive and internationally acclaimed No.1 bestselling book, Capitalist Nigger: The Road to Success, and the novel, The Broederbond Conspiracy. Chika Onyeani, Timbuktu Publishers, 463 North Arlington Avenue, East Orange, New Jersey 07017 Phone: (973) 675-9919 Fax: (973) 675-5704 E-mail: timbuktupublishers@yahoo.com Website: www.thebroederbondconspiracy.com

Travis Otey 42 year old networks operations support specialist his newest book is One Man's Soul: Lessons of a Lifetime, a non-fiction work of Inspirational self-help essays. Travis Otey, Diligent Publishing Company, Post Office Box 390605, Snellville, Georgia 30039 Phone: (404) 409-6025 E-mail: Travis@OneMansSoul.com Website: www.OneMansSoul.com

Renea Overstreet Author of Desire, Duty & Destiny. Always a Bridesmaid is her first work of fiction. Contact Ms. Renea Overstreet, 201 Oak Park Drive, Suite #202, Alvin, Texas 77511 E-mail: mlordolove@yahoo.com

Madge D. Owens A native Atlantan and graduate of Clark College her first novel is To Silence Her Memory (AuthorHouse) She began her career in Georgia government as a legislative aide, before being appointed to the Tours and Special Events Program at the Georgia State Capitol. She is presently on the legislative staff of the Georgia House of Representatives. She owns Write Page Literary Service, Inc., an Atlanta-based business and creative writing firm. Madge D. Owens, Write Page Literary Service Inc., Post Office Box 38288, Atlanta, Georgia 30334 Phone: (404) 280-5029 Fax: (404) 656-0238 E-mail: writepagemo@yahoo.com

Vivian Owens Author of four books, Parenting For Education, Create A Math Environment, Nadanda The Wordmaker (Writer's Digest Best Book Award Winner), and How Oswa Came to Own All Music. Her newspaper articles have appeared in over 200 newspapers across the country, and her magazine articles have appeared in such publications as Upscale Magazine, About…Time Magazine, and The Virginia Science Journal. Contact Ms. Vivian Owens, Eschar Publications, Post Office Box 1194, Mount Dora, Florida 32756 Fax: (352) 357-9695 E-mail: escharpub@earthlink.net Website: www.vivianowens.com

Deadria Farmer-Paellmann Excerpt of "Black Exodus: The Ex-Slave Pension Movement Reader" published in "Should America Pay: Slavery and the Raging Debate on Reparations" by Raymond Winbush, Ph D. Lawyer, Activist, Adjunct Professor, Restitution Study Group, Executive Director. Organization of Tribal Unity, Chair. Deadria Farmer-Paellmann, Post Office Box 1228, New York, New York 10009 Phone: (917) 365-3007 Fax: (201) 656-1981 E-mail: Paellmann@rcn.com

Margaret D. Pagan Author of the book, More Than A Slave: The Life of Katherine Ferguson. The book was a finalist in the 2004 Atlanta Daily World Choice Awards. She has published articles in newspapers, magazines, journals, and newsletters since graduating from Morgan State University. Margaret D. Pagan, 3809 Juniper Road, Baltimore, Maryland 21218 E-mail: mdpagan@verizon.net Website: www.margaretpagan.com

Evelyn Palfrey Author of four novels, Everything In Its Place, Dangerous Dilemmas, Price of Passion, and Three Perfect Men. Palfrey is contributor to two books in the Chicken Soup series, a graduate of Southern Methodist University and the University of Texas Law School and is active with the Austin Writers League, the Austin Romance Writers of America, the Travis County Bar Association, and Links Inc. Nominated for Career Achievement Award, Romantic Times Magazine. Evelyn Palfrey, Post Office Box 142495, Austin, Texas 78714 Phone: (512) 773-8776 E-mail: evelyn@evelynpalfrey.com Website: www.evelynpalfrey.com

Lincoln Park Author of Sculptured Nails and Nappy Hair (2005), and The Brevity of the Selves (2007), in her third novel, Handle Time (2008), Parks, brings you a saucy, searing and Hilarious story which explores the inner workings of an American Call Center. Ms. Lincoln Park, 4465 PReSS, 610-A East Battlefield Road, Suite 279, Springfield, Missouri 65807 Phone: (866) 842-1042 Fax: (775) 257-1286 E-mail: press4465@yahoo.com Website: www.4465press.com

Electa Rome Parks Author of the best-selling novels The Ties That Bind, Loose Ends, and Almost Doesn't Count (August, 2005, Penguin/NAL). After successfully publishing her debut novels, Loose Ends and The Ties That Bind, New American Library, a division of Penguin bought the rights. Parks is also author of These are My Confessions and her latest book is Diary of a Stalker. Electa Rome Parks, 2274 Salem Road, Suite 106, Post Office Box 173, Conyers, Georgia 30013 E-mail: novelideal@yahoo.com Website: www.electaromeparks.com

Monica Payton Author of two novels, *Black Deception,* and Cloning, a sequel and the recipient of an award at the Los Angeles Black Book Expo, 2004. Ms. Monica, Payton, Vision Harmony Publishing, Inc., 13089 Peyton Drive, Suite C201, Chino Hills, California, 91709 Phone: (951) 505-2503 E-mail: monica@monicapayton.com Website: www.visionharmony.com

Pearl Jr. Author of three books, the most recent is Black Women Need Love, too! Contact Pearl Jr., Elbow Grease Productions, 5632 Van Nuys Boulevard #195, Van Nuys, California 91401 E-mail: pearljr@trutalk.us Website: www.BlackWomenNeedLoveToo.com

Arthur Pindle Professor and author of the novel, Bayou St. John, set in 1825, is about two intriguing fugitives with a master/slave relationship who escape to start new lives in New Orleans. Arthur Pindle, 260 18th Street NW, #10216, Atlanta, Georgia 30363 Phone: (404) 931-5365 E-mail: apindle@aim.com

Suzetta M. Perkins Author of Behind the Veil, A Love So Deep, and EX-terminator, Life After Marriage. Contributing author of My Soul to His Spirit, an anthology of short stories that was featured in Ebony magazine (2005) and winner of the 2006 Fresh Voices Award. Cofounder and president of the Sistahs Book Club. Suzetta M. Perkins, Post Office Box 64424, Fayetteville, North Carolina 28306 E-mail: nubianqe2@aol.com Website: www.suzettaperkins.com

M. LaVora Perry Author of a middle-grade novel 'Taneesha Never Disparaging' (Wisdom Publications, 2008). This story is about an urban black Buddhist girl is recommended and praised by national teacher organizations, Teaching Tolerance and Teaching for Change, as well as by a reviewer for the International Reading Association. M. LaVora Perry, 13200 Forest Hill Avenue, East Cleveland, Ohio 44112 E-mail: mlavoraperry@mlavoraperry.com Website: www.mlavoraperry.com

Naresha S. Perry Author. Also founder and publisher of Better Day Publishing, dedicated to children with different learning abilities. Naresha S. Perry, 1152 Westheimer #341, Houston, Texas 77042 Phone: (713) 548-4048 E-mail: contact@betterdaypublishing.com Website: www.betterdaypublishing.com

Roy L. Pickering Author, photographer, poet, and freelance writer his debut novel is Patches of Grey. Roy's monthly column covering prevalent issues in the world of pro sports can be found at suite101.com. In 2003, his prose was featured in two anthologies. Kensington Books put out Proverbs for the People, which includes his short story, Lessons; The Game...Short Stories About the Life (Triple Crown Publications), Mama's Boy, and Enigmas of Desire, an anthology. Roy L. Pickering, 1185 Avenue of the Americas, 26th Floor, New York, New York 10036 E-mail: RoyLPickering@aol.com Website: www.RoyPickering.net

Adriene Pickett Author of Never Forget The Bridge That Crossed You Over. She is a graduate of William Paterson University and learned the art of storytelling firsthand in her home. Ms. Adriene Pickett, Post Office Box 643062, Los Angeles, California 90064 Phone: (310) 351-0378 E-mail: adrienepickett@aol.com Website: www.adrienepickett.com

Naiomi Pitre Author of two books, Broken Vows, and a second book newly released in January 2007, entitled In The Panty Drawer - Journey Into The Mind of a Sexual Woman. This steamy collection of stories offers a uniquely dark view of women thrust into precarious situations. Contact Ms. Naiomi Pitre, 39070 South Angelle Court, Gonzales, Louisiana 70737 Phone: (225) 673-8395 Fax: (225) 296-8858 E-mail: naiomipitre@hotmail.com Website: www.NaiomiPitre.4t.com

Darlene Pitts Author of Haunted Revenge, a novel about a psychic artist who seeks the ultimate revenge on a longtime enemy only to have it backfire in the form of an apparition. She is also the author of Discover Your Intuition & Let's Talk Intuition. Darlene Pitts, Inspiration & Intuition, Post Office Box 391, Smyrna, Georgia 30081 Phone: (770) 434-5240 E-mail: dpitts@inspirationandintuition.com Website: www.inspirationandintuition.com

D.T. Pollard Born in Henderson, Texas, He earned an academic scholarship to the School of Business and Industry at Florida A & M University in Tallahassee, Florida. His first novel The Trophy Wife Network was published in April 2006 followed by Rooftop Diva-A Novel of Triumph After Katrina in September 2006. D. T. Pollard, Post Office Box 541651, Grand Prairie, Texas 75054 E-mail: dtpollard@dtpollard.com Website: www.dtpollard.com

Cheryl Lynn Pope Parenting author of '25 Ways To Make Your Child(ren) Feel Special.' She is currently working on a children's book series that is targeted towards black girls ages 5-9. Cheryl Pope, 6340 Devereaux, Detroit, Michigan 48210 Phone: (313) 598-2710 E-mail: mylilbratz@hotmail.com

M. Quinn Writer, Lecturer and Author of the book Removing the Veil. M. Quinn, Post Office Box 411, Mountain. View, California 94042 E-mail: twentyfirstcentury_writer@yahoo.com

Katina Rankin A native of Magee, Mississippi Katina is WLBT's weekday morning anchor. She received her bachelor's degree in mass communications from Alcorn State University and her master's degree in broadcast journalism from Jackson State University. She has authored two books -- "The Courage to Walk Away" and "Up North, Down South: City Folk Meet Country Folk," a children's book. Katina Rankin, WLBT-TV3, Post Box 1712, Jackson, Mississippi 39215 Phone: (601) 948-3333 E-mail: krankin@wlbt.net Website: www.wlbt.net

Winona Rasheed Freelance writer, author, editor, and entrepreneur with her own online writing and editing business Dream Writers' Essentials. Winona writes children stories and has four published books. Her titles are: (1) Sugar and Spice Fairy Tales for Girls, (2) Smiles and Frowns Through Animal Town's Storybook, (3) Stories From Grandma's Garden, (4) Wohali and the Little People, (5) A New Home for Her Cubs and Broken Voices (her first book for teens). Winona Rasheed, 2426 Otis Street, North East, Washington DC 20018 Phone: (202) 635-3588 E-mail: rasheedwinona@yahoo.com Website: www.winonarasheed.com

Francis Ray A graduate of Texas Woman's University, and author of 33 bestsellers, her titles consistently make bestseller's lists such as Blackboard and Essence Magazine. Incognito, her sixth title, was the first made-for-TV movie for Black Entertainment Television (BET). She has written fourteen single titles and eight anthologies. The Turning Point, her first mainstream, was a finalist for the prestigious HOLT Medallion Award. At the release event for Turning Point in May 2001, she established The Turning Point Legal defense Fund to assist women of domestic violence to help restructure their lives. Her second mainstream, I Know Who Holds Tomorrow in May 2002, made the bestseller's list of The Dallas Morning News, Blackboard, Black Expressions Book Club, and Essence Magazine. Other releases include Chocolate Kisses, January, 2006/NAL and Dreaming of You, September 2006. Ms. Francis Ray, Post Office Box 764651, Dallas, Texas 75276 E-mail: **francisray@aol.com**

Gene T. Reed Author of Here's to My Lady a must-have for men looking to improve their relationships and know what to do and say in almost every situation. Mr. Reed was born and raised in Baltimore, Maryland, where he enjoyed a long and successful career in sales and as a sales trainer. Today, Reed lives in the Los Angeles area and pursues his longtime love of music. Gene T. Reed, 1833 Raleo Avenue, Rowland Heights, California 91748 Phone: (626) 965-8327 Fax: (626) 965-8327 E-mail: **genereed7@msn.com** Website: **www.HerestoMyLady.com**

Gregory J. Reed Author, agent, producer, attorney and specialist in tax and entertainment law, Gregory J. Reed is the author of fourteen books: Tax Planning and Contract Negotiating Techniques for Creative Persons, Professional Athletes and Entertainers (1979), This Business of Boxing and and Its Secrets (1981), This Business of Entertainment and Its Secrets (1985); Negotiations Behind Closed Doors (1992); Economic Empowerment Through The Church (Zondervan, 1994, American Book Award Winner) and This Business of Celebrity Estates. Reed is co-author of the book Quiet Strength, with Mrs. Rosa Parks (Zondervan, 1995), and Dear Mrs. Parks (Lee & Low, 1996). He recently completed Obama Talks and another book, Dear Dr. Mandela. Education: B.S., Michigan State University (Engineering); M.S., Michigan State University (Management Science); J.D., Wayne State University (Master of Taxation Law). He is a recipient of the John Hensel Award for significant contributions to the arts. Gregory J. Reed & Associates, PC, 1201 Bagley, Detroit, Michigan 48226 Phone: (313) 961-3580 Fax: (313) 961-3582 E-mail: **gjrassoc@aol.com** Website: **www.gjreedlaw.com**

Mel Reed An African-Native-Caucasian American motivational speaker and author, whose life is a testimonial to God's love. In 1956 he left Pine Plains High without a diploma to join the Army. Highlights of his service include serving in Thule, Greenland and the Assistant Chief of Staff for Intelligence in the Pentagon. Mel left the service and went to work for IBM until his retirement. IBM positions included serving as an analyst, manager and quality engineer. Consulting activities include Legends Cars the Star Bank of Cincinatti, H/R consultant to Sverdrup-Fleming's $578M Charlotte school bid and small business plans. Mel also wrote and directed a vocational training program while on an IBM leave in the basement of St Francis AME Zion Church in Port Chester, NY. Mel was named 1993 volunteer of the year for motivational seminars by Charlotte parole/probation. Few people knew he did not have a H/S diploma or that his ABM degree came from a college that advertised on a book of matches. The book he wrote is from a miracle that changed his life. Melvin W. Reed, 610-C Sofia Lane, Charlotte, North Carolina 28262 E-mail: **cmelreed@aol.com**

Taryn Reed Author, his first novel was The Other Side of Da Court, and the latest release is The Calm Before The Storm, both published by Publish America. Contact Taryn Reed, 410 Farmington Avenue, Unit L5, New Britain, Connecticut 06053 Phone: (914) 420-8838 E-mail: tarynr@sbcglobal.net

Tom Reed Author, writer, Black music documentaries, Wattstax Revisited and Ray Charles: Words and Music, etc. Producer/host of 'For Members Only' TV, L.A.'s longest running locally produced Black cultural entertainment & information television program. Awards, commendations and plaques grace his walls, given to him because of his competitive spirit and his concern for his fellow man. He holds a B.S. & M.S. Honorary Doctorate in Education (Communications) from City Unit, Los Angeles, 1982. Tom Reed, Post Office Box 27487, Los Angeles, California 90027 Phone: (818) 894-8880

James Reedom Author of The Pro se Attorney Manual: Layman Strategies In The Law. He is a former Pre-Law Professor, Public Administration and Economic and Community Development strategist. He has worked at such universities as Grambling State University and The State University of New York. He ia a former Instructor at TCU Off Campus Continuing Education Program in Political Science Public Administration, Whitehouse Empowerment Conference Participant 1999-2000 and several distinguished community colleges. Mr. James Reedom, Post Office Box 8221, Fort Worth, Texas 76112   E-mail: preed230@netscape.net Website: www.authorhouse.com

Dane Reid Known nationally and internationally on radio and television for his voice over work, Dane Reid is author of Dana The Procrastinator, a childrens book and video. Contact Mr. Dane Reid, Dane Reid Media, Post Office Box 640055, Atlanta, Georgia 30364 Phone: (404) 822-7107 E-mail: DR@DaneReidMedia.com Website: www.danereidmedia.com

Christina E. Reyes Author of Conant Gardens. Contact Ms. Christina E. Reyes, 17228 MacKay Street, Detroit, Michigan 48212 Phone: (313) 463-8797 E-mail: conantgardens@gmail.com Website: www.conantgardens.com

Barbara A. Reynolds Award winning journalist and author of 3 books, No I Won't Shut Up: 30 Years of Telling It Like It Is, Out of Hell and Living Well, and Jesse Jackson: America's David. Born in Columbus, Ohio, Dr. Reynolds received her BA in journalism from The Ohio State University, her Masters Degree from Howard University School of Divinity in 1991, and her doctorate in Ministry from the United Theological Seminary in Dayton, Ohio in 1998. She was awarded an honorary doctorates from Shenandoah University and her alma mater, The Ohio State University. As a professor, she has held the Jessie Ball Dupont Chair in Journalism at Shenandoah University in Winchester, Virginia and was a Freedom Forum Scholar for the 1998 school year in journalism at Florida A&M University. Dr. Barbara A. Reynolds, JFJ Publishing, 4806 Saint Barnabas Road, Suite 598, Temple Hills, Maryland 20757 Phone: (301) 899-1341 E-mail: reynew@aol.com Website: www.reynoldsworldnews.com

Patricia Richardson Author of A Place For Ida and A Time For Jonathan. Patricia Richardson, Leap Of Faith Publishing, Post Office Box 957705, Duluth, Georgia 30095 Phone: (770) 689-6924 E-mail: richprch@aol.com Website: www.leapoffaithpublishing.bravehost.com

Naomi Roberson Author of After Daddy Died, a shocking true story of how a family was affected by their father's psychotic behavior. She is also a producer, director, and camera operator and has produced and directed documentaries, award shows, public service announcements, and interviews for local television and the outlying areas. She has an associate degree in accounting, a bachelor's degree in behavioral science, a master's degree in management and human resources, a doctorate in organizational psychology, and a doctorate in divinity. Dr. Naomi Roberson, GEM, Inc., Post Office Box 557533, Chicago, Illinois 60655 Phone: (312) 458-9812 E-mail: **ncroberson@comcast.net**

Janeen Robichaud Author of two published erotic novels Candy and Candy2, The Sequel; one teen novel about bullying at school and the effects it has on one particular student, Laura Wellington entitled They Killed Me. Janeen has also written numerous poems and short stories; featured in anthologies, Messages from the Universe and Wounds of War (soon to be released). Contact Ms. Janeen Robichaud, 7000 Donald Street, Millville, New Jersey 08332 E-mail: **candyjaneen@aol.com**

Brenetia Adams-Robinson Entrepreneur, trainer, motivational speaker and author, Brenetia is the Founder/President of Epitome' Consulting Services, and of Proverbial Peace Revived Ministries. She is a contributing writer of the acclaimed 100 Words of Wisdom for Women: A 31-Day Exercise in Empowerment, as well as contributor for Entertaining Secrets, an e-book for Christian event planners. Brenetia Adams-Robinson, Epitome' Consulting Services, Post Office Box 743, Jonesboro, Georgia 30237 E-mail: **epitomeconsult@yahoo.com**

C. Kelly Robinson A graduate of Howard University and Washington University in St. Louis, CK self-published his first novel, Not All Dogs while still working in corporate America. In October 2001 Not All Dogs was re-released by Random House/Villard, under the new title Between Brothers. It has been a bestseller on CushCity.com and been favorably reviewed in publications including Essence, Publishers Weekly, and the Chicago Sun-Times. His 2002 release of the romantic comedy No More Mr. Nice Guy also went on to top the April 2003 Essence Best-Seller list. C. Kelly Robinson, Against the Grain Communications, Post Office Box 58, Clayton, Ohio 45315 E-mail: **ckrob7071@aol.com** Website: **www.ckellyrobinson.com**

Cheryl Robinson Author, and host of Just About Books Talk Show, an internet radio talk show with a worldwide audience featuring authors, book reviews, book clubs, and literary events for African American book lovers. Cheryl Robinson, Just About Books Talk Show, 1282 Smallwood Drive, West, Suite 116, Waldorf, Maryland 20603 Phone: (301) 643-2077 E-mail: **JustAboutBooks@yahoo.com** Website: **www.JustAboutBookTalkShow.com**

Christine Young-Robinson Isra the Butterfly Gets Caught for Show and Tell, her first children's book, was inspired by her granddaughter and put into print to share with other children. She has now released her second children's book, Chicken Wing. She is the recipient of the Carrie Allen McCray Award, "Honorable Mention" for Juvenile Fiction given by the South Carolina Writer's Workshop. Presently working on a chapter book and an adult fiction novel. Christine Young-Robinson, Yoroson Publishing, 10120 Two Notch Road, #143, Columbia, South Carolina 29223 Phone: (803) 419-5890 Fax: (803) 865-9001 E-mail: **miraclewriter4u@aol.com** Website: **www.christineyoungrobinson.com**

Michelle Janine Robinson Studied Journalism at New York University. Erotic short story Mi Destino is included in the anxiously awaited Zane anthology, Caramel Flava. Currently working on two novels, You Created a Monster and Pleasure Principle. Ms. Michelle Janine Robinson, 148 East 150th Street, Bronx, New York 10451 E-mail: **Robinson_201@hotmail.com**

Sabra A. Robinson A writer of both children's literature and non-fiction with plans to write in all age groups. She is the author of the multicultural picture book, Micky, Ticky, Boo! Says Hello and founder of the African-American Children's Writers and Illustrators online group AACBWI.com. a collective information-sharing forum for children's authors and illustrators, young and old. She received her bachelor's degree in Sociology from Morgan State University. She was recognized as a finalist out of over 300 applicants for the ABC/Disney New Talent Development program for 2003. Sabra A. Robinson, Post Office Box 620324, Charlotte, North Carolina 28262 E-mail: **sabra@sabrarobinson.com** Website: **www.sabrarobinson.com**

Malaak Compton-Rock Broadway Books, a division of Random House, released her first book, "If It Takes A Village, Build One: How I Found Meaning Through a Life of Service and 100+ Ways You Can Too" on April 6, 2010. She holds a B.F.A. in Arts/Production Management from Howard University and received an honorary doctorate degree from Fairleigh Dickenson University in May 2009. Compton-Rock sits on the board of directors of The Children's Defense Fund and The Triple Negative Breast Cancer Foundation. She is a Global Ambassador for The Susan G. Komen for the Cure Global Promise Fund, a member of New York Women in Communications, The Cause Marketing Forum and The Association of Fundraising Professionals. Recently, she was honored to be a member of the Blue Ribbon Panel who selected the 2009 CNN Hero of the Year and to be chosen as one of Ebony Magazine's 2009 Power 150, Change Agents We Can Believe In. Ms. Malaak Compton-Rock, Box #996, Tenafly, New Jersey 07670 Phone: 201-750-8370 Fax: 201-750-8371 E-mail: **Malaak@angelrockproject.com** Website: **www.angelrockproject.com**

Gayle Rogers A teacher, trainer, and founder and co-paster of L.I.F.E. Outreach Ministries International, Inc., Dr. Rogers has authored several books including Healing the Traumatized Soul. She received her Ph.D. in Women's Studies from Trinity Theological Seminary and certification by the American Society of Development and Training (ASTD) through the University of Oklahoma. Contact Dr. Gayle Rogers, Forever Free, Inc., Post Office Box 390475, Snellville, Georgia 30039 Phone: (678) 344-8638 E-mail: **drgayleforhelp@comcast.net** Website: **www.bforeverfree.org**

Akosua Ali-Sabree Executive director of the Amadi Wellness Connection (AWC) and founder of the Amadi Universal Light Mission (AULM); the program director of the Annual International Locks Conference: Natural Hair, Wholistic Health & Beauty Expo. Dr. Ali-Sabree is an ordained minister with a master's degree in human services/counseling, and a doctorate in divinity. Her published works include We Surrender: A Collection of Inspirational Poems & Lyrical Verse; Hair Piecez: The Anthology; Wholistic Guide to Health and Wellness: How to Achieve Peace, Joy, and a Simple Life; and her latest book Emancipating Your Spirit: A Conscious Guidebook: Affirmations, Meditation, Liberty & Other Soulful Reflections. Dr. Akosua Ali-Sabree, 800 Callowhill Street, Suite 8, Philadelphia, Pennsylvania 19130 Phone: (215) 438-8189 E-mail: **info@BeWellRelax.com** Website: **www.BeWellRelax.com**

Carla Sams Author. Contact Ms. Carla Sams, Now U No Publishing Company, Post Office Box 9501, Cincinnati Ohio 45209 Phone: (513) 226-6450 E-mail: holly.ferguson@nowuno-enterprises.com Website: www.nowunopublishingco.com

Deon C. Sanders (Deno Sandz) embraces and turns southern myths and religion into his second published supernatural/horror novel. Contact Publicist, Dawn Sanders, 2259 West Adams, Chicago, Illinois 60612 Phone: (708) 539-7827 E-mail: dsanders4119@yahoo.com

Marsha D. Jenkins-Sanders A writer of novels and songs Marsha received acclaim in the music industry for lyrics written for Keith Washington's freshmen album project, Make Time for Love. Both "Kissing You" and "Closer" introduced her writing talent and she received award-winning recognition from ASCAP for Writer and Publisher in the R & B genre. "Kissing You" was certified gold and went on to be featured as the background music for love scenes on ABC's soap, General Hospital. "The Other Side of Through", her debut novel was released in February 2007, on the Strebor/Simon & Schuster label. "Jealousy: A Strange Company Keeper" followed in 2008. Marsha D. Jenkins-Sanders, 18455 Miramar Parkway, #162, Miramar, Florida 33029 Phone: (734) 334-3645 E-mail: mrcsdno@yahoo.com

Vince Sanders The author of the book, can't get Here from There (1st Books) and That's Not Funny! (Booksurge), Mr. Sanders is a retired former chief operator of the broadcast division of National Black Network. During more than 35 years of professional radio and television, his assignments included Vice President and General Manager of radio station WWRL in New York City, from 1983 - 1995; and Anchor/Reporter for NBC news from 1971 - 1973. He did on-air stints in the Chicago area at WMAQ-AM radio and TV, WBEE-AM radio, WMPP-AM radio and WCIU-TV. In 1968, he was also special correspondent for KPOI radio in Honolulu, Hawaii. As an actor, Vince traveled with the American Negro Opera Guild and served as Theatrical Consultant to the Chicago Emancipation Centennial Authority in the early 1960's. Vince Sanders, Post Office Box 917358, Longwood, Florida 32791 Phone: (321) 277-7214 Fax: (407) 786-0709 E-mail: vincnet@cfl.rr.com Website: www.vincesanders.com

Viola Sanders Owner and founder of Vii's Services, Inc., an African American Educational company providing seven traveling exhibits. Published in 1995, AFRICAN AMERICAN INVENTORS book and in 2003 published, An African American Tea Ceremony book. Contact Ms. Viola Sanders, Post Office Box 181, Blythewood, South Carolina 29016 Phone: (803) 754-5620 E-mail: vii@viiservices.com

Deno Sandz Husband and father of six, was born in Alabama and raised in Chicago. He is the prolific author of three supernatural/horror novels titled "Miss Mary Weather: A Southern Nightmare, I AM, and his new novel "Pen of Iniquity. Deno Sandz, 2259 West Adams, Chicago, Illinois 60612 Phone: (312) 213-2148 E-mail: dsanders4119@yahoo.com

Luticia Santipriya Psychopathologist, psychologist theoretician, book editor-publisher. Specialist in psycho-archeology and the slave trade. Author of The Ipuwer Chronicles (2005), A Bluejay's Eye: Notes on Our Time from a Psychologist's Daybook (in press 2007) and Rebel Sunrise with a Twist of Sour: A Memoir (in press 2008). Luticia Santipriya, Post Office Box 136, Brooklyn, New York 11231 Phone: (212) 715-6873 E-mail: santipriya@hotmail.com

Yolanda Brunson-Sarrabo A native of Brooklyn, New York, Yolanda Brunson-Sarrabo has worked at various levels of the fashion industry. Along with writing The Ins and Outs of the Fashion Industry she also co-writes a popular monthly newsletter, The Laundry Source. Yolanda's entrepreneurial spirit has led her to form Spitfir Productions, a literary home for authors who want to display their talents in writing. She is currently working on a second novel based on the epidemic of AIDS in the Black community, and lives in Brooklyn with her husband. Yolanda Brunson-Sarrabo, Spitfir Productions, 1454 Rockaway Parkway, Brooklyn, New York 11236 E-mail: **blackwriternew@yahoo.com** Website: **www.ybrunson.com**

Rodney Saulsberry One of the top voice-over talents in the country, Rodney Saulsberry is also author of the book You Can Bank on Your Voice: Your Guide to a Successful Career in Voice-Overs. (August 2004, Tondor). As one of the top trailer voices in the business, movie fans have heard Rodney's voice on radio and television, the internet and videos promoting some of their favorites: Tupac Resurrection, How Stella Got Her Groove Back, Drumline, Undercover Brother, Dumb & Dumberer, Finding Forrester, and many more. A Detroit native and actor on the CBS soap "The Bold and the Beautiful," Rodney has been nominated for an NAACP Image Award for his work. Saulsberry plays Anthony, a homeless man who turns his life around when he gets a job at a local coffee shop. Rodney Saulsberry, Tomdor Publishing, LLC, Post Office Box 1735, Agoura Hills, California 91376 Phone: (818) 207-2682 E-mail: **rodtalks@aol.com** Website: **www.rodneysaulsberry.com**

Deirdre Savoy Native New Yorker Deirdre Savoy's first novel was, SPELLBOUND, published by BET in 1999. Since then Deirdre has published more than a dozen books and two novellas, all of which have garnered critical acclaim and honors. She has won two prestigious Emma awards. Deirdre Savoy, Post Office Box 233, Bronx, New York 10469 Phone: (646) 418-1257 Fax: (718) 994-7343 E-mail: **deesavoy@gmail.com** Website: **www.deesavoy.com**

Beatrice Lee Scott Graduated from Norfolk State University with a degree in Social Work. Author of The Cracked Door (2006, Tate Publishing). Contact Bea Lee, 1310 Holly Avenue, Chesapeake Virginia 23324 Phone: (757) 543-2443 E-mail: **beatricescott_334@msn.com**

Devon Scott Fiction Writer and author of the novels Obsessed and Unfaithful, published in June, 2009 and May 2008 respectively, by Kensington. Mr. Devon Scott, c/o Kensington Publishing Corp, Dafina Books, 850 Third Avenue, New York, New York 10022 E-mail: **info@devonscott.com** Website: **www.devonscott.com**

Sandra J. Scott Founder and executive director of Y.E.S., Inc., Ms. Scott is also the author of three published books: Lord, Let There Be Light, Becoming Whole Before Becoming One, and Baggage Handlers: My road to letting go of life's painful luggage. Sandra Scott, 630 Minnesota Avenue, Suite 206, Kansas City, Kansas 66101 E-mail: **becomingwhole@hotmail.com**

Janet West Sellars The embodiment of her passion is impressively revealed in her first novel, Quiet As It's Kept. She has lived and traveled extensively throughout the US and Europe. She holds a Bachelor's degree in Sociology and a Master's degree in Human Relations. Janet West Sellars, 908 Bellgate Court, Newport News, Virginia 23602 Phone: (757) 897-1015 E-mail: **jsellars@cox.net** Website: **www.janetwestsellars.com**

Earl Sewell Has authored such titles as The Good Got To Suffer With the Bad, Taken For Granted and You're Making Me Wet. When not writing Earl Sewell spends his time training to complete an Ironman Triathlon. Earl resides in Palatine, Illinois, and is currently working on his next title A Hot Mess. Through Thick and Thin is Earl's second BET novel. Earl Sewell, Kicheko Driggins, One BET Plaza West, Washington, DC 20018 E-mail: earl@earlsewell.com Website: www.earlsewell.com

Ntozake Shange Award winning author, poet, playwright and novelist. Contact Author Appearance Coordinator, Simon & Schuster, 1230 Avenue of the Americas, New York, New York 10020 Phone: (212) 698-2808 Fax: (212) 698-4350 Website: www.SimonSaysKids.com

Anesha A. Sharp Director of Charles Martin Ministries, Author, Multi-gifted Motivational Speaker and Youth Minister. Anesha is the author of "Unlocking the Doors to Destiny" an inspirational book of deliverance, healing, and restoration of identity and purpose. Mrs. Anesha Sharp, 4501 North Meridian, Oklahoma City, Oklahoma 73112 Phone: (405) 822-6090 E-mail: asharpauthor06@sbcglobal.net

Jesse Sharpe Writer and self publisher of adult fiction and non-fiction books as well as educational books for children and adults. The authors books include poetry, short story, short novel, workbooks, and educational reference. Contact Jesse Sharpe, 6629 Adrian Street, New Carrollton, Maryland 20784 Phone: (240) 375-6033 E-mail: sharpesolutions@comcast.net Website: www.sharpebooksonline.com

Kali Shirah Author, my work includes non-fiction, career and fiction books, Start Your Own Transcription Business (1-3rd Editions), Real Estate Agent's Yearly Planner/Organizer, and A Dieting Diva's Diary. Fiction, inspirational romance & general romance includes, Romancin' the Reverend, and In Cahoots with the Choir. Kali Shirah, Post Office Box 1088, Tioga, Louisiana 71477 Website: www.kaliannah.com

Yasmin Shiraz Author of six books including the award winner Retaliation, The Novel and the critically acclaimed empowerment series for girls, The Blueprint for My Girls.Yasmin Shiraz, President, Rolling Hills Press, Post Office Box 220053, Chantilly, Virginia 20153 E-mail: yshiraz@yasminshiraz.net Website: www.yasminshiraz.net

Margie Gosa Shivers Voted 2003 Best Self-Published Author, Mahogany Book Club. She also received the Disilgold Mystery Novelist Award of Excellence 2004 and the YOUnity Reviewers Guild Most Sought Book of the Year 2004. Margie Gosa Shivers, 16781 Torrence Avenue #294, Lansing, Illinois 60438 Phone: (708) 889-9886 E-mail: margegosa@aol.com

Della Faye Showunmi Pen name, Della Faye, she is author of the inspirational book, Always Try Just One More Time. Della Faye Showunmi, Post Office Box 743842, Dallas, Texas 75374 E-mail: della@dellafaye.com Website: www.dellafaye.com

Lura Sutton-Sims An author/publisher of "Step by Step Travel Guide for Corporate and Leisure Travel." Lura Sutton-Sims, 5910 Purple Sage, Houston, Texas 77049 Phone: (281) 458-2972 E-mail: luras@msn.com

Irene Smalls Author, storyteller, historian, Smalls is an award winning author of 15 books for children and 3 storytelling CDs. She is the creator of Literacy+Exercise=Literacise. Literacise is book-based book-related exercise and movement based on scientific research that shows that physical exercises increases academic achievement. Literacise storytelling sessions engage students with literature in a physically active way with targeted exercises and movements. Graduate of Cornell University and has an MBA from New York University. Irene Smalls, Post Office Box 990631, Prudential Center, Boston, Massachusetts 02199 Phone: (617) 504-3050 E-mail: **ISmalls107@aol.com** Website: **www.literacise.com**

Andrea Smith Her debut novel received outstanding reviews and is quickly gained bestseller status. Her book Friday Nights At Honeybee's was chosen by Barnes and Noble as a "Discover Great New Writers" selection for Winter 2003, Borders, February 2003 "Original Voices" title and spotlighted on the cover of Black Expressions Book Club's Spring 2003 catalog as special feature. Her second novel (Random House/The Dial Press) is tentatively titled "Canaan Creek. Andrea Smith, c/o Julia Shaw, Shaw Literary Group, 295 Madison Avenue, 21st Floor, New York, New York 10017 E-mail: **shawlit@aol.com** Website: **www.andreamsmith.com**

Horane Smith Award-winning author of six published novels. He's the recipient of the BURLA Award for outstanding contribution to African North American and Caribbean literature. Having worked in radio, television and the print media for nearly twenty years, he took on creative writing seriously in 1999, when his first novel Lover's Leap, based on the Jamaican Legend, was published to international acclaim. He has since written Port Royal, Underground to Freedom, The Lynching Stream, Reggae Silver, and Dawn at Lover's Leap, the sequel to Lover's Leap. Horane Smith, 36 Pinedale Gate, Vaughan, Ontario Canada L4L 8W9, E-mail: **Horane_Smith@hotmail.com** Website: **www.horanesmith.com**

Katherine Smith The Naked Author - Exposing the Myths of Publishing. Formerly co-host of the morning radio show on ABC Radio Networks, Inc., "Classic Soul Hits" format, Ms. Smith is an internationally published writer and the author of The Book Seller's List and Love the Vicious Cycle. She is presently a member of The Writer's Block, Inc., writers group. Katherine "Kat" Smith, Post Office Box 701478, Dallas, Texas 75370 E-mail: **kat@kat-smith.biz** Website: **www.tomkatproductions.com**

Linda Hudson-Smith Currently has 24 titles to her credit, Ice Under Fire her debut Arabesque novel, which has received rave reviews and won the 2000 Gold Pen Award, Soulful Serenade (2000), was selected by Romance In Color as the Best Cover for August 2000. Desperate Deceptions (2001), Fire Beneath the Ice, a sequel to Ice Under Fire (2001), Ladies In Waiting (2002), Thicker Than Water/The Devil's Advocate (2006) was #7 on the Essence Best Seller's list, capturing her the title of national best selling author. Her 25th published title Romancing the Runway was released March 2009 and Destiny Calls (2009). Linda Hudson-Smith,16516 El Camino Real, Box 174, Houston, Texas 77062 Phone: (281) 804- 9092 E-mail: **lindahudsonsmith@yahoo.com** Website: **www.lindahudsonsmith.com**

Peaches Smith Storyteller and author of 13 childrens books. Ms. Smith is also founder of Bullets to Books turning trigger-pullers into page-turners. Contact Ms. Peaches Smith, 108 Ridgewood Street, Hot Springs, Arkansas 71901 E-mail: **peachessmith@sbcglobal.net**

Swanzetta Smith Author of the romance novel, Private Passions. A fiction writer since 1996, Ms. Swanzetta Smith is a member of The Black Writers Alliance, and Romance Writer's of America. She is currently working on her second novel. Contact Swanzetta Smith, 231 East Alessandro Boulevard, #A-107, Riverside California 92507 E-mail: mszetta@earthlink.net Website: www.swanzettasmith.com

M. Lavonte Stanley Syracuse, New York author of the book, The Makings of a Superwoman" by Red Bull. I currently reside in the Tampa, Florida area. M. Lavonte Stanley, Authorhouse Publishing, 1663 Liberty Drive, Suite 200, Bloomington, Indiana 47403 Phone: (888) 519-5121 E-mail: truthshespeaks@yahoo.com Website: www.themakingsofasuperwoman.com

Crystal Perkins-Stell An educator and author, Crystal is a three-time Who's Who inductee. She completed her undergraduate degree at Langston University with scholastic honors and obtained her Master's degree from the University of Oklahoma in Human Relations, where she graduated Summa Cum Laude. She has three novels, Soiled Pillowcases, Hood Rich, and Never Knew a Father's Love. She is a member of Delta Sigma Theta Sorority Inc., and an affiliate of several professional literary and educational organizations. Crystal Perkins Stells, Crystell Publications, Post Office Box 8044, Edmond, Oklahoma 73083 Phone: (405) 414-3991 E-mail: cleva@crystalstell.com Website: www.crystalstell.com

Timothy N. Stelly, Sr. Author of three novels: "Tempest In The Stone," "The Malice of Cain," and "Like A Straight-Up Sucka." He is also a frequent contributor to e-zines useless-knowledge.com and e-zinearticles.com. Timothy N. Stelly, Sr., Post Office Box 1264, Pittsburg, California 94565 Phone: (925) 473-0741 E-mail: stellbread@yahoo.com

Torrance Stephens His work has appeared in print and publications such as NOMMÓ, Creative Loafing, Rolling Out, Talking Drum, the North Avenue Review and other periodicals. He graduated from Hamilton High School in Memphis and attended Morehouse College where he studied, psychology, biology and chemistry. Master's degree, Educational Psychology and Measurement from Atlanta University, and a Ph.D. in Counseling from Clark Atlanta University. Torrance Stephens, Post Office Box 1331, Palmetto, Georgia 30268 Phone: (404) 354-1449 E-mail: torrance_stephens@yahoo.com

Johnnie P. Stevenson BA, MS, Retired Teacher of English and author with special interest in interpreting poetry including Fathers of my Fathers, Dream Crasher, Children of a Far Country, and The Lynching of Laura, novel. Johnnie P. Stevenson, 12720 Nelson Avenue, Spencer, Oklahoma 73084 Phone: (405) 769-3748 E-mail: johnniepstevenson@sbcglobal.com

Lisa St. Hill Author and entertainment fashion and beauty writer for Jolie Magazine and author of a fiction book, Revenge of the Celebrity Assistant. Lisa St. Hill, 28 Hazelplace, Irvington, New Jersey 07111 Phone: (718) 812-1327 E-mail: Lisa_sthill@yahoo.com

Michelle Stimpson Author, Public Teacher. Publications: Boaz Brown (Christian fiction), and 2 upcoming novels with Warner/Walk Worthy Press. Michelle also serves on the writing/editing team for Heartbeat quarterly magazine. Michelle Stimpson, Post Office Box 2195, Cedar Hill, Texas 75106 E-mail: michelle@michellestimpson.com Website: www.michellestimpson.com

Rosalind Stormer Author, Christian Fiction. Ms. Stormer's debut novel entitled Healing The Breach is BlackRefer.com's best pick for Christian Fiction in 2004. Her second book is In The Wrong Hands (2005). Contact Ms. Rosalind Stormer, Heavenly Bound Publishing Company, Post Office Box 12106, Cincinnati, Ohio 45212 Website: www.heavenlybound.org E-mail: rosalind@heavenlybound.org

Cheryl Samuel Stover Author of From the Inside Out: How to Transform Your School to Increase Student Achievement, Elementary Basic Skills Through Black History; and Walk Out of the Shadows: Poetry to Inspire and Encourage Youth in the 21st Century. Dr. Cheryl Samuel Stover, 3516 John G. Richards Road, Post Office Box 153, Liberty Hill, South Carolina 29074 Phone: (803) 273-3772 E-mail: chrylstover@yahoo.com Website: www.wastelandpress.net

Vickie Stringer CEO of Triple Crown Publications, the world leader of urban literature publishing, and the author of the best selling books "Let That Be The Reason" and the sequel "Imagine This," and a third book, Dirty Red. "Let That Be the Reason," is a novel based on the author's real-life experiences. Contact Ms. Vickie Stringer, Triple Crown Publications, P.O. Box 247378, Columbus, Ohio 43224 Phone: (614) 934-1233 Fax: (614) 934-1593 E-mail: admin@triplecrownpublications.com Website: www.triplecrownpublications.com

Debby Stroman Professor in the Sport Administration specialization, has three primary responsibilities for EXSS: instruction, internship coordination, and departmental academic advising. Her courses include administration, finance and economics, marketing, and leadership. As the coordinator of the undergraduate field experience (internship) program, she seeks to provide sport administration students with a valuable practicum that matches their career interest. Dr. Stroman also enjoys working with UNC's Office of Diversity and Multicultural Affairs and the NCAA's Office of Diversity and Inclusion on special projects. She received her degrees from the University of Virginia (B.S.), University of North Carolina (M.A. in Sport Administration), and Capella University (Ph.D. in Organization and Management). Her dissertation topic is "The Critical Success Factors of the Atlantic Coast Conference." Dr. Stroman's research interests are leadership, marketing, entrepreneurship, and social issues of sport. She is the faculty advisor for the Carolina Sports Business Club and Sigma Alpha Lamba, a leadership honors society. She is the 2006 recipient of the state of Maryland's Top MBE Award, which recognizes leadership, and business and entrepreneurial success. She also has experience as a grant writer, philanthropic development officer, and fundraiser for non-profit organizations. Dr. Stroman is the owner of L.A.S.E.R. (Life After Sports With Effective Results), which provides life coaching and transition planning to former athletes, and Soulful Golf, Inc. Contact Dr. Deborah Stroman, Ph.D., CLU, Lecturer/Academic Advisor, Department of Exercise and Sport Science, 04 Smith Building, CB# 3182, University of North Carolina, Chapel Hill, North Carolina 27599 E-mail: dstroman@email.unc.edu

Carol A. Taylor Former Random House book editor and the editor of the bestselling 4 book series, Brown Sugar. She has been in the book publishing business for over 10 years and is a published author, a freelance writer, book editor and an editorial consultant who has worked with book publishers, agents, best selling authors and up and coming writers. For book editing send an e-mail. Carol A. Taylor, Black Star Consulting, 295 Clinton Avenue #E3, Brooklyn, New York 11205 E-mail: carol@brownsugarbooks.com   Website: www.BrownSugarBooks.com

Marlene Taylor Author, Life Is What You Make It, Darlin', and A Silver Tongue, Ms. Taylor is working to offset the potentially devastating drop in literacy levels among black American families. She visits prisons and shelters to speak up about the importance of literacy and how it can affect the overall quality of a person's life. Her book was the first book chosen for the Philadelphia Prison System's inmate reading group and was nominated for an NAACP Image Award for best fiction writing. Graduate of the University of Pennsylvania, Wharton School; publisher of Radio TV Interviews Media Magazine (RTIMM); founder of million dollar corporation. Marlene Taylor, 633 West Rittenhouse Street, Suite B823, Philadelphia, Pennsylvania 19144 Phone: (215) 438-5283 E-mail: **mttw@msn.com**

Michael Taylor Author, publisher, personal development coach and entrepreneur, Mr. Taylor is author of the book Brothers, Are You Listening: A Success Guide For The New Millennium. He is a motivational speaker, workshops, and seminars are designed to help men embrace the changing roles of manhood and to provide guidance and support for men who want to create balance and connection in their lives. Contact Mr. Michael Taylor, 1219 Nikki Lane, Stafford, Texas 77477 Phone: (713) 303-2067 E-mail: **mtaylor@creationpublishing.com** Website: **www.creationpublishing.com**

Ruby L. Taylor Author of Aunt Ruby, Do I Look Like God?, a thought provoking story for young readers. Taylor also became an entrepreneur and formed Connected 2 The Father Publishing, which distributes children's books, DVDs and merchandise that help children build spiritual relationships. She is also author of Love Don't Come Easy and If Only You Knew. Contact Ruby L. Taylor, M.S.W., 3203 Grace Avenue, Bronx, New York 10469 Phone: (718) 813-3363 E-mail: **RLT@connected2theFather.com** Website: **connected2theFather.com**

Susan L. Taylor Author of four books: In the Spirit: The Inspirational Writings of Susan L. Taylor; Lessons in Living; Confirmation: The Spiritual Wisdom That Has Shaped Our Lives, which she coauthored with her husband, Khephra Burns; and her most recent, All About Love, Favorite Selections from In the Spirit on Living Fearlessly. Susan L. Taylor is synonymous with Essence magazine, the brand she built—as its fashion and beauty editor, editor-in-chief and editorial director. For 27 years she authored of one of the magazine's most popular columns, In the Spirit. As the driving force behind one of the most celebrated Black-owned businesses for nearly three decades, Susan is a legend in the magazine publishing world. Susan L. Taylor, National Cares Mentoring Movement, 230 Peachtree Street, Suite 530, Atlanta, Georgia 30303 Phone: (404) 584-2744 Fax: (404) 525-6226 E-mail: **info@caresmentoring.com** Website: **www.caresmentoring.com**

D. L. Teamor Author, founder and pastor of Mt. Calvary House of Prayer in Southfield, Michigan, Teamor teaches Entrepreneurship and Information Technology in the Detroit Public Schools. Released three books, A Harlem Love Song, Womanchild, and Because Our Story Will Never End. Dr. Teamor holds a Bachelor of Science in Business Administration, an MBA, a Ph.D. in Business Marketing, (completed at age 25). Also completed her second Doctorate, a Th.D. in Systematic Theology. Her fourth book is The African Biblical Presence and the Effects of Exclusion on African Americans. Dr. D. L. Teamor, 17360 West Twelve Mile Road, Suite 107, Southfield, Michigan 48076 Phone: (248) 281-1780 Fax: (248) 564-5302 E-mail: **dlteamor@calvaryhouseusa.org** Website: **www.calvaryhouseusa.org**

Willie Tee Author of The Winds of Destiny a nonfiction memoir about his families tragedies and triumphs on a small farm in the rural south from the 1950s to present. Born at Pender County, North Carolina during the 1950's. Retired US Army Staff Sergeant with a Bachelors Degree in Criminal Justice. Member of American Legion and Prince George Rotary. Alumni of Virginia Commonwealth University. Mr. Willie Tee, Post Office Box 5171, Midlothian, Virginia 23112 Phone: (804) 739-8073 E-mail: **dwindsofdestiny@aol.com**

Angela M. Thomas Author and Certified Speaker Angela M. Thomas CPC is a retired Miami-Dade County Correctional Officer. An Inspirational Author and Speaker, and revelatory teacher who exercises her faith through biblical principles that include her spiritual gifts of writing. Angela has a Bachelor's Degree in Business Administration and also, is a graduate from the Professional Speakers Certified Network at Devry University. She is currently a contributing columnist for Trendsetter to Trendsetter Magazine in Atlanta, Georgia. She is also a memeber of Madison's Who's Who among Executives Professionals and have been featured in several newspapers, The Miami Times, The Miami Herald and The South Dade News Leader. She has done a variety of speaking engagements and conferences in the professional and religious spectrum. She speaks and volunteers at middle schools and shelters to inspire, motivate and uplift others. Angela M. Thomas CPC, Post Office Box 700098, Miami, Florida 33177 Phone: (305) 793-1347 E-mail: **topcop137@bellsouth.net** Website: **www.angelamthomas.com**

Brenda L Thomas Essence best selling author of THREESOME, FOURPLAY and the anthology FOUR DEGREES OF HEAT fame, Brenda's third novel is THE VELVET ROPE. She is a Philadelphia-based marketing professional who has made numerous appearances on national television in the wake of the Kobe Bryant case including CNN, Entertainment Tonight, ESPN and Dateline as an expert on the culture surrounding athletes. Also worked as the personal assistant to NBA All-Star Stephon X. Marbury. Brenda Thomas, Admin Ink, Post Office Box 39111, Philadelphia, Pennsylvania 19136 Phone: (215) 331-4554 Fax: (215) 333-8053 E-mail: **brenda@phillywriter.com** Website: **www.phillywriter.com**

Jacquelin Thomas Award winning author with twenty-nine titles in print. Her books have garnered several awards, including two EMMA awards, the Romance In Color Reviewers Award, Readers Choice Award and the Atlanta Choice Award in the Religious & Spiritual category. Other credits include contributions to the Women of Color Devotional Bible and Brides Noir magazine. Her BET Books/New Spirit release is titled Soul Journey. Contact Ms. Jacquelin Thomas, Post Office Box 99374, Raleigh, North Carolina 27624 Website: **www.jacquelinthomas.com**

Carla Thompson An award-winning freelance writer, is the author of "Bearing Witness: Not So Crazy in Alabama" (May 2005, August Press) which chronicles the Harlem native's nearly six years of adventures while living in Montgomery, Alabama. Carla Thompson, 872 Pacific Street, Brooklyn, New York 11238 Phone: (718) 857-9574 E-mail: **cwrite@earthlink.net**

Carlyle Van Thompson Author of Tragic Black Buck: Racial Masquerading in the American Literary Imagination. Mr. Thompson is also Associate Professor of English at Medgar Evers College. Carlyle Thompson, PhD., Medgar Evers College, CUNY, 1650 Bedford Avenue, Brooklyn, New York 11225 E-mail: **kj190@juno.com**

Maxine E. Thompson An award-winning writer, Dr. Thompson has self-published 2 novels, The Ebony Tree and No Pockets in a Shroud and 2 ebooks, her short story collection, A Place Called Home and Second Chances. She has also written The Hush Hush Secrets of Creating a Life You Love, and How To Promote, Market, and Sell Your Book Via eBook Publishing. In May 2002, she edited and published her anthology, Saturday Morning. In February 2003, she published an ebook, The Hush Hush Secrets of Writing Fiction That Sells. In June 2003, her short story, Valley Of The Shadow, was published in Kensington's Proverbs For The People (2005). She is a retired social worker with 23 years of experience, became an editor in 1998, and since that time, she has edited/ghostwritten over 1,000 books, many which have made the best seller's list, including the New York Times Best Seller list. Contact Maxine E. Thompson, Black Butterfly Press, Post Office Box 25279, Philadelphia Pennsylvania, 19119 E-mail: maxtho@aol.com Website: www.maxinethompson.com

Jessica Tilles Best-selling author, award-winning publisher of Xpress Yourself Publishing (recipient of the 2008 African American Literary Award Show Independent Publisher of the Year), founder of The Writer's Assistant and publisher of Erotic Expressions.net, an online eZine. As a native of Washington, DC, Jessica is a creative writer in all genres of fiction, with several titles in print: Anything Goes, In My Sisters' Corner, Apple Tree, Sweet Revenge, Fatal Desire, Unfinished Business, editor of the best-selling anthology, Erogenous Zone: A Sexual Voyage, and Loving Simone. In addition to her many accomplishments, Jessica is a staff writer for Black Men In America.com, has contributed the article Third Shift Blues to Black Romance Magazine, and is the recipient of the Memphis Black Writer's Guild's Rising Star award, and the Jackson Mississippi Reader's Clubs' Outstanding Contributor to Literature award. Jessica Tilles, Post Office Box 1615, Upper Marlboro, Maryland 20773 Phone: (301) 390-3645 Fax: (208) 975-0667 E-mail: JessicaTilles@aol.com Website: www.jessicatilles.com

G.C. Tobias Author. Crime novel entitled, Murder By Dawn. Contact G.C. Tobia, GLC International Book Company, Post Office Box 21225, White Hall, Arkansas 71612 E-mail: gctobiasnovels@yahoo.com Website: www.gctobias.9k.com

Tina Toles Author of four books and President and founder of the Dayton Christian Writer's Guild, Inc., in September 1993. Contact Ms. Tina Toles, Post Office Box 251, Englewood, Ohio 45322 Phone: (937) 836-6600 E-mail: tinatoles@yahoo.com

Pia Townes Author of the novel, Bloodless Affairs: A Tale of Necrophilia (2006). Her follow-up novel is Nighttime Affairs: A Tale of Stalking. She is a graduate of Johnson C. Smith University, 1988 BS in Biology; East Carolina School of Medicine, 1993 Medical Doctorate; Residency/ Psychiatric Medicine, Pitt County Memorial Hospital. Contact Ms. Pia Townes, MD, Post Office Box 668034, Charlotte, North Carolina 28266 Phone: (704) 763-7810 E-mail: pia@piatownes.net Website: www.piatownes.net

Martha Tucker Writer, and author of the suspense thriller The Mayor's Wife Wore Sapphires (Urban Classic Books). Martha is the wife of the late Mayor Walter R. Tucker who served as Compton, California's Mayor for 12 years. Specialties: publishing, book coaching and marketing. Martha Tucker, Urban Classic Books, 6245 Bristol Parkway, # 265, Culver City, California 90230 E-mail: writelink3@yahoo.com Website: www.urbanclassicbooks.com

Bevin Sinclair Turnbull Composer/Educator/Author, my novel is called THE OTHER SIDE OF TOMORROW (Xlibris.com). Executive Director of Bronx Renaissance Community Theater. I am engaged in encouraging youth as well as older folks, involving them in various aspects of musical theater. Masters Degree in Education from East Stroudsburg University in Pennsylvania. Completed my undergraduate degree at Howard University in Washington D.C., and have New York State teacher Certifications in Music and Biology. Currently, 7 albums of my work can be found at CDBaby.com. Bevin Sinclair Turnbull, 1170 East 225th Street, Bronx, New York 10466 Phone: (718) 405-1553 Fax: (718) 231-5681 E-mail: **bjazz7@aol.com**

Brenda C. Turner Adjunct Professor, University of Phoenix-VA Campus, Senior Education Program Specialist, U.S. Department of Education, Researcher, Evangelist and Inspirational Speaker, Published Books: Tithing: Need or Greed Part I and II (2004, 2006, respectively). Dr. Brenda C. Turner, M.Ed., D.D., Post Office Box 44967, Fort Washington, Maryland 20749 Phone: (301) 292-5555 Fax: (301) 229-6876 E-mail: **jbtre2006@verizon.net**

Denise Turney Author of Portia, Love Has Many Faces and the book Spiral. Editor of The Book Lover's Haven. Denise Turney, c/o Chistell Publishing, 2500 Knights Road, Suite 19-01 Bensalem, Pennsylvania 19020 E-mail: **soulfar@aol.com** Website: **www.chistell.com**

Omar Tyree New York Times best-selling author, a 2001 NAACP Image Award recipient for Outstanding Literature in Fiction, and a 2006 Phillis Wheatley Literary Award winner for Body of Work in Urban Fiction, has been cited in 2009 by the City Council of Philadelphia for his work in Urban Literacy, and has published 19 books with 2 million copies sold worldwide that has generated more than $30 million. With a degree in Print Journalism from Howard University in 1991, Tyree has been recognized as one of the most renown contemporary writers in the African-American community. He is also an informed and passionate speaker on various community-related and intellectual topics. Now entering the world of business seminars, urban children's books, feature films and songwriting, Tyree is a tireless creator and visionary of few limitations. Omar Tyree, Post Office Box 562296, Charlotte, North Carolina 28256 E-mail: **Omar8Tyree@aol.com** Website: **www.omartyree.com**

Robert Upton Author of Racism@Work: Among the LORD's People, Mr. Upton is a gifted public speaker, community leader and evangelist. Mr. Robert Upton, Upton Consulting, 1407 Laurel Avenue, South East, Grand Rapids, Michigan 49501 Phone: (616) 243-5129 E-mail: **rsuptongr@sbcglobal.net** Website: **www.robertupton.com**

Eric Velasquez The authors latest book Le Mozart Noir tells the remarkable story of the Chevalier de Saint George, one of the most famous men in 18th Century France. Contact Mr. Eric Velasquez, Harry N. Abrams, 115 West 18th Street, New York, New York 10011 E-mail: **freepub@abramsbooks.com** Website: **www.hnabooks.com**

Carmel S. Victor Author of award-winning novel: "Facing Our Skeletons" and Best Work of Poetry for 2005 "Every Day Again: Real Life through Poetry and Short Stories." Carmel S. Victor, Post Office Box 1132, Union, New Jersey 07083 Phone: (908) 206-0828 E-mail: **carmel@carmelsvictor.com** Website: **www.carmelsvictor.com**

Waithley L. Williams Author, W. Lionel Williams EdD, has years of experience as a teacher consultant, and school administrator. He holds a Doctorate in Educational Administration from Teachers College, Ball State University. His latest book "A Lamb to the Slaughter: Hope and Defeat in a High School Classroom" is a literary fiction work that focuses on the difficult task of managing in Urban classrooms. Mr. Waithley L. Williams, 47 Lincoln Road, Hempstead, New York 11550 E-mail: wlionel@sbasys.net

Darcell Walker Author of the book Godly Ideas: Perceiving and Pursuing God-Given Ideas, a resource designed to help people manifest their ideas, Attorney Walker specializes in matters related to Intellectual Property. He has a B. S. in Electrical Engineering from Prairie View A & M University, his Masters in Engineering from the University of California, Los Angeles, and his Law Degree from University of Texas at Austin, School of Law. Darcell Walker, Esq., Post Office Box 25048, Houston, Texas 77265 Phone: (713) 772-1255 Fax: (877) 523-2178 E-mail: dw0914@sbcglobal.net   Website: www.dwalkerlaw.net

Ethel Pitts Walker Current Chair of Television, Radio, Film and Theatre at San Jose State University where she was a 1999-2000 Teacher Scholar. Selected past accomplishments include: Elected as one of four 2008 University of Missouri College of Arts & Science Distinguished Alumna and a National Black Theatre Festival 2001 Living Legend. This Black Theatre Network two term Founding President was also a CA Educational Theatre Association and CA Legislative Action Coalition for Arts Education former President. In 1999 the American College Theatre Festival honored Walker with its Theatre in Excellence Award plus she was inducted into the National Educational Theatre Association Hall of Fame in 2000. Featured on the cover of Black Masks' July/August 2000 issue, in 2002, Dr. Walker was inducted into The College of Fellows of the American Theatre at the Kennedy Center. She has two books: New/Lost Plays by Ed Bullins: An Anthology and African American Scenebook. Ms. Ethel Walker, The Plaza of San Jose, Thirty East Julian Suite #218, San Jose, California 95112 Phone: (408) 216-9877 E-mail: DRAMART@comcast.net Website: www.africanamericandramacompany.org

Frank X. Walker Author of four poetry collections, Mr. Walker is founding member of the Affrilachian Poets, and editor of America! What's My Name? The Other Poets Unfurl the Flag (Wind Publications, 2007), and Eclipsing a Nappy New Millennium. Contact Mr. Frank X. Walker, 2197 Curtiswood Drive, Lexington, Kentucky 40505 Phone: (513) 375-7221 E-mail: affrilachia@aol.com Website: www.frankxwalker.com

Jacquelyn Dupont-Walker Co-author of the book A Model Of A Servant Bishop (The Ministry of Vinton Randolph Anderson) with Reverands Lee P. Washington, Ronald E. Braxton, Barbara Y. Glenn, and William D. Watley. Contact Ms. Jacquelyn Dupont-Walker, VRA Book Fund, 22 West Sherwood Drive, Overland, Missouri 63114 E-mail: jdupontw@aol.com

Tonya M. Evans-Walls Poet and author of the Literary Law Guide for Authors: Copyright, Trademark, and Contracts in Plain Language, Seasons of Her and SHINE! Her short story, Not Tonight appears in a new anthology titled Proverbs for the People, published by Kensington. An attorney she specializes in the areas of entertainment law. Tonya M. Evans-Walls, Esq., TME Law, 6703 Germantown Avenue, Suite 200, Philadelphia, Pennsylvania 19119 Phone: (215) 438-0468 Fax: (215) 438-0469 E-mail: tme@tmelaw.net Website: www.tmelaw.net

S. Courtney Walton   Columnist, Author, and Editor of "FUNgasa: Free Oneself! The Magazine for African-American Home Educators" and homeschooling columnist for The Good News Herald in Saint Louis, Missouri, "Real Living...Real Learning with S. Courtney Walton." Founder of African-American Unschoolers, a national network of Black Homeschooling families. Courtney Walton, 7549 West Cactus Road #104-340, Peoria, Arizona 85381 Phone: (623) 205-9883 E-mail: **Editor@afamunschool.com** Website: **www.afamunschool.com**

Karen R. Ward   Author of "The King's Men," and the educational book entitled, "It's All About School." An internationally traveled playwright, Ward is an educator who urges young and older to publish their poetry and art. She teaches educational course to both youth and adults. She is founder and chief operating officer of the literary company Gracious Hands. Karen R. Ward, Gracious Hands Literary Company, Post Office Box 20167, Rochester, New York 14602 Phone: (585) 235-2976 E-mail: **kwgracioushands@yahoo.com** Website: **www.Karenrward.com**

Vicki Ward   Writer, publisher and CEO of Nubian Images Publishing which published Life's Spices From Seasoned Sistahs, A Collection of Life Stories From Mature Women of Color in 2005. The book garnered three awards including Book of the Year, Best Anthology, and Honorable Mention. Contact Ms. Vicki Ward, Publisher, Nubian Images Publishing, Post Office Box 1332, El Cerrito, California 94532 E-mail: **vicki@nubianimagespublishing.com** Website: **www.nubianimagespublishing.com**

Shellie R. Warren   Full-time writer in Nashville, Tennessee, Shellie has been published in over 40 publications including Upscale, Honey, NV, CCM and Women's Health and Fitness Magazine. She is an entertainment columnist for a local Gannett publication All The Rage, a co-host on Freestyle, a local talk show, and the author of "Inside of Me: Lessons of Lust, Love and Redemption" (Relevant Books). Ms. Shellie Warren, 3840 Augusta Drive, Nashville, Tennessee 37207 E-mail: **shellie@shellierwarren.com** Website: **www.shellierwarren.com**

Cecil Washington   The author writes science fiction, fantasy and horror, in addition to poetry. Some of his published books include Alien Erotica, A collection of short stories and verses, Walkware, A techno-thriller, Seeing Red---SF short story, sold to Alienskinmag.com, July 2003 issue, Asspitality"---song lyrics written for the "Avenue X" movie soundtrack (lyrics written in September 2003), and Badlands: An Underground Science Fiction Novel. Mr. Washington graduated from Bowie State University in 1993 with a degree in Business Administration, and minors in Marketing, Music, Communications and Economics. He works as a QA Test Analyst in the private sector. He is also the founder of Creative Brother's Sci-Fi Magazine. Cecil Washington, 5701 Galloway Drive, Oxon Hill, Maryland 20745 Phone: (301) 749-1505 E-mail: **cecilwashington@yahoo.com** Website: **www.cecilwashington.com**

Mason Weaver   Author of It's OK to Leave the Plantation, The Rope, and Diamond in the Rough, which discusses the social issues that affect us all and that bind us together. With a degree in Political Science from U.C. Berkeley and experience as a Congressional Aid, Federal Contract Specialist, teacher and entrepreneur, he is gifted with an extraordinary view of government and business and a noted conference speaker and guest lecturer. Mason Weaver, Mason Media Company, 8301 Rio San Diego Drive, #10, San Diego, California 92108 E-mail: **masonweaver@masonweaver.com** Website: **www.masonweaver.com**

Nancy Weaver Recipient of Blackrefer.com Reviewer's Choice Award Outstanding Read for 2004 for her book In Her Presence: A Husband's Dirty Secret.   She was valedictorian of State University of New York Empire State College where she won several scholastic awards, including the Cecil Cohen award for Black Studies. Nancy Weaver, Time & Chance Publishing, 149 Freedom Avenue, Staten Island, New York 10314   Phone: (718) 370-3655 E-mail: contact@timeandchancepublishing.com Website: www.timeandchancepublishing.com

Shaun Webb Author of the new book A Motion For Innocence. Shaun leads a quiet life in Waterford, Michigan with his wife Nancy. They have three children, Bill, Mary and Alycia. They also have two grandchildren, Keller and Ruth Ann. Shaun enjoys travel, sports and the great outdoors. When Shaun isn't writing, he is a card-carrying union laborer who works at various locations in the Detroit metro area. Shaun Webb, 5530 Elizabeth Lake Road, Waterford, Michigan 48327 Phone: (248) 683-4037 E-mail: Dakota0526@gmail.com Website: www.amotionforinnocence.blogspot.com

Kevin M. Weeks Author of The Street Life Series, a collection of crime fiction novels, Weeks is a 2007 New York Book Festival Award Winning Author and MosaicBooks.com 2007 Bestselling Author. His published works include: The Street Life Series: Is It Passion or Revenge? (Xlibris, 2008), and The Street Life Series: Is It Suicide or Murder? (Xlibris, 2006). For his works, Weeks received a 2008 London Book Festival award, 2007 New York Book Festival award, and YOUnity Guild of America Best New Urban Author award. He is currently serving time at the Georgia Department of Corrections in Atlanta, Georgia. Kevin M. Weeks, 3961 Floyd Road; Suite 300, PMB 178, Austell, Georgia 30106 Phone: (404) 806-9542 E-mail: info@thestreetlifeseries.com Website: www.thestreetlifeseries.com

Theressa Gunnels Wesley Author, Wesley edited Published Black American Writers Past and present: A Biographical and Bibliographical Directory (Scare Crow Press, 1975), a two-volume directory listing complete bibliographies and biographies of over 2000 writers. Theressa G. Wesley, 14508 Sara Lynn Drive, Little Rock, Arkansas 72206 E-mail: twesley@aol.com

Carole E. Wharton Author. Founder/Director of The Writer's Corner, a poetry group. Carole Wharton, 1015 Morning View Drive, #210, Escondido, California 92026 Phone: (323) 244-5579 E-mail: eileencarole@sbcglobal.net Website: www.creativejuices.web.officelive.com

Dorrie Williams-Wheeler Entertainment journalist, screenwriter, educator, web designer and author of three books, Sparkledoll Always Into Something, Be My Sorority Sister-Under Pressure and The Unplanned Pregnancy Handbook. She has worked as an educator, curriculum developer and as a computer specialist Intranet/Internet for the Department of Defense. Completed her Masters of Science in Education Degree in Curriculum & Instruction with a major in Instructional Technology and her undergraduate course work at Southern Illinois University at Carbondale. Dorrie Williams-Wheeler, Post Office Box 56173, Virginia Beach, Virginia 23454 E-mail: dorrie@sparkledoll.com Website: www.dorrieinteractive.com

D. S. White Author of Age is Just a Number: Adventures in Online Dating (Vol I). Ms. D.S. White, Divine Truth Press, Post Office Box 145, Whitehall, Pennsylvania 18052 Fax: (530) 504-7094 E-mail: dee@deeswhite.com Website: www.deeswhite.com

Tanya White Editor/Writer of Tanya's Tips weekly international e-newsletter and author of Relationship Reruns: How To Break The Cycle of Choosing The Wrong People For The Right Relationships (August, 2008), and How To Deal With A Difficult Woman. Tanya White, Post Office Box #16635, Louisville, Kentucky 40256 Phone: (502) 449-0157 Fax: (502) 449-0157 E-mail: tanya@tanyawhite.com Website: www.tanyawhite.com

Barbara Joe-Williams Resides in Tallahassee, Florida. However, she was born and raised in Rosston, Arkansas. She spent four years in the U.S. Navy prior to attending college. She holds an A.A. degree in Office Education from Tallahassee Community College. She has a B.S. degree in Business Education and a M.Ed. in Counseling Education from Florida A&M University. She's a freelance writer, a motivational speaker, and an independent publisher who spends her spare time traveling and speaking on writing, publishing, marketing, and marriage. Her latest project was a non-fictional book titled, Moving the Furniture: 52 Ways to Keep Your Marriage Fresh (January 2009). She's been published in two anthologies, How I Met My Sweetheart (2007) and Memories of Mother (2007); She has one other non-fictional title: A Writer's Guide to Self-Publishing & Marketing (2007). In addition, Barbara has authored the following fictional books: Courtney's Collage with Sherille Fisher (2007); Falling for Lies (2006); Dancing with Temptation (2005); and Forgive Us This Day (2004). Barbara Joe-Williams, Amani Publishing, Post Office Box 12045, Tallahassee, Florida 32317 Phone: (850) 264-3341 E-mail: Amanipublishing@aol.com Website: www.amanipublishing.net

Blanche Williams Author of 'How To Design Your Mind for Greatness'; Member: SheSource/Women's Media Center; Social/Political Commentator: BreakingOurSilence.com; Founder/President - National Black Women's Town Hall, Inc.; Management Director & Facilitator-The Souls of Black Girls Film Documentary; Founder-The Sisterhood of Greatness: 21st Century Global Sorority ; Assistant Managing Director-International Association of Eating Disorders Professionals. Radio talk show host. Blanche Williams-Corey, Greatness By Design, LLC, 5900 Princess Garden Parkway, 8th Floor, Lanham, Maryland 20706 Phone: (202) 497-4564 E-mail: blanche@blanchewilliams.com Website: www.greatnessbydesign.com

DWe Williams Accomplished storyteller, playwright, performer and educator. DWe, a graduate of North Carolina A&T State University and SIU Carbondale holds a Master's degree with a double major in Speech and Theater. DWeLo Publications is a joint venture between DWe Williams and Loretta Ford. These two talented women have combined their talents to create a series of children's books entitled "We Were Always There." This series focuses on the contributions and accomplishments of African American heroes. The first book in this series is Bridget "Biddy" Mason: A Walking Sensation. DWe Williams, 2609 North West 38th Street, Oklahoma City, Oklahoma 73112 E-mail: ewdwms@sbcglobal.net

Hubert P. Williams, Jr. An anointed singer, songwriter, and producer Hubert writes poetry and inspirarional messages to uplift the Name of the Lord. He also writes songs and instrumental music for other artists. Currently serves on the following committees: Chair, Cumberland County Coalition on Teen Pregnancy Prevention and Adolescent Parenting; Member of Coalition for Awareness, Resources, and Education of Substances, (C.A.R.E.S). Minister Hubert P. Williams, Jr., Trinity Music Group, 2907 Kingfisher Drive, Fayetteville, North Carolina Phone: (910) 977-7354 E-mail: min.hpwilliams@yahoo.com

Kim Williams   Author of 40 Hours And An Unwritten Rule: The Diary of a Nigger, Negro, Colored, Black, African-American Woman (2004). It follows an African American woman's professional journey told through her personal memoirs. Kim graduated from the University of North Texas with a degree in Radio-TV-Film, 1996. Currently she is writing her second novel. Kim Williams, Butterfly Ink Publishing, Post Office Box 56874, Sherman Oaks, California 91413 E-mail: **kim@butterflyinkpublishing.com** Website: **www.butterflyinkpublishing.com**

Laura Williams   Author, her novel Lead Us Not Into Temptation, depicts the life of a desperate and lonely young woman who's desire for love is so strong that she crosses and destroys all moral boundaries. Laura Williams, 5121 Kenwood Road, Durham, North Carolina 27712 Phone: (919) 471-5121 E-mail: **Godzfavor2@yahoo.com** Website: **www.Godzfavor.com**

Maiya Williams   Began her career as a children's author with the publication of her middle-grade novel The Golden Hour in 2005. The sequel, The Hour of The Cobra, is her second novel. Maiya Williams, Harry N. Abrams, 115 West 18th Street, New York, New York 10010 E-mail: **freepub@abramsbooks.com**

Patricia H. Williams   Author of No Longer Will I Hide The Stranger In My Bed based on a true story of an 18 year Domestic Violence situation. Contact Ms. Patricia H. Williams, RAPHA, Inc, Post Office Box 1184, Groton, Connecticut 06340 Phone: (860) 449-1374 E-mail: **joyindamornin@earthlink.net** Website: **www.patticoupons.com**

Richard Williams   An author and health educator, Dr. Williams' emphasis of study includes psychology, religion, and health. Consultant, he conducts workshops and seminars on the family and on health. He speaks on issues affecting African-Americans and explains why African-Americans must determine their destiny by themselves and for themselves. He is the author of They Stole It But You Must Return It, as a young classic, and Torches On The Road Of Passage is particularly helpful to the growth of the young male's development into manhood and father hood. He has appeared on more that 70 different radio and TV talk shows including The Oprah Winfrey Show and Black Entertainment Network (BET). Dr. Richard Williams, 56 Wildbriar Road, Rochester, New York 14623 Phone: (419) 297-6636 E-mail: **aym@blackfamilysite.com** Website: **www.blackfamilysite.com**

Rozalia Williams   Educator, Publisher, President of Hidden Curriculum Education, Inc., and Author of the College FAQ Book: Over 5,000 Not Frequently Asked Questions About College! She holds an Ed.D. from Harvard University. A college administrator for over twenty years, she has devoted her professional career to creating, implementing and evaluating student development programs. Her experiences as a retention counselor, pre-college program director, assistant to the vice president of student affairs, branch campus director, assistant dean and instructor of first year experience courses at two-and four-year institutions frame the questions for the book and the course. Rozalia Williams, Post Office Box 222041, Hollywood, Florida 33022 Phone: (954) 457-8098 Fax: (954) 457-3331 E-mail: **hiddencurriculum@aol.com**

Shelita Williams   Motivational speaker, goals coach author of How To Reign in Life. Shelita Williams, Post Office Box 533,Sterling Heights,Michigan 48311 Phone: (586) 944-9060 E-mail: **spiritualita@comcast.net** Website: **www.shelitawilliams.com**

Sonja T. Williams Author of the children's book, "Aloma and the Red Suitcase." Sonja T. Williams, STP Publishing, Post Office Box 291712, Columbia, South Carolina 29229 E-mail: sonii_t@yahoo.com

Terrie Williams Author and President / Founder of The Terrie Williams Agency and The Stay Strong Foundation, Terrie Williams' first book The Personal Touch: What You Really Need to Succeed in Today's Fast-Paced Business World (1994 Warner Books) is a best-selling book on developing business practices and includes a foreword by Bill Cosby and a preface by Jonathan M. Tisch, the president and CEO of Loews Hotels. Her other books are Stay Strong: Life Lessons for Teens (Scholastic 2001), and another is A Plentiful Harvest: Creating Balance and Harmony Through Seven Living Virtues (2001 Warner Books. Terrie Williams Agency, 382 Central Park West, Suite 7R, New York, New York 10023 Phone: (212) 316-0305 Fax: (212) 749-8867 E-mail: tmwms@terriewilliams.com Website: www.terriewilliams.com

Ann E. Williamson A professional life coach specializing in assisting individuals make changes in their personal and professional lives, Mr. Williamson is co-author of the Survival Skills for African American Women (2007). Contact Ann E. Williamson, Ph.D., 321 North Cottonwood Drive, Gilbert, Arizona 85234 Phone: (480) 892-7756 E-mail: dranelwi@aol.com Website: www.annewilliamson.com

Emily Means-Willis Educator, author, literary reviewer, columnist. After 37 years as an instructor in secondary education, Emily Means-Willis, recently retired and has published a novel entitled "Looking for that Silver Spoon". She also writes for various magazines. A second novel "Flip Side of the Coin" will be released in 2007. Emily Means-Willis, We, Us and Company, International, 419 Douglas Street, Park Forest, Illinois 60466 Phone: (708) 769-4116 E-mail: pamemi@comcast.net

Jessica Nyel Willis Author, writer of articles for magazines, short stories, film script, teleplays, sitcom and drama scripts, as well as novels for young adults and adults. Contact Jessica Nyel Willis, 8629 144th Street, #2, Jamaica, New York 11435 Phone: (646) 207-1877 E-mail: JessicaNyelWillis@hotmail.com

Anita L. Wills Lecturer, and Historian, Anita's specialty is Free Persons of Color, in Colonial Virginia. Author of numerous articles and two books, Notes And Documents of Free Persons of Color: Four Hundred Years of An American Family History (Lulu Press, 2003) and Pieces of the Quilt: The Mosaic of An African American Family (May, 2009). Anita is also host of a radio show, "Anita Talks Genealogy," geared toward people who are tracing Multi-Racial Ancestors. Anita Wills, 2041 Miramonte Avenue, #12, San Leandro, California 94578 Phone: (510) 586-0529 E-mail: alani2@yahoo.com Website: http://blogtalkradio.com/Anita-Wills

Betty Wilson In her job as a curriculum developer for the City of New York, Betty designs courses and has written well over three-dozen how-to training manuals. She recently published a novel about the funny, sometimes perplexing but always intriguing personalities she met during twenty years as a property manager in city-owned buildings, Mr. Jefferson's Piano & Other Central Harlem Stories, an anthology. Betty Wilson, Post Office Box 50, Hamilton Grange Station, New York, New York 10031 E-mail: wilsonbluez@aol.com

Raymond A. Winbush Director of the Institute for Urban Research at Morgan State University in Baltimore, Maryland. Author of three books, The Warrior Method: A Program for Rearing Healthy Black Boys (2001), Should America Pay?: Slavery and the Raging Debate on Reparations (2003), both published by Amistad/HarperCollins, and recently released, Belinda's Petition: A Concise History of Reparations for the Transatlantic Slave Trade (July, 2009), Mr. Winbush received his Ph.D. from the University of Chicago. Raymond A. Winbush, PhD., 1190 West Northern Parkway, Suite 915, Baltimore Maryland 21210 Phone: (410) 532-2252 Fax: (410) 988-3018 E-mail: **rwinbush@usit.net**

Joel Windsor (Hozeh) Holds a Bachelor of Arts in Liberal Arts from Lafayette College and a Master of Arts in Writing Studies from St. Joseph's University. He's taught in elementary and middle schools in New Jersey and Pennsylvania, and he has won the Hurston/Wright Award for College Writers. His book, The Hip Hop Manifesto, has been read at the collegiate level, and he has performed in New York and in Philadelphia as a rapper and as a spoken word artist. Joel Windsor, 357 West Mount Airy Avenue, #B8, Philadelphia, Pennsylvania 19119 E-mail: **thehozeh@yahoo.com**

Laureen Wishom Nationally known guest speaker and author of five how to business books, The Greater Houston Resource Guide, The Source Newsletter, The Entrepreneur and Career Professionals Newsletter, and The 501(c)3 Newsletter. Her articles have appeared in numerous newspapers, magazines, and online publications. She holds a Bachelor's degree in General Education, a Master's degree in Psychology/Sociology and a Ph.D. in Psychology/Christian Counseling. She holds a Board Goverance and Leadership certification, and certificate for Productivity Education from the Academy of Human Potential. She is a certified hospice volunteer and a commissioned lay Chaplain. Dr. Laureen Wishom, Masterpiece Solutions, LLC, Post Office Box 441234, Houston, Texas 77244 Phone: (281) 584-0348 Fax: (281) 584-0355 E-mail: **drlaureen@drlaureen.com** Website: **www.masterpiecesolutions.biz**

Petra E. Woodard An educator, author, playwright, poet and inspirational speaker, and certified counselor, Petra's debut novel INcomPLETE DENIAL, a suspenseful romance, was published in 2004. Her plays have been performed in various communities for over ten years. Petra Woodard, Post Office Box 273, Arcadia, Oklahoma 73007 Phone: (405) 370-1604 Fax: (405) 396-2290 E-mail: **mpetra@sbcglobal.net**

Alice G. Wootson Author of ten contemporary romance novels. Her 10th novel, Ready to Take a Chance, was released by Kimani/Arabesque in 2006. All of her novels, including Aloha Love and her latest, Perfect Wedding, have been published by BET Books/Arabesque. Her upcoming release is, Love Will Make it Better. Contact Ms. Alice G. Wootson, Post Office Box 18832, Philadelphia, Pennsylvania 19119 E-mail: **agwwriter@email.com** Website: **www.alicewootson.net**

Frances Faye Ward-Worthy Graduated from the Art Institute of Atlanta (music business and video); had classes at Cranbrook Institute (film & video); scriptwriting with Tim Jeffrey. I've been Production Assistant on music videos, documentaries and TV productions. given lectures and workshops on rap/hip hop and the Black Madonna. Ms. Frances Faye Ward-Worthy, 242 Chalmers, Detroit, Michigan 48215 E-mail: **worth23karat@yahoo.com**

Sankofa Camille Yarbrough Award winning performance artist, cultural activist and the author of several young adult and children's books, Yarbrough, is a multi-talented veteran of theater, film, dance, and song. Vanguard Records recorded her first album of original songs and poetry, "The Iron Pot Cooker" in 1975, and re-released it in 2000. Her work as an actress can be heard on the cast album of Lorrain Hansberry's Play, "To Be Young, Gifted and Black." Sankofa Camille Yarbrough, Ancestor House, African American Traditions Workshop, 80 Saint Nicholas Avenue Suite 4G, New York, New York 10026 Phone: (212) 865-7460 E-mail: Yarbroughchosan@aol.com Website: www.ancestorhouse.net

Francine A. Yates The author was born in Jacksonville, Florida the setting of her first book, a novel Carrie O and Me (What A Woman God Made). In 2002, she founded her own publishing company, Yates Publishing, LLC which produced the sequel, Faith Holds the Key (2004). Fran has been a mentor at an Indianapolis public school. She created a book club at the Wheelers Boys & Girls Club of Indianapolis. She studied Business at Indiana University/Purdue University in Indianapolis. Memberships: Urban Arts Consortium of Indianapolis Writer's Group, Authors Supporting Authors Positively (ASAP). Francine, A. Yates, Yates Publishing, LLC, Post Office Box 18982, Indianapolis, Indiana 46218 E-mail: fran3214@yahoo.com Website: www.franyates.net

Zane A New York Times best-selling author and founder/publisher of Strebor Books (1999). Strebor has published over 60 authors, produced numerous best sellers and has recently become an official imprint of Simon and Schuster. Contact Zane, Strebor Books International/Simon and Schuster, Post Office Box 6505, Largo, Maryland 20792 Phone: (301) 583-0616 E-mail: endeavors@aol.com Website: www.streborbooks.com

Roxanne Marie Zeigler Author of "Are You Looking Through The Window of My Soul?" Minister Roxanne Marie Zeigler, Post Office Box 592, Spencer, Oklahoma 73084 Phone: (405) 761-6869 E-mail: roxanneswindow2003@hotmail.com

Zhana Author of Sojourn, a collection of writings by Black women in Britain about Black mother/daughter relationships, sisterhood and friendships (Methuen London Ltd., 1988), and Success Strategies for Black People and Black Success Stories. Zhana, Zhana Books, Post Office Box 12156, London SE5 8ZJ United Kingdom E-mail: zhana2002@hotmail.com Website: www.blacksuccess1.com

Black Studies Programs

Alabama

Director, Dr. Janice Franklin, National Center for the Study of Civil Rights & African-American Culture, Alabama State University, Post Office Box 271, Montgomery, Alabama 36101 Phone: (334) 229-4106 E-mail: **civilrightscenter@alasu.edu** Website: **www.lib.alasu.edu/natctr**

Director, Dr. Kern M. Jackson, Afican-American Studies, University of South Alabama, HUMB 268, Mobile, Alabama 36688   Phone: (251) 460-6146   E-mail: **kemjacks@usouthal.edu** Website: **www.southalabama.edu/bulletin/artafr.htm**

Arizona

Arizona State University, African and African American Studies, 140 Wilson Hall, Post Office Box 874902, Tempe, Arizona 85287 Phone: (480) 965-4399 Fax: (480) 965-7229 E-mail: **aframstu@asu.edu** Website: **www.aaas.clas.asu.edu**

Arkansas

Vice Provost for Diversity, Charles Robinson, University of Arkansas, African and African-American Studies, 416 Old Main, Fayetteville, Arkansas 72701 Phone: (479) 575-3001 E-mail: **cfrobins@uark.edu** Website: **www.catalogofstudies.uark.edu/2009/2905.php**

Director, Matthew Harper, African and African American Studies, University of Central Arkansas, 201 Donaghey Avenue, Conway, Arkansas 72035 Phone: (501) 450-5000 E-mail: **mharper@uca.edu** Website: **http://uca.edu/africanamericanstudies/**

California

Associate Professor, Denise Isom, Ethnic Studies, California Polytechnic State University, Building 38 Room 136, San Luis Obispo, California 93407 Phone: (805) 756-1707 Fax: (805) 756-6188 E-mail: **ethnicstudies@calpoly.edu** Website: **www.cla.calpoly.edu/es.html**

Department Chair, Dorothy Randall Tsuruta, Ph.D., San Francisco State University, Africia Studies, 1600 Holloway Avenue, San Francisco, California 94132 Phone: (415) 338-2352 E-mail: **dtsuruta@sfsu.edu** Website: **http://userwww.sfsu.edu/~afrs/index.html**

Associate Professor, Dr, Charles Toombs, Ph.D., Africana Studies Department, College of Arts and Letters, San Diego State University, 5500 Campanile Drive, San Diego, California 92182 Phone: (619) 594-6532 Fax: (619) 594-0728 E-mail: **ctoombs@mail.sdsu.edu** Website: **http://www-rohan.sdsu.edu/~afras/index.htm**

Colorado

Chair and Professor, Donna Langston, Ethnic Studies, University of Colorado, Campus Box 134, Post Office Box 173364, Denver, Colorado 80217 Phone: (303) 315-3616 Fax: (303) 315-3610 E-mail: ethnic_studies@ucdenver.edu Website: www.ucdenver.edu

Connecticut

Director, Felton O. Best, African American Studies, Central Connecticut State University, 1615 Stanley Street, New Britain, Connecticut 06050 Phone: (860) 832-2910 E-mail: BestF@ccsu.edu Website: http://www.ccsu.edu/page.cfm?p=5376

Delaware

Chair, Dr. Carol E. Henderson, Black Studies Program, University of Delaware, 417 John Ewing Hall, 021 Memorial Hall, Newark, Delaware 19716 Phone: (302) 831-6330 Fax: (302) 831-6063 E-mail: ceh@udel.edu Website: http://www.bams.udel.edu

District of Columbia

Director, E. Ethelbert Miller, Afro-American Studies, Howard University, Post Office Box 746, Washington, D.C. 20001   Phone: (202) 806-7242 E-mail: emiller698@aol.com Website: http://www.coas.howard.edu/afroamerican

Florida

Director, Dr. Sharon Austin, African American Studies, University of Florida, 103 Walker Hall, Post Office Box 118120, Gainesville, Florida 32611 Phone: (352) 392-5724 Fax: (352) 294-0007 E-mail: polssdw@ufl.edu Website: http://www.clas.ufl.edu/afam/history.html

Georgia

Administrator, La Shanda Perryman, African American Studies, Emory University, Candler Library Building 201B, Atlanta, Georgia 30304 Phone: (404) 727-6847 Fax: (404) 727-6848 E-mail: aas@emory.edu Website: www.aas.emory.edu

Coordinator, Dr. Josephine B. Bradley, African & African American Studies and Africana Women's Studies, Clarke Atlanta University, J.P. Brawley Drive, Atlanta, Georgia 30314 Phone: (404) 880-6810 Fax: (404) 880-8534 E-mail: jbradley@cau.edu Website: http://www.cau.edu/Academics_African_and_African_American_Studies_And_Africana_ Womens_Studies.aspx

Illinois

Chairperson, Darlene Clark Hine, African American Studies, Northwestern University, 2-320 Kresge Hall, Evanston, Illinois 60208 Phone: (847) 491-5122 Fax: (847) 491-4803 E-mail: afas@northwestern.edu Website: http://www.afam.northwestern.edu/

Indiana

Director, Dr. Leslie R. James, Ph.D., African American Studies, DePauw University, Post Office Box 37, Greencastle, Indiana 46135 Phone: (765) 658-4800 Fax: (765) 658-4875 E-mail: ljames@depauw.edu Website: http://www.depauw.edu/acad/black

Iowa

Chair, Carin M. Green, African American Studies, University of Iowa, 715 Jefferson Building, Iowa City, Iowa 52242 Phone: (319) 335-3494 Fax: (319) 335-0314   E-mail: timothy-havens@uiowa.edu Website: www.uiowa.edu/~amstud/

Michigan

Chair, Tiya Miles, Afroamerican and African Studies, University of Michigan, Haven Hall, Room 4700, 505 South State Street, Ann Arbor, Michigan 48109 Phone: (734) 764-5513 Fax: (734) 763-0543 E-mail: daas-info@umich.edu Website: http://www.lsa.umich.edu/daas/

Minnesota

African American Student Services Coordinator, Stanley Hatcher, Metropolitan State University, African American Services, 700 East Seventh Street, Saint Paul, Minnesota 55106 Phone: (651) 793-1541 E-mail: Stanley.Hatcher@metrostate.edu Website: www.metrostate.edu

Mississippi

Director, Dr. Charles K. Ross, African-American Studies, University of Mississippi 309 Longstreet Hall, University, Mississippi 38677 Phone: (662) 915-5978 Fax: (662) 915-5675 E-mail: cross@olemiss.edu Website: http://www.olemiss.edu/depts/afro_am/

Missouri

Director, Dr. Wilma King, Black Studies, University of Missouri, 203 Read Hall, Columbia, Missouri 65211 Phone: (573) 882-4612 Fax: (573) 884-6470 E-mail: kingw@missouri.edu Website: www.blackstudies.missouri.edu

Nebraska

Interim Chair, Cynthia L. Robinson, Ph.D., Black Studies, University of Nebraska at Omaha, Room 184, 6001 Dodge Street, Omaha, Nebraska 68182 Phone: (402) 554-2412 Fax: (402) 554-3883 E-mail: fdailey@unomaha.edu Website: http://www.unomaha.edu/blst

New Hampshire

Chair, Antonio D. Tillis, African and African-American Studies, Dartmouth College, 105 Choate House, HB 6134, 34 North Main Street, Hanover, New Hampshire 03755 Phone: (603) 646-0224 E-mail: Antonio.Tillis@Dartmouth.edu Website: www.dartmouth.edu/~african

New Jersey

Chair, Mr. Eddie Glaude, Center for African American Studies, Princeton University, Stanhope Hall, Princeton, New Jersey 08544 Phone: (609) 258-4270 Fax: (609) 258-5095 E-mail: esglaude@princeton.edu Website: http://www.princeton.edu/africanamericanstudies/

New York

Coordinator, Karanja Keita Carroll, Black Studies, State University of New York at New Paltz, 1 Hawk Drive, New Paltz, New York 12561 Phone: (845) 257-2760 Fax: (845) 257-2768 E-mail: blackstudies@newpaltz.edu Website: www.newpaltz.edu/blackstudies

Ohio

Director, Dr. Michael R. Williams, Ph.D., MPH, Black Studies, Cleveland State University, 2121 Euclid Avenue, MC 137, Cleveland, Ohio 44115 Phone: (216) 523-7211 Fax: (216) 687-3655 E-mail: m.williams@csuohio.edu Website: http://www.csuohio.edu/class/blackstudies/

Oklahoma

Chair, Jeanette Davidson, Ph.D., ACSW, African and African American Studies, University of Oklahoma, 633 Elm Avenue, Room 233, Norman, Oklahoma 73019 Phone: (405) 325-2327 Fax: (405) 325-0842 jrdavidson@ou.edu Website: www.ou.edu/cas/afam/1/contact.htm

Pennsylvania

Coordinator, LaTonya Thames Taylor, African American Studies, West Chester University of Pennsylvania, 309 Main Hall, West Chester, Pennsylvania 19383 Phone: (610) 436-2970 E-mail: cmarciano@wcupa.edu Website: www.wcupa.edu

Tennessee

Director, Beverly G. Bond, African and African American Studies, The University of Memphis, 107 Scates Hall, Memphis, Tennessee 38152 Phone: (901) 678-3550 Fax: (901) 678-4831 E-mail: bgbond@memphis.edu Website: http://www.memphis.edu/aaas/

Wisconsin

Chair, Brenda Gayle Plummer, Afro-American Studies, University of Wisconsin, 4141 Helen C. White Hall, 600 North Park Street, Madison, Wisconsin 53706 Phone: (608) 263-7978 Fax: (608) 263-7198 E-mail: bplummer@wisc.edu Website: www.wisconsin.edu

Book Clubs

African American Book Club Summit (AABCS) Annual. Pamela Walker-Williams, Pageturner.net, PMB-120, 2951 Marina Bay Drive, #130, League City, Texas 77573 Phone: (866) 875-1044 E-mail: pwsquare@pageturner.net Website: www.pageturner.net

African American Literature Book Club Founded in 1997 by Troy Johnson, the AALBC website features author profiles, book excerpts, poetry, online discussion boards, chat sessions, contests, and information about upcoming events. AALBC, 55 West 116th Street #195, Harlem, New York 10026 Phone: (866) 603-8394 E-mail: troy@aalbc.com Website: www.aalbc.com

Apooo An online author and reader community dedicated to advancing African-American literature. Features upcoming literary events, book reviews, forthcoming books, bookstore. Yasmin Coleman, A Place of Our Own, 4426 Pinewood Court, Harrisburg, Pennsylvania 17112 E-mail: apooo4u@yahoo.com Website: www.apooobooks.com

ASiS Book Club Post Office Box 211, Lorton, VA 22199 E-mail: asisbookclub@yahoo.com Website: www.asisbookclub.org

Between the Covers Book Club The first WVON radio station book club launched by award-winning air personality, Sharon K. McGhee, former News Director at WVON. Contact Sharon K. McGhee, WVON 1690 AM, 3350 South Kedzie, Chicago, Illinois 60623 Phone: (773) 247-6200 E-mail: Sharon@wvon.com Website: www.wvon.com

BlackBookPlus.com Post Office Box 030064, Elmont, New York 11003 Phone: (718) 267-2833 E-mail: blackbooksmail@gmail.com Website: www.blackbookplus.com

Black Expressions African American book club. Also on-line book seller. Contact Diversity City Media, 225 West 3rd Street, Suite 203, Long Beach, California 90802 Phone: (562) 209-0616 Website: www.blackexpressions.com

BookClubEtc. A group of 15+ African American men and women who meet on a monthly basis to discuss books by and about our people. We also host book signings and poetry readings. Jennifer Belfield, 217 Union Street, Hampton, Virginia 23669 E-Mail: BookClubEtc@aol.com

Brown Baby Reads! 1111 North Wells, Suite 308, Chicago, Ilinois 60610 E-mail: info@brownbabyreads.com Website: www.brownbabyreads.com

Escapade 'A Soulful Circle' Book Club We read books by African American authors of fiction and non-fiction literature. We meet on the fourth Saturday of each month. Contact Escapade Book Club, Post Office Box 3581, San Leandro, California 94578 Phone: (510) 332-9997 E-mail: escapadebookclub@yahoo.com Website: www.escapadebookclub.com

The Grits Online Reading Club Webzine is an interactive publication for men and women who love classic and contemporary literature! The GRITS COM Literary Service, 526 Kingwood Drive, Suite 404, Kingwood, Texas 77339 Website: www.thegritsbookclub.com

Imani Book Club Diverse group of African-American women who enjoy reading. Contact Imani Book Club, c/o Cashana, Post Office Box 240063, Montgomery, Alabama 36124 E-mail: imanivoices@aol.com Website: www.imanivoices.com

Kindred Spirits Book Club African-American women meet to discuss a variety of literary accomplishments with a focus on Black authors. Contact Ms. Sharon Hollis, Kindred Spirits Book Club, 11024 Balboa Boulevard. Suite #634, Granada Hills, California 91344 E-mail: contact@kindredspiritsbookclub.org Website: www.kindredspiritsbookclub.org

Q.U.E.E.N.S. Book Club of Atlanta (Quality Unique Elegance Exquisite & Naturally Sophisticated) is a group who possess a genuine passion in reading thought-provoking novels and having a good time. Contact Q.U.E.E.N.S. Book Club of Atlanta, 2884 Pearl Street, East Point, Georgia 30344 Phone: (404) 543-7183 E-mail: queensbookclubofatlanta@yahoo.com Website: www.queensbookclubofatlanta.webs.com

Rawsistaz Review Founded in September 2000 by Tee C. Royal with a focus on reading and writing (RAW). RAWSISTAZ, Post Office Box 1362, Duluth, Georgia 30096 Phone: (775) 363-8683 Fax: (775) 416-4540 E-mail: tee@rawsistaz.com Website: www.rawsistaz.com

Sistah Circle Book Club, Inc. (The) Founded,1999. Group of avid African American women readers which seeks to promote reading among African American women and their families. The Sistah Circle Book Club, Post Office Box 49022, Denver, Colorado 80249 E-mail: sistahcircle@gmail.com Website: www.thesistahcircle.com

Sistahs Book Club Founded in April, 1999 by cofounder and president Suzetta M. Perkins and Pamela Smith. Sistahs Book Club, Post Office Box 64424, Fayetteville, North Carolina 28306 nubianqe2@aol.com Website: www.suzettaperkins.com

SistahFriend Book Club Book club for all women who share a love and respect for African-American Literature. SistahFriend Book Club, PMB #351, 4611 Hardscrabble Road, Columbia, South Carolina 29229 E-mail: info@sistahfriend.com Website: www.sistahfriend.com

Thumper's Corner Reading group. Thumper's Corner, AALBC, 55 West 116th Street, #195, Harlem, New York 10026 Phone: (866) 603-8394 Website: www.thumperscorner.com

Bookstores

A Different Booklist From Canadian to African-Canadian children and adult books. Events. A Different Booklist, 746 Bathurst Street, Toronto, Ontario M5S 2R6 Phone: (416) 538-0889 Fax: (416) 538-6914 E-mail: info@adifferentbooklist.com Website: www.adifferentbooklist.com

African American Books Online Guide To African-American books. Ther is no cost to list your books on this website. AABooks, 5036 Switch Grass, Naperville, Illinois 60564 E-mail: info@aabooks.com Website: www.aabooks.com

African American Images Founded by Dr. Jawanza Kunjufu. Online bookstore. African American Images, Post Office Box 1799, Sauk Village, Illinois 60412 Phone: (708) 672-4909 E-mail: aarcher@africanamericanimages.com Website: www.africanamericanimages.com

African Enterprise U.S.A. Online bookstore. African Enterprise. Christopher Doyle, Executive Director. African Enterprise USA, 128 East Palm Avenue, Monrovia, California 91016 Phone: (800) 672-3742 E-mail: cdoyle@aeusa.org Website: www.africanenterprise.org

African Imports Since 1990. Operates two super stores in Dallas and Fort Worth, Texas. Raymond and Blessing Odimegwu, Managers. African Imports, South West Center Mall, 3662 West Camp Wisdom, #1067, Dallas, Texas 75237 Phone: (877) 8-AFRICA Fax: (972) 296-9550 E-mail: sales@africanimportsusa.com Website: www.africanimportsusa.com

African Bookstore Black owned and operated bookstore in South Florida. A.H. Harrison, African Bookstore, 3600 West Broward Boulevard, Ft. Lauderdale, Florida 33312 Phone: (954) 584-0460 E-mail: sales@africanbookstore.net Website: www.africanbookstore.net

Afrikan World Books Monday thru Friday 9 a.m. to 5 p.m. Afrikan World Books, 2217 Pennsylvania Avenue, Baltimore, Maryland 21217 Phone: (410) 383-2006 Fax: (410) 383-0511 E-mail: afrikanworldword@aol.com Website: www.afrikanworldbooks.com

Black Book News (BBN) Publishes BBN magazine. Online book seller. Contact Editor, BBN, Post Office Box 030064, Elmont New York 11003 E-mail: blackbooknewsmail@gmail.com Website: www.blackbooknews.com

Black Books Galore!® founded in 1992 by three African American mothers, who, as the result of their challenges in finding quality books reflecting positive images for their children, dedicated themselves to identifying and distributing great African American children's books. Contact Black Books Galore, 65 High Ridge Road, #407, Stamford, Connecticut 06905 Phone: (203) 359-6925 E-mail: bbg@blackbooksgalore.com Website: www.blackbooksgalore.com

Black Book Plus African-American Bookstore. Online bookseller. Contact Black Book Plus, Post Office Box 030064, Elmont, New York 11003   E-mail: blackbooksmail@gmail.com Website: www.blackbookplus.com

Black Classics Books & Gifts Specializes in Black Literature for children and adults, fiction and non-fiction books. Black Classics Books & Gifts, 140 S. Sage Avenue, Suite B, Mobile, Alabama 36606 Phone: (251) 476-1060 Fax: (251) 476-4642 E-mail: blackbkgft@aol.com

BlackPrint Bookstore & Art Gallery Established by Bea Dozier-Taylor. BlackPrint Bookstore & Art Gallery, 162 Edgewood Avenue, New Haven, Connecticut 06511 Phone: (203) 782-2159 E-mail: bea@blackprint.com Website: www.blackprint.com

Brownstone Books African American bookstore. Brownstone Books Literary Camps, 339 MacDonough Street, Brooklyn, New York 11233 Phone: (646) 389-6859 Fax: (347) 586-0289 E-mail: info@brownstonebooks.com Website: www.brownstonebooks.com

B's Books and More, Inc. We are an online store specializing in books written by, about or relevant to African Americans for all ages. B's Books and More, Inc., Post Office Box 1229, Lithonia, Georgia 30058 Phone: (770) 484-6222 Website: www.bsbooksandmore.com

C & B Books Distribution We offer our books for less than the major distributors. Caroline Rogers, C & B Books Distribution, 65-77 160th, Street, #3A, Flushing, New York 11365 Phone: (718) 591-4525 E-mail: cbbookdist@aol.com Website: www.cbbooksdistribution.com

Charis Books & More Poetry and book signings. Charis Books & More, 1189 Euclid Avenue, North East Atlanta, Georgia Phone: (404) 524-0304 E-mail: info@charisbooksandmore.com Website: www.charisbooksandmore.com

Confetti Company Began in 1991. Confetti Company c/o Sandcastle Publishing LLC, 1723 Hill Drive, Postal Box 3070, South Pasadena, California 91031 Phone: (323) 255-3616 E-mail: info@confettibooks4kids.com Website: www.confettibooks4kids.com

Cushcity Bookseller. Cushcity, 13533 Bammel North Houston Road, Houston, Texas 77066 Phone: (281) 444-4265 E-mail: GRichardson@cushcity.com   Website: www.cushcity.com

Everyone's Place Open Monday thru Saturday 9 a.m. to 7 p.m. and Sunday 12 p.m. to 5p.m. Everyone's Place, 1356 West North Avenue, Baltimore Maryland 21217 Phone: (410) 728 0877 E-mail: afrikanworldword@aol.com   Website: www.afrikanworldbooks.com

Hakims Bookstore and Giftshop Contact Hakims Bookstore and Giftshop, 210 South 52nd Street, Philadelphia, Pennsyvania 19139 Phone: (215) 474-9495 Fax: (215) 471-7177 E-mail: hakims_bookstore@verizon.net

Hueman Bookstore & Cafe African-American books. Author signings. Hueman Bookstore & Cafe, 2319 Frederick Douglass Boulevard, New York, New York 10027 Phone: (212) 665-7400 E-mail: info@hueman-bookstore.com Website: www.huemanbookstore.com

Jokae's Bookseller. Jokae's Bookstore, 3223 West Camp Wisdom, Dallas, Texas 75237 Phone: (214) 331-8100 E-mail: jokaesbooks1@sbcglobal.net Website: www.jokaes.com

Knowledge Bookstore Retail. Specializes in African-American and Caribbean book titles and authors, natural skin care products. Knowledge Bookstore, 177 Queen Street West, Brampton Ontario Canada L6Y 1M5 Phone: (905) 459-9875 E-mail: sales@knowledgebookstore.com Website: www.knowledgebookstore.com

LittleAfrica.com Online bookseller. Contact LittleAfrica.com, 8192 Misty Shore Drive, West Chester, Ohio 45069 Phone: (513) 870-9337 E-mail: Market@LittleAfrica.com Website: www.LittleAfrica.com

Lushena Books Distributes and publishes African American Books Contact Lushena Books Inc., 607 Country Club Drive, Unit E, Bensenville, Illinois 60106 Phone: (630) 238-8708 E-mail: lushenabooks@gmail.com Website: www.lushenabks.com

Marcus Books Books by and about Black people. Marcus Books, 1712 Fillmore Street, San Francisco, California 94115 Phone: (415) 346-4222 Website: www.marcusbookstores.com

Marcus Books Books by about Black people. Marcus Books, 3900 Martin Luther King Jr. Way, Oakland, California 94609 Phone: (510) 652-2344 Website: www.marcusbookstores.com

Milligan Books Bookstore Bookseller. Book Publisher. Dr. Rosie Millligan, Milligan Books, 1425 West Manchester Avenue, Suite C, Los Angeles, California 90047 Phone: (323) 750-3592 E-mail: DrRosie@aol.com Website: www.drrosie.com

MochaReaders 893 South Main Street #189, Englewood, Ohio 45322 Phone: (937) 361-7657 E-mail: info@mochareaders.com Website: www.mochareaders.com

Nubian Bookstore Retail Books. Marcus Williams, 2449 Southlake Mall, Morrow, Georgia 30260 Phone: (678) 422-6120

Nubian Express Book Store Monday thru Friday 10 a.m. to 6:00 p.m., Saturday 10: a.m. to 6:00 p.m. Nubian Express Book, 3814 Linwood Avenue, Shreveport, Louisiana 71103 Phone: (318) 635-7505 E-mail: nubian1a@comcast.net Website: http://topcatlive.com/nubian

Pan African Connection Artifacts from the Motherland, African Drums, Books, Paintings, Prints and More! Pan African Connection 828 Fourth Avenue, Dallas, Texas 75226 Phone: (214) 943-8262 E-mail: panafric@airmail.net Website: www.panafricanconnection.com

Pyramid Art Books African American Retail Bookstore. Contact Garbo Hearne, Pyramid Art Books, 1001 Wright Avenue, Suite C, Little Rock, Arkansas 72206 Phone: (501) 372-5824 E-mail: pyramid@aristotle.net

RealEyes Bookstore 2424 North Davidson Street, Suite 112A, North Carolina 28205 Phone: (704) 377-8989 E-mail: jaz@redat28th.com Website: www.redat28th.com

The Shrine Bookstore Bookstore, 3 locations. The Shrine Bookstore, 13535 Livernois Avenue, Detroit, Michigan 48238 Phone: (313) 491-0777 Website: www.shrinebookstore.com

Sister's Uptown Bookstore African centered, homework help, lectures, internet, at 156th Street. Sisters Uptown Bookstore, 1942 Amsterdam Avenue, Harlem, New York 10032 Phone: (212) 862-3680 E-mail: sistersuptownbookstore@yahoo.com

Smiley's Bookstore Bookseller. Mecca of Information. Contact Smiley's Bookstore, 20220 South Avalon Boulevard, Suite A, Carson, California 90746 Phone: (310) 324-8444

Soul On Wheels Books Online retailer. Kenny, Soul On Wheels Books, 294 Sumpter Street, #2F, Brooklyn, New York 11233 Phone: (718) 453-6017 E-mail: soulonwheels@optonline.net Website: www.soulonwheels.com

TimBookTu On-line bookseller. Memphis Vaughan, Jr., TimBookTu, Post Office Box 933, Mobile, Alabama 36601 E-mail: editor@TimBookTu.com Website: www.TimBookTu.com

Tree of Life Bookstore of Harlem Kanya Vashon McGhee Founder. Tree of Life Bookstore of Harlem, 1701 Martin.Luther King Drive SW, Atlanta, Georgia 30314 Phone: (404) 753-5700 E-mail: drkanya9@hotmail.com Website: http://www.naturalusa.com/ads/treeoflife.html

Truth Bookstore African American books and Booksignings. Located in the Northland Mall, Store 779. Truth Bookstore, 21500 Northwestern Highway, Southfield, Michigan 48075 Phone: (248) 557-4824 E-mail: truthbookstore@sbcglobal.net

Umoja Books & Products Wednesday thru Friday 12:00 p.m. - 6:00 p.m., Saturday 10 a.m. - 5 p.m. Asante Sana, Umoja Books & Products, 1006 Surrey Street, Lafayette, Lousiana 70501 Phone: (337) 593-8665 E-mail: gjm3768@louisiana.edu Website: www.umojabookstore.com

The Underground Bookstore A treasure trove of books await readers in this eclectic bookstore. Hours: 11:00 a.m.- 7:00 p.m. Monday thru Saturday; closed Sunday. The Underground Bookstore, 1727 East 87th Street, Chicago, Illinois 60617 Phone: (773) 768-8869

Underground Railroad Reading Station Bookstore Hours: Monday: Closed Tuesday, Thursday and Friday 5:30 p.m. to 8 p.m., Saturday: 10 a.m. to 3 p.m., Sunday: 12:30 p.m. to 3 p.m. Underground Railroad Reading Station Bookstore, 461 Monroe Avenue, Detroit, Michigan 48226 Phone: (313) 961-0325 Fax: (313) 961-0444 E-mail: ugrrbook@aol.com

Zawadi Books, Inc. North America's largest seller of black themed books. Tressa Sanders, Publisher. Zawadi Books, Inc., 2017 Maryland Avenue, Columbus, Ohio 43219 Phone: (614) 327-7131

Columnists

Stacy Hawkins Adams Professional journalist and speaker, Stacy is a nationally acclaimed author of several Christian fiction novels "Watercolored Pearls," "Nothing But the Right Thing" and her book "Speak To My Heart," was voted 2004 Best New Multicultural Christian Fiction, Stacy Hawkins Adams, Post Office Box 25985, Richmond, Virginia 23260 Phone: (804) 768-1292 E-mail: stacy@stacyhawkinsadams.com Website: www.stacyhawkinsadams.com

Keith Alexander Reporter. Keith Alexander, The Washington Post, 1150 15th Street, North West, Washington, DC 20071 Phone: (202) 334-7796 E-mail: Alexanderk@washpost.com Website: www.washpost.com

Tracy Allen Journalist, writer and reporter. Contact Ms. Tracy Allen, Kansas City Call, 1715 East 18th Street, Kansas City, Missouri 64108 E-mail: tracyKccall@hotmail.com

Florence Anthony The host of the daily radio feature "Gossip To Go With Flo" syndicated by Jones Radio Network, "Flo," is also the President/Editor-In-Chief of Black Elegance Magazine, which boasts a national circulation of 200,000 and writes a weekly column called "Go With the Flo" in the New York Amsterdam News, Philadelphia Sunday Sun, BRE and Dallas Examiner. Flo's daily radio feature is in 30 markets which include WJLB Detroit, K-104 Dallas, WAMO Pittsburgh, KMEZ New Orleans and V101.9 Charlotte. A graduate of Howard University, with post-graduate studies at the University of Michigan and Northwestern University, Flo was the first African-American woman to work in the sports and entertainment departments at the New York Post, and the first African-American woman in the nation to work on a gossip page: the Post's highly revered Page Six. When she left the New York Post, she became the first African-American woman to write a column for a tabloid. She headed up the Eye on the Stars column in the National Examiner from 1994-2001. Florence Anthony, Black Noir Magazine, 100 Park Avenue South, Suite 1600, New York, New York 10017 Phone: (201) 408-4306 E-mail: communications@floanthonysblacknoir.comWebsite: www.florenceanthonysblacknoir.com

Jabari Asim Author, columnist, and Deputy Editor of Washington Post Book World. Jbari Asim, 1150 15th Street, North West, Washington, DC 20071 E-mail: asimj@washpost.com Website: www.washingtonpost.com

Alicia Banks Columnist, renowned radio personality, radio producer, host, educator, scholar, rebel public intellectual. Contact Alicia Banks, Post Office Box 55596, Little Rock, Arkansas 72215 E-mail: ambwww@yahoo.com Website: http://aliciabanks.xanga.com

Rose Jackson-Beavers Columnist, Ms. Beavers currently writes as a columnist for the Spanish Word, a local community newspaper. Rose Jackson-Beavers, Post Office Box 2535, Florissant, Missouri 63032 Phone: (314) 741-6789 E-mail: rosbeav03@yahoo.com

Edith Billups Free-lance writer for The Black-owned Washington Informer Newspaper. Reviews theater, music and film and also writes regularly for a travel column, "Pack Your Bags." Ms. Edith Billips, The Gabriel Group, 8720 Georgia Avenue, Suite 906, Silver Spring, Maryland 20910 E-mail: eybillups@aol.com

Aminisha Black Columnist, two columns, The Parents Notebook in Our Time Press newspaper, and Spirited Parent in Single Parent: Raising our Children news magazine. Aminisha Black, Post Office Box 755, Brooklyn, New York 11238 E-mail: parentsnotebook@yahoo.com

Jennifer Elaine Black A writer for Gatekeeper magazine and Virtuous Woman magazine. Also author of several poetry books, speaker and instructor. She teaches writing, and music workshops. Jennifer Black, Post Office Box 56394, Little Rock, Arkansas 72215 Phone: (501) 859-0841 E-mail: booking@thepropheticartist.com

Herb Boyd An award-winning journalist, and author of nine books, including Brotherman: The Odyssey of Black Men in America, an anthology that he co-edited with Robert Allen which received the 1995 American Book Award. Currently teaches at College of New Rochelle in Manhattan. Herb Boyd, Post Office Box #328, Randallstown, Maryland, 21133 Phone: (410) 659-8298 Fax: (410) 521-9993 E-mail: herbboyd47@gmail.com

Donna L. Brazile Weekly contributor and political commentator on CNN's Inside Politics and American Morning. Also columnist for Roll Call Newspaper. Appears regularly on MSNBC's Hardball and Fox's Hannity and Colmes. Donna Braziles, Post Office Box 15369, Washington, DC 20003 E-mail: info@brazileassociates.com Website: www.brazileassociates.com

Crystal C. Brown Freelance journalist and published author. CEO and President of Crystal Clear Communications, an award winning public relations and marketing firm. Crystal C. Brown, 2470 South Dairy Ashford #252, Houston, Texas 77077 Phone: (281) 589-2007 E-mail: cbrown5530@aol.com Website: www.crystalcommunicates.com

Luther Brown, Jr. Author, editor, reporter and producer. B.S. in English, North Carolina A&T State University (1969) where he became the school's first Woodrow Wilson Fellow. Has juris doctorate degree from Georgetown University (1988). He attended graduate school at Rutgers University before going to work for CBS News in 1972. Later he moved to NBC News. Luther Brown, Jr., 918 14th Street, South East, Washington, DC 20003 E-mail: nikmar@pacbell.net

Vonetta Booker Brown An accomplished journalist and writer who has contributed to various publications including Stamford Advocate, Fairfield County Weekly, New Haven Register, MediaBistro.com, HealthQuest, Essence, Vibe, Honey and XXL. Vonetta Brown, Right Hand Concepts, 2020 Pennsylvania Avenue, North West, #341, Washington, DC 20006 Phone: (203) 816-0918 E-mail: vonetta@righthandconcepts.com Website: www.righthandconcepts.com

Lisa-Anne Ray-Byers Licensed and certified speech-language pathologist, and educational consultant her column appears in four local newspapers throughout New York. Lisa-Anne Ray-Byers, 41 East Woodbine Drive, Freeport, New York 11520 Phone: (516) 770-2972 E-mail: speechlrb@yahoo.com Website: www.asklisaanne.com

Monica P. Carter Seasoned writer, with nearly 10 years of professional writing experience and a most sought after speaker and award winning columnist for The Times newspaper in Shreveport, Louisiana. Author, freelancer, she conducts publishing and writing workshops. Monica Carter, RootSky Publishing, Post Office Box 52482, Shreveport, Louisiana 71115 Phone: (318) 617-3267

TonyaSue Carther Associate editor, romance columnist, movie / DVD review specialist and book editor of Black Noir Magazine. TonyaSue Carther, Black Noir Magazine, 100 Park Avenue South, Suite 1600, New York, New York 10017 Phone: (201) 408-4306 E-mail: **communications@floanthonysblacknoir.com** Website: **www.florenceanthonysblacknoir.com**

Mamadou Chinyelu Working journalist since 1977. Contact Mamadou Chinyelu, Post Office Box 32406 Charleston, South Carolina 29417 E-mail: **mchinyelu99@hotmail.com**

Rick Christie Assistant Managing Editor. Palm Beach Post, Post Office Box 24700, West Palm Beach, Florida 33416 Phone: (561) 820-4476 E-mail: **rchristie@pbpost.com**

Denise Clay Education Writer. Denise Clay, The Bucks County Courier Times, 8400 Route 13, Levittown, Pennsylvania 19057 Phone: (215) 949-4195 E-mail: **dclay@phillyBurbs.com**

Ben Clement Author, playwright, journalist, and screenwriter. Ben Clement, Miracle Hands Productions, 2929 West 24th Place, Gary, Indiana 46404 Phone: (219) 944-1201 Fax: (219) 944-1202 E-mail: **ben_clement_99@yahoo.com**

Floyd A. Cray Writes a Holy CD review column monthly for The Tri State Voice Christian Newspaper. Floyd is also alternative Gospel music director at 89.1 WFDU-FM. Contact Floyd A. Cray III, Gospel Vibrations Inc, 114 Shepard Avenue, Teaneck, New Jersey 07666 Phone: (201) 833-0694 E-mail: **GospelVibrations@aol.com** Website: **www.wfdu.fm**

E-K. Daufin Writer. E.K. Daufin, 915 S. Jackson Street Montgomery, Alabama 36101 Phone: (334) 229-6885 E-mail: **ekdaufin@alasu.edu**

Wayne Dawkins Author of Black Journalists: The NABJ Story (August Press) Also editor of the Black Alumni Network Newsletter. Contact Wayne Dawkins, August Press, Post Office Box 6693, Newport News, Virginia 23606 Phone: (757) 727-5437 **wdawkins4bj@aol.com** Website: **www.augustpress.net**

Anita Davis-DeFoe Author, journalist, and television host of caribbeanwomentoday, a segment on Caribbean Weekly; an informational and community affairs program produced by the Duke of Earle Media Group (Florida/Jamaica). Dr. DeFoe is also resident advice guru for She-Caribbean, a St. Lucian magazine that is sold in 16 islands, New York, Atlanta, New Jersey, South Florida, Canada and London. Her articles have appeared in the Saturday Edition (Miami) Carib Life (New York), and others. Anita Davis-DeFoe, She Advice Guru-Straight Talk Column, Contributing Writer, The Mobay Group, Contact Dr. Anita DeFoe, The Defoe Group, Post Office Box 451973, Sunrise, Florida 33345 Phone: (954) 816-9462 E-mail: **dranitadavisdefoe@hotmail.com** Website: **www.dranitadavisdefoe.com**

Eric Deggans Writer. Contact Mr. Eric Deggans, The Saint Petersburg Times, 490 1ˢᵗ Avenue, South, Saint Petersburg, Florida 33701 Phone: (727) 893-8521 Fax: (727) 892-2327 E-mail: **deggans@sptimes.com**

Angela P. Dodson Free-lance editor and writer for magazines, online services, individual authors and book publishers. She is a senior editor of NeWorld Review, a literary magazine and blog and an online editor for DIVERSE Issues in Higher Education. She is the former executive editor of Black Issues Book Review and has been a journalist for more than 30 years. She is a former senior editor and Style editor for the New York Times magazine. She has also done writing and editing for various other magazines and newspapers. She has been a consultant, instructor in media studies and public speaking and is the host of a weekly radio program about black Roman Catholics. Angela P. Dodson, 324 Hamilton Avenue, Trenton, New Jersey 08609 Phone: (609) 394-7632 Fax: (609) 396-7808 E-mail: **angela4bibr@aol.com**

Karen Dumas Newspaper columnist and respected local radio & television personality, she is also president of her own PR firm, Images & Ideas, Inc. She formerly served as Director of Culture, Art & Tourism for the City of Detroit, which included the Detroit Film Office and Eastern Market, and as Director of Community Relations for Mayor Kwame M. Kilpatrick. Dumas graduated from Michigan State University where she received a Bachelor of Science degree from Michigan State University. Karen Dumas, Images & Ideas, Inc., Post Office Box 14724, Detroit, Michigan 48214 Phone: (866) 330-4585 Fax: (313) 824-6987 E-mail: **karendumas2@aol.com** Website: **www.KarenDumas.com**

Ervin Dyer Staff Reporter. Contact Mr. Ervin Dyer, Pittsburgh Post-Gazette, 34 Boulevard of the Allies, Pittsburgh, Pennsylvania, 15222 Phone: (412) 263-1410 Fax: (412) 263-1706 E-mail: **edyer@post-gazette.com**

Deborah Gabriel A multi-skilled journalist with international experience in the UK, Jamaica and Africa, across the mediums of print, TV, radio and online. She is currently the editor of an online news publication and founder and director of Imani Media Ltd, an organization that works closely with social enterprises and voluntary organizations. Contact Ms. Deborah Gabriel, Imani Media Ltd, (Registered Office) 2nd Floor, 145-157 Saint John Street, London EC1V 4PY E-mail: **deborahgabriel@layersofblackness.com** Website: **www.imani-media.com**

Daniel Garrett Writer of journalism, fiction, poetry, and drama and essays that focus on international cultures, philosophy, history, and politics. He has edited music interviews for I/Propaganda. He selected poetry for the male feminist magazine Changing Men. His own poetry has been published by AIM/America's Intercultural Magazine. Mr. Daniel Garrett, 05-63 135ᵗʰ Street, Richmond Hill, New York 11419 E-mail: **dgarrett31@hotmail.com**

Michelle R. Gipson Publisher of Written Magazine, the former Director of Advertising for Black Issues Book Review, and Managing Editor of the Atlanta Daily World's Celebration of Books. Earned her B.A. in Mass Media, and her M.A. in Counseling from Hampton University. Published in Jane, the Atlanta Daily World, and Chicken Soup for the African American Soul. Michelle R. Gipson, Written Magazine, Post Office Box 250504, Atlanta, Georgia 30310 Phone: (404) 753-8315 E-mail: **michelle.gipson@writtenmag.com** Website: **www.writtenmag.com**

C.D. Grant Journalist, essayist, photographer, poet and short story writer, nationally published since 1970, Essence Magazine, Soul, etc. Mr. Grant is co-founder of Blind Beggar Press, based in the Bronx in New York City, since 1977. Blind Beggar Press publishes people of colour. Also a TV show host, Mr. Grant interviews authors, and other guests. C.D. Grant, Publisher, Blind Beggar Press, Post Office Box 437, Bronx, New York 10467 Phone: (914) 282-5747 E-mail: blindbeggar1@juno.com Website: www.blindbeggarpress.org

Vanessa Davis Griggs Author and columnists she pens a column A Peace of My Mind and periodically writes articles for various magazines and newspapers. She is the recipient of numerous recognitions including The Greater Birmingham Millennium Section National Council of Negro Women Inspiration Award (2006). Contact Ms. Vanessa Davis Griggs, Post Office Box 101328, Birmingham, Alabama 35210 E-mail: Vanessa@VanessaDavisGriggs.com Website: www.vanessaDavisGriggs.com

Bernice L. Guity Seasoned award winning journalist reporter and writer, Guity has written numerous front-page stories on issues involving education, health care, real estate, social services and manufacturing for the New York Times Newspaper Group, Knight-Ridder Newspapers, and American City Business Journals. Bernice L. Guity, P & G Communications, Inc., Post Office Box 715, Avondale Estates, Georgia 30002 Phone: (404) 298-7799 Fax: (404) 298-0059 E-mail: pgcommuns@aol.com

Nathasha Brooks Harris Editor of Black Romance and Bronze Thrills magazines. Co-owner of Write On! Literary Consortium, a literary consulting services. Ms. Natasha Brooks Harris, 297 7th Street, Brooklyn, New York 11215 E-mail: nabrooks@aol.com

Adele Hodge A seasoned media communications professional with a solid reputation for strong people management skills Hodge started her television career at WXYZ-TV/ABC in Detroit. She moved to the NBC-TV affiliate, before taking a position as newswriter-producer at the NBC owned and operated WMAQ-TV in Chicago. Adele Hodge, Post Office Box 3584, Phoeniz, Arizona 85030 Phone: (602) 274-7842 E-mail: writers@earthlink.net

Earl Ofari Hutchinson Nationally acclaimed author and journalist, his writings have appeared in such publications as the Los Angeles Times, Ebony, Newsday, Black Scholar, Los Angeles Herald, Harpers and many others. He is a radio host and TV commentator and has received numerous awards for his writings. Dr. Earl Ofari Hutchinson, Hutchinson Communications, 614 East Manchester Boulevard, Suite 204, Inglewood, California 90301 Phone: (323) 296-6331 E-mail: ehutchinson@thehutchinsonreport.com Website: www.thehutchinsonreport.com

Kevin Wayne Johnson Columnist, The Joys of Fatherhood, for The Church Guide of Detroit, Kevin is author of a nine-book series entitled Give God the Glory! Kevin Wayne Johnson, Writing for the Lord Ministries, 6400 Shannon Court, Clarksville, Maryland 21029 Phone: (410) 340-8633 E-mail: kevin@writingforthelord.com Website: www.writingforthelord.com

Tonisha Johnson New York freelance writer, editor and publisher of Gesica Magazine. Tonisha Johnson, Gesica Magazine, Post Office. Box 30231, Staten Island, New York 10303 Phone: (718) 216-3530 E-mail: TonishaJohnson@gmail.com Website: www.gesicaonline.com

Jusbee Jones Worked with professional athletes for over fifteen years in the capacity of sports public relations and marketing. Jones is currently President of a sports entertainment publicity firm and contributes to a monthly sports entertainment column. She is author of Confessions of the Twelfth Man: A Different Game Played Off The Field. Under the pseudonym of Jusbee Jones, sports publicist LaShirl Smith has been associated with sports most of her life. Contact Jusbee Jones, Adnor Books, 15030 Ventura Boulevard, Suite 525, Sherman Oaks, California 91403 E-mail: JusbeeJones@aol.com Website: www.confessionsofthe12thman.com

Marsha Jones A graduate of Purdue University, her works have appeared in such regional publications as about..time magazine, Rochester Business Magazine, and her weekly 411 column in The Buffalo Challenger. Jones has interviewed such notables as filmmaker Spike Lee, poets Nikki Giovanni and Sonia Sanchez, musicians Miriam Makeba, and Wynton, Branford, and Ellis Marsalis, authors Maya Angelou and Antowne Fisher, comedians Bernie Mac and Chris Rock, and actors Malik Yoba and Danny Glover. Marsha Jones, 411 Communications, 97 Culver Parkway, Rochester, New York 14609 E-mail: defdefyingmj@yahoo.com

Eugene Kane Journalist. Writer/ columnist. Contact Mr. Eugene Kane, Milwaukee Journal-Sentinel, 333 West State Street, Milwaukee, Wisconsin 53201 Phone: (414) 223-5521 E-mail: ekane@journalsentinel.com Website: www.journalsentinel.com

Tanya Kersey As one of Hollywood's most respected and well-regarded entertainment journalists and commentators, Tanya has her finger on the pulse of what's happening in the world of urban entertainment. She has developed and earned a reputation for covering the entertainment industry, focusing on celebrities, film, television, music, fashion, award shows, special events and the business of entertainment in a trend-setting, groundbreaking format. She is perhaps best known as the Founder, Publisher and Editor-in-Chief of the online entertainment trade publication, BlackTalentNews.com, and as the Founder the Hollywood Black Film Festival. Tanya Kersey, 8306 Wilshire Boulevard, Suite 2057, Beverly Hills, California 90211 Phone: (310) 203-1336 E-mail: tanya@tanyakersey.com Website: www.tanyakersey.com

Russell LaCour Journalist. Copy Editor. Contact Mr. Russell LaCour, Tulsa World, 315 South Boulder Avenue, Tulsa, Oklahoma 74103 Phone: (918) 581-8327 Fax: (918) 581-8353 E-mail: russell.lacour@tulsaworld.com

Matthew Lynch An author, Mr. Lynch is also a contributing columnist for the Mississippi Link, and Emerging Minds, an online magazine devoted to uplifting the African American community. Mr. Lynch is founder of Project E.P.I.P.H.A.N.Y, a research based mentoring program. Contact Matthew Lynch, 2324 Princess Pine Drive, Jackson, Mississippi 39212 Phone: (601) 373-1552 E-mail: lynch39083@aol.com

Beverly Mahone Veteran journalist who has spent more than 25 years in radio and television. The Ohio University graduate established her own media coaching and consulting business called Soul Solutions/Talk2Bev. She also has a radio talk show. Listen to her live every Thursday at 1 p.m. on 105.3 FM WCOM Radio in Carrboro, North Carolina. Beverly Mahone, Post Office Box 11037, Durham, North Carolina 27703 Phone: (301) 356-6280 E-mail: beverly@talk2bev.com Website: www.beverlymahone.com

Julianne Malveaux As a writer and columnist, her work appears regularly in USA Today, Black Issues in Higher Education, Ms. Magazine, Essence magazine, and the Progressive among others. Well-known for her appearances on national network programs, Dr. Malveaux is a popular guest on CNN. Dr. Julianne Malveaux, Last Word Productions, 1318 Corcoran Street, North West, Washington, DC 20009 Phone: (202) 462-1932 E-mail: info@lastwordprod.com Website: www.juliannemalveaux.com

Roland S. Martin Nationally award winning journalist. Syndicated columnist with Creators Syndicate, founding editor of BlackAmericaweb.com, and a frequent commentator on TV-One, CNN, MSNBC, FOX, and Black Entertainment Television (BET). Roland S. Martin, NuVision Media, Inc., 1327 West Washington Boulevard #102B, Chicago, Illinois 60607   Phone: (312) 543-6000 E-mail: roland@rolandsmartin.com Website: www.rolandsmartin.com

Edward W. Mays Writer. CBORD/Accounts Payable Coordinator, Evans Hall, Washington and Lee University, Lexington, Virginia 24450 Phone: (540) 458-8072 Fax: (540) 458-8074 E-mail: mayse@wlu.edu

Rych McCain Author of the book Black Afrikan Hair and The Insanity of the Black Blonde Psych!, Mr. Rych McCain is an international/nationally syndicated Urban Entertainment Newspaper/Magazine Columnist with 3.5 Million readers. His interviews and print features reads like a who's who of the urban film, TV, stage and recording arenas. His print features and famous photo spreads include Hollywood Red Carpet Movie Premieres, Major Awards Shows, and Press Junkets. Rych McCain, Post Office Box 2272, Beverly Hills, California 90213 Phone: (213) 387-3493 E-mail: rychmccain@sbcglobal.net

Sylvia McClain Contributing writer for Equal Opportunity Publications, Inc, Ms. McClain formerly wrote a weekly column, "Sylvia Speaks" for the Dearborn Press & Guide. She has been featured in the Writer's Digest magazine on-line "Speak Out" section as well as Writer's Digest Writer's Yearbook extra. Guest columnist and contributing writer for the Michigan Chronicle and regularly quoted in The Detroit Free Press and Detroit News as a subject matter expert. Sylvia McClain, 6896 Lakeview Blvd., Apt 20203, Westland, Michigan 48185, Phone: (734) 326-3341 E-mail: sylmcclain@juno.com Website: www.scribalpress.com

Cedric McClester Award winning journalist and author, Cedric wrote, Kwanzaa, Everything You Always Wanted To Know, But Didn't Know Where To Ask, and his latest childrens book, The Legend of Nia Umoja. He is a prolific lyricist who has written over a thousand songs. Has a Masters of Science in Education degree and has written for national and international publications, including the New York Times and the Daily News. Cedric McClester, 1966 First Ave. # 12-K, New York, New York 10029 E-mail: Gandpadamis@aol.com

Jacquelin Salvatto McCord A muti-talented individual with a varied professional background: Naprapath, Educator and Writer, McCord-Harris is the author and publisher of four books and a contributing writer for several magazines, newspapers and books. She conducts workshops for teachers and parents to promote literacy in homes and early childhood centers. Jacquelin S. McCord, Post Office Box 167054, Chicago, Illinois 60616 Phone: (733) 363-6613 Fax: (773) 363-6650 E-mail: jsmc45@aol.com Website: www.jsmccord.com

Sharon K. McGhee Award-winning radio personality and former news director for radio at WVON, Sharon hosted the top rated morning talk show, "Good Morning St. Louis," for five years WVON. Sharon won the prestigious AIR Award on KATZ radio for a series on the death of Emmitt Till. Sharon won the prestigious AIR Award for a five-part series on Breast Cancer. She also launched the first WVON book club, "Between the Covers." Her professional affiliations include, the Association of Black Journalists (ABJ), the Chicago Chapter of the Urban League, and she participates in the yearly Cook County Annual Youth Summit. Contact Sharon K. McGhee, WVON 1690AM, 3350 South Kedzie, Chicago, Illinois 60623 Phone: (773) 247-6200 E-mail: Sharon@wvon.com Website: www.wvon.com

Dorma McGruder A columnist for two years for Detroit Legacy News and the Michigan Chronicle, Dorma is a gifted, national public speaker since the age of four addressing crowds from 10 to 10,000 in political, educational, social and religious venues. She has also completed her first novel, entitled 'I Had No Choice' the truthful fiction story of her life. Contact Ms. Dorma McGruder, Post Office Box 44615, Detroit, MI 48244 Phone: (313) 205-0600 Fax: (313) 531-9141 E-mail: dorma@dormamcgruder.com Website: www.dormamcgruder.com

Michelle Mellon Freelance writer and editor and has had articles published in Imprint and Blue Planet Quarterly, poetry in journals, and anthologies such as Hodgepodge, and Seasons of the Heart, and was co-author of a book chapter on professional mentoring. Contact Ms. Michelle Mellon, 2416 Casa Way, Walnut Creek, California 94597 Phone: (925) 937-1947 E-mail: michelle@mpmellon.com Website: www.mpmellon.com

Denise Meridith A New York City native Ms. Meridith has a BS from Cornell University and a MPA from the University of Southern California. She was the first female professional hired by the US Bureau of Land Management, a natural resource agency, and went on to an illustrious 29 career that took her to six states and the District of Columbia, where she served as the Deputy Director of the agency of 200 offices and 10,000 employees. She retired early in 2002 and has her own public and community relations firm. Since 1998, she has been a regular columnist with the Phoenix Business Journal and was a finalist in the 2004 National Association of Black Journalists' excellence awards. Denise Meridith Consultants Inc, 5515 North 7th Street, Suite 5, Phoenix, Arizona 85014 Phone: (602) 763-9900 E-mail: denisemeridithconsultants@cox.net Website: www.denisemeridithconsultants.com

S. Renee Mitchell M.B.A. Award-winning writer, playwright, spoken word recording artist, author, novelist, empowerment speaker. Renee is a former award-winning newspaper columnist who was nominated twice for the prestigious Pulitzer Prize. She also is a powerful public speaker, who uses poetry and personal experiences to bring audiences to their feet, as well as touch their hearts. Renee, a survivor of domestic violence and sexual assault, experienced decades of low self-esteem and feelings of unworthiness. Her tireless and creative work to support other survivors of domestic violence resulted in her being selected as one of 2006's 21 Leaders of the 21st Century by New York City-based Women eNews, which bestowed Renee with the international Ida B. Wells Award for Bravery in Journalism. Renee also teaches writing workshops. Renee Mitchell Speaks LLC, 6835 South West Capitol Hill Road #34, Portland, Oregon 97219 Phone: (503) 278-8280 E-mail: reneemitchellspeaks@yahoo.com Website: http://www.myppk.com/go/reneemitchellspeaks.aspx

Melissa Monroe Reporter/Writer. Contact Melissa Monroe, San Antonio Express-News, Post Office Box 2171, San Antonio, Texas 78297 Phone: (210) 250-3329 Fax: (210) 250-3232 E-mail: **mmonroe@express-news.net**

Spencer Moon Authored articles published by: American Writer: Journal of the National Writers Union; Cinezine; Release Print; Media Review; Black Film Bulletin of the British Film Institute 1980 - Now. Co-authored, co-published, co-marketed with George Hill, PhD, Blacks in Hollywood: Five Favorable Years, 1987-1991 (Daystar Press, Los Angeles, California 1991). Authored - Reel Black Talk: A Sourcebook of 50 American Filmmakers (Greenwood Press, Westport, Connecticut, 1997}. Education: Master of Arts, Film & Television Production, Columbia Pacific University, San Rafael, California. Bachelor of Arts, Filmmaking, Antioch College, San Francisco, California program. Awards: Service Award, 1984; Media Award, 1997; Lifetime Member Award, 1997. Contact Mr. Spencer Moon, Post Office Box 4510, Atlanta, Georgia 30302 E-mail: **moonrye@aol.com**

Toi Moore Freelance writer for publications such as Billboard, Upscale, The Cause and Saludos Hispanos Magazines to name a few, where she has over 200 published articles in various newspaper and magazines throughout the United States and Canada. Author, Toi has written several short stories, four novels and two screenplays and published her own magazine titled "Mini Romances." Toi also has several bylines to her credit in which she has authored and interviewed a variety of well-known celebrities such as: Oprah Winfrey, Laila Ali, Patti LaBelle, and Jaheim, to name a small few. Toi Moore, Post Office Box 2099, Sun City, California 92586 Phone: (951) 231-1633 E-mail: **toimoore@aol.com** Website: **www.toimoore.com**

Shanté Morgan Writer, editor, educator, and founder of Morgan Communications, a full-service communications company. She is also currently editor of Turning Point Magazine, freelances as a copyeditor and proofreader. also worked as a college instructor teaching journalism. Shanté Morgan, 1710 North Moorpark Road #163, Thousand Oaks, California 91360 Phone: 310-594-9890 E-mail: **ShanteMorgan@aol.com**

Maidstone Mulenga Global Editor. Contact Maidstone Mulenga, Democrat and Chronicle, 55 Exchange Boulevard, Rochester, New York 14614 E-mail: **bamulenga@aol.com**

Daphne Muse Writer, her commentaries and radio essays have been featured on KTOP-FM, KPFA-FM, KQED-FM and NPR. A New Frontiers Radio Essayist, her social commentaries have been published in major newspapers and air on public radio and commercial stations across the country. Daphne Muse, 2429 East 23rd Street, Oakland, California 94601 Phone: (510) 436-4716 E-mail: **msmusewriter@gmail.com** Website: **www.oasisinthediaspora.com**

The Salim Muwakkil Show Saturday 7pm - 10pm. Host, Salim Muwakkil is a Senior Editor of In These Times, and an op-ed columnist for the Chicago Tribune. He is currently a Crime and Communities Media Fellow of the Open Society Institute, examining the impact of ex-inmates and gang leaders in leadership positions in the black community. He is a faculty member of the Associated Colleges of the Midwest's Urban Studies Program, and a former adjunct professor at Columbia College, Northwestern University's Medill School of Journalism and the School of the Art Institute of Chicago. Mr. Salim Muwakkil, WVON 1450AM, 3350 South Kedzie, Chicago, Illinois 60623 Phone: (773) 247-6200 E-mail: **salim4x@aol.com** Website: **www.wvon.com**

Darren Nichols Reporter. Darren Nichols, Detroit News, 615 West Lafayette Avenue, Detroit, Michigan 48226 Phone: (734) 462-2190 Fax: (734) 462-6771 E-mail: **dnichols@detnews.com** Website: **www.detnews.com**

Greg Patterson Editor. Reporter. Contact Greg Patterson, Star Tribune, 425 Portland Avenue, Minneapolis, Minnesota 55488 Phone: (612) 673-7287 E-mail: **gpatterson@startribune.com**

Winona Rasheed Freelance writer and editor. Also a childrens book author, Winona has written 6 books. Winona Rasheed, 2426 Otis Street, North East, Washington DC 20018 Phone: (202) 635-3588 E-mail: **rasheedwinona@yahoo.com** Website: **www.winonarasheed.com**

William Raspberry Washington-based urban and minority affairs columnist, and Pulitzer-prize winning Journalist. William Raspberry, The Washington Post, 1150 15th Street, North West, Washington, DC 20071 Phone: (202) 334-6000 E-mail: **willrasp@washpost.com**

Rashida Rawls Copy Editor/Designer. Rashida Rawls, The Macon Telegraph, 120 Broadway, Macon, Georgia 31201 Phone: (478) 744-4420 E-mail: **miss_rawls19@hotmail.com**

Barbara A. Reynolds Author and an award winning journalist, her syndicated newspapers columns have reached an estimated 10 million people weekly. She has appeared on such major television shows as the "Oprah Winfrey Show," "Politically Incorrect," and "CNN." Dr. Barbara A. Reynolds, JFJ Publishing, 4806 Saint Barnabas Road, Suite 598, Temple Hills, Maryland 20757 Phone: (301) 899-1341 E-mail: **reynew@aol.com** Website: **www.reynoldsnews.com**

Eric L. Robinson Black Tokyo webmaster and site owner, Eric L. Robinson (Zurui) is a Detroit, Michigan native and has lived and worked in Asia for about two decades. Having spent a little over 16-years in Japan, his Black Tokyo blog posts have been mentioned on CNN, CNN Political Blog, France 24, The Guardian, The Huffington Post, The Japan Times and others. Robinson earned a Bachelor of Science degree from the University of the State of New York, diplomas from the Defense Language Institute-Foreign Language Center in Basic and Intermediate Korean language, and is completing a Master of Arts in National Security Affairs. Eric L. Robinson, Black Tokyo, 3-16-1-2 Takada, Toshima-ku, Tokyo 117-0033 Phone: 011-81-902-338-4435 E-mail: **info@blacktokyo.com** Website: **www.blacktokyo.com**

Wanda Sabir Columnist and Arts Editor, at the San Francisco Bay View Newspaper. Contact Ms. Wanda Sabir, Post Office Box 30756, Oakland, California 94604 Phone: (510) 261-8436 E-mail: **wsab1@aol.com** Website: **www.wandaspicks.com**

Yolanda Brunson-Sarrabo Along with writing The Ins and Outs of the Fashion Industry she also co-writes a popular monthly newsletter, The Laundry Source. Contact Ms. Yolanda Brunson-Sarrabo, Spitfir Productions,1454 Rockaway Parkway, Brooklyn, New York 11236 E-mail: **blackwriternew@yahoo.com** Website: **www.ybrunson.com**

Matthew Scott Personal Finance Editor. Contact Matthew Scott, Black Enterprise Magazine, 130 Fifth Avenue, New York, New York 10011 Phone: (212) 886-9589 Fax: (212) 886-9610 E-mail: **scottm@blackenterprise.com**

Terence Shepherd   Weekend Business Editor, The Miami Herald. Terence Shepherd, The Miami Herald, One Herald Plaza, Miami, Florida 33132 Phone: (305) 376-3596 Phone: (954) 764-7026 E-mail: tshepherd@herald.com

Stan Simpson   Columnist. Stan Simpson is host of The Stan Simpson Show, an entertaining and insightful current affairs talk show that can been seen 24/7 or Saturdays at 6:30 a.m. on Fox CT. Stan Simpson, The Hartford Courant, 285 Broad Street, Hartford, Connecticut 06115 Phone: (860) 241-6521 E-mail: stansimpson@comcast.net Website: www.ctnow.com/stan

Ken Smikle   President and founder of Target Market News, and editor and publisher of its publications, is considered one of the leading authorities on marketing, advertising and media directed to the African-American market. Contact Mr. Ken Smikle, Tarket Market News, 228 South Wabash Avenue, Suite 210, Chicago, Illinois 60604 Phone: (312) 408-1881 E-mail: info@tarketmarketnews.com Website: www.targetmarketnews.com

Erma Somerville   Wrote Negotiating For Love, also wrote short stories in Black Romance magazines for Sterling MacFadden publications. Erma Somerville, 2000 Lee Road, Suite 100, Cleveland Heights, Ohio 44118 Fax: (216) 397-0645 E-mail: Lermaj@aol.com

Larry D. Starks   Sports Editor, St. Louis Post-Dispatch, 900 North Tucker Boulevard, Saint Louis, Missouri 63101 Phone: (314) 340-8000 E-mail: lstarks@post-dispatch.com Website: www.post-dispatch.com

Torrance Stephens   Currently, senior Op-Ed writer for Rolling Out Urban weekly. His work has appeared in print and publications such as NOMMO, Creative Loafing, Rolling Out, Talking Drum, the North Avenue Review and other periodicals. He graduated from Hamilton High School in Memphis and attended Morehouse College where he studied, psychology, biology and chemistry. Torrance Stephens, Post Office Box 1331, Palmetto, Georgia 30268 E-mail: torrance_stephens@yahoo.com

Lisa St. Hill   Author and entertainment fashion and beauty writer for Jolie Magazine, Ms. Hill's debut book is Revenge of the Celebrity Assistant (2010). Lisa St. Hill, 28 Hazelplace, Irvington, New Jersey 07111 Phone: (718) 812-1327 E-mail: Lisa_sthill@yahoo.com

Robert Taylor   Journalist. Editor of the online digital newspaper: The National Black News Journal, and the Black History Journal - a weekly email-distributed journal detailing the most important Black historical events of each week. Taylor earned his Masters Degree in Mass Communications from Columbia University in New York City. Robert Taylor, Taylor Media Services, 1517 T Street, South East, Washington, D.C. 20020 Phone: (202) 657-8872 E-mail: taylormediaservices@yahoo.com Website: www.freewebs.com/blacknewsjournal

Juanita Torrence-Thompson   a nationally acclaimed poet, author, and freelance writer publishes a weekly poetry column in The Culvert Chronicles, New York and a monthly poetry column in Point of View in Massachusetts. Editor-in-Chief, Publisher of 27-year old non-profit Mobius, The Poetry Magazine. Juanita Torrence-Thompson, Post Office Box 671058, Flushing, New York 11367 E-mail: poetrytown@earthlink.net Website: www.poetrytown.com

Richard Thompson Business Writer. The Commercial Appeal, 495 Union Avenue, Memphis, Tennessee 38103 Phone: (901) 333-2011 E-mail: **spkyjuice@bellsouth.com**

Mark J. Tuggle Freelance Writer. Contact Mr. Mark J. Tuggle, 102 West 109th Street, Apartment #1B, New York, New York 10025 E-mail: **mjt579@msn.com**

Ismail Turay, Jr. Journalist, writer and reporter. Ismail Turay, Jr., Dayton Daily News, 45 South Ludlow Street, Dayton, Ohio 45402 E-mail: **liberian_1@man.com**

Raymond Tyler Freelance Writer/Photographer, Essence Magazine, The Source, and Vibe magazines. Columnist, About Time, The National Impact, AC Weekly. Talk Show Host/Producer, The National Impact radio show Friday's 10am-11am, The Wayback Machine 11am-1pm on 91.7 FM WLFR (WLFR.FM). Mr. Raymond Tyler, Dark Seed Communications, 6701 Black Horse Pike, Suite A-4, EHT, New Jersey 08234 Phone: (609) 816-5589 E-mail: **nationalimpact@gmail.com**

Monica Z. Utsey Freelance writer & editor, Ms. Utseys work has appeared in national publications, including Heart & Soul and Upscale Magazines. Ms. Monica Z. Utsey, 201 I Street South West, #531, Washington, DC 20024 Phone: (202) 479-9222 Fax: (202) 484-5680 E-mail: **monicautsey@aol.com** Website: **www.southerndcmochamoms.com**

Denise T. Ward Sports Writer. Denise T. Ward, San Diego Union Tribune, 350 Camino De La Reina, San Diego, California 92108 Phone: (619) 718-5304 Fax: (619) 293-2443 E-mail: **denise.ward@uniontrib.com**

Jerry W. Ward, Jr. Professor of English at Dillard University, Ward is a poet, literary critic, and editor. He compiled and edited Trouble The Water: 250 Years of African American Poetry (Mentor, 1997). Contact Jerry W. Ward, Jr., Department of English, Dillard University, 2601 Gentilly Boulevard, New Orleans, Louisiana 70122 E-mail: **jerryward31@hotmail.com**

Tamika Washington Writer. Contact Ms. Tamika Washington, 2201 Hayes Road, Suite #4215, Houston, Texas 77077 E-mail: **markusmond@hotmail.com**

Rod Watson Urban affairs editor and columnist. Contact Rod Watson, The Buffalo News, One News Plaza, Post Office Box 100, Buffalo, New York 14240 Phone: (716) 849-5598 Fax: (716) 847-0207 E-mail: **lcoles@njn.org**

George White Vice President (print) of The Black Journalist Association of Southern California (BJASC). Contact Mr. George White, UCLA Center for Communications, 3701 Stocker Street, Suite 204, Los Angeles, California 90008 Phone: (310) 206-2189 Fax: (310) 206-2972 E-mail: **geowhite@ucla.edu** Website: **www.uclaccc.ucla.edu**

Dera R. Williams Free lance writer travel, and contributor to literature manual. Also a literary columnist at Dera's Den. Contact Ms. Dera R. Williams, CocoWriter Book & Tea Parlor, 4316 Rilea Way Suite 2, Oakland, California 94605 E-mail: **dwillautho@aol.com** Website: **www.apooobooks.com**

Emily Means-Willis Educator, literary reviewer, columnist. She is involved in doing numerous literary reviews and critiques for noted authors and poets. She also writes for various magazines. A second novel "Flip Side of the Coin" will be released in 2007. Emily Means-Willis, We, Us and Company, International, 419 Douglas Street, Park Forest, Illinois 60466 Phone: (708) 769-4116 E-mail: pamemi@comcast.net

Freddie Willis Sports Copy Editor, The Times Picayune, 3800 Howard Avenue, New Orleans, Louisiana 70140 Phone: (504) 826-3405 E-mail: fwillis@timespicayune.com

Gloria Dulan-Wilson Freelance writer/photographer, screenwriter and public speaker who has covered the Black political arena of New York and Northern New Jersey. She has interviewed and profiled such luminaries as Ossie Davis, Min. Louis Farrakhan, Floyd Flake, Kweisi Mfume, interviewed Diana Ross, Don King, the late Johnnie Cochran, Rosa Parks, and the late Mrs. Coretta Scott King, among others. She has written for the Daily Challenge News, New York Beacon, Positive Community Magazine, and numerous others. Gloria Dulan-Wilson, 90 Church Street, Suite 3343, New York City, New York 10008 E-mail: geemomadee@yahoo.com

Alecia Goodlow-Young Author, columnist, and a freelance writer. Civil Rights Chair, National Writers Union. Alecia Goodlow-Young, 28490 Tavistock Trail, Southfield, Michigan 48034 Phone: (313) 796-7949 Fax: (313) 541-6638 E-mail: aleciawrites@sbcglobal.net

Susan L. Taylor
Writer * Author * Journalist
Editorial Director

Susan L. Taylor has been the driving force behind one of the most celebrated African American owned business success stories of the past three decades, *ESSENCE* magazine,   As former editorial director, she oversaw the editorial operations of the magazine and wrote the popular *In the Spirit* column each month. A fourth-generation entrepreneur, Taylor was the founder of her own company, Nequai Cosmetics, before becoming *ESSENCE's* fashion and beauty editor and, in 1981, its editor-in-chief. She is the author of three books: *In the Spirit: The Inspirational Writings of Susan L. Taylor* and *Lessons in Living and Confirmation: The Spiritual Wisdom That Has Shaped Our Lives*, the latter co-authored with her husband, Khephra Burns.

In 1999, Taylor became the first African-American woman to receive *The Henry Johnson Fisher Award* from the Magazine Publishers of America, the magazine industry's highest honor. In 2002, she was inducted into the American Society of Magazine Editors' (ASME) Hall of Fame, which celebrates the career-long records of excellence, creativity and impact of a select group of highly influential magazine journalists. She is a member of the National Association of Black Journalists and the American Society of Magazine Editors. She is also an avid supporter of a host of organizations dedicated to moving the Black community forward serving as a member of the Commission on Research in Black Education, among others.

She is currently co-chair of a capital campaign with actor Danny Glover to raise money to build housing in the rural areas of South Africa.

Competitions/Awards

The African American Literary Award Show The brainchild of Yvette Hayward, president of Y. Hayward, Inc., a public relations company that has been a powerful resource in the literary field for over a decade. The AALAS Awards is the first of its kind and the most comprehensive awards show ever to recognize, honor, celebrate and promote the outstanding achievements and contributions that authors and writers make to the publishing, arts and entertainment industries. Contact Ms. Annual. Yvette Hayward, The African American Literary Awards Show, Inc., Post Office Box 162, New York, New York 10039   E-mail: yvette@literaryawardshow.com Website: www.literaryawardshow.com

Black Filmmakers Hall Of Fame Inc. Features film presentations and festivals of works by independent black filmmakers. Annual film, video and screenplay competition. BFHFI also publishes an annual catalogue featuring biographical material about filmmakers being inducted into the Black filmmakers Hall Of Fame. Felix Curtis, Executive Director, BFHFI, 410 14th Street, Oakland, California 94612 E-mail: bfhfinc@aol.com

The Black Caucus Literature Awards Recognizes excellence in adult fiction and nonfiction by African American authors published in the previous year, recognition of a first novelist, as well as a citation for Outstanding Contribution to Publishing. John S. Page, BCALA Awards, 3003 Van Ness Street, North West, W522, Washington, DC 20008 Phone: (202) 274-6030 Fax: (202) 274-6012 E-mail: newsletter@bcala.org Website: www.bcala.org

The Coretta Scott King Award Presented annually by the Coretta Scott King Task Force of the American Library Association's Ethnic Multicultural Information Exchange Round Table (EMIERT). Recipients are authors and illustrators of African descent whose distinguished books promote an understanding and appreciation of the "American Dream." Contact Tanga Morris, ALA, Office of Literacy and Outreach Services, 50 East Huron Street, Chicago, Illinois 60611 Phone: (800) 545-2433 Website: www.ala.org/ala/srrt/corettascottking/corettascott.htm

Film Life Movie Awards Star-studded awards ceremony celebrating Black cinema established in 1997, by Jeff Friday, President and CEO of Film Life, Inc. Held as the culminating event of the American Black Film Festival it recognizes the achievement of persons of African descent in Hollywood, as well as to showcase and reward the work of the independent filmmaker. Jana Elise Taylor, Film Life, Inc., Post Office Box 688, New York, New York 10012 Phone: (212) 966-2411 Fax: (212) 966-2411 E-mail: info@thefilmlife.com Website: www.thefilmlife.com

Hurston/Wright LEGACY Award The first national award presented to published writers of African descent by the national community of Black writers. This award, is underwritten by Borders Books & Music. Contact The Hurston/Wright Foundation, 6525 Belcrest Road, Suite 531, Hyattsville, Maryland 20782 Phone: (301) 683-2134   Fax: (301) 277-1262 E-mail: info@hurstonwright.org Website: www.hurstonwright.org

LISTEN AND EXCHANGE[TM] Annual Competition. Creative songwriters/composers/music producers from all over the world submit ORIGINAL music, and compete to be named as the LISTEN AND EXCHANGE Grand Prize winning top music producer. Attendees consiste of filmmakers, celebrity VP music producers, record label executives, publishing company executives, and more. Dedra S. Davis, 26 Broadway, Suite 400, New York, New York 10004 Texas: 7322 Southwest Freeway, Suite 1100, Houston, Texas, 77242 Phone: (713) 981-3861 Fax: (713) 981-3862 E-mail: DEDRADAVIS@musiclw.com Website: www.musiclw.com

NAACP Image Award Event celebrating the outstanding achievements and performances of people of color in the arts as well as those individuals or groups who promote social justice/ NAACP Image Awards, 4929 Wilshire Boulevard, Suite 310, Los Angeles, California 90010 Phone: (323) 938-5268 Fax: (323) 938-5045 E-mail: imageawards@naacpnet.org Website: www.naacpimageawards.net/main.html

OBS Pilot Competition Cash awards for winning pilot scripts to be read by major production companies and top talent agencies (UTA, Edmonds Entertainment, UPN, Disney, Fox TV). Winners receive Professional Table Reading. OBS Pilot Competition, Organization of Black Screenwriters, Inc., 1968 Adams Boulevard, Los Angeles, California 90018 Phone: (323) 735-2050 E-mail: sfranklin@obswriter.com Website: www.obswriter.com

Philadelphia Writers' Conference, Inc. Contest. Submit manuscripts in advance for criticism by the workshop leaders. About a dozen contest categories. Cash prizes and certificates are given to first and second place winners, plus full tuition for the following year's conference to first place winners. Contact PWC Registrar, D. O. Haggerty, 535 Fairview Road, Medford, New Jersey 08055 E-mail: info@pwcwriters.org Website: www.pwcwriters.org

Romance Slam Jam Competition Awards Ema Rogers Award. Annaual conference.recognize the authors of this remarkable genre, and to celebrate their craft with their avid fans Romance Slam Jam, 90-06 Merrick Boulevard, Jamaica, New York 11432 E-mail: romanceslamjam2005@yahoo.com Website: www.romanceslamjam.com

Sistahfaith Conference Writing Contest Winner awarded a publishing contract with Amani Publishing, LLC. Contact Ms. Marilynn Griffith, Amani Publishing, Post Office Box 12045, Tallahassee, Florida 32317 Phone: (850) 264-3341 E-mail: Marilynngriffith@gmail.com Website: www.amanipublishing.net

YOUnity Reviewers Guild of America Awards Show Hosted by "The Literary Legends Ball Online" every New Year's Eve along with live celebrations commemorating award winners of excellence. Heather Covington, Disilgold, Post Office Box 652, Baychester Station, Bronx, New York 10469 Phone: (718) 547-0499 E- mail: Disilgold@aol.com Website: www.disilgold.com

Composers/Songwriters

Jillina "J-Bax" Baxter Website Journalist – The Hive/Blaze 1 Radio at blaze1graphixs.com in Atlanta, Georgia. J-Bax has written a catalog close to 300 consisting of Rap & R&B songs and poetry pieces. Other projects include a number of books, a fictional novel, and a coffee table book "A Pictorial Purpose." Jillina "J-Bax" Baxter, 184 Second Avenue, Albany, New York 12202 Phone: (518) 210-3518 E-mail: **jbmeow@yahoo.com**

Richard Jess Brown, Jr. Musician, composer, teacher, performer, professor of Doublebass studies at Belhaven University in Jackson, Mississippi. Only person chosen to represent Mississippi in first European tour at age 14. A graduate of the University of Memphis with a Master of Music degree from DePaul University. Became a member of the Memphis Symphony Orchestra at age 19. Performed in Europe, Canada, South America, Central America and the U.S. including Alaska. Worked with many legendary jazz and classical artist such as Eddie Harris, the Marsalis family, Ella Fitzgerald, Cassandra Wilson, George Solti, and many others. Richard Jess Brown, Jr., 2570 Prosperity Street, Jackson, Mississippi 39213 Phone: (769) 233-7418 E-mail: **jessbrown37@comcast.net** Website: **www.rjessbrownjr.com**

Troy Buckner A songwriter/lyricist and literary writer, Buckner was the Producer and Executive Producer for the theatrical production, 'Tell Hell I Aint Comin', starring Tommy Ford from the sitcom, 'Martin & New York Undercover' and Tony Grant from the Grammy nominated R & B Group, 'Az Yet' on the La Face Record label. She has managed and co-produced Gospel Renown Artist and Stella Award Winner, Kenny Smith and Vernessa Mitchell from the Motown's Grammy Award winning R & B Group, 'Hi-Energy. Ms. Troy Buckner, Hy'tara Entertainment, Post Office Box 19049, Anaheim, California 92817 Phone: (714) 227-5000 E-mail: **birdinflight@aol.com** Website: **www.abirdinflight.com**

Mary Kathryn Cannon Published poet, writer, author and songwriter. The song Hold On was recorded in 2002. I am a member of ASCAP music Industry. I began writing in 1988. Nominated Who's Who in poetry 2004 by the International Library of Poetry and published in Eternal Portraits in 2004. Nominated Five Thousand Personalities of the World in 1994. Golden Poet Award in 1989, Silver Poet in 1992. Contact Ms. Mary Kathryn Cannon,19643 Donovans Road, Georgetown Delaware 19947 E-mail: **kittymaryq@aol.com**

Bil Carpenter A songwriter, Bil's songs have been recorded by Grammy nominees David "Pop" Winans and Candi Staton, among others. Over the last decade, he has worked both as a music journalist and a record label publicist. He has also written liner note essays for various CD compilations for Sony/BMG Music, Malaco, Warner Bros, and EMI Records. His company, a small public relations firm has worked extensively with gospel artists such as Vickie Winans, Bishop T.D. Jakes, CeCe Winans, and Donald Lawrence & the Tri-City Singers, among many others. Bil Carpenter, Capital Entertainment, 217 Seaton Place North East, Washington, D.C. 20002 Phone: (202) 506-5051 E-mail: **carpbil@aol.com** Website: **www.bilcarpenter.com**

Gordon Chambers Grammy Award winner currently signed to L.A. Reid's prestigious Hitco Music publishing company where he has written for over 60 recording artists, including household names, Aretha Franklin, Queen Latifah, Brandy, Gladys Knight, Chaka Khan and Marc Anthony. He is best known for his 1994 Grammy winning hit "I Apologize" for Anita Baker and his 1995 #1 Grammy-nominated smash "If You Love Me" for the trio Brownstone (which was later featured as the theme song of the film "Living Out Loud"). Gordon Chambers, 171 Adelphi Street, Brooklyn, New York 11205 Phone: (212) 696-6774 Fax: (718) 852-1886 E-mail: **gordon@gordonchambers.com** Website: **www.gordonchambers.com**

Harry Walter Cooper, Jr. Lyricist and composer. Most well know song "ON The Other Side of Through." The song was recorded by James Bignon and reached #17 on the gospel billboard charts. Number one in Atlanta for 3 weeks in 1998. Harry Walter Cooper, Jr., 210 South Euclid Avenue, San Diego, California 92114 Fax: (619) 264-9049 E-mail: **sepastor@yahoo.com**

Kolade Daniel Poet, Songwriter, Scriptwriter. Kolade Daniel, 17 Igun Street, Itire Surulere, Lagos 23401 Nigeria Phone: 234 806650672 E-mail: **koladedaniel@praize.com**

Arthur Douse Vice President, writer, and HipHop artist. Publishing company. Arthur Douse, Fat Boy Hits Music Group, 1244 Herkamer, Brooklyn, New York 11233 Phone: (718) 216-5334 E-mail: **celsiusbk@aol.com**

Kenneth Gamble Co-founder/Chairman of Gamble-Huff Music. Grammy winners and BMI songwriters awards honorees, Mr. Gamble and his partner, Leon Huff wrote or co-wrote over 3,000 songs in 35 years including R and B #1 hits, pop #1 hits, gold and platinum records. Contact Mr. Kenneth Gamble, Gamble-Huff Music, 309 South Broad Street, Philadelphia, Pennsylvania 19107 Phone: (215) 985-0900 E-mail: **chuckgamblepir@aol.com** Website: **www.gamble-huffmusic.com**

Kyra Gaunt Kyra a.k.a. "Professor G" is a singer-songwriter and an associate professor of ethnomusicology at New York University who lectures nationally and internationally on African American music and issues of race, gender and the musical body. Her 2006 book The Games Black Girls Play: Learning the Ropes from Double-Dutch to Hip-hop (New York University Press, 2006) creates a new way of thinking about how black musical style and taste is learned and developed through interactions between the sexes and between genres. Contact Ms. Kyra Gaunt, 1 Washington Square Village #5-H, New York, New York 10012 Phone: (646) 831-0615 E-mail: **kyraocity@yahoo.com**

Forest Garfield Hairston Poet, script and songwriter, Forest Garfield Hairston is author of the book "Spirit Ran Free", an emotional saga about love and courage. Poems from the book include Caged Soul, Even Further, Ever America, Truth, and Across This Land. Contact Mr. Forest Hairston, Producer, ForGen Productions, 3654 Barham Boulevard, Suite Q301, Los Angeles, California E-mail: **fgprod@forgen.com** Website: **www.blackvillage.com**

Vernon Hairston Composer, jazz pianist. Original Compositions. Composer for hire. Music Transcription services. Contact Vernon Hairston, Hairstonning Music, Post Office Box 91194, Columbus, Ohio 43209 E-mail: **vh@vernonhairston.com** Website: **www.vernonhairston.com**

Fred Hammond Songwriter, bass player, vocalist, and producer whose credits include Commissions' release "State of Mind." A gifted musical arranger and producer. Hammond's work as a producer has landed him in the #1 spot among gospel producers according to the Gospel Music Round-up. His projects have received and been nominated for every major award including the Grammy, and the N.A.A.C.P. Image, Stellar, Dove, and GMWA Excellence Awards. Morris Townsend, Face To Face, Inc., 2812 Sonterra Drive, Cedar Hill, Texas 75104 Phone: (972) 293-2885 Fax: (972) 293-6866 E-mail: facetofacemgt@aol.com

Joseph Harrison Songwriter. Demo production/multimedia packages using our original music. Contact Mr. Joseph Harrison, Post Office Box 2742, Prairie View, Texas 77446 E-mail: Joseph_Harrison@pvamu.edu Website: www.GrooveDepot.com

Leon Huff Co-founder and Vice Chairman of Gamble-Huff Music Company, Huff helped to bring the genre of Philadelphia soul music to the world. He and partner Kenny Gamble wrote or co-wrote over 3,000 songs in 35 years including R and B #1 hits, pop #1 hits, gold and platinum records, Grammy winners and BMI songwriters awards honorees. Leon Huff, Gamble-Huff Music, 309 South Broad Street, Philadelphia, Pennsylvania 19107 Phone: (215) 985-0900 E-mail: chuckgamblepir@aol.com Website: www.gamble-huffmusic.com

Rodney Jenkins Musician, songwriter, producer, President/CEO of Dark Child, Inc., a music and song production company. Dubbed "Hitman" by the music industry, Rodney is one of the most sought after pop, R&B and Gospel music producers in the industry. Grammy (s) Award winner, he has written, produced and co-wrote songs for such artists as Michael Jackson, Whitney Houston, Britney Spears, N'Sync, Backstreet Boys, Mark Anthony, Kenneth "Babyface" Edmunds, to name a few. Contact Mr. Rodney Jenkins, Dark Child, Inc. E-mail: info@darkchild.com Website: www.darkchild.com

Darryl D. Lassiter Composer, Writer, Producer-Director/Filmmaker, Lassiter has written screenplays to Dead End Street and the remake of Bill Cosby and Sidney Poitier's Uptown Saturday Night. In development now is the movie, REVENGE. .He recently was given a proclamation from the mayor of his hometown, inducted into the National Black College Alumni Distinction Hall Of Fame a Lifetime Achievement Literacy Classic Award, (2003), and the coveted Stellar Award 2004 for "Video Of The Year." Contact Darryl D'Wayne Lassiter, Post Office Box 50374, Atlanta, Georgia 30302 Phone: (770) 732-0484 Fax: (770) 819-9153 E-mail: sales@ddlentertainment.com Website: www.ddlentertainment.com

Cedric McClester Award winning journalist and author, Cedric is also a prolific lyricist who has written over a thousand songs. He is also a motivational speaker who speaks to various groups across the country. McClester has a Masters of Science in Education from Fordham University, and has written for national and international publications, including the New York Times. Contact Mr. Cedric McClester, 1966 First Ave. # 12-K, New York, New York 10029 E-mail: Gandpadamis@aol.com

Charles E. McClinon African-American author, singer, songwriter and playwright. Enjoy writing fiction, drama and musicals. Charles E. McClinon, 8307 Mayfair Street, Cincinnati, Ohio Phone: (513) 417-9465 E-mail: cmcclinon@yahoo.com

Roy Dennis Merriwether   A contemporary, classic composer Mr. Merriwethers' music is rooted in a strong gospel tradition, infused with jazz, blues, and rock elements, all intertwined with classical influences. His compositions range from jazz ballads to big band arrangements to folk operas (scored for vocal chorus, orchestra and dances) to compositions orchestrated for an 85-piece orchestra. His earlier works include: "The Alma Mater," a ballad, "March Tempo," for Thomas Edison State College, Trenton, NJ, "The All Nighter," jazz/funk, 1984 and "Sister City, Let It Be Done," inspirational and commissioned for the celebration of sister cities, Trenton, New Jersey and The Lenin District of Moscow, Russia, 1985. He wrote "A Song For Sarah," a ballad, co-written by Blaine Collins, 1986. Contact Mr. Roy Dennis Merriwether   E-mail: **heavengoal@aol.com** Website: **www.roymeriwether.biz**

Carman Moore Composer, Author, Music Critic Carman began composing for symphony and chamber ensembles while writing lyrics for pop songs, gradually adding opera, theatre, dance and film scores to his body of work. His work in popular music included lyrics and arrangements for ex-Rascals leader Felix Cavaliere. Among his early commissioned symphonic works were Wildfires and Field Songs for the New York Philharmonic conducted by Pierre Boulez and Gospel Fuse for the San Francisco Symphony with Seiji Ozawa conducting and Cissy Houston the vocal soloist. Among other of his works for symphony orchestra have been Concerto for Blues Piano and Orchestra (for Jay McShann). Among Moore's scores for theatre have been Yale Rep's production of Shakespeare's Timon of Athens (starring James Earl Jones and directed by Lloyd Richards) and When The Bough Breaks at LaMama E.T.C., directed by Lawrence Sacharow. Carman Moore, 152 Columbus Avenue, New York, New York 10023 Phone: (212) 580-0825 E-mail: **skycarmuse@mindspring.com**

Kevin Neal Pastor, singer and BMI registered songwriter. Kevin Neal, 4173 Wellington Hills Drive, Snellville, Georgia 30039 Phone: (770) 972-9632 E-mail: **1kdneal@bellsouth.net**

Dariel Raye Author, composer, editor. Dariel Raye, 655 Welworth Street, Mobile, Alabama 36617 Phone: (251) 661-3464 E-mail: **darielraye@yahoo.com**

Marsha D. Jenkins-Sanders Author, songwriter, she received acclaim for lyrics written for Keith Washington's freshmen album project, Make Time for Love. Both "Kissing You" and "Closer" introduced her writing talent and she received award-winning recognition from ASCAP in the R & B genre. Marsha D. Jenkins-Sanders, Markei Publishing, Post Office Box 395, Garden City, Michigan 48136 Phone: (734) 334-3645 E-mail: **mdjswrites@yahoo.com**

James Tatum Composer, Jazz concert pianist, teacher, performer and recording artist, Tatum has composed major jazz works; the Contemporary Jazz Mass, Return of Joshua, and many others. He is listed in Who's Who Among African-Americans 2003. Contact Mr. James Tatum, James Tatum Trio, Inc., Post Office Box 32240, Detroit, Michigan 48232 Phone: (313) 537-1265 Fax: (313) 255-9015 E-mail: **clejam@sbcglobal.net** Website: **www.jamestatum.com**

Roosevelt "Rozie" Turner   Singer, emcee, songwriter, producer, actor, recording artist, emcee, and one of the most versatile up and coming artists in the music and entertainment industry. Mr. Roosevelt Turner IV, Post Office Box 32713, Oklahoma City, Oklahoma 73123 Phone: (405) 255-6716 E-mail: **rozieturner@cox.net**

Narada Michael Walden   Producer, composer, singer, songwriter, musician, he has been honored by his colleagues with a Grammy Award for Best R&B Song in 1985 (*Freeway of Love*), co-writing and producing two smash hits for Franklin, *Freeway* and *Who's Zoomin' Who?*, which opened the way for Franklin to garner her first platinum record in thirty years of record making. Contact Mr. Narada Michael Walden, Tarpan Studios, 1925 East Francisco Boulevard, Suite L, San Rafael, California 94901 Phone: (415) 485-1999 Fax: (415) 459-3234 E-mail: **inquiries@tarpanstudios.com** Website: **tarpanstudios.com**

Hubert P. Williams, Jr.   Singer/songwriter/producer/poet, Mr. Williams is currently Chair, Cumberland County Coalition on Teen Pregnancy Prevention and Adolescent Parenting; Member of Coalition for Awareness, Resources, and Education of Substances, (C.A.R.E.S); and an Executive Board member for the Adolescent Pregnancy Prevention Coalition of North Carolina.   Rev. Hubert P. Williams, Jr., Trinity Music Group, 2907 Kingfisher Drive, Fayetteville, North Carolina Phone: (910) 977-7354 E-mail: **min.hpwilliams@yahoo.com**

Kenneth Wilson   An accomplished writer, keyboardist, director, producer, publisher, and minister of the gospel, Kenneth Wilson is one of the most fruitful and anointed songwriters of our time, producing over 100 new gospel songs ready for any Sunday morning praise and worship service. Kenneth Wilson & the Kenneth Wilson Chorale, Post Office Box 21100, Detroit, Michigan 48221 Phone: (313) 496 3999 E-mail: **kennethwilson2@netzero.com** Website: **www.cdbaby.com**

Bevin Sinclair Turnbull   Composer/Educator/Author, my novel is called THE OTHER SIDE OF TOMORROW (Xlibris.com). Executive Director of Bronx Renaissance Community Theater. Currently, 7 albums of my work can be found at CDBaby.com. Contact Mr. Bevin Sinclair Turnbull, 1170 East 225th Street, Bronx, New York 10466 Phone: (718) 405-1553 Fax: (718) 231-5681 E-mail: **bjazz7@aol.com**

Narada Michael Walden
Songwriter * Composer
Producer * Recording Artist

Producer and composer Narada Michael Walden has used his formidable musical knowledge to craft a string of pop smashes that have established him as one of the finest and most successful producers working in the record industry today. Known as the "man who helped the Queen of Soul, Aretha Franklin, land her first platinum album", he has produced and co-written three #1 smash hits for Whitney Houston, established himself as a drumming wunderkind while playing alongside guitar aces Jeff Beck and John McLaughlin and has parlayed a healthy solo career into a writing, producing and performing profession, resulting in over ten solo albums. Walden has been honored by his colleagues with a Grammy Award for Best R&B Song in 1985 (*Freeway of Love*), co-writing and producing two smash hits for Franklin, *Freeway* and *Who's Zoomin' Who?*, which opened the way for Franklin to garner her first platinum record in thirty years of record making. He produced *How Will I Know?* from Whitney Houston's multi-platinum 1985 Arista debut and produced and co-wrote the hits, *I Wanna Dance With Somebody*, *Where Do Broken Hearts Go* and *So Emotional*, from her 1987 follow up, *WHITNEY*. Walden also produced and won a Sports Emmy For Houston's *One Moment In Time*, taken from the 1988 Olympics LP.

Other Walden projects have included the 1987 Aretha/George Michael duet *I knew You Were Waiting*, which followed the Walden-produced, *Nothing's Gonna Stop Us Now* (by Starship) into the #1 slot, and the Aretha/Elton John hit duet *Through The Storm*. Besides establishing a "user friendly" studio in San Rafael, Tarpan Studios, and getting back to being a solo artists, he's enjoying in the success of his four #1 single hits including Mariah Carey's Vision Of Love, and I Don't Wanna Cry, Whitney Houston's *All The Man That I Need*, and Lisa Fischer's *How Can I Ease The Pain*? He has also written and completed a number of projects for such artists as Shanice Wilson, Tevin Campbell and Al Jarreau.

Other Top 10 hits written and/or produced by this very talented musician and composer include *Songbird* (Kenny G); *Baby Come To Me* (Regina Belle); *Put Your Mouth On Me* (Eddie Murphy); and *We Don't Have To Take Our Clothes Off* (Jermaine Stewart); *Kisses In the Moonlight* (from the George Benson album, *While The City Sleeps*); *We're Not Making Love Anymore* (Barbra Streisand's album, *Barbra Streisand's Greatest Hits*); and *I Do* (Natalie Cole's Album, *Good To Be Back*)

Conferences/Expos

African American Arts Festival Annual county-wide celebration of African American Arts, Culture and Heritage. Atelier provides an environment for visual exposure, educational exchange and a showcase for African American art and artists. African American Atelier, 200 North Davie Street, Box 14, Greensboro, North Carolina 27401 Phone: (336) 333-6885 E-mail: info@africanamericanatelier.org Website: www.africanamericanatelier.org

African American Book Club Summit Annual, the AABCS is an excellent opportunity for book clubs to gather to discuss books, exchange ideas, develop strategies, and meet some of the country's finest authors. Contact Ms. Pamela Walker-Williams, AABCS, Pageturner, PMB-120, 2951 Marina Bay Drive, Suite #130, League City, Texas 77573 Phone: (866) 875-1044 E-mail: E-mail: pwsquare@pageturner.net Website: www.pageturner.net

Atlanta African Dance & Drum Festival Afrikan Djeli Cultural Institute (ADCI) coordinates classes, workshops and conferences for African Dance and Drum. Also coordinates drum and dance for programs, weddings and many types of events. ADCI, Post Office Box 50130, Atlanta, Georgia 30302 Phone: (404) 753-8933 Fax: (480) 275-3612 Website: www.aaddf.org

African American Heritage Festival Annual festival celebration of African American culture. AAHF is a week of educational and cultural programs culminates with a weekend of social and recreational activities. Arican American Heritage Festival, The Multicultural Center, 4th Floor, Ohio Union, 1739 North High Street, Columbus, Ohio 43210 Phone: (614) 688-8449 E-mail: multiculturalcenter@osu.edu Website: www.multiculturalcenter.osu.edu/afam

African American Pavilion at Book-Expo America Founded in 2004. Annual conference event showcases African American books, authors, products and publishers. Contact Tony Rose, Publisher. Contact Mr. Tony Rose, Amber Communications Group, Inc., 1334 East Chandler Boulevard, Suite 5-D67, Phoenix, Arizona 85048 Phone: (480) 460-1660 Fax: (480) 283-0991 E-mail: amberbk@aol.com Website: www.amberbooks.com

The African Diaspora Film Festival (ADFF) Presents an eclectic mix of urban, classic, independent and foreign films that depict the richness and diversity of the life experience of people of African descent and Indigenous people all over the world. ArtMattan Productions, The African Diaspora Film Festival, 535 Cathedral Parkway, Suite 14B, New York, New York 10025 Phone: (212) 864-1760 E-mail: info@nyadff.org Website: www.nyadff.org

African World Festival (AWF) The largest public outreach program of the year with attendance topping one million, this festival is a dynamic, colorful mix of people and cultures of the African Diaspora. Contact AWF, The Museum Of African American History, 315 East Warren Avenue, Detroit, Michigan 48201 Phone: (313) 494-5824 Fax: (313) 494-5855 E-mail: dhamm@maah-detroit.org Website: www.maah-detroit.org

Afro-American Historical and Genealogical Society, Inc. Host annual authors' luncheon held in different cities each year. Focus is on authors of Black history or genealogical books. Contact AAHGS, Post Office Box 73067, Washington, DC 20056 Phone: (202) 234-5350 E-mail: khadmatin@earthlink.net Website: www.aahgs.org

American Black Film Festival Annual. Founded in 1997 by Jeff Friday, President and CEO of Film Life, Inc. Showcases the cinematic work of independent artists of vision and emerging talent. Contact Mr. Jeff Friday, ABFF c/o of Film Life, Post Office Box 688, New York, New York 10012 E-mail: abff@thefilmlife.com Website: www.abff.com

ASALH Annual convention to celebrate and study Africana life and history hosted by The Association for the Study of African American Life and History (ASALH). Also hosts an annual Black History Month Luncheon and co-sponsors with the National Education Association the annual Carter G. Woodson Award. Sylvia Cyrus, ASALH, CB Powell Building, 525 Bryant Street, North West, Suite C142, Washington, DC 20059 Phone: (202) 865-0053 Fax: (202) 265-7920 E-mail: executivedirector@asalh.net Website: www.asalh.org

Birmingham Civil Rights Institute Host annual events, exhibitions, archives, and online resource gallery. Serves as a depository for civil rights archives and documents. Contact BCRI, 520 Sixteenth Street North, Birmingham, Alabama 35203 Phone: (205) 328-9696 Fax: (205) 251-6104 E-mail: award@bcri.org Website: www.bcri.org

Black Business Professionals and Entrepreneurs Conference Annual BBPE national conference whose mission is to service the minority business community. Ms. Jewel Daniels, BBPE, Post Office Box 60561, Savannah, Georgia 31420 Phone: (912) 354-7400 E-mail: jewel@blackbusinessprofessionals.com Website: www.blackbusinessprofessionals.com

Black Caucus of the American Library Association (BCALA) National association of black librarians. Host annual conference and awards. Newsletter. Andrew P. Jackson, President. BCALA, VA State Library, Richmond, Virginia 23219 Phone: (804) 786-2332 Fax: (804) 786-5855 E-mail: andrew.p.jackson@queenslibrary.org Website: www.bcala.org

Black College Radio Convention Annual forum for black college broadcasters, professional broadcasters and members of the music industry. Lo Jelks, Chairman. National Association of Black College Broadcasters, Post Office Box 3191, Atlanta, Georgia 30302 Phone: (404) 523-6136 Fax: (404) 523-5467 E-mail: bcrmail@aol.com Website: www.blackcollegeradio.com

Black Events Central (BEC) Provides information on events for the African-American community ranging from concerts to lectures, networking socials to fundraisers, book signings, festivals. Contact Black Events Central, 244 5th Avenue, #G282, New York, New York 10001 E-mail: events@blackeventscentral.com Website: www.blackeventscentral.com

Black Film & Media Conference A venue where Black filmmakers can expand and broaden their craft consisting of programs and promotions (film screenings, workshops, expert panels). BFMC, 923 Spring Garden Street, Suite 300, Philadelphia, Pennsylvania 19123 E-mail: info@phillybfmc.com Website: www.phillybfmc.com/index.html

Black Literary Marketplace Expo (BLMPE) Annual. Four events are held each year, Winter, Summer, Fall and Winter. Author sigining vendors and exhibits. Contact BLMPE, The Grace Company, 829 Langdon Court, Suite 45, Rochester Hills, Michigan 48307 Phone: (248) 651-6775 E-mail: graccointern@msn.com Website: www.blackliterarymarketplaceexpo.com

Black Writers On Tour This annual event gives exposure to Black authors and writers, increase their book sales, motivate, and develop aspiring new writers and authors. Milligan Books, 1425 West Manchester Avenue, Suite C, Los Angeles, California 90047 Phone: (323) 750-3592 Fax: (323) 750-2886 E-mail: DrRosie@aol.com Website: www.blackwriters.org

Black Writers Reunion and Conference Annual conference held for Black authors that allows them to interact with other authors, playwrights, editors, and writers from across the country. Also, features relevant workshops and speeches. Contact Dr. Rosie, Milligan Books, 1425 West Manchester Avenue, Suite C, Los Angeles, California 90047 Phone: (323) 750-3592 Fax: (323) 750-2886 E-mail: DrRosie@aol.com Website: www.blackwriters.org

Hollywood Black Film Festival Tanya Kersey Founder & Executive Director. Hollywood Black Film Festival, 8306 Wilshire Blvd., Suite 2057, Beverly Hills, California 90211 E-mail: tanya@hbff.org Website: www.hbff.org

Indiana Black Expo, Inc. (IBE) Founded in Indianapolis in 1970 by a group of religious and civic leaders. In 1971, the same group created an exposition at the Indiana State Fairgrounds that showcased the achievements of African-Americans in the areas of culture, art, history and economics. Ms. Tanya Bell, CEO/President. Contact Indiana Black Expo, Inc., 3145 North Meridian Street, Indianapolis, Indiana 46208 Phone: (317) 925-2702 Fax: (317) 925-6624 E-mail: tbell@indianablackexpo.com Website: www.indianablackexpo.com

International Black Writers & Artists (IBWA) Annual conference designed to improve skills, knowledge, and career opportunities for artists of all media. Features workshops, discussions, booksignings and an awards dinner dance banquet. IBWA, Post Office Box 43576, Los Angeles, California 90043 Phone: (323) 964-3721 E-mail: info@ibwa.org Website: www.ibwa.org

Juneteenth Celebrated annually, the oldest known celebration of the ending of slavery. Dating back to 1865, it was on June 19th that the Union soldiers, landed at Galveston, Texas with news the war had ended and that all slaves were now free. Birmingham Civil Rights Institute, 520 Sixteenth Street North, Birmingham, Alabama 35203 Phone: (205) 328-9696 Fax: (205) 251-6104 E-mail: award@bcri.org Website: www.bcri.org

Los Angeles Black Book Expo Itibari M. Zulu, Executive director. Contact Itibari M. Zulu, Amen-Ra Theological Seminary Press, Post Office Box 44572, Los Angeles, California 90044 E-mail: imzsr@yahoo.com Website: www.labbx.com

Midwest Regional Black Theatre Festival Held at venues throughout Greater Cincinnati and the surrounding areas, the Festival offers an exhibit of new and established African American plays and musicals; and other activities. Black Theatre Company, 5919 Hamilton Avenue, Cincinnati, Ohio 45224 Phone: (513) 241-6060 E-mail: cbtsherman@hotmail.com

National Association For The Study and Performance Of African American Music (NASPAAM) Newsletter/Professional Organization. The organization serves its members and others by increasing the awareness of Black Music and its contribution to the arts, culture, and society. Frank Suggs, President. NASPAAM, 1201 Mary Jane, Memphis, Tennessee 38116 Phone: (901) 396-2913 E-mail: f.suggs@naspaam.org Website: www.naspaam.org

National Association Of Black Accountants (NABA) Annual convention. Publishes newsletters and video tapes. Carla Welborn, Director. Contact Gregory Johnson, NABA, 7249-A Hanover Parkway, Greenbelt, Maryland 20770 Phone: (301) 474-6222 Fax: (301) 474-3114 E-mail: gjohnson@nabainc.org Website: www.nabainc.org

National Association Of Black Owned Broadcasters (NABOB) We host two management conferences annually of African-American owners of radio and television stations across the country. Contact James Winston, NABOB, 1155 Connecticut Avenue, North West, Washington, DC 20036 Phone: (202) 463-8970 E-mail: info@nabob.org Website: www.nabob.org

National Black Arts Festival NBAF is one of the premier national and international celebrations of the art, music and culture of people of African descent. Stephanie Hughley, Executive Producer. Contact National Black Arts Festival, 659 Auburn Avenue, #254, Atlanta, Georgia 30312 Phone: (404) 224-3468 Fax: (404) 730-7104 E-mail: info@nbaf.org Website: www.nbaf.org

National Black Book Festival (NBBF) Annual book conference. Contact Ms. Gwen Richardson, Cushcity.com, 14300 Cornerstone Village Drive, Suite 370, Houston, Texas 77014 Phone: (281) 444-4265 Fax: (281) 583-9534 E-mail: grichardson@cushcity.com Website: www.nationalblackbookfestival.com

National Black Expo Inc. Founded in 1990, by Susan F. Stanley, NBE's mission is to improve the economic viability of minority owned business enterprises. Through the exhibition portion of the NBE thousands of small businesses have increased their viability by reaching thousands of new customers. National Black Expo Inc., 400 West 76th Street #202, Chicago, Illinois 60620 E-mail: stantley@nationalblackexpo.com Website: www.nationalblackexpo.org

The National Black Theatre Festival The North Carolina Black Repertory Company hosts the famous "The National Black Theatre Festival." A large number of workshops and seminars are available at the Festival. NCBRC, 610 Coliseum Drive, Winston-Salem, North Carolina 27106 Phone: (336) 723-2266 E-mail: playrite@earthlink.net Website: www.nbtf.org

National Society Of Black Engineers (NSBE) Annual national convention, hosting over 8,000 attendees. Chancee Lundy, National Chairperson. NSBE, 1454 Duke Street, Alexandria, Virginia 22314 Phone: (703) 549-2207 E-Mail: info@nsbe.org Website: www.nsbe.org

The Pan African Film Festival (PAFF) Since 1992, PAFF presents and showcases one of America's largest fine art shows featuring black artists and fine crafts including poets, musicians and storytellers. PAFF, 6820 La Tijera Blvd., Suite 200, Los Angeles, California 90045 Phone: (310) 337-4737 Fax: (310) 337-4736 E-Mail: info@paff.org Website: www.paff.org

Philadelphia Writers' Conference, Inc. Annual, traditionally held in early June; offers from 14 workshops, seminars, several "manuscript rap." Cash prizes and certificates given plus full tuition to first place winners. Contact D. O. Haggerty, PWC Registrar, 535 Fairview Road, Medford, New Jersey 08055 E-mail: info@pwcwriters.org Website: www.pwcwriters.org

Romance Slam Jam The conference grew out of an early desire to recognize the authors of this remarkable genre, and to celebrate their craft with their avid fans. Slam Jam, 90-06 Merrick Boulevard, Jamaica, New York 11432 E-mail: romanceslamjam2005@yahoo.com Website: www.romanceslamjam.com

San Francisco Black Film Festival (SFBFF) Celebration of African American cinema and the African cultural Diaspora. Festival showcases a diverse collection of films from emerging and established filmmakers that highlight the beauty and complexity of the African and African American experience. Contact SFBFF, Post Office Box 15490, San Francisco, California 94115 Phone: (415) 771-9271 Fax: (415) 346-9046 E-mail: info@sfbff.org Website: www.sfbff.org

Urban Network Magazine Annual industry conference. Launched in 1988 by founder, editor, Mary Nichols, aka DJ Fusion. A bi-monthly newsletter is also sent to several million opt in subscribers at the website urbannetwork.com/newsletter.html. Contact Mary Nichols, FuseBox Radio/BlackRadioIsBack.com, Post Office Box2465, Waldorf, Maryland 20604 Phone: (347) 252 4032 E-mail: djfusion5@Yahoo.com Website: www.blackradioisback.com

Women's Empowerment Expo Since 1994, in honor of Women's History Month, expo was designed to enhance the lives of African American women by addressing issues that specifically impact their "health, hearts and pocketbooks." NTR/Special Events, Radio One, Raleigh, 8001 Creedmoor Road, Suite 101, Raleigh, North Carolina 27613 Phone: (919) 848.9736 E-mail: info@womensempowermentexpo.com Website: www.womensempowermentexpo.com

Women's Leadership Summit Annual, hosted by the National Association of Black Female Executives in Music & Entertainment, Inc. (NABFEME) Founded in 1999 by record industry trailblazer Johnnie Walker, NABFEME supports and empowers professional women of color, executives, managers, and technicians in the music and entertainment industries. Contact: NABFEME, 59 Maiden Lane, 27th Floor, New York, New York 10038 Fax: (201) 313-1192 E-mail: info@NABFEME.org Website: www.nabfeme.org

Zimbabwe International Book Fair The largest and most diverse exhibition of books, magazines, journals, CD-ROM and publishing and printing technology and services in sub-Saharan Africa," Is the main book trade event for the African publishing industry. ZIBF, 5 Woodlane, Borrowdale, Zimbabwe Phone: 870834-5/852371-2/852892-5 Fax: 851161 E-mail: dpi@trendtotrendmag.com Website: www.zibf.org.zw

Gregory J. Reed, Esq.
Author * Agent * Producer

Gregory J. Reed is active in areas of sports, corporate, entertainment, and taxation laws. He is the first African American to receive a Master of Taxation Laws in Michigan. He is the first African American lawyer to Chair a Sports and Entertainment Lawyers Section in the United States. Reed is a producer and represents sports figures, entertainers, firms, and numerous persons from TV to Broadway, including Anita Baker, Wynston Marsalis, The Winans, and First Black Miss USA, Carole Gist and many other artists. He is the only attorney to represent six world champion boxers. He has produced such plays as the Pulitzer Prize winning production, *A Soldier's Play*, which was developed into a screenplay by Columbia Pictures as *A Soldier's Story*, awarded an Oscar. Reed has produced and represented the following Broadway plays: "Ain't Misbehavin"; "For Colored Girls Who Have Considered Suicide When the Rainbow Is Enuf"; "What The Wine Sellers Buy"; "The Wiz"; "Your Arms Too Short To Box With God"; and Rosa Parks "More Than a Bus Story," co-authored with Von Washington. Reed also staged the largest tour entertainment tribute in the U.S. in honor of Dr. Martin Luther King Jr., with Emmy winner Al Eaton in *We Are The Dream*. He produced a documentary of the Last Poets, originators of Rap music, whom he reunited for a national tour.

Author of fourteen books, Reed wrote the first exclusive contract negotiating guide explaining tax aspects of entertainment and sports law in the U.S. entitled *Tax Planning and Contract Negotiating Techniques for Creative Persons, Professional Athletes and Entertainers* (1979). His second book, *This Business of Boxing and Its Secrets* (1981) the only book of its kind, made the New York Times bestseller list, and was cited as an international authority on the subject matter. Other releases include *This Business of Entertainment and Its Secrets* (1985) and *Negotiations Behind Closed Doors* (1992). A fifth book, entitled *Economic Empowerment Through The Church* (1994, Zondervan Publishing House, 1994 American Book Awards Winner) is about mass organization, religion, communication, tax planning. Reed's sixth book is *This Business of Celebrity Estates*. Reed is co-author of the book *Quiet Strength* with Mrs. Rosa Parks (Zondervan Publishing House, 1995) and *Dear Mrs. Parks* (1996, Lee & Low Publishing).

In October 1992, Reed purchased the original manuscript on the Autobiography of Malcolm X which included the handwritten notations of both Alex Haley and Malcolm X. He established an exhibition and several media related projects based on the notations. Reed is the founder of the Gregory J. Reed Scholarship Foundation that aids students in the field of arts, engineering and law.

Reed's accomplishments have been cited by the Detroit News as one of the top lawyers in the legal profession, and he is listed in "*Who's Who in Entertainment, Who's Who Among Black Americans, Who's Who Among American Law, and Who's Who in Finance.*" In October 1992 he was inducted into the Black Entertainment and Sports Lawyers Association Hall of Fame.

Consultants

Abdul-Jalil al-Hakim President/CEO of Superstar Management. Mr. Abdul-Jalil al-Hakim negotiates and drafts all agreements for all publishing, merchandising and licensing; commercial advertisements and product endorsements; corporate sponsorships and affiliations; motion picture, television, radio and personal appearances; professional personal services contracts; electronic multimedia, literary, publishing, merchandising, licensing, concerts, tours, broadcasting, and video. He was the first African-American in the field and has taught and lectured Entertainment Law for 30 years. Abdul-Jalil al-Hakim, Superstar Management, 7633 Sunkist Drive, Oakland California 94605 E-mail: (510) 638-0808 Fax: (510) 638-8889 E-mail: **jalil@superstarmanagement.com** Website: **www.superstarmanagement.com**

Carolyn L. Bennett Author, writer, and instructor, Dr. Bennett's essays on current affairs appear regularly in the Dallas Examiner, Buffalo Criterion, Philadelphia New Observer, AIM and About Time magazines. She is a journalist-educator (graduate of Michigan State University, Ph.D. in education; and American University, M.A. in journalism) who has taught editorial and opinion writing, magazine article and feature writing, news writing and editing, journalism issues and ethics at Howard University, the University of Maine, Rowan University and others. She offers writing services and workshops through CMAL Writing Associates. Contact Carolyn L. Bennett, CMAL Writing Associates, 221 Greystone Lane, Rochester, New York 14618 Phone: (585) 442-8507 E-mail: **cwriter85@aol.com**

Ed Bullins Author, playwright. Distinguished Artist-in-Residence, Northeastern University. Mr. Bullins is the author of eight books, including Five Plays By Ed Bullins, The Duplex, The Hungered One, Four Dynamite Plays, The Theme is Blackness, and The Reluctant Rapist. He wrote and produced for the theatre several commission works, including *Rainin' Down Stairs* for the 1992 San Francisco Theatre Artaud, and has been editor for a number of theatre magazines and publications. He was producer of *Circles of Times,* Boston's Lyric Theatre in August 2003. Among his awards and grants is three Obie Awards, four Rockefeller Foundation Playwriting Grants, two Guffenheim Playwriting Fellowships, an NEA Playwriting Grant, the AUDELCO Award. Mr. Bullins' latest book is ED BULLINS: 12 Plays and Selected Writings (U of Michigan Press, 2006). Mr. Ed Bullins, 37 Vine Street Roxbury, Massachusetts 02119 Phone: (617) 442-6627 E-mail: **rct9@verizon.net** Website: **www.edbullins.com**

Charles L. Chatmon Author of The Depths of My Soul and The Voices of South Central, two books of poems. Currently executive director of the Los Angeles Black Book Expo, and a co-founder of the California Writers Collective. He is also a freelance writer and a former English and writing lab instructor. As part of the CWC, Charles coordinates writers workshops and assist new authors just starting out with interviews, resources and networking. He is also the co-host of an internet radio show called Mixed Matters bringing the best in up and coming authors, writers and poets. Charles L. Chatmon, Post Office Box 1924, Vallejo, California 94590 Phone: (707) 235-6520 E-mail: **chatwrites2@yahoo.com**Website: **http://charleslchatmon.com**

Angela P. Dodson Free-lance editor and writer for magazines, online services, individual authors and book publishers. Dodson has been a consultant, instructor in media studies and public speaking and is the host of a weekly radio program about black Roman Catholics. She is a journalism graduate of Marshall University and has a master's degree in journalism and public affairs from the American University in Washington, D.C. She has led workshops on writing and editing for many organizations. Angela P. Dodson, 324 Hamilton Avenue, Trenton, New Jersey 08609 Phone: (609) 394-7632 Fax: (609) 396-7808 E-mail: **angela4bibr@aol.com**

Latorial Faison Author, poet and instructor, Latorial has taught English and Writing at several colleges and universities including Coker College and Johnson C. Smith University. She is the founding editor of PoeticallySpeaking.net. She currently teaches for Robert Morris College and ITT and resides in North Chicago. Latorial Faison, Post Office Box 145, Highwood, Illinois 60040 E-mail: **Latorial@PoeticallySpeaking.net** Website: **Latorial@PoeticallySpeaking.net**

Kyra Gaunt Kyra a.k.a. "Professor G" is a singer-songwriter and an associate professor of ethnomusicology at New York University who lectures nationally and internationally on African American music and issues of race, gender and the musical body. Her 2006 book The Games Black Girls Play: Learning the Ropes from Double-Dutch to Hip-hop (NYU Press, 2006) creates a new way of thinking about how black musical style and taste is learned and developed through interactions between the sexes and between genres. Kyra Gaunt, 1 Washington Square Village #5-H, New York, New York 10012 Phone: (646) 831-0615 E-mail: **kyraocity@yahoo.com**

Idris Goodwin Playwright, performer, director, and educator, Idris Goodwin is the recipient of the NEA/TCG Theatre Residency Program for Playwrights for 2004. He holds a BA in Film & Video from Columbia College, Chicago and an MFA in Writing from the School of the Art Institute of Chicago. Since 1999, he has been creating original hip-hop music as a solo artist and in collaboration, releasing CD's independently and for the Chicago based Naiveté Records. As an educator, Goodwin has taught writing and performance workshops all over the city in for numerous programs. Mr. Idris Goodwin, 1721 West Huron, Apartment 2f, Chicago, Illinois 60622 E-mail: **Idris@hermitsite.com** Website: **www.Idrisgoodwin.com**

International Black Writers & Artists Los Angeles (IBWA/LA) Founded in Los Angeles in 1974 by Mrs. Edna Crutchfield, IBWALA is a network of authors, publishers, visual artists, community and educators dedicated to making sure our writers and artists are published, read, seen, and heard. Contact IBWA/LA, Post Office Box 43576, Los Angeles, California 90043 Phone: (323) 964-3721 E-mail: **webmaster@ibwala.com** Website: **http://www.ibwala.com**

N. Kali Mincy Speaker, Coach for Writers, Kali shows executives in all fields and writers at all levels how to produce top-quality written communications and books that generate more business and increased sales. A former English and Writing instructor for Columbia College, Kali served as Public Relations Manager for Long & Silverman Publishing where she began as Senior Editor. Her client list includes business, education, literary, and marketing writers from Harvard, Yale, Columbia and Georgetown. Her work with C-level executives, professional writers and authors has since produced national bestseller *The Baron Son*, a business and personal finance book featured on the *Forbes* Book Club Notable list. N. Kali Mincy, 2020 Pennsylvania Avenue NW #368, Washington, DC 20006 Website: **www.baronseries.com**

Motown Alumni Association, Inc. We help with all genre of music: artists, performers, and musicians to move forward as professional entertainers. Most of our consulting services are free. We are an education based organization. We deal with amateurs, semi-professionals and Professional entertainers. Contact Mr. Billy J. Wilson, Founder, President, Motown Alumni Association, Inc., 621 Orleans #65, Detroit, Michigan 48207 Phone: (734) 972-7582 E-mail: Billy_j_wilson@yahoo.com Website: www.motownalumniassociation.com

Motown Writers Network The largest online organization to network, market, and educate writers on and off the Internet founded by Sylvia Hubbard webmistress for 4 websites, founder of Write Steps 101, and owner of Hub Books Publishing. Sylvia Hubbard, Post Office Box 27310, Detroit, Michigan 48227 Phone: (313) 289-8614 E-mail: sylviahubbard1@yahoo.com Website: www.SylviaHubbard.com

Daphne Muse Author, writer, social commentator, her editorial service works with emerging and established writers to move them from Concept to Manuscript. Daphne Muse, 2429 East 23rd Street, Oakland, California 94601 Phone: (510) 436-4716 E-mail: msmusewriter@gmail.com Website: www.oasisinthediaspora.com

Pat McLean-RaShine A poet and author, Pat presently co-facilitates poetry and creative writing workshops at Temple University's Pan-African Studies Community Education Program (PASCEP) and at Drexel University, both of Philadelphia. She was recently published in "BMa: The Sonia Sanchez Literary Review – Legends and Legacies." Pat McLean-RaShine, 632 Elkins Avenue, Philadelphia, Pennsylvania 19120 Phone: (215) 683-3620 E-mail: PMcPoet@aol.com

Roz Private coaching and workshop consultant, Roz has worked on Broadway, in major motion pictures and on numerous TV shows, directed many short films and started a production company. She was specifically chosen by Margie Haber, whose celebrity clients include Brad Pitt, Halle Berry and Heather Locklear among many others, to be the East Coast representative of her world-famous acting studio and to teach her Cold Reading Technique. She has taught students at The Actors Center, ACT, Actor's Connection, Howard University and Duke Ellington School of the Arts and conducted acting workshops at film festivals around the country. Served as on-set acting coach during the second season of HBO's "In Treatment." Contact Roz, Red Wall Productions, 400 West 43rd Street, New York, New York 10036 Phone: (646) 374-8403 E-mail: rozactingcoach@gmail.com Website: www.redwallproductions.com

Julia Shaw Literary publicist for over 15 years. Consultant, specialist in public relations, sales, marketing, and publicity of African American books and authors. Julia Shaw, Shaw Business Group, LLC, 1204 Washington Avenue, Suite 401, Saint Louis, Missouri 63103 Phone: (917) 501-6780 E-mail: info@shawbizgroupinc.com Website: www.shawbizgroupinc.com

Carol A. Taylor Former Random House book editor, Carol has been in the book publishing business for over 10 years and is a published author, a freelance writer, book editor and an editorial consultant who has worked with book publishers, agents, best selling authors and up and coming writers. For book editing or consulting queries send an e-mail. Carol A. Taylor, Black Star Consulting, 295 Clinton Avenue #E3, Brooklyn, New York 11205 E-mail: carol@brownsugarbooks.com Website: www.BrownSugarBooks.com

Art Thomas Vice President of program development and acquisitions for CoLours TV. Also, co-founder of Denver Entertainment Group a coalition of 15 companies from five countries - including the United Kingdom, Singapore and Japan - includes all segments of media and entertainment production. Art Thomas, Post Office Box 3773 Englewood, Colorado 80155 Phone: (303) 331-0339 E-mail: **info@mainmanfilms.com** Website: **www.mainmanfilms.com**

Garland Lee Thompson, Sr. Co-Founder/Executive Director of The Frank Silvera Writers' Workshop Foundation, Inc., a theatre arts organization and playwright development program for emerging playwrights, directors and artists. Garland Thompson, Post Office Box 1791, Manhattanville Station, New York, New York 10027 Phone: (212) 281-8832 E-mail: **playrite@earthlink.net** Website: **www.fsww.org**

C. Sade Turnipseed Professor and executive producer of: educational and literary concept developments for film, television, radio, live stage events and festivals. Also international consultant for film festivals and literary performances. C. Sade Turnipseed, Red Clay Publishing, Post Office Box 4221, Greenville, Mississippi 38704 Phone: (662) 773-2048 E-mail: **khafre@peoplepc.com** Website: **www.khafre.us**

Ethel Pitts Walker Current Chair of Television, Radio, Film and Theatre at San Jose State University where she was a 1999-2000 *Teacher Scholar*. A former San Francisco Arts Commissioner, Walker was selected as one of four 2008 University of Missouri College of Arts & Science *Distinguished Alumna,* and a National Black Theatre Festival 2001 *Living Legend.* Ethel Walker, Thirty East Julian, Suite #218, San Jose, California 95112 Phone: (408) 216-9877 E-mail: **DRAMART@comcast.net** Website: **www.africanamericandramacompany.org**

Gary Watson Specialist in music, motion picture, and television entertainment legal services, Gary has been a guest lecturer for several seminars and conferences, as well as, courses for the University of California. Gary A. Watson, Esq., Gary A. Watson & Associates, 1875 Century Park East, Suite 1000, Los Angeles, California 90067 Phone: (310) 203-8022 Fax: (310) 203-8028 E-mail: **gwatson@garywatsonlaw.com** Website: **www.garywatsonlaw.com**

Kevin Craig West Director, producer and actor working in film, television, radio and stage and also a member of The Barrow Group in NYC, Chair member of Upstate Independents and in addition to being a Voice Acting Teacher and Producer for Voice Coaches, he also works as a Teacher/Artist with Symphony Space. Kevin West, MoBetta Films, Post Office Box 484, Troy, New York 12181 E-mail: **contact@kevincraigwest.com** Website: **www.kevincraigwest.com**

Crystal E. Wilkinson Served as writing mentor and taught creative writing classes for the center at Carnegie Center for Literacy and Learning, and at the University of Kentucky. Currently assistant professor of Creative Writing in Indiana University's MFA program. Crystal E. Wilkinson, 1428 North Forbes, Lexington, Kentucky 40511 Phone: (859) 381-8133 E-mail: **WilkinsonCrystal@aol.com** Website: **www.mythiumlitmag.com**

Write On! Literary Consortium Literary consulting services. Founder, Natasha Brooks-Harris. Write On! Literary Consortium, 297 7th Street, Brooklyn, New York 11215 E-mail: **nabrooks@aol.com**

Critics/Reviewers

Allbooks Reviews Company provides professional book reviews and author promotion at very reasonable fees. We also offer editing, advertising and guest speaking services. Listed in 101 Best Websites for Writers. Allbooks Reviews will review POD as well as traditional. Shirley Roe, Allbooks Review, 6540 Falconer Dr. # 38, Mississauga, Ontario L5N 1M1 Canada Phone: (416) 454-3643 E-mail: allbookreviews@aol.com

A Place of Our Own (Apooo) Information regarding African American Literature founded by Ms. Yasmin Coleman. Features upcoming literary events, book reviews, books, forthcoming books, bookstore. American literature. Ms. Coleman has over 20 years of marketing experiences and is a seasoned veteran at marketing, advertising, promotions, and publicity and has honed her craft via stints with several Fortune 500 packaged goods companies including Kraft Foods, RJR/Nabisco and Hershey Foods. Currently the Director of Marketing for a major state agency. Ms. Yasmin Coleman, A Place of Our Own, 4426 Pinewood Court, Harrisburg, Pennsylvania 17112 E-mail: apooo4u@yahoo.com Website: www.apooobooks.com

Edith Y. Billups Free-lance writer and critic for The Washington Informer Newspaper. Edith reviews theater, movies and music, and has written several travel articles for the paper's travel column, "Pack Your Bags." Contact Ms. Edith Y. Billups, The Gabriel Group, Post Office Box 13403, Silver Spring, Maryland 20911 Phone: (301) 562-5460 Fax: (240) 562-5468 E-mail: eybillups@aol.com

Black Issues Book Review Founded in 1998 by William E. Cox, President of Cox, Matthews & Associates, Inc., BIBR regular features include Between the Lines, affectionately known as BTL, the inside scoop on what's happening in the publishing industry. BIBR also provides up-to-date news on forthcoming author events, publications, conferences, shows and exhibits. Contact BIBR, Empire State Building, 350 Fifth Avenue, Suite 1522, New York, New York 10118 Phone: (212) 947-8515 Fax: (212) 947-5674 E-mail: bibredit@cmapublishing Website: www.bibookreview.com

Monique Miles Bruner Graduated from the University of Oklahoma with a Bachelors and Masters degree in Public Administration and a Masters of Human Relations. She has also completed the requirements for her doctoral degree in Adult Education from Oklahoma State University. She writes book reviews for a website that features African American authors at Looseleaves.org. Monique Miles Bruner, 6409 Braniff Drive, Oklahoma City, Oklahoma 73105 Phone: (405) 615-6711 E-mail: n2delta@yahoo.com

Anna Dennis Author and book reviewer for The LineUp's Bookworm Column, and co-host of The DR BookChat Radio Show, 97.7 and 88.1 FM (KECG/More Public Radio). She is co-founder of The Bay Area Book Writers Guild (BBWG). Anna Dennis, Apex Publishing, Post Office Box 5077, South San Francisco, California 94083 E-mail: apexpublishing@aol.com

Daniel Garrett Writer of journalism, fiction, poetry, and drama. Recently he has written a series of in-depth film essays for the web magazine, Offscreen.com, essays that focus on international cultures, philosophy, history, and politics. Previously, Garrett attended Baruch College, where he edited and wrote for The Reporter, before transferring as an undergraduate to the New School for Social Research, where he studied literature, politics, and philosophy and from which he graduated. He edited music interviews for I/Propaganda. He selected poetry for the male feminist magazine Changing Men. His own poetry has been published by AIM/America's Intercultural Magazine, Black American Literature Forum, The City Sun, The Humanist, Illuminations, and a few small book anthologies. Daniel Garrett, 05-63 135th Street, Richmond Hill, New York 11419 E-mail: **dgarrett31@hotmail.com**

Edward W. Hudlin Jr. Reviews books and films. Teaches and published in all areas of philosophy with specialties in Black Studies, film, and Asian Studies. Director and writer of educational television and radio. Harvard Fellow at the Institute for Afro-American Research. Edward W. Hudlin, Jr., 187 Lake Hillcrest, Glen Carbon, Illinois 62034 Phone: (618) 288-5545

Sharon Hudson Book reviewer. Also, editing provides services for authors - manuscripts, novels, poems, and any literary work. Provides on-line book reviews, critiques of literary events. Contact Sharon Hudson, Loose Leaves Enterprises, Post Office Box 548, Tyrone, Georgia 30290 Phone: (770) 314-5932 E-mail: **akaivyleaf@looseleaves.org** Website: **www.looseleaves.org**

Jacquie Jones An award-winning writer, director and producer of documentary films. In addition to her filmmaking, she is a widely published critic of popular culture and was formerly the editor of the internationally respected journal, Black Film Review. She is also Executive Director of the National Black Programming Consortium (NBPC). Jones holds a BA in English from Howard University and an MA in documentary filmmaking from Stanford University. Jacquie Jones, NBPC, 68 East 131st Street, 7th Floor, Harlem, New York 10037 Phone: (212) 234-8200 Fax: (212) 234-7032 E-mail: **jacquie@nbpc.tv** Website: **www.nbpc.tv**

Winnie MacGregor Writes various articles for the custom car industry. Publishes NationWide Riders 411, a monthly newsletter covering car shows and events and profiles various custom car enthusiasts. Winnie MacGregor, NationWide Riders, LLC, 25422 Trabuco Road #105, Lake Forest, California 92630 Phone: (949) 263-4594 E-mail: **NWRiders@aol.com**

Daphne Muse Social commentator, and poet, Daphne's commentaries and radio essays have been featured on KTOP-FM, KPFA-FM, KQED-FM and NPR. She has written more than 300 feature articles, essays, reviews and op-ed pieces for major newspapers and academic journals. Ms. Daphne Muse, 2429 East 23rd Street, Oakland, California 94601 Phone: (510) 436-4716 E-mail: **msmusewriter@gmail.com** Website: **www.oasisinthediaspora.com**

RAWSISTAZ Reviewers Leading reviewers in the literary industry with a focus on promoting the works of books by and about African-American Authors. Tee C. Royal is founder of Rawsistaz. She is also senior editor of BlackBoard Magazine; Books Editor of Mommy Too and TCBW Magazine. Rawsistzaz also offers literary services. The RAWSISTAZ Reviewers, Post Office Box 1362, Duluth, Georgia 30096 Phone: (775) 363-8683 Fax: (775) 416-4540 E-mail: **info@rawsistaz.com** Website: **www.blackbookreviews.net**

Real Page Turners Provides book reviews for readers. We post book reviews on various online sites, newsletters and online magazines. Monique "Deltareviewer" Bruner, Real Page Turners, Post Office Box 13204, Oklahoma City, Oklahoma 73113 E-mail: deltareviewer@yahoo.com

Cheryl Robinson Veteran broadcaster on radio and television throughout the years, Ms. Robinson is the host of Just About Books Talk Show, an internet radio talk show which provides book reviews of the books by interviewed authors. Ms. Cheryl Robinson, 1282 Smallwood Drive, West, Suite 116, Waldorf, Maryland 20603 Phone: (301) 643-2077 E-mail: JustAboutBooks@yahoo.com Website: www.JustAboutBooksTalkShow.com

Alvin C. Romer Editor of The Romer Review and Co-Owner of Write On! & Literary Consortium. Alvin C. Romer, Editor, The Romer Review, 415 North West 58th Street, Miami, Florida 33127 Phone: (786) 356-8119 E-mail: n4wiz51@yahoo.com

Wanda Sabir Columnist, and Arts Editor, at the San Francisco Bay View Newspaper. Contact Ms. Wanda Sabir, Post Office Box 30756, Oakland, California 94604 Phone: (510) 261-8436 E-mail: wsab1@aol.com Website: www.wandaspicks.com

Brenda M. Tillman Has been editor of several newsletters and magazines, written book reviews, a contributing writer for former Atlanta magazine, Strictly Jazz. Brenda M. Tillman, Jobrelika Enterprises International, LLC, Post Office Box 311223, Atlanta, Georgia 31131 Phone: (404) 556-7534 E-mail: shadesofmandingo@yahoo.com

Jeanette Toomer Drama in Education Specialist. MA, Educational Theatre; teacher; curriculum consultant; freelance writer; theatre critic; contributing editor. Jeanette Toomer, Post Office Box 1092, Cathedral Station, New York, New York 10025 Phone: (917) 405-1710 E-mail: nettoomer@yahoo.com

Ethel Pitts Walker Current Chair of Television, Radio, Film and Theatre at San Jose State University where she was a 1999-2000 *Teacher Scholar*. A former San Francisco Arts Commissioner, selected past accomplishments include: Elected as one of four 2008 University of Missouri College of Arts & Science *Distinguished Alumna* and a National Black Theatre Festival 2001 *Living Legend*. Ethel Pitts Walker, San Jose State University, Theatre Arts Department, One Washington Square, San Jose, California 95192 Phone: (408) 924-4586 E-mail: DRAMART@comcast.net Website: www.africanamericandramacompany.org

Jerry W. Ward, Jr. Professor of English at Dillard University, Jerry Washington Ward, Jr., is a poet, literary critic, and editor. His current projects include The Richard Wright Encyclopedia and Reading Race, Reading America, a collection of social and literary essays. He compiled and edited Trouble The Water: 250 Years of African American Poetry (Mentor, 1997). Jerry W. Ward, Jr., Department of English, Dillard University, 2601 Gentilly Boulevard, New Orleans, Louisiana 70122 E-mail: jerryward31@hotmail.com

Dera R. Williams Free lance writer. Also, a literary columnist for Dera's Den at apooo.org. Contact Dera R. Williams, CocoWriter Book & Tea Parlor, 4316 Rilea Way, Suite #2, Oakland, California 94605 E-mail: dwillautho@aol.com Website: www.apooobooks.com

Emily Means-Willis Educator, author, literary reviewer, columnist. After 37 years as an instructor in secondary education, Emily Means-Willis, recently retired and has published a novel entitled "Looking for that Silver Spoon". She also writes for various magazines. A second novel "Flip Side of the Coin" will be released in 2007. Emily Means-Willis, We, Us and Company, International, 419 Douglas Street, Park Forest, Illinois 60466 Phone: (708) 769-4116 E-mail: pamemi@comcast.net

Monique Baldwin Worrell Founded Flavah Reviewers. Features book and author interviews. Monique Baldwin Worrell, 1959 North Peace Haven Road, Suite 205, Winston Salem, North Carolina 27106 E-mail: anutwist@anutwistaflavah.com Website: www.anutwistaflavah.com

Directories

African American Yearbook Lists African American organizations, media publications, radio stations, Church resources, and more. Contact TIYM Publishing Company, Inc., 6718 Whittier Avenue, Suite 130, McLean, Virginia 22101 Phone: (703) 734-1632 Fax: (703) 356-0787 E-mail: tiym@tiym.com Website: www.africanamericanyearbook.com

Arizona's Black Pages A full service advertising agency specializing in reaching the Urban/Black community in Arizona & Nevada. Publishers of Arizona's Black Pages, Neveda's Black Pages (nvbp.com) and Arizona Jazz Magazine (AZJazz.com). Contact Publisher/CEO, D.A. Peartree. Contact Arizona's Black Pages, 822 East Montecito Avenue, Suite 4, Phoenix, Arizona 85014 Phone: (602) 230-8161 E-mail: editor@AZBP.com Website: www.azbp.com

Black Authors & Published Writers Directory Black Literary Marketplace listing of: authors, writers, song, film, and playwrights, poets, publishers, producers, agents, bookstores, distributors, librarians, columnists, critic reviewers, e-publications, newspapers, magazines, journals, TV news reporters, talk shows, voice-over artists, publishing services, audio and video production services, and much more. Editor and Publisher, Grace Adams. BAPWD c/o The Grace Publishing Company, 829 Langdon Court, Rochester Hills, Michigan 48307 Phone: (248) 613-6395 E-mail: graccointern@msn.com Website: www.bapwd.com

Black Film Report A comprehensive report on the financial performance of black films by author Tanya Kersey. Her most recent endeavors are as the host and producer of "Inside Urban Hollywood" on BlogTalkRadio and the CEO of BlackHollywoodUniversity.com. Contact Ms. Tanya Kersey, The Black Film Report, 8306 Wilshire Boulevard, Suite 2057, Beverly Hills, California 90211 Phone: (310) 203-1336 E-mail: tanya@tanyakersey.com Website: www.tanyakersey.com

BlackExperts.com A unique online directory that allows African American experts to profile themselves in front of journalists, TV/radio producers, meeting planners, and each other. We are not another speakers bureau, we are a directory! Contact Diversity City Media: 750-Q Cross Pointe Road, Columbus, Ohio 43230 Phone: (866) 910-6277 E-mail: sales@diversitycity.com Website: www.blackexperts.com

Black History Theme Book and Learning Resource Materials (The) Published by The Association for the Study of African American Life and History (ASALH-The Founders of Black History Month). ASALH was founded by Dr. Carter G. Woodson, the Father of Black History in 1915. ASALH sets the Black History Theme for each year and publishes a theme book which includes essays, articles, selected reading lists, curriculum guides, and more. Contact Dr. Sylvia Cyrus-Albritton, ASALH, CB Powell Building, 525 Bryant Street, North West, Suite C142, Washington, DC 20059 Phone: (202) 865-0053 Fax: (202) 265-7920 E-mail: executivedirector@asalh.net Website: www.asalh.org

Black Pages USA National Publication. Circulation 50,000. Annually, we will reach all segments of the African-American community including (but not limited to) youth, retirees, and the working class. Contact Gerry McCants, Publisher. Thomas-McCants Media, 355 Crawford Street, #402, Portsmouth, Virginia 23704 Phone: (757) 399-4153 Fax: (757) 399-0969 E-mail: gerry@blackpagesusa.com Website: www.blackpagesusa.com

Black Press Yearbook A national directory with complete listings of the Black and minority media. Contact Black Press Foundation, 1629 K Street, NW 3rd Floor, Washington, DC 20006 Phone: (646) 322-3047 Fax: (203) 738-3047 E-mail: blackpressmagazine@yahoo.com Website: www.blackpress.org

Black News Features daily African-American news. The site publishes a weekly e-mail newsletter featuring the top Black news stories of each week. Contact Black News, Diversity City Media, 225 West 3rd Street, Suite #203, Long Beach, California 90802 Phone: (562) 209-0616 E-mail: support@blacknews.com Website: blacknews.com

Black Speakers Online A division of Speakers Etc. The brainchild of Norma Thompson Hollis BSO offers a directory of Black speakers from a wide range of budgets, geographical areas, topics, talents and entertainments. Provides meeting planners the opportunity to connect with Black speakers and talent. Contact Ms. Norma Thompson, Black Speakers, Etc., 1968 West Adams Boulevard, Suite 208, Los Angeles, California 90018 Phone: (323) 734-7144 E-mail: info@blackspeakersonline.com Website: www.blackspeakersonline.com

Nevada's Black Pages Established in 2003, currently circulating 50,000 copies. Annually. Publisher/CEO, D.A. Peartree. Editor: M. Fitzhugh-Craig. Nevada's Black Pages, 822 East Montecito Avenue, Suite 4, Phoenix, Arizona 85014 E-mail: editor@nvbp.com Website: www.nvbp.com

Talk of the Town A physical minority business directory interactive website serving business professionals in the state of Kentucky & Southern Indiana. Janeice R. Black, Post Office Box 18088, Louisville, Kentucky 40261 Phone: (502) 287-0278 Fax: (502) 287-0278 E-mail: talklou@win.net Website: www.talkofthetown-lou.com

The Urban Hollywood Resource Directory National and international directory listings of the African-American film industry. Tanya Kersey, editor and Publisher. Also, publishes the Black Talent News Newsletter. Contact Editor, Tanya Kersey, Lacy Street Production Center, 2630 Lacy Street, Los Angeles, California 90031 Phone: (310) 203-1336 Fax: (310) 943-2326 E-mail: tanya@tanyakersey.com Website: www.tanyakersey.com

Editorial Services

A KEEN EYE Copyediting Group Since, 2005. Consists of a team of experienced editors with backgrounds in Journalism and Education. After years of editing and proofreading business plans, short stories, novels, brochures, and other documents, they decided that the self-published author is where they would like to focus their efforts and attention. The Group is dedicated to providing excellent service and feedback to first-time writers, as well as those who have published multiple novels. Each member of the editing group is an avid reader of different styles of literature which makes them especially competent in editing many genres of books, including fantasy, urban African-American literature, commentary, romance, mystery, erotica, and horror. Contact Ms. Teowonna Clifton, Copyediting Group, Post Office Box 3907, Columbia, South Carolina 29230 Phone: (803) 348-5847 E-mail: **editor@akeeneyecopyediting.com** Website: **www.akeeneyecopyediting.com**

Better Day Publishing Company Book, brochure and catalog design, copyright application, direct marketing, editorial services, graphic design illustration, material design book publishing. Naresha S. Perry, Publisher. Contact Better Day Publishing Company, 1152 Westheimer, #341, Houston, Texas 77042 Phone: (713) 548-4048 E-mail: **contact@betterdaypublishing.com** Website: **www.betterdaypublishing.com**

Black Star Consulting Former Random House book editor, Carol A.Taylor has been in the book publishing business for over 10 years. She is a published author, a freelance writer, book editor and an editorial consultant who has worked with book publishers, agents, best selling authors and up and coming writers. For book editing or consulting queries send an e-mail. Carol A. Taylor, Black Star Consulting, 295 Clinton Avenue #E3, Brooklyn, New York 11205 E-mail: **carol@brownsugarbooks.com** Website: **www.BrownSugarBooks.com**

Magdalene Breaux Publishing services, technical writing, book production consulting for independent authors and TV production and editing. Contact Ms. Magdalene Breaux, Post Office Box 67, Fairburn, Georgia 30213 Phone: (770) 842-4792 Fax: (770) 964-1875 E-mail: **magbreaux@mindspring.com** Website: **www.familycurse.com**

EBM Professional Services Specializes in content editing, copyediting, proofreading, and technical editing for ALL document types. Since 2003, the editors at EPS have proofread and edited more than 100,000 pages for clients worldwide Michelle Chester, EBM Professional Services, Post Office Box 118900, Carrollton, Texas 75011 Phone: (469) 222-3418 E-mail: **michelle@ebm-services.com** Website: **www.ebm-services.com**

Milligan Literary Agency Editorial consultant and book agent. Ghost writing, book evaluation, book rewriting for mainstream publishing submission; book rewrite when requested. Milligan Literary Agency, 1425 West Manchester Avenue, Suite C, Los Angeles, California 90047 Phone: (323) 750-3592 E-mail: **DrRosie@aol.com** Website: **www.drrosie.com**

Daphne Muse   Through her more than ten year old editorial service, she works with emerging and established writers; move them from Concept to Manuscript.   Contact Ms. Daphne Muse, 2429 East 23rd Street, Oakland, California 94601   Phone: (510) 436-4716   Fax: (510) 261-6064   E-mail: **msmusewriter@gmail.com**   Website: **www.oasisinthediaspora.com**

Novel Ideal Publishing & Editorial Services Company   Full service editorial service offering copy editing, content editing and proofreading services.   Novel Ideal Publishing & Editorial Services Company, 2274 Salem Road, Suite 106, Post Office Box 173, Conyers, Georgia 30013   E-mail: **novelideal@yahoo.com**   Website: **www.electaromeparks.com**

Taylor Media Services   Press/News Releases, copy writing and editoral services.   Founder, President Robert Taylor.   Approximately, 40,000 people read his newsletter weekly.   Also edits the Black History Journal - a free weekly email-distributed journal detailing the most important Black historical events of each week.   Mr. Taylor received his BA from Howard University in Washington, D.C., and his Masters Degree in Mass Communications from Columbia University in New York City.   Mr. Robert S. Taylor, Taylor Media Services, 1517 T Street, South East, Washington, D.C. 20020   Phone: (202) 657-8872   E-mail: **taylormediaservices@yahoo.com**   Website: **www.freewebs.com/blacknewsjournal**

Write On! Literary Consortium   Company provides literary consulting services. Founder, Natasha Brooks-Harris is a full-service copy editor, line editor, and proofreader of novel and short fiction manuscripts.   She has edited several full-length novels and is working on several more.   She has worked in the publishing field since 1987.   Currently, Nathasha is the editor of Black Romance and Bronze Thrills magazines.   She is the author of Panache, a contemporary romance novel.   Contact Ms. Natasha Brooks-Harris, Write On! Literary Consortium, 297 7th Street, Brooklyn, New York 11215   E-mail: **nabrooks@aol.com**

Write Page Literary Service, Inc.   An Atlanta-based business and creative writing firm. President and primary consultant, Ms. Madge D. Owens is an author and native Atlantan and graduate of Clark College (now Clark Atlanta University).   Contact Ms. Madge D. Owens, Write Page Literary Service, Inc., Post Office Box 38288, Atlanta, Georgia 30334   Phone: (404) 280-5029   Fax: (404) 656-0238   E-mail: **writepagemo@yahoo.com**

Editors

Book

Malaika Adero Senior Editor. Malaika Adero, Atria Books/Simon & Schuster, Simon & Schuster, Inc., 1230 Avenue of the Americas, New York, New York 10020 Phone: 212-698-7000 E-mail: malaika.adero@simonandschuster.com Website: www.simonsays.com

Dawn Davis Vice Presdent and Publisher. Interested in general, non-fiction and fiction related to the Black experience. Contact Ms. Christina Morgan, Assistant, Amistad, HarperCollins Publishers, 10 East 53rd Street, New York, New York 10022 Phone: (212) 207-7000 Website: www.harpercollins.com

Glenda Howard Executive Editor. We publish a variety of outstanding mainstream fiction titles that predominately feature African-American characters. Our editorial features a broad range of genres such as: commercial women's fiction, historical fiction and romantic suspense. Submission Guidelines: Please send a detailed synopsis and three sample chapters to: Glenda Howard, Executive Editor, Kimani Press. Kimani Press, 233 Broadway, Suite 1001, New York, New York 10279 Phone: (212) 553-4217 Website: www.eharlequin.com

Selena James Executive Editor, Dafina Books. African-American fiction and nonfiction, including inspirational, young adult, romance, and pop culture. Query only by e-mail. Do not attach manuscripts or proposals to e-mail queries. Selena James Dafina/Kensington/Penguin, Kensington Publishing Corp., 850 Third Avenue, New York, New York 10022 Phone: (877) 422-3665 E-mail: sjames@kensingtonbooks.com Website: www.kensingtonbooks.com

Erroll McDonald Vice President and Executive Editor. Pantheon/Random Imprints. Interested in adult, fiction and non-fiction books. Contact Mr. Erroll McDonald, Pantheon/Random Imprints, 1745 Broadway, New York, New York 10019 Phone: (212) 940-7741 E-mail: EMcDonald@randomhouse.com Website: www.randomhouse.biz

Evette Porter Editor. Imprint Kimani TRU. Interested in young Adult fiction. Manuscript word length approximately 60,000 - 70,000 words. Evette Porter, Editor, Kimani Press, 233 Broadway, Suite 1001, New York, New York 10279 Website: www.eharlequin.com

Magazine

Susan Benjamin Editor-in-Chief of Family Digest Magazine, the leading family magazine in the United States, and the #1 publication for Black families nationwide. Features family and parenting tips and advice, stories, quotes, culture and home, beauty and style, health and fitness. Susan Benjamin, Editor-in-Chief, Family Digest, Post Office Box 342374, Austin, Texas 78734 Fax: (512) 795-2078 E-mail: editor@familydigest.com Website: www.familydigest.com

Carla D. Bluitt Editor and Publisher of Say So! Magazine, a free Christian resource magazine with bi-monthly distribution in the Baltimore/Washington Metropolitan Area. Carla D. Bluitt, Say So! Magazine, 6030 Daybreak Circle, Suite A150/151, Clarksville, Maryland 21029 Phone: (301) 807-5445 E-mail: **cbluitt@saysomagazine.com** Website: **www.saysomagazine.com**

Nathasha Brooks-Harris Editor of Black Romance and Bronze Thrills magazines and the co-owner of Write On! Literary Consortium, provides literary consulting services. Contact Ms. Natasha Brooks-Harris, 297 7th Street, Brooklyn, New York 11215 E-mail: **nabrooks@aol.com**

Caleen Burton-Allen Publisher/Editor-In-Chief of ONYX Style Magazine. Contact Ms. Caleen Burton-Allen, ONYX Style Magazine, 8787 Woodway Drive, Suite 4206, Houston, Texas 77063 Phone: (832) 467-9377 Fax: (832) 467-9378 E-mail: **caleen@onyxstyle.com** Website: **www.onyxstyle.com**

Algie deWitt Publisher and Editor-in-Chief of MAMi Magazine. Internationally distributed title, Mami Magazine is the now of fashion, lifestyle, luxury magazine. Contact Mr. Algie deWitt, MAMi Magazine, 4408 Aberdeen Lane, Blackwood, New Jersey 08012 E-mail: **algie@mamimagazine.com** Website: **www.mamimagazine.com**

Alfred Edmond Jr. Senior Vice President and Editor-in-Chief of BlackEnterprise.com. Also host The Urban Business Roundtable radio show at WVON. The show promotes engaging dialogue and debate about the impact of business and economic trends on the African-American community. At Black Enterpris.com, Mr. Edmond is responsible for the long-term planning and development of the Website's content, as well as the hiring and overall supervision of the editorial staff, which consists of editors, writers/bloggers, and contributing editors. Mr. Alfred Edmond, Jr., WVON 1450AM, 3350 South Kedzie, Chicago, Illinois 60623 Phone: (773) 247-6200 E-mail: **monews74@hotmail.com** Website: **www.wvon.com**

Dawn Fobbs Author, and Creative publisher of Stand Magazine for 2 years. Stand is committed to providing solid information for entrepreneurs and business owners. Contact Ms. Dawn Fobbs, Stand Magazine, Post Office Box 6667, Katy, Texas 77491 Phone: (281) 587-4054 E-mail: **msdawwn@sbcglobal.net** Website: **www.standmagazine.biz**

Michelle Fitzhugh-Craig CEO/Editor-In-Chief, Shades Magazine. Editor of Arizona's Black Pages, a full service advertising agency specializing in reaching the Urban/Black community in Arizona & Nevada. President, Arizona Association of Black Journalists. Contact Ms. Michelle Fitzhugh-Craig, Shades Magazine, Post Office Box 46325, Phoenix, Arizona 85063 E-mail: **shadesmagazine1@gmail.com** Website: **www.myshadesmagazine.net**

Nancey Flowers Editor-In-Chief of Game Sports Magazine and publisher of Flowers In Bloom Publishing, Inc., Nancey attended Morgan State University in Baltimore, Maryland, where she received her bachelor's degree in mass communications with a minor in journalism. She served as Program Director for The Harlem Book Fair, a contributor to Black Issues Book Review and former Managing Editor of QBR, The Black Book Review. Contact Ms. Nancey Flowers, Flowers In Bloom Publishing, Post Office Box 473106, Brooklyn, New York 11247 E-mail: **nanceyflowers@msn.com** Website: **www.flowersinbloompublishing.com**

Michelle R. Gipson Publisher of Written Magazine, and former Director of Advertising for Black Issues Book Review and Managing Editor of the Atlanta Daily World's Celebration of Books. She earned both her B.A. in Mass Media and her M.A. in Counseling from Hampton University. She has been published in Jane, Black Issues Book Review, the Atlanta Daily World and Chicken Soup for the African American Soul, and Chicken Soup for the Recovering Soul. Michelle R. Gipson, Written Magazine, Post Office Box 250504, Atlanta, Georgia 30325 Phone: (404) 753-8315 E-mail: michelle.gipson@writtenmag.com   Website: www.writtenmag.com

L A Hughes (aka Linda Atkins Hughes) Editor-in-chief of IBWALA's newsletter / literary magazine, Black Expressions. An active member of IBWALA since 1978, Hughes has been associate editor on two IBWALA anthologies and has been the primary editor for several outside projects, fiction and nonfiction. Contact Ms. L A Hughes, International Black Writers & Artists, Los Angeles, Post Office Box 43576, Los Angeles, California 90043 Phone: (323) 964-3721 E-mail: ahughes@ibwa.org Website: www.ibwa.org

Roxann Latimer Editor in Chief of the award winning multicultural magazine, Women In Motion. Roxann also works as a television producer with her company WIM Media and as Publisher. Roxann Latimer, WIM Media, 3900 West 22nd Lane #10G, Yuma, Arizona 85364 Phone: (928) 343-9729 E-mail: wimmedia@yahoo.com Website: www.roxannlatimer.com

Shanté Morgan Editor of Turning Point Magazine, Shanté Morgan has worked for over a decade as a reporter, writing for both newspapers and magazines, covering everything from Hollywood trends to presidential campaigns. Shanté Morgan, Morgan Communications, 1710 North Moorpark Road #163, Thousand Oaks, California 91360 Phone: (310) 594-9890 E-mail: ShanteMorgan@aol.com

Salim Muwakkil A Senior Editor of In These Times, and an op-ed columnist for the Chicago Tribune, Mr. Muwakkil is currently a Crime and Communities Media Fellow of the Open Society Institute, examining the impact of ex-inmates and gang leaders in leadership positions in the black community. Also host his own radio show The Salim Muwakkil Show at WVON 1450AM in Chicago. Muwakkil is a frequent contributor to Chicago Tonight and Beyond the Beltway with Bruce Dumont, two Chicago-based public affairs programs. Salim Muwakkil, WVON 1450AM, 3350 South Kedzie, Chicago, Illinois 60623 Phone: (773) 247-6200 E-mail: salim4x@aol.com Website: www.inthesetimes.com

Tee C. Royal Senior Editor of BlackBoard Magazine; Books Editor of Mommy Too and TCBW Magazine. Founder of RAWSISTAZ Reviewers, the leading reviewers in the literary industry. Review and promote books by both mainstream and independent authors. Also offers literary services. Tee C. Royal, Post Office Box 1362, Duluth, Georgia 30096 Phone: (775) 363-8683 Fax: (775) 416-4540 E-mail: tee@rawsistaz.com Website: www.therawreviewers.com

Oasis Owner/Editor-In-Chief, Man Up Magazine. The thing which makes Man Up Magazine unique is that 90% of its contributors are either prisoners or ex-convicts whose life has been changed through adversity and now strives to enhance the quality of life. Oasis Publishing Group c/o Man Up Magazine, Post Office Box 19101, Cleveland, Ohio 44119 Phone: (216) 633-2397 E-mail: manup@oasisnovels.com Website: www.oasisnovels.com

Newspaper

Roland S. Martin Nationally award winning journalist and syndicated columnist with Creators Syndicate, the founding editor of BlackAmericaweb.com and formerly the executive editor of The Chicago Defender, is a frequent commentator on TV-One, CNN, MSNBC, FOX, and Black Entertainment Television (BET). He is also the author of Speak, Brother! A Black Man's View of America. Roland S. Martin, NuVision Media, Inc., 1327 West Washington Boulevard #102B, Chicago, Illinois 60607 Phone: (312) 543-6000 E-mail: **roland@rolandsmartin.com** Website: **www.rolandsmartin.com**

Wanda Sabir Arts Editor and Columnist at the San Francisco Bay View Newspaper. Also host an online radio show Wanda Picks at blogtalkradio.com. Contact Wanda Sabir, Post Office Box 30756, Oakland, California 94604 Phone: (510) 261-8436 E-mail: **wanda@wandaspicks.com** Website: **www.wandaspicks.com**

Ken Smikle President and founder of Target Market News, and editor and publisher of its publications, is considered one of the leading authorities on marketing, advertising and media directed to the African-American market. The company also distributes news and information on the latest developments in marketing and media through its Web site. Ken Smikle, Target Market News, 228 South Wabash Avenue, Suite 210, Chicago, Illinois 60604 Phone: (312) 408-1881 E-mail: **info@tarketmarketnews.com** Website: **www.targetmarketnews.com**

Robert Taylor Currently Editor of the online digital newspaper: The National Black News Journal. Approximately, 40,000 people read his newsletter weekly. Contact Mr. Robert S. Taylor, National Black News Services, Taylor Media Services, 1517 T Street, South East, Washington, D.C. 20020 Phone: (202) 657-8872 E-mail: **taylormediaservices@yahoo.com** Website: **www.freewebs.com/blacknewsjournal**

Kathy Reevie Editor Assistant, The Baltimore Times Newspaper. Publisher, Joye Bramble. Contact Ms. Kathy Reevie, The Baltimore Times, 2513 North Charles, Baltimore, Maryland 21218 Phone: (410) 366-3900 Fax: (410) 243-1627 E-mail: **kreevie@btimes.com** Website: **www.btimes.com**

ePublications

Africabiz Online Online e-newsletter on investing and trading in Africa. Mr. Khalid Thomas, President. Contact Dynamic Group Ltd, Businessafrica, 1106 Carlyon Road, Cleveland, Ohio 44112 Phone: (347) 534-9329 E-mail: editor@africabiz.org Website: www.africabiz.org

AACBWI.com The African-American Children's Writers and Illustrators online group is a collective information-sharing forum for children's authors and illustrators, young and old founded by author, Sabra A. Robinson. AACBWI.com, Post Office Box 620324, Charlotte, North Carolina 28262 E-mail: sabra@sabrarobinson.com Website: www.aacbwi.com

Afropop WorldWide eNewsletter. Premier destination for web denizens interested in contemporary music of Africa and the African Diaspora. Our mission of connecting world class veteran and emerging artists from Africa, the Caribbean and the Americas with music lovers everywhere will find new pathways in the web world. Afropop worldwide producer, Sean Barlow is the Project Director. He edits the weekly Afropop e-Newsletter. Afropop Worldwide, 688 Union Street, Storefront, Brooklyn New York 11215 Website: www.afropop.org

Afropulse Website Publication. Focus is reggae, African, Caribbean and world music, information, news, reviews, interviews, discographies and cultural features to an international audience of avid music fans. Mr. Jay Nelson is Editor. He is also a Photographer and host The Beat website. Contact Jay Nelson, The Beat Magazine, Post Office Box 65856, Los Angeles, California 90065 Phone: (818) 500-9299 Fax: (818) 500-9454 E-mail: jay@afropulse.com Website: www.afropulse.com

AllAfrica Successor to the non-profit Africa News Service, which produced prize-winning print and broadcast reporting for major media such as National Public Radio, the Washington Post and the BBC for two decades, prior to developing an online venture. Reed Kramer, founder, chief executive officer and director. Contact AllAfrica, 920 M. Street, South East, Washington, DC 20002 Phone: (202) 546-0777 Fax: (202) 546-0676 Website: www.allafrica.com

BackList Monthly publishing and literary newsletter of African-American interest. Each issue is an intelligent and timely discussion of publishing, writing, and reading trends. Features include: Q&A with Industry Professionals, Book Commentary and Reviews, Publishing News, Author Profiles, Events and Literary Announcements. Read issues online. Galleys, ARC's and press releases, mail to Felicia Pride, Backlist, 55 West 116th Street, Suite 455, New York, New York 10026 E-mail: felicia@thebacklist.net Website: www.thebacklist.net

Black Book Reviews Leading African American Book Reviews in the industry. Publishes a Daily newsletter of black book reviews which can be found on our site. The RAWSISTAZ Reviewers, Post Office Box 1362, Duluth, Georgia 30096 Phone: (775) 363-8683 Fax: (775) 416-4540 E-mail: info@rawsistaz.com Website: www.blackbookreviews.net

Black Britain Launched in July 1998 to deliver immediate and regular news and information services to the Black and ethnic minority communities, and to address the shortcomings of mainstream media which continued to cover Black and ethnic minority news interest negatively and/or inadequately. Black Britain c/o The Colourful Network, Suite 5, 2nd Floor, Culvert House, Culvert Road, London SW11 5AP Phone: 08700 76 5656 Fax: 08700 76 5757 Text: 07779 66 5858 E-mail: **publisher@live247.co.uk** Website: **www.live247.co.uk**

Black Coffee Magazine Online magazine, recognize successful African Americans in Business, Entertainment and the Arts. Also a book club and online bookstore. Crystal Cornell, Publisher. Crystallized Publishing, 16208 Eucalyptus Ave #21, Bellflower, California 90706 Phone: (562) 685-4609 E-mail: **crystal@blackcoffeemag.com** Website: **www.blackcoffeemag.com**

Black Collegian Online The electronic version of the national career opportunities magazine. Features commentary by leading African-American writers, lifestyle/entertainment features, general information on college life, and news of what's happening on college campuses today. Black Collegian Online, 140 Carondelet Street, New Orleans, Louisiana 70130 Phone: (832) 615-8871 E-mail: **stewart@imdiversity.com** Website: **www.black-collegian.com**

Black Commentator.com Core audience is African Americans. Features commentary, analysis and investigation, elements of political dialogue that are absolutely essential to the creation of movements for social change. Co-publisher, Peter Gamble. Contact BlackCommentator.com, Suite 473, 93 Old York Road, Jenkintown Pennsylvania 19046 Phone: (202) 318-4032 E-mail: **publisher@blackcommentator.com** Website: **www.blackcommentator.com**

Black Enterprise.co.uk Directory of UK businesses and development / support agencies. BE's mission is to facilitate the development, growth and long-term sustainability of business enterprise. It has the only regular publication of news and information to the African Caribbean business community. Contact Black Enterprise.co.uk c/o The Colourful Network, Suite 5, 2nd Floor, Culvert House, Culvert Road, London SW11 5AP Phone: 08700 76 5656 Fax: 08700 76 5757 Text: 07779 66 5858 E-mail: **publisher@live247.co.uk** Website: **www.live247.co.uk**

Black Literary Players Monthly on-line newsletter update for Black Authors & Published Writers Directory on our website. Features the Black Literary Marketplace: authors, writers, song, film and playwrights, poets, agents, producers, publishers, and much more. Grace Adams, Editor. The Grace Company, 829 Langdon Court, #45, Rochester Hills, Michigan 48307 Phone: (248) 425-7083 E-mail: **info@bapwd.com** Website: **www.bapwd.com**

Black Living Network focusing on today's black woman providing news, entertainment, career, health, fitness, beauty, business, personal finance and more! Gloria Sawyers, Publisher. Black Women's Network, 601 E. Palomar, #264, Chula Vista, California 91911 Phone: (619) 254-1704 Fax: (619) 863-5719 E-mail: **editor@blackliving.com** Website: **www.blackliving.com**

Black News Features daily African-American news. The site publishes a weekly e-mail newsletter featuring the top Black news stories of each week. Contact Black News, Diversity City Media, 225 West 3rd Street, Suite #203, Long Beach, California 90802 Phone: (562) 209-0616 E-mail: **support@blacknews.com** Website: **blacknews.com**

Black Speakers Online A division of Speakers Etc. The brainchild of Norma Thompson Hollis BSO offers a directory of Black speakers from a wide range of budgets, geographical areas, topics, talents and entertainments. Provides meeting planners the opportunity to connect with Black speakers and talent. Contact Ms. Norma Thompson, Black Speakers, Etc., 1968 West Adams Boulevard, Suite 208, Los Angeles, California 90018 Phone: (323) 734-7144 E-mail: info@blackspeakersonline.com Website: www.blackspeakersonline.com

Black Students   Publishes a weekly e-mail newsletter featuring the latest news, tips, and opportunities for African-American students. Contact Black Students, Diversity City Media, 225 West 3rd Street, Suite #203, Long Beach, California 90802 Phone: (562) 209-0616 E-mail: support@blackstudents.com Website: blackstudents.com

Black Tokyo Site for Africans and African-Americans in Tokyo. Webmaster and site owner Eric L. Robinson (Zurui). Features news and discussion on Japan from an Afro perspective: life in Japan, business, economy and finance, government, politics and security. News, discussions, and many other topics. BT was created to provide a voice and a network for Blacks living in Japan. Black Tokyo, 3-16-1-2 Takada, Toshima-ku, Tokyo 117-0033 Phone: 011-81-902-338-4435 E-mail: info@blacktokyo.com Website: www.blacktokyo.com

Black Voices   African-American and Black culture community.   Publication features news, lifestyle, career and entertainment online for African-Americans. Black Voices, Tribune Tower, 435 North Michigan Avenue, Suite LL2, Chicago, Illinois 60611 Phone: (312) 222-4326 Fax: (312) 222-4502 E-mail: dsquires@corp.blackvoices.com Website: www.blackvoices.com

de Griot Space   Online writing workshop. Our primary purpose as an online writing workshop is to offer a psychologically safe space to African descended writers. A. Hodari, dGS Moderator. de Griot Space, Post Office Box 110637, Birmingham, Alabama 35211 Phone: (205) 910-7952 E-mail: dgs@igc.org

DelawareBlack.com   Mission is to provide the African-American community an online resource which will help promote the growth of Black-Owned businesses and encourage the support for African-American events. Darryl Wilson, Delawareblack.com, 560 Peoples Plaza #288, Newark, Delaware 19702 Phone: (302) 250-4425 E-mail: dwilson@delawareblack.com Website: www.delawareblack.com

Detroit Gospel A Gospel music and entertainment E-zine providing comprehensive coverage of the Metro-Detroit gospel scene. Also maintains database of Detroit's gospel music artists; lists of Detroit's gospel media outlets, record labels, and management companies. Mary Crosby, Editor, Detroit Gospel, 18701 Grand River Avenue, #134, Detroit, Michigan 48223 Phone: (313) 531-1141 E-mail: editor@detroitgospel.com Website: www.detroitgospel.com

Emerging Minds Online Magazine Launched in 2003 EM online is a news and cultural magazine for writers of all ages to present their perspectives on the current issues and events. Saadiq Mance, Managing Director, Emerging Minds Magazine, 541 Tenth Street, North West, Suite 318, Atlanta, Georgia 30318 E-mail: emergingminds@emergingminds.org Website: www.emergingminds.org

EXODUS Newsmagazine Published on the internet. The newsmagaine's goal is to bring news from international, national and San Francisco Bay Area perspectives readers find useful and informative. EXODUS Newsmagazine, 1009 East Capitol Exp. #323, San Jose, California 95121 Phone: (408) 821-2916 Fax: (630) 982-3171 E-mail: hampton@exodusnews.com Website: www.exodusnews.com

Family Digest Online Founded by Darryl L. Mobley, FDM is the leading family magazine in the United States, and the #1 publication for Black families nationwide. Features family and parenting tips and advice, stories, quotes, culture and home, beauty and style, health and fitness. Susan Benjamin, Editor-in-Chief. Family Digest, Post Office Box 342374, Austin, Texas 78734 Fax: (512) 795-2078 E-mail: editor@familydigest.com Website: www.familydigest.com

Gesica Magazine The Premiere Urban Entertainment Experience. Tonisha Johnson, Editor and Publisher. Gesica Magazine, Post Office. Box 30231, Staten Island, New York 10303 Phone: (718) 216-3530 E-mail: TonishaJohnson@gmail.com Website: www.gesicaonline.com

Kay3Musik An Online gospel/Christian music publication serving the mainstream and independent sections of the industry. Resources and inspirational articles, also provides artist promotion. Contact Mr. Robert Kennedy III, Kay3Music, 210 Mill Street, Suite 166, Lancaster, Massachusetts 01523 E-mail: info@kay3music.com Website: www.kay3music.com

Live247 Provides a single point of reference on the internet for multicultural events and entertainment in the UK. Primary target market is the UK urban community - 12 - 29 year olds. Live247.co.uk c/o The Colourful Network, Suite 5, 2nd Floor, Culvert House, Culvert Road, London SW11 5AP Phone: 08700 76 5656 Fax: 08700 76 5757 Text: 07779 66 5858 E-mail: publisher@live247.co.uk Website: www.live247.co.uk

The Mail & Guardian Online Internet-based news publication in Africa. Launched in early 1994, it is one of South Africa's and Africa's major news publishers and is reputed internationally for its quality content. The Mail & Guardian Online, Post Office Box 9166, Auckland Park, Johannesburg 2006 South Africa E-mail: editoronline@mg.co.za Website: www.mg.co.za

Man Up Magazine Bi-monthly via the internet targets avid readers and art enthusiast who frequent cultural events. Features the syndicated column Reality On Ice. Its columns range from author features to business and investing. Oasis, is owner and Editor-In-Chief. Contact Oasis Publishing Group c/o Man Up Magazine, Post Office Box 19101, Cleveland, Ohio 44119 Phone: (216) 633-2397 E-mail: manup@oasisnovels.com Website: www.oasisnovels.com

Mirror-Gibbs Magazine Weekly on-line magazine with over 300,000 readers a month. Frank Jones, Publisher, Mirror-Gibbs Publications, Post Office Box 6573, Oakland, California 94603 Phone: (510) 409-9571 E-mail: pinoquit@hotmail.com Website: www.gibbsmagazine.com

MMR e-News E-mail-distributed newswire that features profiles of companies that have expertise in reaching multicultural consumers. Multicultural Marketing Resources, Inc., 286 Spring Street, Suite 201, New York, New York 10013 Phone: (212) 242-3351 Fax: 212) 691-5969 E-mail: lisa@multicultural.com Website: www.multicultural.com

The National Black News Journal The nation's leading Black-interest E-newsletter. It is distributed weekly to nearly 10,000 subscribers. Robert "Siraj" Taylor, National Black News Journal, 2315 Lincoln Road, North East, #207 Washington, DC 20002 Phone: (202) 486-8103 E-mail: blacknewsjournal@yahoo.com Website: www.freewebs.com/blacknewsjournal

Quarterly Book Review Dedicated to books about the Africana experience; fiction, nonfiction, poetry, children's books, health, lifestyle management, writers from Africa and the Caribbean. Max Rodriguez, Publisher. QBR, 9 West 126th Street, New York, New York 10027 Phone: (212) 348-1681 Fax: (212) 427-9901 E-mail: mrodz@qbr.com Website: www.qbr.com

Radio Facts E-zine covers all areas of the industry including: television, music, radio, books, movies, clubs and production from an industry perspective.   Contact Mr. Kevin Ross, Radio Facts, 595 Piedmont Avenue North East, Suite 320-314, Atlanta, Georgia 30308   E-mail: kevin.ross@radiofacts.com Website: www.radiofacts.com

SFBayView Online version of the national Black newspaper San Francisco Bay View. Contact San Francisco Bay View, 4917 Third Street, San Francisco, California 94124 Phone: (415) 671-0789 Fax: (415) 671-0316 E-mail: editor@sfbayview.com Website: www.sfbayview.com

The Talking Drum A yearly publication of academic articles on African and African American Music by a variety of writers published by The National Association for the Study and Performance of African American Music (NASPAAM). Contact Mr. Frank Suggs, President, NASPAAM, 1201 Mary Jane, Memphis, Tennessee 38116 Phone: (901) 396-2913 E-mail: f.suggs@naspaam.org Website: www.naspaam.org

Talk of the Town A physical minority business directory interactive website serving business professionals in the state of Kentucky & Southern Indiana. Janice R. Black, Post Office Box 18088, Louisville, Kentucky 40261 Phone: (502) 287-0278 Fax: (502) 287-0278 E-mail: talklou@win.net Website: www.talkofthetown-lou.com

Trendsetters to Trendsetters Magazine National publication reaches thousands of homes and businesses bi-monthly via hardcopy and internet. Willie Stewart, Chief Executive Officer and Publisher. Trendsetters to Trendsetters Magazine, 3007 Panola Road, Suite 283C, Lithonia, Georgia 30038 Phone: (404) 437-4311 E-mail: wstewart@trendtotrendmag.com Website: www.trendtotrendmag.com

Triangle Offense On-line informative and interactive publication, which promotes the writings of graduate students, employees of community-based organizations, and aspiring journalists and creative writers. La Caille Nous Publishing, Inc., 328 Flatbush Avenue, Suite 240, Brooklyn, New York 11238 Phone: (212) 726-1293 Fax: (212) 591-6465 E-mail: info@lncpub.com Website: www.lcnpub.com

Women in Focus FORUM Newsletter A professional business network mentoring and supporting women, men and students. Women in Focus Forum Newsletter, Post Office Box 1334, Rialto, California 92377 Phone: (909) 873-5055 E-mail: Info@wifforum.com Website: www.wifforum.com/meetings001.htm

Molefi Kete Asante
Author * Educator * Painter * Poet

Molefi Kete Asante is Professor, Department of African American Studies at Temple University. He is also a Guest Professor, Zhejiang University in Hangzhou, China. Dr. Asante has published 70 books, among the most recent are Maulana Karenga: An Intellectual Portrait, (2010); Erasing Racism, 2nd edition, (2009); Encyclopedia of African Religion, (2009), co-edited with Ama Mazama; The History of Africa, (2008); Global Intercultural Communication (2007); Cheikh Anta Diop: An Intellectual Portrait (2006); Spear Masters: An Introduction to African Religion (2006), co-authored with Emeka Nwadiora; Handbook of Black Studies, (2005), co-edited with Maulana Karenga; Encyclopedia of Black Studies, (2004), co-edited with Ama Mazama; Race, Rhetoric, and Identity: The Architecton of Soul (2005); Ancient Egyptian Philosophers (2000); Scattered to the Wind, Custom and Culture of Egypt, and 100 Greatest African Americans. He has recently been recognized as one of the most widely cited scholars. In the 1990s, he was recognized as one of the most influential leaders in American education.

Dr. Asante was born in Valdosta, Georgia in the United States, of Sudanese and Nigerian heritage, one of sixteen children. He is a poet, dramatist, and a painter. He is the founding editor of the Journal of Black Studies (1969) and was the President of the Civil Rights organization, the Student Non-Violent Coordinating Committee chapter at UCLA in the 1960's. He completed his M.A. at Pepperdine and received his Ph.D. from the University of California, Los Angeles, at the age of 26, and was appointed a full professor at the age of 30 at the State University of New York at Buffalo. At Temple University he created the first Ph.D. Program in African American Studies in 1987. He has directed more than 130 Ph.D. dissertations. He has written more than 300 articles for journals and magazines and is the founder of the theory of Afrocentricity. His work on African language, multiculturalism, and human culture and philosophy has been cited by journals such as the Africalogical Perspectives, Quarterly Journal of Speech, Journal of Black Studies, Journal of Communication, American Scholar, Daedalus, Western Journal of Black Studies, and Africaological Perspectives. The Utne Reader called him one of the "100 Leading Thinkers" in America. In 2002 he received the distinguished Douglas Ehninger Award for Rhetorical Scholarship from the National Communication Association. He regularly consults with the African Union. In 2004 he was asked to give one of the keynote addresses at the Conference of Intellectuals of Africa and the Diaspora in Dakar, Senegal. He was inducted into the Literary Hall of Fame for Writers of African Descent at the Gwendolyn Brooks Center at Chicago State University in 2004, and is the recipient of more than 100 national and international awards, including three honorary degrees.

In 1995 he was made a traditional king, Nana Okru Asante Peasah, Kyidomhene of Tafo, Akyem, Ghana.

Journals

African American Review First published in 1967 as Negro American Literature Forum, and then as Black American Literature Forum, African American Review is published quarterly in at Saint Louis University. Each issue includes essays on African-American literature, theatre, film, visual arts, and culture generally; interviews; poetry; fiction; and book reviews. Nathan Grant, African American Review, Saint Louis University, 317 Adorjan Hall, 3800 Lindell Boulevard, Saint Louis, Missouri 63108 Phone: (314) 977-3688 Fax: (314) 977-1514 E-mail: moodyjk@slu.edu Website: www.aar.slu.edu

African Studies Quarterly Since, 1977, information on authors and a link to the University of Florida. African Studies program, articles, book reviews. ASQ, Post Office Box 115560, 427 Grinter Hall, Gainesville, Florida 32611 Phone: (352) 392-2187 Fax: (352) 392-2435 E-mail: asq@africa.ufl.edu Website: www.africa.ufl.edu/asq

The Afro-Hispanic Review A bilingual journal of Afro-Hispanic literature and culture, is published by the Department of Romance Languages and Literatures of the University of Missouri-Columbia. It appears twice yearly. Publishes literary criticism, book reviews, translations, creative writing, and relevant developments in the field. Dr. Marvin Lewis, Institute Director. Afro-Romance Institute for Languages & Literatures of the African Diaspora, 318 Arts & Science Building, Columbia, Missouri 65211 Phone: (573) 884-0593 Fax: (573) 884-0595 E-mail: LewisM@missouri.edu Website: www.missouri.edu

Black Business Journal All-business, technology insight and financial information magazine for African-Americans and non-Blacks who do business in the community published twice a month. Chido Nwangwuf, Black Business Journal, USAfrica Digital Media Networks, 8303 South West Freeway, Suite 100, Houston, Texas 77074 Phone: (713) 270-6500 Fax: 713-270-8131 E-mail: business@bbjonline.com Website: www.bbjonline.com

The Black Employment and Entrepreneur Journal African-American business and career magazine. Contact Pamela Burke, Black Employment and Entrepreneur Journal, 22845 Savi Ranch, Suite A, Yorba Linda, California 92887 Phone: (800) 487-5099 Fax: (714) 974-3978 E-mail: pburke@blackeoejournal.com Website: www.blackeoejournal.com

Black History Journal A free weekly email-distributed journal detailing the most important Black historical events of each week. Robert Taylor, Editor, Taylor Media Services, Taylor Media Services, 1517 T Street, South East, Washington, D.C. 20020 Phone: (202) 657-8872 E-mail: taylormediaservices@yahoo.com Website: www.freewebs.com/blacknewsjournal

Black Journalism Review Information, for and about the Black Press in America, BJR, 2062 National Press Building, Washington, DC 20045 Phone: (202) 298-9519 Fax: (202) 234-7437 E-mail: editor@blackjournalism.com Website: www.blackjournalism.com

The Black Scholar Every issue of the Journal focuses on a subject of major concern in the African American community: Features book reviews, announcements, and employment listings by colleges and universities. Robert Chrisman, Editor-in-Chief & Publisher. Robert Chrisman, The Black Scholar, Post Office Box 22869, Oakland, California 94618 Phone: (510) 547-6633 Fax: (510) 547-6679 E-mail: BlkSchlr@aol.com Website: www.theblackscholar,net

Callaloo Publishes original works by, and critical studies of black writers worldwide: fiction, poetry, plays, critical essays, interviews, and annotated bibliographies. Interviews, and visual art, as well as special thematic issues. Contact Journals Manager, Callaloo, The Johns Hopkins University Press, 2715 North Charles Street, Baltimore, Maryland 21218 Phone: (410) 516-6900 E-mail: webmaster@jhupress.jhu.edu Website: www.muse.jhu.edu/journals/callaloo

Caribbean Writer International literary anthology with a Caribbean focus. The Caribbean should be central to the work, or the work should reflect a Caribbean heritage, experience or perspective. Submit poems (5 maximum), short stories, personal essays, (2 maximum not to exceed 15 pages each), and one-act plays. Marvin E. Williams, Editor, CW, University of the Virgin Islands, RR 1 Box 10000, Kingshill Virgin Island 00850 Phone: (340) 692-4152 E-mail: info@thecaribbeanwriter.org Website: www.thecaribbeanwriter.org

Context Journal on community issues and news coverage published by the Center for Community and Communications. George White, UCLA Center for Communications, 3701 Stocker Street, Suite 204, Los Angeles, California 90008 Phone: (310) 206-2189 Fax: (310) 206-2972 E-mail: geowhite@ucla.edu Website: www.uclaccc.ucla.edu

The Journal of African American History Published quarterly by the founders of Black History Month, The Association for the Study of African American Life and History (ASALH). Sylvia Cyrus, Executive Director. ASALH, CB Powell Building, 525 Bryant Street, North West, Suite C142, Washington, DC 20059 Phone: (202) 865-0053 Fax: (202) 265-7920 E-mail: executivedirector@asalh.net Website: www.asalh.net

The Journal of the Afro-American Historical and Genealogical Society Semi-annual publication provides a medium for the publication of original manuscripts, articles, and information on African and African American history and genealogy. Sylvia Polk-Burriss, Editor, AAHGS Journal, 14340 Rosetree Court, Silver Spring, Maryland 20906 E-mail: spburriss@aol.com Website: www.aahgs.org

Mythium Literary Journal The Journal of Contemporary Literature for writers of color who represent the many various narratives of indigenous and diasporic peoples. We take submissions all-year-round in the categories of poetry, fiction and creative non-fiction. Mythium Literary Journal, Post Office Box 3988, Midway, Kentucky 40347 E-mail: editor@mythiumlitmag.com Website: www.Mythiumlitmag.com

The Network Journal Founded in 1993 by Aziz Gueye Adetimirin, the magazine is dedicated to educating and empowering Black professionals and small business owners. The Network Journal, 29 John Street, Suite1402, New York, New York 10038 Phone: (212) 962-3791 Fax: (212) 962-3537 E-mail: editors@tnj.com

The North Star   Journal of African American religious history.   Contact Ms. Judith Weisenfeld, Associate Professor, Department of Religion, Vassar College, Post Office Box 205, 124 Raymond Avenue, Poughkeepsie, New York 12604 E-mail: **juweisenfeld@vassar.edu** Website: **www.northstar.vassar.edu**

Obsidian III: Literature in the African Diaspora Literary journal, biannually. Solicits essays, fiction, poetry, and reviews by creative writers. Obsidian III, English Department, North Carolina State University, Post Office Box 8105, Raleigh, North Carolina 27695 Phone: (919) 515-4153 E-mail: **obsidian@chass.ncsu.edu** Website: **www.ncsu.edu/chass/obsidian**

Palara A multi-lingual journal devoted to African diaspora studies, is housed in the Institute and published annually by the Afro-Romance Institute of the University of Missouri-Columbia, and the Department of African and African American Studies of the Pennsylvania State University. Dr. Marvin Lewis, Institute Director. Palara publishes research. Afro-Romance Institute for Languages & Literatures of the African Diaspora, 318 Arts & Science Building, Columbia, Missouri 65211 Phone: (573) 884-0593 Fax: (573) 884-0595 E-mail: **LewisM@missouri.edu** Website: **www.missouri.edu**

PLUCK Frank X. Walker is editor of PLUCK! The Journal of Affrilachian Arts and Culture, and a founding member of the Affrilachian Poets and a Cave Canem fellow. Frank X Walker, Northern Kentucky University, Department of Literature and Language, 207A Landrum Academic Building, Highland Heights, Kentucky 41099 E-mail: **affrilachia@aol.com**

Ruby Dee
Author * Actor * Playwright

Ruby Dee's career in acting has crossed all major forms of media over a span of eight decades. Although she was born Ruby Ann Wallace in Cleveland, Ohio, Ms. Dee considers herself a product of Harlem, where she grew up and began her career as a member of the American Negro Theatre. She received her B.A. from Hunter College in 1945, with degrees in French and Spanish and later studied acting with Paul Mann, Lloyd Richards and Morris Carnovsky. Some of her favorite roles on stage and screen include Lutiebelle in *Purlie Victorious* (written by her late husband, Ossie Davis); Ruth in A *Raisin in the Sun;* Lena in *Boesman and Lena,* for which she received and Obie and a Drama Desk award; and Mary Tyrone in *A Long Day's Journey Into Night,* for which she received a Cable ACE award. Other notable credits include *Anna Lucasta, Wedding Band, St. Lucy's Eyes, The Jackie Robinson Story, Uptight* (which she co-wrote), *Buck and the Preacher, Countdown at Kusini* (which she co-produced with Delta Sigma Theta sorority), *Do The Right Thing, Jungle Fever, Peyton Place, Go Tell It on the Mountain, The Stand,* and *Having Our Say.* She has received several Emmy nominations, and in 1991, won an Emmy for her performance in *Decoration Day.* She completed work as the lead in Number 2, a New Zealand comedy-drama, and is featured with Julie Harris in the independent drama, *The Way Back Home.* She was also featured in the television production of *Their Eyes Were Watching God* (for which performance she won an Audie Award).

In 1988, Ruby was inducted into the Theatre Hall of Fame. With her late husband, Mr. Ossie Davis, she has been inducted into the NAACP Image Award Hall of Fame, awarded the Silver Circle Award by the Academy of Television Arts and Science. In December 2004, Ms. Dee and Mr. Davis were recipients of the John F. Kennedy Center Honors. In 1995, Davis and Dee were celebrated as "national treasures" when they received the National Medal of Arts Honor, and in 2000, they received the Screen Actors Guild's highest honor, the Life Achievement Award. She is a member of Actors' Equity Association, the Screen Actors Guild, the American Federation of Television and Radio Artists, and the Writers Guild.

Ruby Dee is author of children's books, <u>Tower to Heaven and Two Ways to Count to Ten</u>; a book of poetry and short stories, <u>My One Good Nerve</u> (which she has adapted into a solo performance piece); and <u>With Ossie and Ruby: In This Life Together,</u> a joint autobiography co-authored with her late husband. She has also narrated several audio books, including Zora Neale Hurston's Their Eyes Were Watching God.

Librarians

Eric Acree Director of African Library, buys. Mr. Eric Acree, Cornell University, 309 Uris Library, Ithaca, New York 14853 Phone: (607) 255-4625 Fax: (607) 255-5229 E-mail: ea18@cornell.edu   Website: www.cornell.edu

Rosie L. Albritton Director, University Library Services. Rosie L. Albritton, Prairie View A&M Univeristy, John B. Coleman Library, FM 1098 Road & University Drive, Prairie View, Texas 77446 Phone: (936) 261-1500 Fax: (936) 261-1539 E-mail: rlalbritton@PVAMU.edu

Carolyn Henderson Allen Dean of Libraries. Carolyn H. Allen, University of Arkansas Libraries, 365 North McIlroy Avenue, Fayetteville, Arkansas 72701 Phone: (479) 575-6702 Fax: (479) 575-6656 E-mail: challen@uark.edu

Michael Baker Director. Buys and reviews books. Contact Mr. Michael Baker, Carter G. Woodson Regional Library, 5403 South Aberdeen, Chicago, Illinois 60609 Phone: (312) 747-6900 E-mail: mbaker@chipublib.org

Rochelle Ballard Digital Resources Coordinator, Technical Services. Ms. Rochelle Ballard, Princeton University, One Washington Road, Princeton, New Jersey 08544 Phone: (609) 258-7115 Fax: (609) 258-0441 E-mail: rballard@Princeton.edu Website: www.princeton.edu

Danita Barber Library Director. Contact Ms. Danita Barber, Farmers Branch Manske Library, 13613 Webb Chapel, Farmers Branch, Texas 75234 Phone: (972) 919-9800   E-mail: danita.barber@farmersbranch.info

Deborah Barrow Library Director. Former Director of Sunnyvale California Public Library. Ms. Deborah Barrow, San Diego Public Library, Central Library, 820 East Street, San Diego, California 92101 Phone: 619-236-5870 E-mail: LibraryDirector@sandiego.gov

Rebecca Batson Head Librarian (Acting). Rebecca Batson, William C. Jason Library-Learning Center, Delaware State University, 1200 North DuPont Highway, Dover, Delaware 19901 Phone: (302) 857-7887 Fax: (302) 857-6177 E-mail: rbatson@desu.edu

Thomas C. Battle Library Director. Dr. Battle is widely published and is frequently called upon to lecture and to make presentations at workshops, and has appeared on radio, television, and in various video productions. Mr. Thomas C. Battle, Moorland-Spingarn Research Center, Howard University, Moorland-Spingarn Research Center, 500 Howard Place NW, Washington, D.C. 20059 Phone: (202) 806-7240 Fax: (202) 806-6405

Billy Beal Dean of Learning Resources. Contact Billy Beal, Library, Meridian Community College, 910 Highway 19, North Meridian, Mississippi 39307 Phone: (601) 483-8241 E-mail: bbeal@MCC.CC.MS.US

Gladys Smiley Bell Peabody Librarian. Ms. Gladys Smiley Bell, Hampton University, 130 East Tyler Street, Hampton, Virginia 23668　Phone: (757) 727-5371　Fax: (757) 727-5952　E-mail: **gladys.bell@hamptonu.edu**　Website: **www.hamptonu.edu**

Valerie Bell Assistant Director of Public Services. Former Chief Librarian of Branch Services. Ocean County Library, 101 Washington Street, Toms River, New Jersey 08753 Phone: (732) 349-6200　Fax: (732) 473-1356　E-mail: **vbell@theoceancountylibrary.org**

Stephanie Bernard Acquisitions Librarian　Robert W. Woodruff Library, Clark Atlanta University, Atlanta University Center, 111 James P. Brawley Drive, South West, Atlanta, Atlanta, Georgia 30314　Phone: (404) 978-2075　E-mail: **sbernard@auctr.edu**

Stanton F. Biddle Librarian. Stanton Biddle, Baruch College, 17 Lexington Avenue, New York, New York 10010　Phone: (646) 312-1653　E-mail: **Stanton_Biddle@baruch.cuny.edu**

Yolanda Bolden Manager of Outreach Services and MJEW Heritage Center. Yolanda Bolden, Forsyth County Public Library, 1110 East 7th Street, Winston Salem, North Carolina 27101 Phone: (336) 703-2950 E-mail: **boldenyf@forsyth.cc**

Lisa M. Boyd Consumer Health Librarian. Lisa M. Boyd, National Library of Medicine, NIH, 8600 Rockville Pike, Building 38, Room B1-E03, Bethesda, Maryland 20894 Phone: (301) 496-4777　Fax: (301) 480-1467　E-mail: **boydl@mail.nlm.nih.gov**

Richard Bradberry Library Dean. Richard Bradberry, Ph.D., Thurgood Marshall Library, Bowie State University, 14000 Jericho Park Road, Bowie, Maryland 20715　Fax: (301) 860-3848　E-mail: **rbradberry@bowiestate.edu**

Orella R. Brazile Library Director. Southern University at Shreveport, University Library, 3050 Martin Luther King, Jr. Drive, Shreveport, Louisiana 71107　Phone: (318) 674-3401　Fax: (318) 674-3403　E-mail: **obrazile@susla.edu**

Richard Brazile Chair of the Learning Center. Richard Brazile, Wilbur Wright College, 4300 North Narragansett, Chicago, Illinois 60634　Phone: (773) 481-8408　E-mail: **rbazile@ccc.edu**

Irene Briggs Associate Director for Public Services. Ms. Irene Briggs, Prince George County Memorial Library System Public Services, 6532 Adelphi Road, Hyattsville, Maryland 20782 Phone: (301) 699-3500　Fax: (301) 985-5494　E-mail: **Irene.Briggs@pgcmls.info**

Charles M. Brown Director of Libraries. Charles M. Brown, The Public Library of Charlotte and Mecklenburg County, 310 North Tryon Street, Charlotte, North Carolina　Phone: (704) 336-4146　Fax: (704) 336-2677　E-mail: **cbrown@plcmc.org**

Wanda Brown Associate Director. 2006-2008 BCALA President. Ms. Wanda Brown, Wake Forest University, Z. Smith Reynolds Library, 1834 Wake Forest Road, Winston-Salem, North Carolina 27106　Phone: (336) 758-5094　Fax: (336) 758-3694　E-mail: **brownw@wfu.edu**

LaTanya S. Burno Executive Director. LaTanya S. Burno, J. Lewis Crozer Public Library, 620 Engle Street, Chester, Pennsylvania 19013 Phone: (610) 494-3454 Fax: (610) 494-8954 E-mail: crozerlibrary@delco.lib.pa.us

Jean Currie Church Chief librarian. Certified Archivist, Society of American Archivists. Jean Currie Church, Moorland-Spingarn Research Center, Howard University, 500 Howard Place, North West, Washington, DC 20059 Phone: (202) 806-7497 E-mail: jchurch@howard.edu

Regina Clark Librarian.   Assistant Head of Media Services. Contact Ms. Regina Clark, Emerson College, 120 Boylston Street, Boston, Massachusetts 02116 Phone: (617) 824-8409 E-mail: regina_clark@emerson.edu

Rudolph Clay Head of Reference. Rudolph Clay, Washington University Libraries, Campus Box 1061, One Brookings Drive, Saint Louis, Missouri 63130 Phone: (314) 935-5059 E-mail: rudolphc@wustl.edu

Erin Daix M.L.S. Associate Librarian Reference Department. Contact Erin Daix, University of Delaware Library, Newark, Delaware 19717 Phone: (302) 831-6943 Fax: (302) 831-1046 E-mail: daix@udel.edu

Trevor A. Dawes Circulation Services Director. Trevor A. Davis, Princeton University Library, One Washington Road Princeton, New Jersey 08544 Phone: (609) 258-3231 Fax: (609) 258-0441 E-mail: tdawes@Princeton.edu

Rose T. Dawson Director. Contact Ms. Rose T. Dawson, Alexandria Library, 5005 Duke Street, Alexandria, Virginia 22304 Phone: (703) 746-1701 Fax: (703) 746-1738 E-mail: rdawson@alexandria.lib.va.us

Bobbie P. Fells Acquisitions Librarian. Ms. Bobbie Fells, J. D. Boyd Library, Alcorn State University, 1000 Alcorn State University Drive 539, Alcorn State, Mississippi 39096 Phone: (601) 877-6354 E-mail: bpfells@lorman.alcorn.edu Website: jdboyd.alcorn.edu

Janice Franklin Library Director. Contact Ms. Janice Franklin, PhD, Alabama State University Library, 915 South Jackson Street, Montgomery, Alabama 36104 Phone: (334) 229-6890 E-mail: nfoulger@alasu.edu Website: www.lib.alasu.edu

Marilyn Pringle Gibbs Head librarian. Contact Marilyn Pringle Gibbs, Claflin University, 400 Magnolia Street, Orangeburg, South Carolina 29115 Phone: (803) 535-5309 Fax: (803) 535-5091 E-mail: mpringle@claflin.edu Website: www.claflin.edu

Valerie Griffith Librarian. Valerie Griffith, Greenburg Public Library, 300 Tarrytown Road, Elmsford, New York 10523 Phone: (914) 993-1600 E-mail: vgriffith@greenburghlibrary.org

Ana Guthrie Librarian. Ana Guthrie, Nathan W. Collier Library, 15800 North West 42nd Avenue, Miami, Florida 33054 Phone: (305) 626-3786 E-mail: aguthrie@fmuniv.edu

Roland Barksdale-Hall Managing Editor BCALA Newsletter. Contact Mr. Roland Barksdale-Hall, BCALA, 939 Baldwin Avenue, Suite 1 Sharon, Pennsylvania 16146 Phone: (724) 346-0459 Fax: (724) 342-1808 E-mail: **newsletter@bcala.org**

Lorraine Hall Assistant Professor /Acting Head of Reference. Contact Lorrain Hall, Grambling State University, 100 Main Street, Grambling, Louisiana 71245 Phone: (318) 274-2227 E-mail: **ashtonc@gram.edu** Website: **www.gram.edu**

Sylvia Sprinkle-Hamlin Library Director. Sylvia Sprinkle-Hamlin, Forsyth County Public Library, 660 West Fifth Street, Winston-Salem, North Carolina 27101 Phone: (336) 703-3016 Fax: (336) 727-2549 E-mail: **hamlinss@forsyth.cc**

Lee Hampton Director. Lee Hampton, Amistad Research Center, 6823 St. Charles Avenue, New Orleans, Louisiana 70118 Phone: (504) 862-3222 E-mail: **lhampto3@tulane.edu**

S.D. Harris Interim Editor BCALA Newsletter. S.D. Harris, BCALA, Post Office Box 1288, Norwalk, Connecticut 06856 Phone: (203) 299-1226 E-mail: **sdh.newsletter@bcala.org**

Ernestine L. Hawkins Deputy Director. Ms. Ernestine L. Hawkins, East Cleveland Public Library, 14101 Euclid Avenue, East Cleveland, Ohio 44112 Phone: (216) 541-4128 E-mail: **ernestine.hawkins@ecpl.lib.oh.us**

Allene Hayes Digital Projects Coordinator. Acquisitions and Bibliographic Access Directorate. Contact Allene Hayes, Library of Congress, Washington, DC 20540 Phone: (202) 707-1499 Fax: (202) 707-7161 E-mail: **ahay@loc.gov**

Jos N. Holman County Librarian. Jos N. Holman, Tippecanoe County Public Library, 627 South Street, Lafayette, Indiana 47901 Phone: (765) 429-0118 E-mail: **jholman@tcpl.lib.in.us** Website: **www.bcala.org/association/exec_board.htm**

Ernestine Holmes Librarian. Ernestine Holmes, Florida A & M University Libraries, G7 Coleman Library, Tallahassee, Florida 32307 Phone: (850) 599-3314 Fax: (850) 599-8157 E-mail: **ernestine.holmes@famu.edu**

Brenda Hunter Collection Development Manager. Brenda Hunter, Atlanta-Fulton Public Library 1 Margaret Mitchell Square, North West Atlanta, Georgia 30303 Phone: (404) 730-1714 E-mail: **bhunter@af.public.lib.ga.us**

Julie Hunter Director of the African American Research Library and Cultural Center. Julie Hunter, Director, AARLCC, 2650 Sistrunk Boulevard, Fort Lauderdale, Florida 33311 Phone: (954) 357-7430 E-mail: **jhunter@browardlibrary.org** Website: **www.broward/aarlcc**

Andrew P. Jackson Librarian. Mr. Andrew P. Jackson, Langston Hughes Community Library Cultural Center, Queens Borough Public Library, 100-01 Northern Boulevard, Corona, New York 11368 Phone: (718) 651-1100 E-mail: **andrew.p.jackson@queenslibrary.org**

Carol King   Senior Library Associate.   Carol King, DeWitt Wallace Library, 1600 Grand Avenue, Saint Paul, Minneapolis 55105 Phone: (651) 696-6000 E-mail: **king@macalester.edu**

Em Claire Knowles Assistant Director. Simmons College, 300 The Fenway, Boston, Massachusetts 02115 Phone: (617) 521-2798 E-mail: **knowles@simmons.edu**

LeRoy (Lee) LaFleur Liaison Librarian for Public Policy & Management. Contact Leroy Lafleur, Arlington Campus Library, George Mason University, 3401 North Fairfax Drive, Arlington, Virginia 22201 Phone: (703) 993-8268 E-mail: **llafleur@gmu.edu**

Rhea Brown Lawson Director. Nominated as the sixth director in the 101-year history of the Houston Public Library, Texas, she has served as deputy director of the Detroit Public Library, since 2003. Dr. Rhea Lawson, Houston Public Library, 500 McKinney Street Houston, Texas 77002 Phone: (832) 393-1300 Fax: (832) 393-1324 E-mail: **library.director@houstontx.gov** Website: **www.hpl.lib.tx.us**

Karen Lemmons Library Media Specialist. Contact Ms. Karen Lemmons, Howe Elementary School, 2600 Garland, Detroit, Michigan 48214 Phone: (313) 642-4801 Fax: (313) 642-4802 E-mail: **camaraife@aol.com**

Jane Moore McGinn Director, Information and Library Science. Contact Ms. Jane McGinn, PhD., Southern Connecticut State University, 501 Crescent Street, New Haven, Connecticut 06515 Phone: (203) 392-5086 E-mail: **mcginnj1@southernct.edu**

Dianna McKellar M.L.S. Senior Assistant Librarian Reference Department. Dianna McKellar, University of Delaware Library Newark, Delaware 19717 Phone: (302) 831-0790 Fax: (302) 831-1046 E-mail: **mckellar@udel.edu**

Gennette McLaurin Associate Chief Librarian. Gennette McLaurin, Schomburg Center for Research in Black Culture, 515 Malcolm X Boulevard, New York, New York 10037 Phone: (212) 491-2200 E-mail: **gmclaurin@nypl.org** Website: **www.nypl/research/sc/sc**

R. Meeker Reference and Electronic Resource Librarian. R. Meeker, Paul and Emily Douglas Library, Chicago State University, 9501 South Martin Luther King Drive, Chicago, Illinois 60628 Phone: (773) 995-2542 E-mail: **R-Meeker@csu.edu** Website: **www.csu.edu/Library**

Rose Mitchell Black Resource Center Librarian. Contact Rose Mitchell, AC Bilbrew Library, 150 E. El Segundo Boulevard, Los Angeles, California 90061 Phone: (310) 538-0059 E-mail: **brc@library.lacounty.gov**

Rosemary Mokia Assistant Professor. Director of Library Services. Dr. Rosemary Mokia, Grambling State University, 100 Main Street, Grambling, Louisiana 71245 Phone: (318) 274-6122 E-mail: **mokiar@gram.edu** Website: **www.gram.edu**

James Murray Librarian. Buys, reviews. NAACP, Henry Lee Moon Library, 4805 Mt. Hope Drive, Baltimore, Maryland 21215 Phone: (410) 580-5767 E-mail: **jmurray@naacpnet.org**

Charleszine Nelson Manager. Charleszine Nelson, Blair-Caldwell African American Research Library, 2401 Welton Street Denver, Colorado 80205 Phone: (720) 865-2401 E-mail: tnelson@denverlibrary.org Website: www.aarl.denverlibrary.org

Lut Nero Dean of Library & Media Services. Lut Nero, The Leslie Pinckney Hill Library, Cheyney University, 1837 University Circle, Post Office Box 200, Cheyney, Pennsylvania 19319 Phone: (610) 399-2069 E-mail: lnero@cheyney.edu Website: www.cheyney.edu

John Page Associate Dean, University of the District of Columbia, 4200 Connecticut Avenue Washington, DC 20008 Phone: (202) 274-6030 Fax: (202) 274-6012 E-mail: jpage@wrlc.org

Lorna Peterson Library Science Educator. Contact Ms. Lorna Peterson, Sunny-Buffalo Sils University Library, 534 Baldy Hall, Buffalo, New York 14260 Phone: (716) 645-2412 E-mail: lpeterso@buffalo.edu

Bobby Player Head, Acquisitions Department. Bobby, Player, Howard University Libraries, Washington, DC 20059 Phone: (202) 806-7255 E-mail: bplayer@howard.edu

Bobbie Pollard Librarian. Stanton Biddle, Baruch College, 17 Lexington Avenue, New York, New York 10010 Phone: (646) 312-1619 E-mail: bobbie_pollard@baruch.cuny.edu

Jocelyn Poole Librarian. Jocelyn Poole, Zach Henderson Library, Georgia Southern University, Statesboro, Georgia 30460 Phone: (912) 486-7818 E-mail: jpoole@georgiasouthern.edu

Kevin Pothier Head of Acquisitions. Contact Mr. Kevin Pothier, Thurgood Marshall Library. Bowie State University, 14000 Jericho Park Road, Bowie, Maryland 20715 Phone: (301) 860-3994 E-mail: Kpothier@bowiestate.edu Website: www.bowiestate.edu

Ellen Renaud Academic librarian. Contact Ms. Ellen Renaud, Hudson County Community College, 900 Bergen Avenue, Jersey City, New Jersey 07306 Phone: (201) 714-2229 E-mail: erenaud@hccc.edu

Ira Revels Instruction Librarian. Ira Revels, Cornell University, 309 Uris Library, Ithaca, New York 14853 Phone: (607) 255-1569 Fax: (607) 255-7922 E-mail: ir33@cornell.edu Website: www.cornell.edu

LeRoy Robinson Manager/Librarian. Leroy Robinson, Houston Public Library, 7200 Keller, Houston, Texas 77012 Phone: (832) 393-2480 E-mail: leroy.robinson@cityofhouston.net

C. P. Roddey Director. Dr. C. P. Roddey, Richard L. Fisher Memorial Library, Clinton Junior College, 1029 Crawford Road, Rock Hill, South Carolina 29730 Phone: (803) 327-7402 E-mail: cproddey@comporium.net

Mae L. Rodney Director. Dr. Mae L. Rodney, PhD, C. G. O'Kelly Library, Winston Salem University, Campus Box 19543, Winston Salem, North Carolina 27110 Phone: (336) 750-2440 E-mail: rodneyml@wssu.edu Website: www.wssu.edu/library/librarians/rodney.asp

Cynthia Rollins Acquisitions librarian. Cynthia Rollins, Schomburg Center for Research in Black Culture, 515 Malcolm X Boulevard, New York, New York 10037 Phone: (212) 491-2254 E-mail: crollins@nypl.org   Website: www.nypl/research/sc/sc

Carol A. Rudisell Librarian. Carol A. Rudisell, Reference Department, Morris Library, Room 117A, 181 South College Avenue, University of Delaware, Newark, Delaware 19717 Phone: (302) 831-6942 Fax: (302) 831-1631 E-mail: **Rudisell@udel.edu**

Blanche Sanders Dean of Library Services. Blanche Sanders, Boyd Library, Alcorn State University, 1000 ASU Drive 539, Alcorn State, Mississippi 39096 Phone: (601) 877-6354 E-mail: blanche@alcorn.edu   Website: www.alcorn.edu

Lauren Sapp Director. Lauren Sapp, Ph.D., Florida A& M University Libraries, 307 Coleman Library, Tallahassee, Florida 32307 Phone: (850) 599-3370 E-mail: lauren.sapp@famu.edu

Ronald Shelton Libriarian. Ronald Shelton, L. Douglas Wilder Library, 1500 North Lombardy Street, Richmond, Virginia 23220 Phone: (804) 257-5721 E-mail: **RShelton@vuu.edu**

Robert Skinner University librarian. Mr. Robert Skinner, Xavier University of Louisiana, 1 Drexel Drive, New Orleans, Louisiana 70125 E-mail: rskinner@xula.edu

Brenda Stephens Regional Director. Brenda Stephens, Hyconeechee Regional Library, 300 West Tryon Street, Hillsborough, North Carolina 27278 E-mail: **bstephens@co.orange.nc.us**

Willette F. Stinson Director. Dr. Willette F.Stinson, Wilberforce University, Rembert E. Stokes Library, Rembert E. Stokes Library, Room 210, 1055 North Bickett Road, Wilberforce, Ohio 45384 Phone: (937) 708-5629 E-mail: **WStinson@wilberforce.edu**

Sheila A. Stuckey Director of Libraries. Sheila A. Stuckey, Kentucky State University, Paul G. Blazer Library, 400 East Main Street, Frankfort, Kentucky 40601 Phone: (502) 597-6852 E-mail: sheila.stuckey@kysu.edu

Joanna Thompson Director of Library Services. Joanna Thompson, Bluefield Campus, Bluefield State College, 219 Rock Street, Bluefield, West Virginia 24701 Phone: (304) 327-4050 E-mail: jthompson@bluefieldstate.edu Website: www.bluefield.wvnet.edu

Karolyn S. Thompson Interlibrary Loan Coordinator. Cook Memorial Library, University of Southern Mississippi, Post Office Box 5053, Hattiesburg, Mississippi 39406 Phone: (601) 266-5111 Fax: (601) 266-4410 E-mail: karolyn.thompson@usm.edu

Rhea Ballard-Thrower Director of the Law Library. Associate Professor of Law. Rhea Ballard-Thrower, Howard University, School of Law Library, 2929 Van Ness Street, NW, Washington DC 20008 Phone: (202) 806-8045 Fax: (202) 806-8400 E-mail: **RBallard@law.howard.edu**

Deborah J. Tucker Librarian. Deborah J. Tucker, Wayne State University, 213 Kresge, Detroit, Michigan 48202 Phone: (313) 577-2005 E-mail: deborah.tucker@wayne.edu

Laura Turner Librarian. Branch Manager. Laura Turner, 4215 Medgar Evers Blvd, Jackson, Mississippi 39213 E-mail: lturner@jhlibrary.com

Danny Walker Senior librarian. Mr. Danny Walker, Blair-Caldwell African American Research Library, 2401 Welton Street, Denver, Colorado 80205 Phone: (720) 865-2401 E-mail: dwalker@denverlibrary.org Website: www.aarl.denverlibrary.org

Michael C. Walker Associate Librarian for Public Services. Michael C. Walker, James Hugo Johnston Memorial Library, Virginia State University, 1 Hayden Drive, Post Office Box 9406, Petersburg, Virginia 23806 Phone: (804) 524-6946 E-mail: mcwalker@vsu.edu

Roberta V. Webb District Chief. Roberta V. Webb, Chicago Public Library, South District Office, 2107 West 95th Street, Chicago, Illinois 60643 Phone: (312) 747-0171 Fax: (312) 745-4974 E-mail: rwebb@chipublib.org

Lainey Westbrooks Technology Operations Manager. Ms. Lainey Westbrooks, East Cleveland Public Library, 15300 Terrace Road, East Cleveland, Ohio 44112 Phone: (216) 541-4128 E-mail: lwestbrooks@ecpl.lib.oh.us

Joel White Head of Main Library. Contact Mr. Joel White, Durham County Library, 300 North Roxboro Street, Durham, North Carolina 27101 Phone: (919) 560-0114 E-mail: whitejw@Durhamcountylibrary.org

Beacher Wiggins Director of Acquisitions & Bibliographic Access. Beacher Wiggins, Library of Congress, 101 Independence Avenue, SE, Washington, DC 20540 Phone: (202) 707-6118 E-mail: bwig@loc.gov

C. Michael Williams Assistant Librarian. Michael Williams, New River Community/Technical College, 101 Church Street, Lewisburg, West Virginia 24901 Phone: (304) 647-6574 E-mail: cwilliam@access.k12.wv.us

James Williams Dean. Mr. James Williams, University of Colorado at Boulder Libraries, 184 UCB, 1720 Pleasant Street, Boulder, Colorado 80309 Phone: (303) 492-7511 Fax: (303) 492-1881 E-mail: James.Williams@Colorado.EDU

Lois Williams Librarian. Lois Williams, Vance H. Chavis Library 900 South Benbow Road, Greensboro, North Carolina 27406 Fax: (336) 412-5960 E-mail: ann81@hotmail.com

Bobby C. Wynn Director of Library Services. Bobby Wynn, Charles W. Chesnutt Library,1200 Murchison Road, Fayetteville, North Carolina 28301 Phone: (910) 672-1111 Fax: (910) 672-1312 E-mail: bwynn@uncfsu.edu

H. Jamane Yeager Librarian. H. Jamane Yeager, Belk Library, Elon University, Elon, North Carolina 27244 Phone: (336) 278-6576 Fax: (336) 278-6639 E-mail: jyeager@elon.edu

Magazines

about...time Magazine Offers stories about black people and events rarely seen in other markets. The mission of about...time is to build a sense of community. about...time Magazine, 283 Genesee Street, Rochester, New York 14611 Phone: (716) 235-7150 Fax: (716) 235-7195 E-mail: **atmag@abouttimemag.com** Website: **www.abouttimemag.com**

African American Golfer's Digest A nationally distributed publication launched in March 2003 focusing on news, tips and activities in the 'soulful' world of golf. The only print publication of its kind in the U.S., the magazine is subscription based with controlled circulation. Debert Cook, Publisher, African American Golfer's Digest, 80 Wall Street, Suite 720, New York, NY 10005 Phone: (212) 571-6559 E-mail: **Publisher@AfricanAmericanGolfersDigest.com** Website: **www.africanamericangolfersdigest.com**

African Voices Magazine Poetry magazine featuring book reviews and profiles. African Voices Communications, Inc., 270 West 96th Street, New York, New York 10025 Phone: (212) 865-2982 E-mail: **africanvoices@aol.com** Website: **www.africanvoices.com**

Afrique Magazine Monthly French magazine that features current news about popular African entertainment stars and celebrities, interviews, health, beauty, fashion culture, music, tourism and sports. E-mail: **afriquemagazine@cba.fr** Website: **www.afriquemagazine.com**

American Legacy Magazine The premier magazine of African-American history and culture, impacting not just African-Americans but society as a whole. American Legacy Magazine, 7 West Broad Street, Suite 201, Mt. Vernon, New York 10552 Phone: (914) 371-6796 E-mail: **editorial@americanlegacymag.com** Website: **www.americanlegacymag.com**

Atlanta Tribune: The Magazine Black Atlanta's leading source for relevant, thought-provoking news and information on business and wealth-building. We educate our readers and present ideas, viewpoints and possible solutions that economically, politically and socially empower them. Atlanta Tribune, 875 Old Roswell Road, Suite C-100, Roswell, Georgia 30076 Phone: (770) 587-0501 E-mail: **info@atlantatribune.com** Website: **www.atlantatribune.com**

Arizona Jazz Magazine (AZJM) Quarterly. Covers the Arizona jazz scene. Publisher, D.A. Peartree. Arizona Black Pages, 822 East Montecito Avenue, Suite 4, Phoenix, Arizona 85014 Phone: (602) 230-8161 E-mail: **editor@azjazz.com** Website: **www.AZJazz.com**

Black Collegian Magazine Since, 1970. Career and self-development magazine targeted to African-American students; job opportunities, and study abroad programs. Black Collegian Magazine, IMDiversity, 140 Carondelet Street, New Orleans, Lousiana 70130 Phone: (832) 615-8871 E-mail: **sales@imdiversity.com** Website: **www.blackcollegian.com**

Black Enterprise Magazine Founded in 1968 by Earl G. Graves, Sr.   Magazine serves to seek out, analyze and disseminate information that is helpful to African American business people. Black Enterprise Magazine, 130 Fifth Avenue, 10th Floor, New York, New York 10011 Phone: (212) 242-8000 E-mail: beeditors@blackenterprise.com Website: www.blackenterprise.com

Black History Bulletin Black History Magazine. Published by the Association for the Study of African American Life and History (ASALH - Founder's of Black History Month). ASALH, Howard Center, 2225 Georgia Avenue, NW, Suite 331, Washington, DC Phone: (202) 238-5910 E-mail: info@asalh.org Website: www.asalh.org

Black MBA Magazine Official publication of the National Black MBA Association. Contact Robin Melton, NBMBA, 180 North Michigan Avenue, #1400, Chicago, Illinois 60601 Phone: (312) 236-2622 Fax: (312) 236-0390 E-mail: mail@nbmbaa.org Website: www.nbmbaa.org

Black Noir Magazine TonyaSue Carther, Associate Editor. Contact Black Noir Magazine, 100 Park Avenue South, Suite 1600, New York, New York 10017 Phone: (201) 408-4306 E-mail: Gigone2112@cs.com Website: www.floanthonysblacknoir.com

Books2Mention Magazine Features articles on authors, conduct author interviews, provide book reviews, display newly released books and discuss up-coming. Books2Mention Magazine, 2260 Talbot Ridge, Jonesboro, Georgia 30236 E-mail: Info@Books2Mention.com Website: www.Books2Mention.com

Class Magazine The social events and profiles glossy magazine for Africans in the United States and North America. The 'Ebony' magazine for the African professional class. Chido Nwangwuf, Founder. Class Magazine, USAfrica Digital Media Networks, 8303 Southwest Freeway, Suite 100, Houston, Texas 77074 Phone: (713) 270-5500 Fax: (713) 270-8131 E-mail: class@classmagazine.tv Website: www.Classmagazine.tv

Con Brio The official voice of the National Association for the Study and Performance of African American Music (NASPAAM). Publishes articles on African American music, educators, performers and composers. Frank Suggs, President. Contact NASPAAM, 1201 Mary Jane, Memphis, Tennessee 38116 Phone: (901) 396-2913 E-mail: frank.suggs@naspaam.org Website: www.naspaam.org

Crisis Magazine Bi-monthly. One of the oldest Black periodicals in America, Crisis Magazine is the official voice of the NAACP, and the crusading voice for civil rights. Open and honest forum for discussing critical issues confronting people of color, American society and the world in addition to highlighting historical and cultural achievements. Founded in 1910 by W.E.B. Du Bois. The Crisis Magazine, 4805 Mount Hope Drive, Baltimore, Maryland 21215 Phone: (866) 636-2227 E-mail: thecrisiseditorial@naacpnet Website: www.thecrisismagazine.com

Cuisine Noir Magazine Offers a unique way to reach African-American food and wine lovers. Contact Cuisine Noir Magazine, V. Sheree Publishing, LLC, 1714 Franklin Street, #100-130, Oakland, California 94612 Phone: (510) 922-9702 E-mail: info@vshereepublishing.com Website: www.cuisinenoirmag.com

Diverse: Issues in Higher Education Magazine covering issues affecting African Americans and other minorities and underrepresented groups in our nation's colleges and universities. Diverse Education, Cox, Matthews & Associates, 10520 Warwick Avenue, Suite B-8, Fairfax, Virginia 22030 Phone: (703) 385-2981 E-mail: diversebooks@diverseeducation.com Website: www.diverseeducation.com

Ebony and Jet Magazines World's largest Black-owned publishing company is the home of Ebony and Jet magazines. The late John H. Johnson, who founded the privately-held company in November 1942, with Negro Digest, was Publisher and Chairman. Ebony Editorial, 820 South Michigan Avenue, Chicago, Illinois 60605 Website: www.ebony.com

Ebony Cactus Magazine Published twice a month, a full color magazine distributed free by subscription over the Internet. Showcases new and established businesses in Arizona, Nevada and Southern California. The Ebony Cactus Magazine, Post Office Box 24982, Tempe, Arizona 85285 Phone: (602) 821-8191 Fax: (602) 437-8852 E-mail: Publisher@theebonycactus.com

Essence Magazine Magazine for African-American and Caribbean women. Features personal-growth articles, celebrity profiles, and well-reported pieces on political and social issues. We are also looking for how-to pieces on careers, money, health and fitness, and relationships. Editor, Essence, 135 West 50th Street, 4th Floor, New York, New York 10020 Phone: (212) 642-0600 E-mail: letters@essence.com Website: www.essence.com

Everybody's General interest Caribbean-American magazine, since, 1977. Serves Caribbean-American consumers from Alaska to Louisiana to New York. Readership of affluent consumers. Herman Hall Communications, Inc., 1630 Nostrand Avenue, Brooklyn, New York 11226 Phone: (718) 941-1879 E-mail: everybodys@msn.com Website: www.everybodysmag.com

Focus Magazine Since 1972. Covers national issues to a leadership audience. Over 18,000 readers, nearly half of whom are black elected officials. Focus Magazine, Joint Center, 1090 Vermont Avenue, North West, Suite 1100, Washington, DC 20005 Phone: (202) 789-3500 Fax: (202) 789-6390 E-mail: ralpheverett@jointcenter.org Website: www.jointcenter.org

Gospel Truth Magazine Premier lifestyle magazine for African Americans who have a passion for church and gospel music. Gospel Truth Magazine, Post Office Box 38218, Houston, Texas 77382 Phone: (832) 912-7700 Fax: (832) 912-7733 E-mail: ibroussard@gtmmedia.com Website: www.gospeltruthmagazine.com

Heart & Soul Edwin V. Avent is the president, CEO and publisher of Heart & Soul Magazine, the nation's leading health, fitness and life solutions magazine targeting African-American women. Heart & Soul Enterprises, LLC 2514 Maryland Avenue Baltimore, Maryland 21218 (215) 785-3049 E-mail: info@heartandsoul.com Website: www.heartandsoul.com

MAMi Magazine Internationally distributed title, Mami Magazine focuses on latino and black women with such issues as fashion, music, culture and arts. Algie deWitt currently publisher and Editor in Chief. MAMi Magazine, 4408 Aberdeen Lane, Blackwood, New Jersey 08012 E-mail: algie@mamimagazine.com Website: www.mamimagazine.com

MBE Magazine Bi-monthly, serves as a nationwide forum for minority and women business owners, corporations and government agencies concerned with minority enterprise development. MBE, 3528 Torrance Boulevard, Suite 101 Torrance, California 90503 Phone: (310) 540-9398 E-mail: gconrad@mbemag.com Website: www.mbemag.com

Mosaic Books Since, 1998. Showcases and honestly critique African American and Hispanic literature. Ron Kavanaugh, Publisher/Editor in Chief. Mosaic Books, 314 West 231 Suite #470, Bronx, New York 10463 E-mail: listing@mosaicbooks.com   Website: www.mosaicbooks.com

Pride Magazine A local publication that is distributed in Charlotte, North Carolina. For over 16 years, the magazine has highlighted the accomplishments of African Americans and promoted social and cultural awareness throughout the community with regard to men, women, business and health. Pride Magazine, 312 West Trade Street, Suite 600, Charlotte, North Carolina 28202 Phone: (704) 375-9553 Fax: (704) 375-9550 Website: www.pride-communications.net

Real Health Magazine Quarterly magazine Real Health is a leading online and offline resource for African American health. Kate Ferguson, editor in chief. Real Health Magazine, 462 Seventh Avenue, 19th Floor, New York, New York 10018 Phone: (212) 242-2163 Fax: (212) 675-8505 E-mail: katef@smartandstrong.com Website: www.smartandstrong.com

Shades Magazine Michelle Fitzhugh-Craig, CEO/Editor in Chief. Celebrating women of color Shade Magazine features news, lifestyle, health, mind and body, book reviews, voices. Shades Magazine, Post Office Box 46325, Phoenix, Arizona 85063 Phone: (415) 633-6327 E-mail: shadesmagazine1@gmail.com Website: www.myshadesmagazine.net

Sister 2 Sister Magazine National consumer magazine marketed toward Black women. Features news, entertainment, lifestyle, health. Publisher, Jamie Foster Brown. Sister 2 Sister Magazine, 6930 Carroll Avenue, Suite 200, Takoma Park, Maryland 20912 Phone: (301) 270-5999 Fax: (301) 270-0085 E-mail: s2smagazine@aol.com   Website: www.s2smagazine.com

Say So! Magazine A free Christian resource magazine with bi-monthly distribution in the Baltimore/Washington Metropolitan Area. Carla D. Bluitt, Editor and Publisher. Say So! Magazine, 6030 Daybreak Circle, Suite A150/151, Clarksville, Maryland 21029 Phone: (301) 807-5445 E-mail: cbluitt@saysomagazine.com Website: www.saysomagazine.com

SpokenVizions® Magazine Our goal is to shine globally through literature, music production, film, poetry, dance and performances. Publishes poetry from students ages 10 to 17 years of age. Floyd Bokins, Jr., Editor. SpokenVizions Entertainment Group, Post Office Box 373, Florissant, Missouri 63032 Phone: (314) 517-8764 E-mail: Floyd.BoykinJr@spokenvizions.com Website: www.spokenvizions.com

Today's Black Woman For todays modern African-American woman includes information on fashion, beauty, relationships. Steve Gross, Publisher. Founder/host, Jennifer Kreitt, TBW Publishing Group, 441 Lexington Avenue, Suite 1203, New York, New York 10017 Phone: (212) 490-1895 Fax: (212) 490-1074 E-mail: editor@todaysblackwoman.com Website: www.todaysblackwoman.com

Trendsetters to Trendsetters Magazine National publication that reaches thousands of homes and businesses bi-monthly via hardcopy and internet. Willie Stewart, Chief Executive Officer and Publisher. Trendsetters to Trendsetters Magazine, 3007 Panola Road, Suite 283C, Lithonia, Georgia 30038 Phone: (404) 437-4311 E-mail: wstewart@trendtotrendmag.com Website: http://trendtotrendmag.homestead.com/aboutus.htm

Turning Point UrBiz Bi-monthly. Each Issue, offers insight into those companies that partner with us to provide quality information and programs for our readers. Contact Ms. Patricia A. Means, publisher, Turning Point Communications, Post Office Box 8746, Los Angeles, California 90009 Phone: (323) 299-6000 Fax: (323) 299-6006 E-mail: turningp@aol.com Website: www.tpurbiz.com

Upscale Magazine For the affluient lifestyle. Contact Editorial Office, Upscale Magazine, 600 Bronner Brothers Way, South West, Atlanta, Georgia 30310 Phone: (404) 758-7467 E-mail: letters@upscalemag.com Website: www.upscalemagazine.com

Vibe Premier destination for the hip-hop generation, urban music, entertainment, culture and lifestyle for the aspirational 18-34 year old. Vibe Lifestyle network represents over 25 sites and reaches over 19 million unique users per month. Vibe, 113 East 125th Street, 2nd Floor, New York, New York 10035 Website: www.vibe.com

Women In Motion An award winning multicultural magazine. Ms. Roxann Latimer, Publisher and Editor in Chief. Contact Ms. Roxann Latimer, WIM Media, 3900 West 22nd Lane #10G, Yuma, Arizona 85364 Phone: (928) 343-9729 E-mail: wimmedia@yahoo.com Website: www.roxannlatimer.com

Written Magazine Created in 2006, Written Magazine is a bi-monthly publication whose mission is to celebrate the reader and to celebrate the word. Written is a lifestyle publication nationally syndicated as an insert to African American newspapers. Within Written are reviews and critiques, books, movies music...any thing with a written component. Michelle R. Gipson, Publisher. Written Magazine, Post Office Box 250504, Atlanta, Georgia 30325 Phone: (404) 753-8315 E-mail: michelle.gipson@writtenmag.com Website: www.writtenmag.com

Young Urban Viewz Created for African American teens and young adults in mind. Young Urban Viewz, Post Office Box 4657, Upper Marlboro, Maryland 20775 Phone: (301) 637-4280 E-mail: contactonline@youngurbanviewz.com Website: www.youngurbanviewz.com

CARMAN MOORE

Composer * Librettist * Critic
Author * Conductor

Born in Lorain, Ohio and growning up in nearby Elyria, Carman Moore earned his Bachelor of Music Degree at Ohio State University before moving to New York City, where he studied composition privately with Hall Overton and at the Julliard School with Luciano Berio and Vincent Persichetti where he earned his Masters Degree with distinction. Mr. Moore then began composing for symphony and chamber ensembles while writing lyrics for pop songs, gradually adding opera, theatre, dance and film scores to his body of work. His work in popular music included lyrics and arrangements for ex-Rascals leader Felix Cavaliere both on Cavaliere's first solo album FELIX CAVALIERE, his second DESTINY, and on the Foghat single "Rock'n'Roll Outlaws."

Among Mr. Moore's early commissioned symphonic works were Wildfires and Field Songs for the New York Philharmonic conducted by Pierre Boulez and Gospel Fuse for the San Francisco Symphony with Seiji Ozawa conducting and Cissy Houston the vocal soloist. Among others of his works for symphony orchestra have been Concerto for Blues Piano and Orchestra (for Jay McShann); Four Movements for A Five-Toed Dragon, conducted by Isaiah Jackson with the American Symphony Orchestra and The Symphony of the Sorbonne (Paris); Hit; A Concerto for Percussion and Orchestra (Jackson and the Rochester Philharmonic); and Concerto for Flute, Pi-pa, and Orchestra (premiere pending). In 1980 Mr. Moore founded the innovative electro-acoustic SKYMUSIC ENSEMBLE, which since has performed in America, Europe and Asia, including at La Scala in Milan, Geneva's Made-In-America Festival, and at the 9th Hong Kong Ready-to-Wear Show.

A dedicated educator, and author of two youth-oriented books: Somebody's Angel Child: The Story of Bessie Smith (Dell), and Rock-It (a music history and theory book for Alfred Music Publishers), Mr. Moore has taught at the Yale University School of Music, Queens and Brooklyn Colleges, Carnegie-Mellon University, Manhattanville College, and The New School for Social Research. He is presently creating a pop music album based in Outer Space and featuring Dante and Beatrice for the new SKYBAND. He just completed CONCERTO FOR ORNETTE AND ORCHESTRA for jazz legend and 2006 Pulitzer prize winner Ornette Coleman. Mr. Moore recently received a fellowship from the New York State Council on the Arts for a commissioned work for the Continuum Ensemble and as well received a Civitella Ranieri Fellowship to work in Italy Summer, 2010.

Management Companies

Big Fish Productions, Inc   Artists Management/Indielabel/Productions. We do any/everything from Artist Management to Director of Events. James Carter, President. Carter Management, Big Fish Productions, Inc., Post Office Box 782. Bronx, New York 10462 Phone: (212) 860-3639 E-mail: jcarter891@aol.com Website: www.bigfishproductioninc.com

Black Speakers Online Offers directory of Black speakers. Norma Thompson, Black Speakers, Etc., 1968 West Adams Boulevard, Suite 208, Los Angeles, California 90018 Phone: (323) 734-7144 E-mail: info@blackspeakersonline.com Website: www.blackspeakersonline.com

Capital Entertainment   Bil Carpenter runs Capital Entertainment, a small public relations company that has worked extensively with gospel artists such as Vickie Winans, Bishop T.D. Jakes, and CeCe Winans, among many others. Bil has written liner note essays for various CD compilations for Sony/BMG Music, and Warner Bros. Bil Carpenter, Capital Entertainment, 217 Seaton Place North East, Washington, D.C. 20002 Phone: (202) 506-5051 E-mail: carpbil@aol.com Website: www.uncloudydays.com

Celestial Music Studio Booking Agent: live bands for Mardi Gras, special evens, casinos, anniversaries, and club entertainment. We help musicians, band, performers, and entertainers get bookings. Voice, Piano, Drums, Saxophone, Bass, Guitar and Keyboard lessons. Eddie Corley, Music Director. Celestial Music Studio, 2218 22nd Avenue, Gulfport, Mississippi 39501 Phone: (228) 216-2558 E-mail: eddiecorley1@aol.com Website: www.celestialmusicproduction.com

Chew Entertainment Nationally recognized premier event management firm, specializing in event production - ranging from celebrity concerts to fundraising galas. Founders of Chew Entertainment Ray Chew & Vivian Scott Chew. Ray Chew has been at the helm of award winning live and televised musical events featuring performances by the world's brightest stars including Alicia Keys, Sting, Rihanna, Prince, Jennifer Hudson, Barry Manilow, Dionne Warwick, ElvisCostello, Smokey Robinson, Pastor Shirley Caesar, Aretha Franklin and Quincy Jones. Ray's work behind the scenes includes a long recording career with top selling artists, as well as film and television scoring. As a musician, composer and producer, some of Ray's credits include NBC's The Singing Bee, Showtime At the Apollo, Saturday Night Live, BET's Sunday Best, BET Honors, the BET Awards, Miss Universe, MissUSA and the Neighborhood Ball: An Inauguration Celebration. Contact Mr. Ray Chew, Chew Entertainment, 460 Queen Anne Road, 1B, Teaneck, New Jersey 07666 Phone: (201) 928-1696 Phone: (201) 928-1999 E-mail: info@chewentertainment.com Website: www.chewentertainment.com

Emtro Gospel Artist itinerary management. Our session musicians are amongst the finest to be found anywhere. Services include publishing, mastering, marketing, promotions, shopping Artist Project to Record Labels. Emtro Gospel, 420 College Drive, Middleburg, Florida 32068 Phone: (904) 213-1330 E-mail: info@Emtro.com   Website: www.emtro.com

Herman Hall Communications Producer/Promoter of Caribbean plays, calypso & soca concerts in the U.S. Also, agent for soca/calypso artists to perform. Provides management for calypso star, Shadow. Herman Hall, Herman Hall Communications, Inc., 1630 Nostrand Avenue, Brooklyn, New York 11226 Phone: (718) 941-1879 E-mail: everybodys@msn.com Website: www.everybodysmag.com

Hy'Tara Entertainment Troy Buckner is Founder/CEO of Hy'Tara. She has managed and co-produced Gospel Renown Artist and Stella Award Winner, Kenny Smith and Vernessa Mitchell from the Motown's Grammy Award winning R & B Group, 'Hi-Energy'. She is currently writing, managing, and producing several upcoming artists. Ms. Troy Buckner, Hy'tara Entertainment, Post Office Box 19049, Anaheim, California 92817 Phone: (714) 227-5000 E-mail: birdinflight@aol.com Website: www.abirdinflight.com

JFK Entertainment & Sports Management Company Mmanags all types of theatrical productions, represent playwrights, actors, producers and publishers. John F.Kilgore, JFK Entertainment & Sports Management Company, 2266 5ᵗʰ Avenue #77, New York, New York 10037 Phone: (917) 309-4415 Fax: (201) 487-7818 E-mail: jfkentertainment@yahoo.com

Major Money Entertainment Music/entertainment company founded by Terry McGill. Artist management; marketing and promotional strategies. All artist and actor negotiations; negotiate distribution agreements. Current projects include: Pimpsta, Tony Terry, Khia, Don Vito, Atlanta Based Producer/ Business Partner Production and remix credits include: Lil' Jon, Paster Troy, Lil' Scrappy, Blu Cantrell, Mya, Sole`, OutKast, and Ghetto Mafia. Joint venture with Dallas based Koast to Koast. Terry McGill, CEO, Major Money Entertainment, 908 Audelia Road, Suite 200, #229, Richardson, Texas 75081 Phone: (214) 282-8933 Fax: (516) 908-3743 E-mail: majormoney@earthlink.net Website: www.majormoneyentertainment.com

Marshalen Martin & Associates Booking firm. President Marshalen Martin is a professional radio broadcaster since 1980. Each week she features interviews with a veritable who's who of the gospel world on KDYA Gospel 1190FM. Marshalen Martin & Associates, 3260 Blume Drive, Suite 520, Richmond, California 94806 Phone: (510) 222-4242 Fax: (510) 262-9054 E-mail: marshalenmartin@gospel1190.net Website: www.gospel1190.net

Millennium Entertainment Group (MEG) A wholly integrated entertainment and sports management company specializing in Personal Management, Intellectual Property Development, Alternative Marketing and Special Event Production. MEG is the management company behind successful career directions of Eight Time Grammy Winner - CeCe Winans, Creator & Host of BET's #1 Program - Bobby Jones Gospel and Video Gospel, Grammy Nominated - Dr. Bobby Jones, Interscope/B' Rite, Artist, Grammy Nominated - Gospel Gangstaz & other. MEG was instrumental in acquiring multi-platinum recording artist, Two Time Grammy Winner - Kurumt for Death Row's "Dogg Pound", Roscoe - a young rapper signed to Priority Records, and MTV's-The Cut Winner, Silk-E. MEG also provided consulting to the civil rights activist, the late Mrs. Rosa Parks, best selling author Iyanla Vanzant, Queen of Gospel-Shirley Caesar, co-star of the famed House Party 1,2, and 3. Richard Manson, Millennium Entertainment Group, 1223 5th Ave North Germantown, Nashville, Tennessee 37208 Phone: (615) 254-1600 Fax: (615) 891-2407 E-mail: richard.manson@themansongroup.com Website: www.themansongroup.com

Talent Link Inc.   The nation's top black talent agency with a 90% placement rate.   Vince Paul, Talent Link, Inc., Post Office Box 480035, Charlotte, North Carolina 28269 Phone: (704) 335-0027 info@talent-link.com Website: www.talent-link.com

SpokenVizions Entertainment Group, LLC   Management Company.   Contact Quashana Foster, SpokenVizions Entertainment Group, LLC, Post Office Box 373, Florissant, Missouri 63032 Phone: (847) 414-1710 E-mail: QuashanaFoster@spokenvizions.com

Terrie Williams Agency   Management entertainment company.   Company has handled the biggest names in entertainment, sports, business and politics. Contact Terrie Williams Agency, 382 Central Park West, Suite 7R, New York, New York 10025 Phone: (212) 316-0305 Fax: (212) 749-8867 E-mail: tmwms@terriewilliams.com Website: www.terriewilliams.com

Tim Greene Films Film, song and music producer, management and production company; entertainment acts and rappers, etc. Producer, Tim Greene. Contact Mr. Tim Greene Films, Post Office Box 20554, Philadelphia, Pennsylvania 19138 Phone: (213) 399-0600 E-mail: timgreene2009@yahoo.com Website: www.timgreenefilms.com

Tim Greene

Film Actor * Songwriter
Record Producer * Radio & Television Host

D.J. radio personality and film and music video director, Tim Greene is owner of Tim Green Films in Hollywood, California. He is a national Dean's list graduate and Sony Innovators Award finalist of Shaw University with a B.S. Degree in Business Management, with a communications minor. He was heard on L.A.'s top radio station, FM 92 the Beat-KKBT, and FM 102.3 the Rhythm-KJLH, as D.J. "Jammin Jay Williams," where he often took time to speak on the subject of radio and television producing to students. He still enjoys motivating students on the importance of education and positive career endeavors.

As a record producer, Tim has written and produced over 17 national record releases. He managed 68 year-old rap artists, Vivian Smallwod, known as "The Rappin Granny". He was producer, director and host of "Dance City From Hollywood," a television show for the Japanese market and as a regular fundraiser participant in local celebrity tennis tournaments has won over 120 trophies.

Film producer, hip-hop pioneer in four work-filled years, Tim won Best Writer, Producer, Director at the Philadelphia International Film Festival for the parady "Ya Grandma's A Gangsta". Three features, "*Ya Grandma's A Gangsta*", "*Raykwan Cuties*", and *Creepin'*, hundreds of coupons, and thousands of dollars in rebate checks later, Tim Greene has birthed a body of work on which he looks with pride.

Museums

A. Phillip Randolph Pullman Porter Museum Information, African American, labor history museum. Gift shop. Randolph Pullman Porter Museum, Post Office Box 6276, Chicago, Illinois 60680 Phone: (773) 928-3935 Fax: (773) 928-8372 E-mail: **blhmuseum-website@yahoo.com** Website: **aphiliprandolphmuseum.com** j

African American Museum Cleveland Ohio, preservation, information, of African descent. Contact AAM, 1765 Crawford Road, Cleveland, Ohio 44106 Phone: (216) 791-1700 Fax: (216) 791-1774 E-mail: **ourstory@aamcleveland.org** Website: **www.aamcleveland.org**

African American Museum Dallas. The only museum in the Southwestern United States devoted to the preservation and display of African American artistic, cultural and historical materials. It also has one of the largest African American folk art collections in the United States. The African American Museum incorporates a wide variety of visual art forms and historical documents that portray the African American experience in the United States, Southwest, and Dallas. Contact African American Museum Dallas, 3536 Grand Avenue, Dallas, Texas 75210 Phone: (214) 565-9026 Website: **www.aamdallas.org**

African American Museum and Library at Oakland Research library. Contains materials on the Northern California African American community, with an emphasis on the East Bay. AAMLO features exhibitions and programs. Goal is to reach out and educate the community. Rick Moss, Branch Manager, African American Museum and Library at Oakland, Oakland Public Library, 659 Fourteenth Street, Oakland, California 94612 Phone: (510) 637-0200 E-mail: **rmoss@oaklandlibrary.org** Website: **www.oaklandlibrary.org/AAMLO/index.html**

African American Museum in Phillidelphia Exhibits, events, educational programs, membership, general information. AAMP, 701 Arch Street, Philadelphia, Pennsylvania 19106 Phone: (215) 574-0380 Fax: (215) 574-3110 Website: **www.aampmuseum.org**

African American Research Library and Cultural Center The AARLCC has displayed over 38 major exhibits and offered 184 cultural programs to over 895,000 customer, celebrities, noted authors and international speakers who have made AARLCC a thriving center, a vital component of our community. The AARLCC also offers classes in computer technology and educational, recreational, and cultural programs on a regular basis. Contact AARLCC, Broward County Library, 2650 Sistrunk Boulevard, Fort Lauderdale, Florida 33311 Phone: (954) 625-2800 Website: **www.broward.org/library/aarlcc.htm**

Anacostia Museum The Smithsonian Institution's museum of African American history and culture Explores American history, society, and creative expression. Anacostia Museum, 1901 Fort Place South East, Washington, DC 20020 Phone: (202) 287-3306 E-mail: **AMinfo@si.edu** Website: **www.si.edu/anacostia**

Arna Bontemps African American Museum and Cultural Arts Center   The restored childhood home of Arna Bontemps - poet, author, anthologist, and librarian - who was considered the leading authority of the Harlem Renaissance. The period - sometimes referred to as the "New Negro" movement - is when young Black writers went to Harlem to share the Black experience through their writing. ABAAM, 1327 Third Street, Alexandria, Louisiana 71301 Phone: (318) 473-4692 Fax: (318) 473-4675 Website: **www.arnabontempsmuseum.com**

Birmingham Civil Rights Institute   Our mission is to encourage communication and reconciliation of human rights issues worldwide, and to serve as a depository for civil rights archives and documents. Annual Events, Exhibitions, Archives, Online Resource Gallery. BCRI, 520 Sixteenth Street North, Birmingham, Alabama 35203 Phone: (205) 328-9696 Fax: (205) 251-6104 E-mail: **bcri@bcri.org**   Website: **bcri.bham.al.us**

Black American West Museum and Heritage Center   Tells the forgotten story of the African American pioneers who helped to shape the West. This small musuem is housed in the former home of Dr. Justina Ford, Colorado's first African American female doctor. BAWMHC, 3091 California Street, Denver Colorado 80205 Phone: (303) 292-2566 Fax: (303) 382-1981 E-mail: **director1@blackamericanwest.org** Website:**www.blackamericanwest.org**

Boston African American National Historic Site Includes 15 pre-Civil War structures relating to the history of Boston's 19th century African-American community, including the African Meeting House, the oldest standing African-American church in the United States. Boston African American National Historic Site, 14 Beacon Street, Suite 503, Boston, Massachusetts 02108 Phone: (617) 742-5415 Fax: (617) 720-0848 Website: **www.nps.gov/boaf**

California African American Museum The Museum contains African American art, history, and culture. The mission of the California African American Museum is to research, collect, preserve and interpret for public enrichment, the history, art and culture of African Americans with emphasis on California and the western United States. Ms. Charmaine Jefferson, Executive Director. Contact California African American Museum, 600 State Drive, Exposition Park, Los Angeles, California 90037 Phone: (213) 744-2060 E-mail: **info@caamuseum.org**   Website: **www.caamuseum.org**

Central Pennsylvania African American Museum Artifacts, arts, papers, books, photographs, describe history, culture, African Americans. Old Bethel African Methodist Episcopal Church, 119 North Tenth Street, Reading, Pennsylvania 19601 Phone: (610) 371-8713 Fax: (610) 371-8739 Website: **www.homestead/cpaam/index**

Charles H. Wright Museum of African American History Founded, 1965 by Dr. Charles Wright, the museum exists to serve Metropolitan Detroit and national communities by providing exceptional exhibitions and programs. Three major exhibitions were added, A is for Africa, a hands-on exhibit for children; Without Sanctuary: Lynching Photography in America; and the new blockbuster core exhibition, And Still We Rise: Our Journey Through African American History and Culture. Charles H. Wright Museum of African American History, 315 East Warren Avenue, Detroit, Michigan 48201 Phone: (313) 494-5800 Fax: (313) 494-5855 E-mail: **wphillip@maah-detroit.org** Website: **www.maah-detroit.org**

Chattanooga African American Museum Collection, multi-media presentations, rare artifacts, African Art, original sculptures, paintings, musical recordings, Black newspapers. Chattanooga African American Museum, 200 East Martin Luther King Boulevard, Chattanooga, Tennessee 37403 Phone: (423) 266-8658 Fax: (423) 267-1076 Website: www.caamhistory.com

Dunbar House State Historic Site Permanent exhibit, writer's life, young poet, national spokesman. Dunbar House, Post Office Box 1872, Dayton, Ohio 45401 Phone: (937) 224-7061 E-mail: lwf@coax.net Website: www.coax.net/people/lwf/dunbar.htm

DuSable Museum of African American History Founded in 1957, Dr. Margaret T. and Charles G. Burroughs, Chicago. DuSable Museum of African American History, 740 East 56th Place, Chicago, Illinois 60637 Phone: (773) 947-0600 Website: www.dusablemuseum.org

Hammonds House Museum Fine arts venue whose mission is to preserve, exhibit, and increase public awareness about the contributions that visual artists of African descent have made to world culture. Site of one of the first private kindergartens in Atlanta (ca.1911). Features more than 350 art works dating from the mid-19th century. Myrna Anderson-Fuller, Executive Director, Hammonds House Museum, 503 Peeples Street, SW, Atlanta, Georgia 30310 Phone: (404) 612-0500 Website: www.hammondshouse.org

Museum For African Art We present major exhibitions in our Main Gallery, and smaller changing exhibitions in our Focus Gallery. In addition, we maintain a lively calendar of events for visitors of all ages and a Museum Store. Contact Museum For African Art, 36-01 43rd Avenue at 36th Street, Long Island City, New York 11101 Phone: (718) 784-7700 Fax: (718) 784-7718 E-mail: museum@africanart.org Website: www.africanart.org

Museum of Afro American History Boston. Dedicated to preserving the contributions of African-Americans. Museum of Afro American History, Administrative Office, 14 Beacon Street, Suite 719, Boston, Massachusetts 02108 Phone: (617) 725-0022 Fax: (617) 720-5225 E-mail: history@afroammuseum.org Website: www.afroammuseum.org

Museum of the African Diaspora MoAD's goal is to foster a greater understanding of human history and promote cross-cultural communication. As a first voice museum, MoAD will capture the essence of the African Diaspora experiences. V. Denise Bradley, Executive Director. Museum of the African Diaspora, 685 Mission Street, San Francisco, California 94105 Phone: (415) 358-7200 Fax: (415) 358-7252 E-mail: vdb@moadsf.org Website: www.moadsf.org

National Afro-American Museum and Cultural Center Dayton Ohio, national 1950's exhibition From Victory To Freedom. Michael L. Sampson, Afro-American Museum, 1350 Brush Row Road, Post Office Box 578, Wilberforce, Ohio 45384 Phone: (937) 376-4944 E-mail: naamcc@erinet.com Website: http://ohsweb.ohiohistory.org/places/sw13/index.shtml

National Civil Rights Museum Located at the Lorraine Motel, the site of Dr. Martin Luther King's assassination; exhibitions, and educational programs. Contact National Civil Rights Museum, 450 Mulberry Street, Memphis, Tennessee 38103 Phone: (901) 521-9699 Fax: (901) 521-9740 E-mail: contact@civilrightsmuseum.org Website: www.civilrightsmuseum.org

National Museum Of African Art Center for the visual arts of Africa, exhibitions, collections, research, and public programs. NMAFASI, MRC 708, Post Office Box 37012, Washington, DC.20013 Phone: (202) 633-1000 Fax: (202) 357-4879 E-mail: **nmafaweb@nmafa.si.edu** Website: **http://africa.si.edu**

October Gallery Founded July 1985, October Gallery has sponsored hundreds of traveling art shows. Produced and sponsored by October Gallery these shows were "Black Art Shows" held in Atlanta, Chicago, New York, Los Angeles, Oakland, Jacksonville, Sarasota, Washington DC, Baltimore, Montreal, Detroit, and a host of other cities. Contact October Gallery, 68 North 2nd Street, Philadelphia, Pennsylvania 19106 Phone: (215) 629-3939 Fax: (215) 923-4737 E-mail: **customerservice@octobergallery.com** Website: **www.octobergallery.com**

San Francisco African American Museum Presents select exhibits on African and/or African American artists. SFAAHCS, Fort Mason Center, Building C, San Francisco, California 94123 Phone: (415) 441-0640

Tubman African American Museum Art, history, and culture. Contact Tubman African American Museum, 340 Walnut Street, Macon, Georgia 31201 Phone: (478) 743-8544 Fax: (478) 743-9063 E-mail: **adra@tubmanmuseum.com** Website: **www.tubmanmuseum.com**

Newsletters

Black Alumni Network Newsletter Published monthly by Columbia University Journalism Alumni. Editor Wayne Dawkins. Black Alumni Network Newsletter, Post Office Box 6693, Newport News, Virginia 23606 Phone: (757) 727-5437 wdawkins4bj@aol.com Website: www.augustpress.net

BCALA Newsletter The BCALA Newsletter goes to all of the approximately 1,000 members of the Black Caucus of the American Library Association 6 times a year. BCALA, Post Office Box 1738, Hampton, Virginia 23669 Phone: (804) 786-2332 Fax: (804) 786-5855 E-mail: newsletter@bcala.org Website: www.bcala.org

Black Congressional Monitor Published twice-monthly newsletter covering the US Federal Government. Reports on available grant awards, contract and subcontract opportunities, small business set-asides, scholarships, fellowships, internships, Government publications, reports to and by Congress, public notices and meetings. Founding editor and publisher, Lenora Moragne. Len Mor Publications, Post Office Box 75035, Washington, DC 20013 Phone: (202) 488-8879 Fax: (202) 554-3116 E-mail: LMoragne@verizon.net Website: www.bcmonitor.com

Black Excel Quarterly Newsletter. Since its founding in 1988, Black Excel has helped young people and their parents all across the country to navigate the difficult college admission process. Black Excel services have expanded over the years to include an updated 350+ Scholarship List; a personalized College Help Package; a reference guide to 143 Historically Black Colleges, detailed profiles of individual schools; and a Medical School Help Package. Founder Isaac J. Black. Contact Black Excel, 244 Fifth Avenue, Post Office Box H281, New York, New York 10001 Phone: (212) 591-1936 E-mail: ijblack@blackexcel.org Website: www.blackexcel.org

Black, Indian, Hispanic, and Asian Women In Action Newsletter (BIHA) Established in 1983, BIHA serves as a forum for translating current concerns (family violence, racism, ageism, AIDS, chemical abuse) within communities of color. Published Quarterly. Circulation of 1,000. Provides education, information and advocacy for and by Communities of Color. Alice O. Lynch, Executive Director. BIHA, 1830 James Avenue North, Minneapolis, Minnesota 55417 Phone: (612) 521-2986 Fax: (612) 529-6745 E-mail: info@biha.org Website: www.biha.org

Black Students Quarterly print newsletter featuring the latest news, tips, and opportunities for African-American students. Contact Diversity City Media, 225 West. 3rd Street, Suite #203, Long Beach, California 90802 Phone: (562) 209-0616 E-mail: support@blackstudents.com Website: blackstudents.com

Con Brio Newsletter focuses on preserving, promoting, and advancing the tradition of African American music. Frank Suggs, Publisher. NASPAAM, 1201 Mary Jane, Memphis, Tennessee 38116 Phone: (901) 396-2913 E-mail: f.suggs@naspaam.org Website: www.naspaam.org

National Black MBA Association Newsletter   Circulation 3,500. Newsletter published quarterly and one special edition.   Contact National Black MBA Association, 180 North Michigan Avenue, Suite 1820, Chicago, Illinois 60601 Phone: (312) 236-2622 Fax: (312) 236-4131 E-mail: mail@nbmbaa.org Website: www.nbmbaa.org

News Plus   National Association of Black Accountants publication.   Contact NABA, 7249-A Hanover Parkway, Greenbelt, Maryland 20770   Phone: (301) 474-6222 Fax: (301) 474-3114 Website: www.nabainc.org

Statement   Newsletter focuses on current National Coalition of One Hundred Black Women (NCBW), issues and devotes attention to (NCBW) programs. Published twice a year. Contact NCBW, 38 West 32nd Street, Suite 1610, New York, New York 10001 Phone: (212) 947-2196 Fax: (212) 947-2477 E-mail: NC100BW@aol.com Website: www.ncbw.org

Voices in Black Studies Ohio State University National Council for Black Studies. Circulation 1,500. Advertising accepted. Contact Mr. James Devers, Voices in Black Studies, Ohio State University, 1030 Lincoln Tower, Columbus, Ohio 48210 Phone: (614) 292-3922

Newspapers

African-American News & Issues Since 1996. Targeting African-American, readers weekly delivered to more than 100,000 homes and available at more than 5,000 locations. AANI, 6130 Wheatley Street, Houston, Texas, 77091 Phone: (713) 692-1288 Fax: (713) 692-1183 E-mail: news@aframnews.com Website: www.aframnews.com

Afro-American Newspapers The leading news provider for African-Americans in the Baltimore/Washington, DC metropolitan area and longest running African-American, family-owned newspaper in the nation. Chairman of the Board/Publisher, John J. Oliver Jr.   Contact Afro-American News & Issues (AAN), 2519 North Charles Street, Baltimore Maryland 21218 Phone: (410) 554-8200 Fax: (877) 570-9297 Website: www.afro.com

Amsterdam News Voice of the Black constituency. National, international and New York news, politics and business. Amsterdam News, 3200 13th Street, North West, Washington, DC 20010 E-mail: info@amsterdamnews.com Website: www.amsterdamnews.org

Arizona Informant Local newspaper published weekly covering news worthy events affecting the Arizona African American Community. Arizona Informant, 1746 East Madison, Suite 2, Phoenix, Arizona 85034 Phone: (602) 257-9300 E-mail: azinformantnews@earthlink.net Website: www.arizonainformantnewspaper.com

Atlanta Tribune The Magazine Black Atlanta's leading source for relevant, thought-provoking news and information on business, careers, technology, wealth-building, politics and education. Pat Lottier, Publisher. Contact Atlanta Tribune, 875 Old Roswell Road, Suite C-100, Roswell, Georgia 30076 Phone: (770) 587-0501 Fax: (770) 642-6501 E-mail: info@atlantatribune.com Website: www.atlantatribune.com

Baltimore Times Fridays. Circulation 32,000. 10,000 in the Baltimore County, 5,000 in the Prince George County Times, and 5,000 in The Annapolis Times. Publisher, Joye Bramble, Editor, Dena Wane. Baltimore Times, 2513 North Charles, Baltimore, Maryland 21218 Phone: (410) 366-3900 Fax: (410) 243-1627 E-mail: dwane@btimes.com Website: www.btimes.com

Birmingham Times Circulation 16,500. Weekly publication. Thursday. Contact Mr. James E. Lewis, Publisher, Birmingham Times, 115 Third Avenue West, Birmingham, Alabama 35204 Phone: (205) 251-5158 Fax: (205) 323-2294 E-mail: jlewis@birminghamtimes.com Website: www.thebirminghamtimes.com

BlackPressUSA National website features news exclusively from African-American journalists and Black community publications. Contact BlackPressUSA, 3200 13th Street North West, Washington, DC 20010 Phone: (202) 588-8764 E-mail: info@blackpressusa.com Website: www.BlackPressUSA.com

Black Reign News Weekly New York City-based award-winning African American newspaper. Reviews books. Contact Rance Huff, Blackreign News, Post Office Box 30231, Staten Island, New York 10303 Phone: (718) 216-3530

The Black Voice News Established 1972. Weekly newspaper published on Thursdays. Reviews books, films, plays, concerts. Cheryl and Hardy L. Brown, Publishers. Contact Brown Publishing Company, Post Office Box 1581, Riverside, California 92502 Phone: (909) 682-6070 E-mail: hardybrown@blackvoicenews.com Website: www.blackvoicenews.com

Capitol Outlook Weekly, Thursdays. Circulation 12,500. Reviews books, movies, plays, and songs, advertising. Publisher, Roosevelt Wilson. Capital Outlook, 602 North Adams Street, Tallahassee Florida 32301 E-mail: coutlook@aol.com Website: www.capitaloutlook.com

Dallas Examiner Published Thursdays; total readership of 100,000. Sample distribution/drop-off points: Churches, high schools and colleges, banks, etc. Mollie Finch Belt, Publisher. Dallas Examiner, 1516 Corinth Street, Dallas, Texas 75215 Phone: (214) 428-3446 Fax: (214) 428-3451 E-mail: mbelt@dallasexaminer.com Website: www.dallasexaminer.com

Dallas Post Tribune Published Thursdays. Circulation 18,100. T.R. Lee Jr., Publisher/Owner. Dallas Post Tribune, Post Office Box 763939, Dallas, Texas 75376 Phone: (214) 946-7678 Fax: (214) 946-6823 E-mail: posttrib@airmail.net Website: www.dallaspost.com

Final Call Founded in the 1930s as the Final Call to Islam, the newspaper evolved into Muhammad Speaks in the 1960s and boasted a circulation of 900,000 a week, with monthly circulation of 2.5 million. Today, the weekly Final Call Newspaper serves a readership of diverse economic and educational backgrounds, including circulation in North America, Europe, Africa and the Caribbean. Final Call Publishing, 236 Massachusetts Avenue North East, Suite 610, Washington, DC 20002 Phone: (202) 543-7796 Website: www.finalcall.com

Florida Dollar Stretcher Newspaper Serving the African-American communities of Tampa and Plant City, Florida since October 1971. Free. Circulation, 125,000 weekly readers. Sabrina Anette Barnes, Florida Dollar Stretcher, 2002 West Busch Boulevard, Suite C, Tampa, Florida 33612 Phone: (813) 930-9599 Fax: (813) 930-9698 E-mail: dollarstretcher1@aol.com

Freedom Socialist Newspaper Quarterly. Luma Nichol, Organizer. Socialist Feminist political party dedicated to eradicating injustice and inequality. Freedom Socialist Newspaper, 5018 Rainier Avenue South, Seattle, Washington 98118 Phone: (206) 722-2453 Fax: (206) 722-2453 E-mail: fspseattle@mindspring.com Website: www.socialism.com

Frost Illustrated Weekly African American newspaper established in 1968. Editor, Fort Wayne. Contact Frost Illustrated, 3121 South Calhoun Street, Fort Wayne Indiana 46806 Phone: (260) 745-0552 E-mail: frostnews@aol.com Website: www.frostillustrated.com

Grand Rapids Times Published weekly. Circulation 6,000. Issues that pertain to the African American community. Dr. Patricia Pulliam, Owner/Editor. Contact Grand Rapids Times, 2016 Eastern, Grand Rapids, Michigan 49510 Phone: (616) 245-8737 E-mail: staff@grtimes.com

Green County Democrat An African-American oriented newspaper. Published weekly on Wednesdays. Circulation 4,200. We also review books, plays, movies. Contact John Zippert, Publisher, Green County Democrat, Post Office Box 598, Eutaw, Alabama 35462 Phone: (205) 372-3373 Fax: (205) 372-2243 E-mail: **jzippert@aol.com**

Haitian Times Covers Haitian and Haitian-American news: Arts & leisure: entertainment, reviews, profiles, social events, business. Sports: Haitian and American soccer, basketball, tennis. Columns: news from Boston, New York, Miami, and Haiti. The Haitian Times, Inc., 610 Vanderbilt Avenue, Brooklyn, New York, 11238 Phone: (718) 230-8700 Fax: (718) 230-7172 E-mail: **info-ht@haitiantimes.com** Website: **www.haitiantimes.com**

Ink Northeast Indiana's premier Newspaper delivering information, news and knowledge for and about local African Americans. Since, October 2001. Vince Robinson, Publisher. Contact Ink, 1301 Lafayette Street, Suite 202, Fort Wayne, Indiana 46802 Phone: (260) 420-3200 Fax: (260) 420-3210 E-mail: **editor@inknewsonline.com** Website: **www.inknewsonline.com**

The Inland Valley News Since 1992. We service portions of over thirteen cities in the heart of the Inland Valley. Readership in excess of 45,000. Co-Publishers, Gloria Morrow and Tommy Morrow. Shining Glory Publications, Inc., 2249 North Garey Avenue, Pomona, California 91767 Fax: (909) 392-6917 E-mail: **IVNews@aol.com** Website: **www.inlandvalleynews.com**

Insider News Bi-weekly. Circulation 10,000. Ken Lumpkin, Publisher. Insider News, 1661 Douglas Avenue, Racine, Wisconsin 53404 Phone: (262) 632-9370 E-mail: **insider@wi.net**

Long Beach Times Newspaper serving Long Beach, Carson, Compton and surrounding communities; estimated weekly readership 33,000. Richard A. Love, Publisher/Editor. Long Beach Times, 121 Linden Avenue #105, Long Beach, California 90802 Phone: (562) 436-9221 E-mail: **lbtimes@aol.com** Website: **www.lbtimes.net**

Los Angeles Sentinel Largest Black-owned newspaper in the West. Thursdays. Circulation, 125,000. Contact Danny Bakewell, Executive Publisher. Los Angeles Sentinel, 38 Crenshaw Boulevard, Los Angeles, California 90008 Phone: (323) 299-3800 Fax: (323) 299-3896 Website: **www.losangelessentinel.com**

Los Angeles Wave African American newspaper. Contact Editor, The Los Angeles Wave, 4201 Wilshire Boulevard, Suite 600, Los Angeles, California 90010 Phone: (323) 556-5720 Fax: (323) 556-5704 Website: **www.wavenewspapers.com**

Milwaukee Community Journal Weekender Published weekly. Patricia O'Flynn Pattillo, Publisher/CEO. Milwaukee Community Journal Weekender, 3612 North Martin Luther King Drive, Milwaukee, Wisconsin 53212 Phone: (414) 265-5300 Fax: (414) 265-1536 E-mail: **editorial@communityjournal.net** Website: **www.communityjournal.net**

Milwaukee Times Weekly Circulation 15,000. Contact The Milwaukee Times Weekly, 1938 Martin Luther King Drive, Milwaukee, Wisconsin 53212 Phone: (414) 263-5088 E-mail: **miltimes@execpc.com** Website: **www.themilwaukeetimesweekly.com**

The Mississippi Link Weekly publication. L. Socrates Garrett, Publisher. Nikki Burns, Editor. The Mississippi Link, 2659 Livingston Road, Jackson, Mississippi 39213 Phone: (601) 355-9103 Fax: (601) 355-9105 E-mail: **mslink@misnet.com** Website: **www.mississippilink.com**

The New York Beacon Walter Smith Jr., Publisher. The New York Beacon, Smith Haj Group Inc., 341 West 38th Street, Suite 8R, New York, New York 10018 Phone: (212) 213-8585 Fax: (212) 213-6291 E-mail: **newyorkbeacon@yahoo.com** Website: **www.newyorkbeacon.com**

The Old Gold & Black The student newspaper of Wake Forest University. Published Thursdays during the school year. Old Gold & Black, Post Office Box 7569, Winston-Salem, North Carolina 27109 Phone: (336) 758-5279 Fax: (336) 758-4561 Send guest editorials to: E-mail: **business@ofh.wfu.edu** Website: **www.ogb.wfu.edu**

The Pasadena/San Gabriel Valley Journal News Since 1989, serving Altadena, Pasadena, Monrovia and Duarte and surrounding cities in the west San Gabriel Valley area. Joe C. Hopkins, publisher. The Pasadena/San Gabriel Valley Journal News, 1541 North Lake Avenue, Suite A, Pasadena, California 91104 Phone: (626) 798-3972 Fax: (626) 798-3282 E-mail: **pasjour@pacbell.net** Website: **www.pasadenajournal.com**

The Sacramento Observer Founded, 1962. Dr. William H. Lee, founder and publisher. Contact The Observer Newspapers, 2330 Alhambra Boulevard, Sacramento, California 95817 Phone: (916) 452-4781 Fax: (916) 452-7744 E-mail: **whlee@sacobserver.com** Website: **www.SacObserver.com**

San Francisco Bay View National Black newspaper. San Francisco Bay View, 4917 Third Street, San Francisco, California 94124 Phone: (415) 671-0789 Fax: (415) 671-0316 E-mail: **editor@sfbayview.com** Website: **www.sfbayview.com**

The Seattle Medium Circulation exceeds 91,000 with a combined readership of more than 321,000 weekly. Radio stations include KRIZ 1420, KZIZ 1560, KYIZ 1620, Seattle/Tacoma and KBMS 1480 - Portland, Oregon. Publisher, Chris B. Bennett. Contact The Seattle Medium Newspaper Group, 2600 South Jackson Street, Seattle, Washington 98144 Phone: (206) 323-3070 E-mail: **mediumnews@aol.com** Website: **www.seattlemedium.com**

Organizations

African American Atelier, Inc. A non-profit, fine arts gallery organization whose mission is promoting an awareness, appreciation and sensitivity to the visual arts and culture of African Americans and working in harmony with other ethnic groups. Celebrating the contributions of past, present and emerging African American and ethnic artists, Atelier was conceived by Alma Adams and the late Eva Hamlin Miller, who were joined by six local artists and community patrons and chartered in 1990. The gallery opened to the public on January 13, 1991 in the Greensboro Cultural. Alma Adams, The African American Atelier, 200 North Davie Street, Box 14, Greensboro, North Carolina 27401 Phone: (336) 333-6885 Fax: (336) 373-4826 E-mail: **info@africanamericanatelier.org** Website: **www.africanamericanatelier.org**

African American Research Library and Cultural Center (AARLCC) Von D. Mizell Branch Library is a research library and cultural center for scholars, students and the general public. The library contains more than 75,000 books, documents, artifacts and related materials that focus on the experiences of people of African descent. AARLCC, 2650 Sistrunk Boulevard, Fort Lauderdale, Florida 33311 Phone: (954) 625-2800 E-mail: **aarlcc@browardlibrary.org** Website: **www.broward.org/aarlcc**

African American Women in Cinema AAWC is a non profit organization whose mission is to support minority women filmmakers by providing resources in the film industry. Incorporated by the organization's president, Terra Renee in 2000. Contact AAWC, 545 Eighth Avenue, Suite 401, New York, New York 10018 Phone: (212) 769-7949 Fax: (212) 871-2074 E-mail: **info@aawic.org** Website: **www.aawic.org**

African Voices Communications, Inc. Founded 1992. Non profit cultural arts organization. Sponsors literary readings, art exhibitions, writing workshops and other programs. Publishes literary magazine African Voices. Layding Kaliba, Managing Director. Contact Layding Kaliba, African Voices, 270 West 96th Street, New York, New York 10025 Phone: (212) 865-2982 E-mail: **africanvoices@aol.com**   Website: **www.africanvoices.com**

Afro-American Cultural Center Organization purpose is to develops processes, functions and attributes throughout Yale and the city of New Haven that are reciprocal and interactive, resulting in a sense of community, cultural vision, competence, efficacy permanence, spiritual well-being, and integrity. Contact Ms. Pamela George, Director. Afro-American Cultural Center, 211 Park Steet, New Haven, Connecticut 06520 Phone: (203) 432-4132

Afro-American Historical and Genealogical Society, Inc. AAHGS is non-profit, membership organization committed to the preservation of the history, genealogy, and culture of the African-Ancestored populations of the local, national, and international community. Contact Afro-American Historical and Genealogical Society, Inc., Post Office Box 73067, Washington, DC 20056 Phone: (202) 234-5350 E-mail: **info@aahgs.org** Website: **www.aahgs.org**

Afro-Lousiana Historical & Genealogical Society An organization dedicated to expanding the knowledge base, sources, community consciousness, and education regarding the historical, cultural, and genealogical heritage of African-Americans in general and Louisianans in particular. Mrs. Edna Jordan Smith, founder. African American Historical & Genealogical Society, Post Office Box 2123, Baton Rouge, Louisiana 70821 Phone: (225) 387-1370 E-mail: info@alhgs.com Website: www.alhgs.com

Birmingham Civil Rights Institute The Birmingham Civil Rights Institute is a multi-media facility that houses exhibitions devoted to highlighting the American Civil Rights Movement (particularly in Birmingham, Alabama) and the Human Rights Movement worldwide. BCRI provides the community with scores of educational programs and special events and houses an archival department that has been used by researchers across the world. Birmingham Civil Rights Institute, 520 16th Street North, Birmingham, Alabama 35203 Phone: (866) 328-9696 Fax: (205) 251-6104 E-mail: Lpijeaux@bcri.org   Website: www.bcri.org

100 Black Men of Greater Cleveland, Inc. Mentoring, education, health and wellness, economic development. Contact 100 Black Men of Greater Cleveland, Inc., 4415 Euclid Avenue, Suite 331, Cleveland, Ohio 44103 Phone: (216) 361-9146 Fax: (216) 361-9148 E-mail: info@100blackmencleveland.org Website: www.100blackmencleveland.org

Black Broadcasters Alliance National organization of Black broadcasters. The BBC is comprised of owners and professionals who want to see equality and real opportunity for African Americans employed in the broadcasting industry and or who are in pursuit of ownership. The BBC is comprised of broadcasters representing television, radio and cable who are employed or operating in major markets across the United States. Mr. Eddie Edwards, Sr., Chairman. Black Broadcasters Alliance, 711 West 40th Street, Suite 330, Baltimore, Maryland 21211 Fax: (410) 662-0816 E-mail: e-mail@thebba.org Website: www.thebba.org

Black College Radio and Television Organization Provides an annual forum for black college broadcasters, professional broadcasters and members of the music industry to meet and discuss ways and means to increase minority participation in the broadcasting industry. Lo Jelks, Chairman. Contact BCR, Post Office Box 3191, Atlanta, Georgia 30302 Phone: (404) 523-6136 Fax: (404) 523-5467 E-mail: bcrmail@aol.com Website: www.blackcollegeradio.com

Black Press International Non-profit communications and research think tank organization incorporated to mobilize and motivate interest in government and public policies that have direct impact on African-American society. William Reed, President, Black Press International, 405 16th Street, Southeast, Washington, DC 20003 Phone: (202) 547-4125 Fax: (202) 592-1997 E-mail: wreed@blackpressinternational.com Website: www.blackpressinternational.com

Black Speakers Online A division of Speakers Etc. The brainchild of Norma Thompson Hollis BSO offers a directory of Black speakers from a wide range of budgets, geographical areas, topics, talents and entertainments. Provides meeting planners the opportunity to connect with Black speakers and talent. Contact Ms. Norma Thompson, Black Speakers, Etc., 1968 West Adams Boulevard, Suite 208, Los Angeles, California 90018 Phone: (323) 734-7144 E-mail: info@blackspeakersonline.com Website: www.blackspeakersonline.com

The CAAPCO Group Incorporated in January 1997. CAAPCO is a coalition of a number of professional and community organizations that have similar objectives, a commitment to community service, including youth programs, educational forums and economic empowerment. The collective membership of CAAPCO's sponsoring organizations exceeds 7,000 members. The CAAPCO Group, Post Office Box 214014, Dallas, Texas 75221 Phone: (214) 658-1188 E-mail: info@caapco.org Website: www.caapco.org

Center for Black Music Research (CBMR) A research unit of Columbia College Chicago devoted to research, preservation, and dissemination of information about the history of black music on a global scale. Contact CBMR, Columbia College Chicago, 600 South Michigan Avenue, Chicago, Illinois, 60605 Phone: (312) 344-7559 Fax: (312) 344-8029 E-mail: contact@cbmr.colum.edu Website: www.cbmr.colum.edu

The Centre for the Study of Black Cultures in Canada Endeavours to serve as a stimulus to and focal point for faculty, graduate and undergraduate students, as well as independent scholars who are pursuing research in African Canadian Studies, at York University, and elsewhere. The Centre sponsors conferences and other events, and on-going research projects. The website which began in 1998 provides information on African Canadian artists and their work. Contact Professor Leslie Sanders, The Centre for the Study of Black Cultures in Canada, York University, 4700 Keele Street, Toronto, ON M3J 1P3 Phone: (416) 736-2100 E-mail: leslie@yorku.ca Website: www.yorku.ca/aconline/index.html

Charlotte African-American Writers Group The group is comprised of male and female writers who possess volumes of writing experience that we are willing to share with other writers. We represent a diverse and talented group of individuals that express a keen interest in the development of our writing skills. Clayton F. Brown, Founder/President. Contact Charlotte African-American Writers Group, Post Office Box 29155, Charlotte, North Carolina 28229 E-mail: claytonfbrown@msn.com Website: www.caawnc.net

Coffee Chatter, Inc. Motto: "Chatting With Showbiz Pros." Coffee Chatter provides professionals from the entertainment industry to come and speak for informative purposes only to aspiring actors. Past Guest have included; Actress Anne Marie Johnson, Actress Nicey Nash (From Reno 911), Actor Joseph Marcell, (From TV series Fresh Prince Of Bel Air), and many others. Founder: Actress Lynne Burnett. Coffee Chatter, Inc., 16420 Stagecoach Avenue, Palmdale, California 93591 Phone: (661) 264-4696 E-mail: coffeechatter1@cs.com

The Color Of Film Collaborative Non-profit organization that works to support media makers of color and others who have an interest in creating and developing new and diverse images of people of color in film, video and performing arts. TCOF sponsors film screenings and work-in-progress previews annually and throughout the year. Ms. Lisa Simmons, Executive Director. Contact The Color of Film Collaborative, Post Office Box 191901, Roxbury, Massachusetts 02119 Phone: (617) 445-6051 E-mail: info@coloroffilm.com Website: www.coloroffilm.com

The Dayton Christian Writer's Guild Inc. Organized in September 1993, under the leadership of Ms. Tina Toles. Contact Ms. Tina Toles, Post Office Box 251, Englewood, Ohio 45322 Phone: (937) 836-6600 E-mail: tinatoles@yahoo.com

Focus: Joint Center For Political and Economic Studies National nonprofit research and public policy institution founded in 1970 by black intellectuals professionals to provide training and technical assistance to newly elected black officials. Vice President for Communications and Policy and Chief of Staff, Janice F. Joyner. Contact Focus, 1090 Vermont Avenue, North West, Suite 1100, Washington, DC 20005 Phone: (202) 789-3500 Fax: (202) 789-6390 E-mail: jjoyner@jointcenter.org Website: www.jointcenter.org

International Black Writers & Artists Los Angeles Founded in Los Angeles in 1974 by Mrs. Edna Crutchfield and other black writers, IBWALA is a network of authors, publishers, visual artists, educators and community members dedicated to making sure our writers and artists are published, read, seen, and heard by providing workshops and conferences, information and resources as well as cultural outlets, scholarships, publishing opportunities. Linda A. Hughes, Board Member and Co-conference Planner. IBWALA, Post Office Box 43576, Los Angeles, California 90043 Phone: (323) 964-3721 E-mail: info@ibwa.org Website: www.ibwa.org

KHAFRE Writer's colony, now known as: The Harriet Tubman Village, for Writers and Artist is a bed and breakfast facility located in the "Historic South" that provides all the conveniences a writer needs to hone their skills. Khafre, Post Office Box 4221, Greenville, Mississippi 38704 Phone: (662) 773-2048 E-mail: khafre@peoplepc.com Website: www.khafre.us

Langston Hughes Community Library and Cultural Center Public Library and Cultural Center. Home of the Black Heritage Reference Center of Queens County, housing over 45,000 volumes of print and non-print circulating items, books and audio-visual materials, on the Black Experience. Andrew P. Jackson, Langston Hughes Community Library and Cultural Center, Queens Library, 100-01 Northern Boulevard, Corona, New York 11368 Phone: (718) 651-1100 E-mail: andrew.p.jackson@queenslibrary.org   Website: www.queenslibrary.org

Moorland-Spingarn Research Center One of the world's largest and most comprehensive repositories for the documentation of the history and culture of people of African descent in Africa, the Americas, and other parts of the world. As one of Howard University's major research facilities, the MSRC collects, preserves, and makes available for research a wide range of resources chronicling the Black experience. Dr. Thomas C. Battle, Director. Jean Currie Church, Chief Librarian. Howard University, 500 Howard Place, North West, Washington, DC 20059 Phone: (202) 806-7240 Fax: (202) 806-6405 E-mail: Jchurch@howard.edu Website: www.founders.howard.edu/moorland-spingarn/default.htm

Motown Writers Network A 9 year old literary organization for Michigan writers founded by Sylvia Hubbard. Mission: Impact the literary community by bringing readers in touch with local writers. With 300 members strong, offers a monthly newsletter, website promotion. Motown Writers Network, Post Office Box 27310, Detroit, Michigan 48227 Phone: (313) 289-8614 E-mail: motownwriters@yahoo.com Website: www.MotownWriters.homestead.com

Multicultural Marketing Resources Marketing news/Travel news. Editor and Publisher, Ms. Lisa Skriloff. Contact Editor, Multicultural Marketing Resources, Inc., 101 5th Avenue Suite 10B, New York, New York 10003 Phone: (212) 242-3351 Fax: (212) 691-5969 E-mail: lisa@multicultural.com Website: www.multicultural.com

The National Black Programming Consortium (NBPC) Non-profit national media arts organization committed to the presentation, funding, promotion, distribution and preservation of positive images of African Americans and the African Diaspora. Sets the standard and one of the leading providers of historically accurate programming about the African American experience on public television. Jacquie Jones, Executive Director. Mable Haddock, Member and Founding Director. NBPC, 68 East 131st Street, 7th Floor, Harlem, New York 10037 Phone: (212) 234-8200 Fax: (212) 234-7032 E-mail: info@nbpc.tv Website: www.nbpc.tv

National Coalition Of One Hundred Black Women (NCBW) Founded 1981, NCBW is a nonprofit organization with approximately 7,500 members in 62 chapters in 25 states and the District of Columbia. Annual Candace Award ceremony. Jewell Jackson McCabe, Founder and Chair. Leslie A. Mays, President. National Coalition of One Hundred Black Women, 38 West 32nd Street, Suite 1610, New York, New York 10001 Phone: (212) 947-2196 Fax: (212) 947-2477 E-mail: NC100BW@aol.com Website: www.ncbw.org

National Council Of Negro Women (NCNW) Founded in 1935 by Dr. Mary Mcleod Bethune with the goal of improving the lives of black women and their families NCNW acts as central source for planning and seeks to fill the gaps that exist in our communities. Conference. Dr. Dorothy I. Height, Chair. Contact NCNW, 633 Pennsylvania Avenue, North West, Washington, DC 20004 Phone: (202) 737-0120 Fax: (202) 737-0476 Website: www.ncnw.org

National Society Of Black Engineers (NSBE) Offers academic excellence programs, scholarships, leadership training, professional development and access to career opportunities for thousands of members annually. 10,000 members. Annual National Convention, hosting over 8,000 attendees. Features and sells books. Chancee` Lundy, National Chairperson. Contact NSBE, World Headquarters, 1454 Duke Street, Alexandria, Virginia 22314 Phone: (703) 549-2207 Fax: (703) 683-5312 E-mail: info@nsbe.org Website: www.nsbe.org

National Urban League, Inc. The nation's oldest and largest community-based movement empowering African Americans to enter the economic and social mainstream. E-store and annual conference. Scholarship program. President and CEO, Marc Morial. Contact The National Urban League, Inc., 120 Wall Street, New York, New York 10005 Phone: (212) 558-5300 Fax: (212) 344-5332 E-mail: info@nul.org Website: www.nul.org

Organization of Black Screenwriters, Inc. (OBS) Organized in 1988 to support Black screenwriters. Our primary function is to assist screenwriters in the creation of works for film and television, Jennifer William, President. Contact Organization of Black Screenwriters, Inc., Golden State Mutual Life Insurance Building, 1999 West Adams Boulevard, Room Mezzanine, Los Angeles, California 90018 Phone: (323) 735-2050 E-mail: sfranklin@obswriter.com Website: www.obswriter.com

Ralph J. Bunche Center for African American Studies at UCLA Darnell Hunt, Interim IDP Chair. Contact Darnell Hunt, Ralph J. Bunche Center for African-American Studies, UCLA, 160 Haines Hall, Box 951545, Los Angeles, California 90095 Phone: (310) 825-7403 E-mail: lbritton@bunche.ucla.edu Website: www.bunchecenter.ucla.edu

The RAWSISTAZ Reviewers (TRR) Founded in September 2000 by Tee C. Royal, the Rawsistaz Reviewers are the leading reviewers in the literary industry with a focus on promoting the works of books by and about African-American Authors. Daily newsletter of black book reviews can be found on our site. The RAWSISTAZ Reviewers, Post Office Box 1362, Duluth, Georgia 30096 Phone: (775) 363-8683 Fax: (775) 416-4540 E-mail: info@rawsistaz.com Website: www.blackbookreviews.net

Schomburg Center for Research in Black Culture National research library devoted to collecting and documenting the experiences of peoples of African descent throughout the world. Gennette McLaurin, Associate Chief Librarian. Schomburg Center for Research in Black Culture, 515 Malcolm X Boulevard, New York, New York 10037 Phone: (212) 491-2200 E-mail: gmclaurin@nypl.org Website: www.nypl/research/sc/sc

The Writer's Block, Inc. (WBI) Non-profit organization of African-American writers/authors, aspiring and published, of all genres, who are dedicated to the growth and advancement of its members. WBI also promotes African-American literary events, literature and authors. We support young African-American writers through a scholarship fund. Black Writers Group, The Writer's Block, Inc., Post Office Box 170875, Dallas, Texas 75217 Phone: (972) 223-3074 Fax: (972) 223-3075 E-mail: afields121@yahoo.com Website: www.writersblockinc.org

Writers Resource Center (WRC) A 501(3)c non-profit writers organization. Janie P. Bess, Founder. WRC, 1500 Oliver Road, Suite K, PMB 265, Fairfield, California 94534 Phone: (707) 399-9169 E-mail: jpbrites2@sbcglobal.net Website: www.writersresourcecenter.com

Photographers

Cliff Chandler Photographer - German School of Photography, Jazz Musician - The New Muse, Brooklyn, New York, and an editorial writer for a local newspaper. Fine Art Major, Pratt Institute, Brooklyn, New York, Masters Writing courses at New York University, and Editing classes at The New School. His photographs hang in private collections all over the world and in museums here in America. Cliff Chandler, 2492 Tredway Drive, Macon, Georgia 31211 E-mail: CDuke23@aol.com   Website: www.authorsden.com/cliffchandler

Lynisha O. Childers Photographer, poet and author. Lynisha O. Childers Founder/CEO, GreekWorks Entertainment and Infinite Greek Appeal, 550 Palisades Drive South, #102, Birmingham, Alabama 35209 Phone: (205) 940-7566 E-mail: lynisha_childers@hotmail.com

Algie deWitt A Creative writer, photographer, web/graphics designer, and publisher of MaMi Magazine. Mr. Algie deWitt, MAMi Magazine, 4408 Aberdeen Lane, Blackwood, New Jersey 08012 E-mail: algie@mamimagazine.com Website: www.mamimagazine.com

Emtro Music Production Artist Itinerary Management. Our session musicians are amongst the finest to be found anywhere. Other services we provide include: Publishing, Mastering, Marketing and Promotions, Shopping Your Artist Project to Record Labels, Remote and Live Recording Services, Radio and Retail Support, Manufacturing, Tour Support, Graphic Design and Photography. Welcomes all songwriters to submit copy written material to be considered for future projects. Emtro Music Production, Post Office Box 12760, Jacksonville, Florida 32209 E-mail: kishia@theintegritysolution.com Website: www.emtro.com

C.D. Grant Writer, poet, photographer and journalist whose work has appeared in numerous periodicals. He completed a course in professional photography with the New York Institute of Photography and is a member of National Press Photographers Association. C.D. Grant, Blind Beggar Press, Post Office Box 437, Bronx, New York 10467 Phone: (914) 282-5747 E-mail: blindbeggar1@juno.com Website: www.blindbeggarpress.org

Joaquin M. Holloway Jr. Artistic photographer. The collection of color photographs (all matted and framed) has been shown in many galleries throughout the state of Alabama. Contact Joaquin M. Holloway Jr., 2206 De Kruif Court, Mobile, Alabama 36617 Phone: (251) 478-5525 E-mail: joaquinholloway@aol.com

Rob Jay Currently works in both radio and television. He is the morning show host on WYJS 105.9 F.M., an all new blues radio station in central Mississippi. Rob does freelance reporting for Major Black College Sports on the MBC network, sideline reporting for Jackson State Football radio and basketball. Rob Jay, WLBT-TV3, Post Box 1712, Jackson, Mississippi 39215 Phone: (601) 948-3333 E-mail: robj@wlbt.net Website: www.wlbt.net

Rych McCain His features and famous photo spreads include Hollywood Red Carpet Movie Premieres, Major Awards Shows, Press Junkets, Exclusive One to One interview/photo shoots, Concerts, Club Promotional Parties, Forums, Conferences, Private Celebrity Parties to you name it. Rych McCain, Post Office Box 2272, Beverly Hills, California 90213 Phone: (213) 387-3493 E-mail: rychmccain@sbcglobal.net

Gerard McLeod CEO of P.B.G.'s Productions (Photos by Gerard), and Editor-in-Chief of Long Island's first bi-lingual urban music magazine called Strong G Island Biz (SGIB). As a freelance publicity photographer for over 25 years McLeod has supplied photos to and has written for a variety of publications including Where It's At Magazine and Jet Magazine, among others. Has photographed Richard Burton, James Brown, Crystal Gayle, Chuck Berry; cover photographer for "Cosmopolitan" magazine. Gerard Mcleod, Post Office Box 1926, West Babylon, New York 11704 E-mail: SGIBmagazine@aol.com Website: www.sgibmagazines.com

Jay Nelson Photographer. Host of The Beat website. Jay Nelson, The Beat Magazine, Post Office Box 65856, Los Angeles, California 90065 Phone: (818) 500-9299 Fax: (818) 500-9454 E-mail: jay@afropulse.com Website: www.afropulse.com

Keith Saunders Marion Designs founder, Keith Saunders designs book covers, business cards, posters, postcards, marketing materials, and logo design. Several of our book covers have made the Essence best seller list. Also performed work for top names such as Cingular wireless, AT&T, Simon & Schuster, and Fox studios (Garfield movie promotions). Marion Designs, 225 Sunderland Way, Suite # U, Stockbridge, Georgia 30281 Phone: (678) 641-8689 Phone: (678) 641-8689 E-mail: mariondesigns@bellsouth.net Website: www.mariondesigns.com

Raymond Tyler Freelance Writer/Photographer, Essence Magazine, The Source, and Vibe magazines. Columnist, About Time, The National Impact, AC Weekly. Talk Show Host/Producer, The National Impact radio show Friday's 10am-11am, The Wayback Machine 11am-1pm on 91.7 FM WLFR (WLFR.FM) Contact Mr. Raymond Tyler, Dark Seed Communications, 6701 Black Horse Pike, Suite A-4, EHT, New Jersey 08234 Phone: (609) 816-5589 E-mail: nationalimpact@gmail.com

WideVision Photography Photographer, Anthony Wilson. Principle photographer: Marcia Wilson. Our staff's work has appeared in Vibe, Publishers Weekly, Black Issues Book Review, Caribbean Times, LA Weekly, and QBR. WideVision's team of photographers have exhibited at The National Black Writers Conference, Medgar Evers College. Contact Marcia, WideVision Photography, 30a Hampton Place, Brooklyn, New York 11217 Phone: (347) 495-5459 E-mail: marcia@widevisionphotography.com Website: www.widevisionphotography.com

Gloria Dulan-Wilson A freelance writer/photographer, screenwriter and public speaker, Wilson is a seasoned photo-journalist and public speaker who has covered the Black political arena of New York and Northern New Jersey. She has interviewed and profiled such luminaries as Ossie Davis, Min. Louis Farrakhan, Cong. Charles Rangel, Floyd Flake, Kweisi Mfume, interviewed Diana Ross, Don King, the late Johnnie Cochran, Rosa Parks, the late Mrs. Coretta Scott King, among others. Gloria Dulan-Wilson, 90 Church Street, Suite 3343, New York City, New York 10008 E-mail: geemomadee@yahoo.com

Playwrights

Sonya Alexander Journalist, screenwriter, editor, researcher. Contact Ms. Sonya Alexander, Post Office Box 480832, Los Angeles, California 90048 E-mail: **sonyaa2@yahoo.com**

Y. Jamal Ali An eclectic blend of artist, scientist, historian and esotericist. Author of over six hundred fifty poems, in addition to numerous essays, articles, short stories and plays, Jamal has been writing seriously for over 25 years. Y. Jamal Ali, Post Office Box 332, San Pedro, California 90733 Phone: (310) 876-9332 E-mail: **PtahOgun@yahoo.com**

Franklin J. Anderson Playwright, screenwriter, Mr. Andersons' play CLASS ran Off-Broadway at Tribeca Theatre in New York in 1994. Co-writer of screenplay Street Tales of Terror. Contact Mr. Franklin J. Anderson, 2610 Harvest Moon, Missouri City, Texas 77489 Phone: (281) 438-1062 E-mail: **f_anderso@hotmail.com**

Stanley Bois Screen writer currently writing for Roc Box Films. My current play is titled Innocence Lost, a stop the violence script dealing with black on black crimes. Contact Mr. Stanley Bois, 1207 SE Curry Street, Port St. Lucie, Florida 34983 Phone: (772) 634-4838 E-mail: **stanleybois@hotmail.com**

Kenneth Bowens Author and playwright and an improv artist and actor, Kanko has written and produced three plays. Contact Mr. Kenneth (Kanko) Bowens, 1208 Northwest 106th Street, Oklahoma City, Oklahoma 73114 E-mail: **kennethbowens1@kennethbowens.com** Website: **www.kennethbowens.com**

Ed Bullins Artist-in-Residence, Northeastern University and the author of six books, including Five Plays By Ed Bullins, The Duplex, The Hungered One, Four Dynamite Plays, The Theme is Blackness, and The Reluctant Rapist. His latest book is ED BULLINS: 12 Plays and Selected Writings (U of Michigan Press, 2006). Ed Bullins, 37 Vine Street, #1, Roxbury, Massachusetts 02119 Phone: (617) 442-6627 E-mail: **rct9@verizon.net** Website: **www.edbullins.com**

L. Guy Burton My screenplay Latent Blood won honorable mention in a Writer's Digest contest. As founder and Director of The Warwick Valley Writers' Association, I have, through this local writers' group, been able to polish, complete and promote several Works in various genres. L Guy Burton, The Warwick Valley Writers' Association, 12 Burton Lane, Warwick, New York 10990 E-mail: **el_guybur@hotmail.com** Website: **www.warwickinfo.net**

Stanley Bennett Clay Author/playwright, wrote the stage plays "Lovers" and "Armstrong's Kid," as well as the musical "Street Nativity," commisioned by National League of Negro Women. He has received three NAACP Theater Awards for writing, directing, and coproducing the critically acclaimed play, Ritual. Mr. Stanley Bennett Clay, 1155 4th Avenue Los Angeles, California 90019 Phone: (323) 737-2612 E-mail: **sbcpublishers@earthlink.net**

Ben Clement Author, playwright, journalist, and screenwriter. His credits include three independent films, a musical stage production also produced on DVD, newspaper and magazine articles, scripts for five television programs, award winning poetry, and a rap song entitled, "Hit Man." Ben Clement Miracle Hands Productions, 2929 West 24th Place, Gary, Indiana 46404 Phone: (219) 944-1201 Fax: (219) 944-1202 E-mail: ben_clement_99@yahoo.com

Ebony Rose Custis A poet working in various mediums including fiction and dramatic writing. Ebony is author of an award winning one-act drama 'Strange Reflections' and one full length drma 'Taylor's Gift.' Ebony also won First Prize in the Dramatic Writing division of the Margaret Walker College Language Association writing competition for her short play 'Strange Reflections.' She has studied creative writing at the University of Ghana under the instruction of Kofi Awoonor and Kofi Anyidaho. Ms. Ebony Rose Custis, 13211 Vanessa Avenue, Bowie, Maryland 20720 Phone: (301) 602 5918 E-mail: ebony.custis@gmail.com

Jackie Daughtry Pseudonyms: Ayani_Meli Journey Shanise Rhodes is an accomplished poet and playwright, as well as a digital storyteller. She also taught drama at Talbot Academy, an alternative school in Savannah serving the needs of behaviorally challenged youth. Ms. Jackie Daughtry, Post Office Box 32, Sylvania, Georgia 30467 Phone: (912) 687-5546 E-mail: ayani.meli@gmail.com

Gerri DeWitt Screenwriter. Contact Gerri DeWitt, The Corporate Catalysts, 590 Means Street, Suite 200, Atlanta, Georgia 30318 Phone: (404) 223-2438 E-mail: gerri@corpcatalysts.com

Penelope Flynn Author and Screenwriter of Erotica, Science Fiction, Fantasy, Sensual Romance, Paranormal Romance, Legal comedy and drama and Horror. Penelope Flynn, 824 North Marsalis Avenue, Suite C, Dallas, Texas 75203 Phone: (214) 371-7366 Fax: (214) 942-0980 E-mail: penelope@penelopeflynn.com

Papi Kymone Freeman Writer/producer, playwright and poet, Papi Kymone Freeman is the founder of the National Black LUV Festival. He is currently a board member for Words Beats & Life. Papi Kymone Freeman, Frederick Douglas Station, Post Office Box 31243, Banneker City, Washington, DC 20030 Phone: (202) 547-2459 E-mail: kymone@prisonpoetry-theplay.com Website: www.prisonpoetry-theplay.com

Nancy Gilliam Her screenplay, Mercury in Retrograde, won a coveted spot to be pitched before the 2009 SIP Panel during the Philadelphia Film Festival. Contact Ms. Nancy Gilliam, 5525 West Girard Avenue, Philadelphia, Pennsylvania 10131 Phone: (267) 847-5110 E-mail: melodicg2003@hotmail.com

Idris Goodwin Playwright, performer, director, and educator. Recipient of the NEA/TCG Theatre Residency Program for Playwrights for 2004. BA in Film & Video from Columbia College, Chicago and an MFA in Writing from the School of the Art Institute of Chicago. He has written and co-produced eight full-length plays. Since 1999, Idris has been creating original hip-hop music as a solo artist and in collaboration, releasing CD's independently and for the Chicago based Naiveté records. Mr. Idris Goodwin, 1721 West Huron, Apartment 2f, Chicago, Illinois 60622 E-mail: Idris@hermitsite.com Website: www.hermitsite.com

Forest Hairston   Songwriter-music producer, screenwriter and poet. Mr. Forest Hairston, ForGen Productions, 3654 Barham Boulevard, Suite Q301, Los Angeles, California Phone: (323) 851-1225 E-mail: **theater@forgen.com** Website: **www.forgen.com**

William Hairston   Author, playwright and poet, his produced plays include: Walk In Darkness (NYC); Swansong Of The 11th Dawn (NYC); Ira Aldridge (The London Conflict), the winner of the Group Theatre's Playwriting Award, (Seattle, WA, 1987-1988); Double Dare (Theatre Festival, Washington, DC); Black Antigone (NC). He is the recipient of a National Endowment for the Arts Literary Grant and a Ford Foundation Theatre Fellowship; graduated from the University of Northern Colorado, BA. William Hairston, 5501 Seminary Road, #511-S, Falls Church, Virginia 22041 Phone: (703) 845-1281 E-mail: **WilliamRHairston1@msn.com**

Terence E. Jackson   Singer, playwright, poet, and novelist of the controversial novel Nigger's Heaven. Mr. Terence E. Jackson, 690 Durant Place, North East, Suite #2, Atlanta, Georgia 30308 E-mail: **terenceejackson@uspacegallery.com** Website: **www.uspacegallery.com**

Roland S. Jefferson   Author of 6 published novels and four screenplays. Received the NAACP Image Award for Writing (1979); NAACP Special Award of Merit by Black American Cinema Society (1990); 1st Place Award For Drama by Black Filmmakers Hall of Fame (1979). Contact: Roland S. Jefferson, 3870 Crenshaw Boulelvard. #215, Los Angeles, California 90008 Phone: (310) 285-3325 E-mail: **rsjeff@hotmail.com** Website: **www.rolandsjefferson.com**

Melvin Ishmael Johnson   Screenwriter/Playwright/Director. Dramastage-Qumran Recovery Theater, 1335 North La Brea, #2179, Hollywood, California 90028 Phone: (323) 850-4436 E-mail: **bymel2004@yahoo.com** Website: **www.dramastage-qumran.org**

Ralph P.J. Johnson   Has written and directed several screenplays. My company also offers website and software development, video/film productions, and music production. Ralph P.J. Johnson, President, Hi-Tech Media Corp., RR11 Box 11005, Stroudsburg, Pennsylvania 18360 E-mail: **pj@htechmedia.com** Website: **www.htechmedia.com**

Raenell Jones   Published author of poetry book titled Healing Psalms. Recited original poetry on television show titled Spending a Little Time With Poetry Education: UCLA Screenwriting Professional Program, Los Angeles, California (July 2007). Recognition and Accomplishments: Reached semi-finalist position in the 2009 Organization of Screenwriters (OBS) Screenwriting Competition. Made top 15% of 2007 Don and Gee Nicholls Screenwriting competition. Raenell Jones, 1622 West 25th Street, #4, Los Angeles, California 90007 Phone: (310) 775-7244 E-mail: **rdjones08@yahoo.com**

Barbara Kensey   Work has also been produced on stage to critical acclaim by several Chicago theater companies. Barbara Kensey, 5212 South Dorchester Avenue, Chicago, Illinois 60615 Phone: (773) 288-8776 Fax: (312) 454-7454 E-mail: **Kenseycomm@sbcglobal.net**

Nwenna Kai Writer & Film Producer. Contact Nwenna Kai, Full Moon Productions, 311 San Pascual, Los Angeles, California 90042 Phone: (323) 337-7381 Fax: (323) 936-5691 E-mail: **nwenna@excite.com**

Darryl D'Wayne Lassiter PAY THE PRICE, Mr. Lassiter's first full-length feature as writer/producer/director won for him the first-place prize "Best Family Drama," New York International Film Festival. He has written screenplays to Dead End Street and the remake of Bill Cosby and Sidney Poitier's Uptown Saturday Night. His film career began in 1991 working on the set of CBS' In The Heat Of The Night. He has produced and directed nearly 50 music videos. Darryl D'Wayne Lassiter, Post Office Box 50374, Atlanta, Georgia 30302 E-mail: darryl@ddlentertainment.net Website: www.ddlentertainment.net

Tracey Michae'l Lewis Author, poet, screenwriter, and playwright, Ms. Lewis has spent a lifetime cultivating poetry, short stories, and plays devoted to examining the human search for Spirit. Lewis has completed work on several screenplays, and the critically acclaimed stage play, KHEPERA, which ran off-Broadway in 2002. She is a professor of English at New Jersey City University and Essex County College. Ms. Tracey Michae'l Lewis, 1845 West Superior, #1R, Chicago, Illinois 60622 E-mail: traceylewis33@yahoo.com

Garry Moore Chicago native, Garry is a news anchor and senior producer of News 25 Today. His journalism and musical career have taken him to South Africa, Ghana, Senegal, The Gambia, The Dominican Republic, Cuba, Brazil, and Haiti. He is a writer and producer of several successful theatre arts productions, including "Black to the Future," "Dancing My Sisters Back Home," and "The Ghosts of Haiti." Contact Mr. Gary Moore, WEEK-TV, 2907 Springfield Road, East Peoria, Illinois 61611 Phone: (309) 698-2525 Fax: (309) 698-9335 E-mail: gmoore@week.com Website: www.week.com

MWALIM Artist, writer, filmmaker, educator, Mwalim has distinguished himself as a playwright, director, and actor. He received his formal training from New African Company in Boston and his work has been presented throughout the United States and Canada, including his award-winning plays, "Look At My Shorts: An Evening of Short Plays"; "A Party at the Crossroads"; and "OM!: A Street Corner Griot's Comedy." His performance piece "Backwoods People" was presented at the 1999 National Black Drama Festival in Winston Salem, North Carolina. Mwalim, English Department, University of Massachusetts, 285 Old Westport Road, North Dartmouth, Massachusetts 02747 Phone: (508) 999-8304 E-mail: mwalim@gmail.com

Crystal Rhodes She has written 21 plays, 19 of which have been produced in theatres throughout the United States. Her play, The Trip, has been published in two play anthologies: Center Stage: An Anthology of 21 Contemporary Black Playwrights (University of Illinois Press) and Black Women's Blues: A Literary Anthology, 1934-Present (G.K. Hall & Co.). Crystal Rhodes, Crystal Ink Publishing, Post Office Box 53511, Indianapolis, Indiana 46253 E-mail: writetome@crystalrhodes.com Website: www.crystalrhodes.com

Alan Sharpe HIV+ playwright/screenwriter. His body of work focused primarily on contemporary African-American Gay and Lesbian life and culture. He is author of plays including, "Auld Lang Syne", "BrotherHOODs", "Christmas Gifts", "Chump Changes", "Family Business", "HeartBeats", "Storm Signals" and the film, "Party." And, Is the Artistic Director of African-American Collective Theater (ACT) based in Washington, DC. Mr. Alan Sharpe, 1848 Columbia Road, North West, #24, Washington, DC 20009 Phone: (202) 745-3662 E-mail: asharpebgm@msn.com Website: www.alansharpe.org

Tristan Spirit Writes original movie scripts and consults for independent television and independent films. Tristan Spirit, Spiritstyle Enterprises, Inc., 651 West 188th Street, Suite 1-H, New York, New York 10040 Phone: (212) 414-5426 E-mail: badassclothes@yahoo.com

Timothy N. Stelly, Sr. Native of northern California and the author of five novels, Mr. Stelly writes crime-drama, sci-fi noir and hip-hoppolitical satire. He has also rewritten both "Tempest" and "Malice," which he hopes to republish in 2011. Mr. Stelly is the author of more than thirty screenplays. Timothy N. Stelly, Sr., Post Office Box 1264, Pittsburg, California 94565 E-mail: stellbread@yahoo.com

Corean Strong Native of Vicksburg, Mississippi, Corean graduated with honors from Jackson State University in Jackson, Mississippi with a B.S. degree in Computer Science. Founder & CEO of NaeRoc Productions, a Christian based Theatre Ministry. She has written several plays, one of which is All God's Children Got Shoes which appeared off Broadway in 2007 and has been nominated for the 2008 Agape Gospel Academy award for 'most inspiring play.' She also has an adaptation of The Glory Train which is also touring for the second year. Corean Butler, 146 Triangle Street, Danbury, Connecticut 06810 Phone: (203) 885-3190 Fax: (203) 826-7686 E-mail: director@naerocproductions.com Website: www.naerocproductions.com

Antoinette Oglesby Taylor Playwright/Writer. I have 6 plays that have been stage read in Louisville Kentucky. I have been writing for 20 plus years and have done greeting cards and poems and short stories. Antoinette Oglesby Taylor, 6411 Shirley Avenue, Prospect, Kentucky 40059 Fax: (502) 228-9775 Phone: (502) 228-4573 E-mail: jtnursing@aol.com

Jackie Taylor Founder, Producer, Actor and the Executive Director of the Black Ensemble Theater Company in Chicago, Illinois, Taylor has written more than 100 plays including the nationally renowned "The Jackie Wilson Story", "Doo Wop Shoo Bop" and "The Other Cinderella." Contact Ms. Jackie Taylor, Black Ensemble Theater Corporation, 4520 North Beacon Street, Chicago, Illinois 60640 Phone: (773) 769-4451 Fax: (773) 769-4533 E-mail: BlackEnsemble@aol.com Website: www.blackensembletheater.org

T. Tara Turk Graduated from Eugene Lang at The New School in New York and went on to get her MFA from Sarah Lawrence College in 1998. She was a Van Lier Fellow at New York Theatre Workshop in 2001. Her plays have been read at such esteemed institutions as Ensemble Studio Theatre, New Federal Theatre, and Frederick Douglas Creative Arts Center. Her plays include Grim Foster's Love Song, FAM, Indigos, Sistaz On The DL, Newly Dead, Thistory, If Eve Left..., east outer drive, the collaborative piece Bryant Park, Garbage in Eden and Vist or Days. She has just recently finished her novel, Things Fall Together, and a screenplay, Smoke and Mirrors. Ms. T. Tara Turk, 4970 Fountain Avenue, Los Angeles, California 90029 E-mail: scruffdiva@yahoo.com

Van Whitfield Award-winning author, and a hit TV sitcom writer since 2000. Writes the BET hit profile show, TurnStyle and is currently writing the authorized biography of former DC mayor, Marion Barry. He also writes scripts for UPN's hit sitcom, EVE. Mr. Van Whitfield, Post Office Box 941, Lanham, Maryland 20706 E-mail: vanwhitfield@vanwhitfield.com Website: www.vanwhitfield.com

Jessica Nyel Willis Author, writer of articles for magazines, short stories, film script, teleplays, sitcom and drama scripts, as well as novels for young adults and adults. Contact Jessica Nyel Willis, 8629 144th Street, #2, Jamaica, New York 11435 Phone: (646) 207-1877 E-mail: JessicaNyelWillis@hotmail.com

Sylvia Wilson Vocalist, Actress, Playwright, Lyricists, Music Educator. Sylvia Wilson, SylkySmoove Entertainment, Post Office Box 7593, Columbus, Georgia 31908 Phone: (706) 604-7473 E-mail: sylkydiva2003@yahoo.com

David D. Wright Author/Theatre Company/Producer. Orisha Tales Repertory Radio Theatre Company, 133 East 96th Street, Brooklyn, New York 11212 Phone: (718) 735-8905 E-mail: osungumi@aim.com

Alecia Goodlow-Young Author, screenwriter, poet, columnist, and a freelance writer. Alecia Goodlow-Young, 28490 Tavistock Trail, Southfield, Michigan 48034 Phone: (313) 796-7949 Fax: (313) 541-6638 E-mail: aleciawrites@sbcglobal.net

Poets

Octavia McBride-Ahebee Writer of poetry, short stories and plays. Her newest collection of poetry is Where My Birthmark Dances (2011). Her collection of poetry, Assuming Voices, is published by Lit Pot Press. Octavia lived for nine years in Cote d'Ivoire, West Africa. Her poetry gives voice to women who historically have not been heard; African women, women in refugee camps, and women who are victims of civil war, immigrants and rural, battling such health issues as breast cancer and obstetric fistula. Ms. Octavia McBride-Ahebee, Lit Pot Press, 3909 Reche Road, Suite 96, Fallbrook, California 92028 Phone: (215) 877-2502 E-mail: **obmcbride@hotmail.com** Website: **http://omcbride-ahebee.blogspot.com**

Y. Jamal Ali An eclectic blend of artist, scientist, historian and esotericist. Author of over six hundred fifty poems, in addition to numerous essays, articles, short stories and plays. Jamal has been writing seriously for over 25 years. Y. Jamal Ali, Post Office Box 332, San Pedro, California 90733 Phone: (310) 876-9332 E-mail: **PtahOgun@yahoo.com**

Paul Alleyne A published writer (poetry and fiction), as well as a visual artist Mr. Paul Alleyne is the author of Whatever It Takes (2005), and These Are Our Stories (2007). Contact Mr. Paul Alleyne, 2643 Bridgewater Drive, Grand Prairie, Texas 75054 Phone: (323) 230-9336 Website: **www.redbubble.com/people/bambooo**

Michele Barkley Author of the book Wayfaring Stranger-Poems and producer of the videopoem In View Of A Cup Half-Full. Ms. Barkley is also a visual artist. Ms. Michele Barkley, PMB 88, 3703 South Edmunds Street, Seattle, Washington 98118 Phone: (206) 818-1091 E-mail: **artuncommon@yahoo.com**

Jillina "J-Bax" Baxter Website Journalist – The Hive/Blaze 1 Radio at blaze1graphixs.com in Atlanta, Georgia. J-Bax has written a catalog close to 300 consisting of Rap & R&B songs and poetry pieces. Other projects include working on a number of books (poetry "Vision Though Verses", semi-autobiography "Web Celeb", a fictional novel "The Strangers We Call Friends" and a coffee table book "A Pictorial Purpose". Jillina "J-Bax" Baxter, 184 Second Avenue, Albany, New York 12202 Phone: (518) 210-3518 E-mail: **jbmeow@yahoo.com**

Rose Jackson-Beavers CEO of Prioritybooks Publications, Rose grew up in East St. Louis, and received her Bachelor and Master degrees from Illinois State and Southern Illinois Universities. She has worked as a Freelance writer for the A-Magazine, a St. Louis Publication and as an Opinion Shaper for the North County Journal Newspaper. Currently writes as a columnist for the Spanish Word, a local community newspaper. Published books: "Back Room Confessions" (2004), "Summin to Say, "a book of poems and Essays about everyday life" (2001-2002), and "Quilt Designs and Poetry Rhymes" was co-written with nationally known fabric artist, Edna Patterson-Petty. Rose Jackson-Beavers, Post Office Box 2535, Florissant, Missouri 63032 Phone: (314) 741-6789 E-mail: **rosbeav03@yahoo.com** Website: **www.prioritybooks.com**

Gayle Bell An African American womanist whose work has appeared in "Diversity 2000" published by the Austin International Poets; "Broken Sky" benefiting the Walt Whitman Community School; "Poetic Healings" published by Chinwe Odeluga; "Sinister Wisdom", Healing Issue; and "Kente Cloth, Southwest Voices of the African Diaspora", UT Southwest, James Mardis, Editor. Ms. Bell has 2 published books of poetry, "Benediction" and "Primal Gospel", both published by Genuien Lizard Press. A third book, "Open Song", is to be published this year. Gayle Bell, 17617 Midway Road #134, Dallas, Texas 75287 Phone: (214) 440-8125 E-mail: linnbell2002@yahoo.com

Jennifer Elaine Black Author of several poetry books including "Issues of Life" and "The Healing Tree for all Nations." She is a speaker and instructor for The End Times Arts Movement International founded by herself. She teaches youth to be empowered through the use of their own creativity. She teaches acting, praise dance, writing, and music workshops. She is also a writer for Gatekeeper magazine and Virtuous Woman magazine. Jennifer Elaine Black, The End Times Arts Movement International, Inc., Post Office Box 56394, Little Rock, Arkansas 72215 Phone: (501) 859-0841 E-mail: booking@thepropheticartist.com Website: www.thepropheticartist.com

Kennedy Brazier Author of published Poetry Collection, When The June Bugs Come Out in August (Publish America, 2007). Currently seeking representation for 2 novels. Education: Masters in English/Communications, also a fitness model. Contact Mr. Kennedy Brazier, 4387 Brookmere Drive, Kentwood, Michigan 49512 E-mail: Kennedy-lynne@hotmail.com

Traci Brooks Poet, public speaker and writer, Stepping Into Womanhood is Ms. Brooks' first published work. Since graduating from San Francisco State University in 1991, she has continued to seek knowledge and understanding of self in order to learn, grow and teach. She is dedicated to the empowerment and uplifting of Black people and seeks to express that spirit in her poetry. Currently she is at work on her second title. Ms. Traci Brooks, Black Buttafly Publishing, Post Office Box 200251, San Antonio, Texas 78220 E-mail: yalonna@swbell.net

Gregory Bryant Author, writer, Gregory Bryant was born and raised in Atlantic City, New Jersey. He attended Atlantic City High School where he graduated in 1981. In 1984 he entered the United States Air Force and was stationed at Norton Air Force Base in San Bernardino, California. He received an honorable discharge in 1988 and moved to Greensboro, North Carolina where he works for the United States Postal Service. He released his first book called "Poems of the Heart" in 2002 with his sophomore effort "Visions" being released in 2003. He has established his own publishing company called Feel the Flow Publishing to provide other poets information on publishing. His company has released 4 books with the 2004 release of "From the Hearts of Women" and His present book "Diary of an Open Mind" was released April, 2006. Gregory W. Bryant, Feel the Flow Publishing, 2319 Pinecroft Road, Greensboro, North Carolina 27407 Phone: (336) 601-0954 E-mail: gb_xpress@yahoo.com

Jacquelyn A. Bryant Holds an AAS in Early Childhood Education. I have a story that will be featured in Zane's Choc Flava 2 scheduled out in August 07. I currently have a book of poetry published it is titled, "Love Sweet Love." Jacquelyn A. Bryant, 1821 Foulkrod Place, Philadelphia, Pennsylvania 19124 E-mail: mslovelieladie@yahoo.com

L Guy Burton Published writer of Follow The Right Leader (Quill Publishers, 1991), novels Jack In The Pulpit (Xlibris, 2004), and Come Die With Me (PublishAmerica, 2006), magazine articles, poetry, and a movie script. My articles and poetry have appeared in Interrace magazine, and my screenplay Latent Blood—which won honorable mention in a Writer's Digest contest—was represented by The Berzon Agency of Glendale, California. As founder and Director of The Warwick Valley Writers' Association, I have, through this local writers' group, been able to polish, complete and promote several Works in various genres, as well as help others to do the same. L Guy Burton, The Warwick Valley Writers' Association, 12 Burton Lane, Warwick, New York 10990 E-mail: el_guybur@hotmail.com

Eileen Carole Founder/Director of The Writers Corner (poetry group). She is an author of two volumes of poetry and co-author/publisher of six anthologies. Her published books are "If Ever You Have Loved", "On A Musical Note," "Hair Stories," "Peace Pages," and "Renaissance Pages." Ms. Carole is also a book producer and graphic artist. Eileen Carole, 1151 Morning View Drive, Unit 110, Escondido, California 92026 E-mail: eileencarole@sbcglobal.net

Cliff Chandler An award winning author of three novels his accomplishments include Poetry Awards, Short Story Awards, Marquis Who's Who In The East, and the JADA Award Mystery Novel Of The Year 2004. Education: BFA, Pratt Institute, Brooklyn, New York, Masters Writing courses at New York University, and editing classes at The New School. Contact Mr. Cliff Chandler, 2492 Tredway Drive, Macon, Georgia 31211 E-mail: CDuke23@aol.com Website: www.authorsden.com/cliffchandler

Charles L. Chatmon Author of The Depths of My Soul and The Voices of South Central, two books of poems about love, social issues, tales of despair and hope. Current executive director of the Los Angeles Black Book Expo, and a co-founder of the California Writers Collective. As a freelance writer, contributed to local college and community newspapers in addition to a few start up magazines. Former English and writing lab instructor. As part of the CWC, coordinates writers workshops and assist new authors just starting out with interviews, resources and networking. Also co-host of an internet radio show called Mixed Matters bringing the best in up and coming authors, writers and poets. Charles L. Chatmon, Post Office Box 1924, Vallejo, California 94590 Phone: (707) 235-6520 E-mail: chatwrites2@yahoo.com

James E. Cherry   A nationally and internationally published poet and fiction writer whose work has been featured in Callaloo, African American Review, Crab Orchard Review, The Other Half, Sable, Crossroads, Bum Rush the Page (Crown), Beyond the Frontier (Black Classic Press), Roll Call (Third World Press) and others. James E Cherry, Post Office Box 614, Jackson, Tennessee 38302 Phone: (731) 422-2524 E-mail: monksdream@hotmail.com

Lynisha O. Childers A poet, photographer, and an aspiring attorney, Lynisha received her Bachelor of Arts in Political Science from Georgia State University. Currently, she is a law student at Birmingham School of Law specializing in Child Advocacy. She is the author of Woman I Am (1995) and The Key to My Diary: Caught Between Happiness and Pain, A Collection of Poems and Thoughts. She is also Founder/CEO, of GreekWorks Entertainment and Infinite Greek Appeal. Contact Ms. Lynisha O. Childers, 550 Palisades Drive South, #102, Birmingham, Alabama 35209 Phone: (205) 940-7566 E-mail: lynisha_childers@hotmail.com

Wanda Coleman Winner of the prestigious Lenore Marshall prize in 1999 for Bathwater Wine, Coleman continues to prove herself one of the more innovative poets writing today. If Coleman's love of language were not so apparent on every page, her major theme - birth and femininity, slavery and history - might well get lost in mundane polemics. She is the author of Mad Dog Black Lady (1983, 1987), Imagoes (1989), A War of Eyes and Other Stories (October, 1989, Black Sparrow Press), Mambo Hips and Make Believe (1999), and Mercurochrome (National Book Awards Nomination 2001). Her book Ostinato Vamps was published by the University of Pittsburg Press in 2003. A former medical secretary, magazine editor, journalist and scriptwriter, Coleman has received fellowships from the National Endowment for the Arts and the Guggenheim Foundation for her poetry. Wanda Coleman, GuyJoyee Productions, Post Office Box 451621, Los Angeles, California 90045 E-mail: **GuyJ@comcast.net**

Anthony Carlton Cooke The author's fiction and poetry have appeared in the anthologies, "Bardic Tales and Sage Advice: An Anthology of Fantasy, Horror, and Science Fiction" (winner and honorable mention in the 2005 Bards and Sages Writing Contest), "Gathering of the Minds," as well as the journal, "Cherry Bleeds." His work is also scheduled to appear in the anthology, "In Their Own Words: A Generation Defining Itself, Vol.7," due out late 2007. He lived in San Francisco for twelve years, where he was a featured reader at the Art and Divinity Poetry Series, the North Beach Poetry Festival, and read at many other venues while completing "Symmetry," an experimental speculative fiction novel. Currently, Anthony lives in New York, where he is working on a second novel while pursuing his degree in English Literature and Africana Studies. Mr. Anthony Cooke, 450 Circle Road, Building A, Apt. 101A, Stony Brook, New York 11790 Phone: (718) 869-3708 E-mail: **cooke_ac@hotmail.com**

Heather Covington Poet. Ms. Heather Covington, Disilgold, Post Office Box 652, Baychester Station, Bronx, New York 10469 Phone: (718) 547-0499 E-mail: **disilgold@aol.com** Website: **www.disilgold.com**

Nandi SoJourn Asantewaa Crosby Poet and dramatic reader, Nandi is the first Women's Studies hire in the history of CSU, Chico. She completed her B.A. in Psychology from St. Mary's College of Maryland, an M.A. in Africana Women's Studies at Clark Atlanta University with a thesis called Black Lesbian Feminist Theory or How to Start a Black Women's (R)Evolution. She received her Ph.D. in Sociology from Georgia State University with a dissertation on The Souls of Black Men: Male Discourse and Critical Implications for Rethinking Black Feminist Thought. Nandi is a poet and performance artist who has won more than 50 awards for her performances. Most recently she shared the stage with Saul Williams in a Spoken Word event in Harlen Adams Theatre. Nandi Crosby, Assistant Professor in Women's Studies and Sociology, California State University, Chico, Center for Multicultural and Gender Studies, Butte 611, Chico, California 95929 Phone: (530) 898-5249 Fax: (530) 898-5986

Ebony Rose Custis A poet working in various mediums including fiction and dramatic writing and author of two collections of poetry: My Moments, and Defining the Color of Ebony. She is also author of an award winning one-act drama 'Strange Reflections' and one full length drama "Taylor's Gift." Ebony is presently touring with her second book, Defining the Color of Ebony. Contact Ms. Ebony Rose Custis, 13211 Vanessa Avenue, Bowie, Maryland 20720 Phone: (301) 602 5918 E-mail: **ebony.custis@gmail.com** Website: **www.roseprose.com**

Dahveed Born in Greensboro, North Carolina, Dahveed's first book of poetry and prose is "Through The Eyes of A Foster Child: A Poetic Journey." He served several years in the United States Marine Corps before pursuing a career in the field of Mental Health. Contact Dahveed, Post Office Box 881403, San Diego, California 92168 E-mail: dvv@dahveed.com Website: www.dahveed.com

Kolade Daniel Poet, Songwriter, Scriptwriter. Daniel Kolade, 17 Igun Street, Itire Surulere, Lagos 23401 Nigeria Phone: 23 480 66506 72 E-mail: koladedaniel@praize.com

Jackie Daughtry Pseudonyms: Ayani_Meli Journey Shanise Rhodes is an accomplished poet and playwright, as well as a digital storyteller. She is working on a novel, a book of poetry and several plays. Jackie Daughtry, Post Office Box 32, Sylvania, Georgia 30467 Phone: (912) 687-5546 E-mail: ayani.meli@gmail.com Website: www.newbirthpowercenter.com

Vernon J. Davis Jr. His first book,"LOVE, IS, THE BEAUTIFUL BLACK WOMAN" is a tribute to all Black Women. Vernon's first published poem, "Beautiful Black Woman", the basis for his book came out in 1978 in a magazine called Black Forum. More poetry followed in other magazines like SoulWord and Dawn, a magazine supplement to the Los Angeles Sentinel. He has also taught Creative Writing. Mr. Vernon J. Davis, Jr., 3993 Spring Mountain Road #160, Las Vegas, Nevada 89102 Phone: (702) 812-5221 E-mail: vernjdavis@yahoo.com Website: www.loveisthebeautifulblackwoman.com

Deborah Day A Bay Area poet, Deborah is the author of the Mindful Messages Healing Thoughts for the Hip and Hop Descendants from the Motherland, and is the creator of the Mindful Messages Mentoring Program. Contact Ms. Deborah Day, Ashay by the Bay, Post Office Box 2394, Union City, California 94587 Phone: (510) 520-2742 Fax: (510) 477-0967 E-mail: poetashay@aol.com Website: www.ashaybythebay.com

Don P. Demyers Professor of Biology at the University of the District of Columbia in Washington, D.C., writer and poet of over 100 poems. His poem, "I Think" won an Editors choice award from the International Society of Poets. He was awarded the Outstanding Achievement in Poetry Award, Merit Silver Award Bowl, Who's Who in Poetry Award and the Bronze Commemorative Award Medallion as a member of the International Society of Poets. Don P. Demyers, Ph.D., 12007 Fort Washington Road, Fort Washington, Maryland 20744 Phone: (301) 203-9166 E-mail: ddem776975@aol.com

Rita Frances Dove African-American writer and teacher Rita Frances Dove was poet laureate of the United States in 1993-95. Pulitzer Prize for Poetry, 1987. Fulbright, Guggenheim Fellowships, 2 National Endowment For The Arts Grants. She is Professor of English at the University of Virginia Member of PEN Club; Literary Lion of New York Public Library. Contact Ms. Rita Frances Dove, University of Virginia, Post Office Box 400121, Charlottesville, Virginia 22904 Phone: (434) 924-6618 Fax: (434) 924-1478 E-mail: rfd4b@virginia.edu Website: www.people.virginia.edu/~rfd4b

John D. Evans National award winning poet and author. John D. Evans, TEPC, Inc., Post Office Box 2177 Oak Park, Illinois 60303 Phone: (708) 214-0706 E-mail: jdpoetry1@aol.com

Latorial Faison   Her poetry has been published in various literary magazines, journals, and poetry sites. She is author of Secrets of My Soul (2001) and Immaculate Perceptions (2003, CK Press). A native of Courtland, Virginia, she studied English at the University of Virginia, and Virginia Tech. Latorial Faison, Cross Keys Press, Post Office Box 145, Highwood, Illinois 60040 E-mail: Latorial@PoeticallySpeaking.net Website: www.PoeticallySpeaking.net

Peggy M. Fisher   Holds an MA from Teachers College, Columbia University.   Retired, Ms. Fisher is the author of "Lifting Voices: Voices of the Collective Struggle" (1999). Her poems have appeared in several anthologies including Commemorating Excellence: the 1998 Presidential Awards. She is one of the featured authors in an anthology of essays, The Story That Must Be Told, published by Loving Healing Press in June 2007. She completed a memoir, and book "Search Lights for My Soul," (2006). Peggy Fisher, Post Office Box 2775, Camden, New Jersey 08101 E-mail: pyramidcl@cs.com Website: www.pmmfisher.com

Rebera Elliott Foston   Author, poet, Dr Foston has published an inspirational journal entitled Peace on Earth, and 20 books of poetry which include No Stoppin' Sense, The Parade and In God's Time. You Don't Live On My Street, the signature volume of this collection was first published in 1991 and remains a favorite because of her sassy poem, "You Don't Live On My Street." Contact Dr. Rebera Elliott Foston, M.D., DMin, Post Office Box 726, Clarksville, Tennessee 37041 Phone: (800) 418-0374 Fax: (931) 645-3500 E-mail: minfoston@aol.com Website: www.drfoston.com

Delores King-Freeman   Poet, author, TV producer and host, Dee Freeman has published well received books of poetry entitled "Oceans of Love: To Us From Us" and Poetry She Wrote I: Oh, Magnify Him." A number of her poems have appeared in magazines, anthologies and newspapers and have been recognized with awards. She was presented with a commendation for the City and City Council during Black History Month in 2005. She continues to provide the Lansing State Journal with an article, book review or word of inspiration on a monthly basis. She co-hosts "poetry slams" held at various locations throughout the Greater Lansing area. Her Poetree-N-Motion TV program shares information of community events, history tidbits, book reviews and has guests with current community issues. Freeman is also a talented musical lyricist. Alumnus of Northwood University of Midland and former financial analyst for General Motors. Dee Freeman, 1127 Alexandria Drive, Lansing, Michigan 48917 Phone: (517) 321-3122 E-mail: deekfreeman@yahoo.com Website: www.deepoette.com

Papi Kymone Freeman   Writer/producer, playwright and poet, Freeman is the founder of the National Black LUV Festival which was a Mayor's Art Award Finalist for Excellence in Service to the Arts in 2006, and is currently a board member for Words Beats & Life. He is the subject of one chapter of the book, Beat of A Different Drum: The Untold Stories of African Americans Forging Their Own Paths in Work and Life (Hyperion). In addition, he is the author of a book of poetry entitled, Blood Sweat & Tears. He is a founding member with Genesis Poets and has studied under the tutelage of the legendary independent filmmaker Haile Gerima. Freeman produced his screenplay, Starrchildren in 2007. In 2005, Prison Poetry was awarded the 22nd Annual Larry Neal Award for Drama. Contact Papi Kymone Freeman, Frederick Douglas Station, Post Office Box 31243, Banneker City, Washington, DC 20030 Phone: (202) 547-2459 E-mail: kymone@prisonpoetry-theplay.com Website: www.prisonpoetry-theplay.com

Andrea Gager Poet and an author Andrea has written one book of poetry, a play and is currently working on a second one. Andrea Gager, 830 Amsterdam Avemue, #8C, New York, New York 10025 Phone: (917) 392-0202 E-mail: Pastrel1@aol.com

Bettye A. Gaines Poems, Poetry, Prose Food for the Soul. Evangelist Bettye Gaines, Women of Excellence Ministries, Post Office Box 21651, Columbia, South Carolina 29221 Phone: (803) 409-8712

Daniel Garrett Writer of journalism, fiction, poetry, and drama, Garrett's book reviews have appeared in American Book Review, The Quarterly Black Review of Books, and Rain Taxi. He selected poetry for the male feminist magazine Changing Men. His own poetry has been published by AIM/America's Intercultural Magazine, Black American Literature Forum, Red River Review, and a few small book anthologies. Garrett's essay "The Inner Life and the Social World in the Work of James Baldwin" was published by IdentityTheory.com. Mr. Daniel Garrett, 05-63 135th Street, Richmond Hill, New York 11419 E-mail: dgarrett31@hotmail.com

Carolyn Gibson A native of Boston, Massachusetts, and a Simmons College graduate, Gibson is author of a novel, "Repairman Jones" and a collection of 60 poems titled Urban Poetry. Carolyn Gibson, Carolyn's Corner, Post Office Box 300160, Jamaica Plain, Massachusetts 02130 Phone: (617) 298-7484 Fax: (617) 298-1018 E-mail: Carolynscorner@aol.com Website: www.Carolynscorner.com

Richard Charles Gibson The authors first book of short stories Life Lessons was published in 2003. Contact Mr. Richard Charles Gibson, 2517 West Harrison Street, Chicago, Illinois 60612 Phone: (312) 243-5343 E-mail: gibsonsnoopy@aol.com

Michael Glover Author of My Soul Speaks Wisdom: A Collection of Life, Love and Inspirational Poems for Everyday Living. He received a music scholarship to Johnson C. Smith University to play the snare drum where he majored in History and aspired to become a teacher, but instead became an actor. He was encouraged by friends and family to pursue acting because of his comedic talent. Michael started his career in North Carolina at the John Casablancas Modeling and Career Center. In New York, he studied and completed training at The American Academy of Dramatic Arts. Michael has appeared in numerous films, TV shows, and commercials. He also has performed in Off Broadway shows in New York City; one notable show was "One Flew over the Cuckoo's Nest". Michael Glover, 599 Franklin Avenue, #4R,Brooklyn, New York 11238 E-mail: mysoulspeakswisdom@gmail.com

C.D. Grant A nationally-published, versatile writer, poet and journalist since 1970 whose work has appeared in Essence Magazine (for which he was Music Editor for 5 Quindaro (Kansas), Suburban Styles (Westchester, New York), and numerous other periodicals. He is a scholarly writer who has presented papers at Howard University, Pace University and Berkeley and an article has been included in the Educational Resource Information Center (ERIC) of Columbia University as a reference for African and African American music. He has two published books of poetry Keeping Time and Images in a Shaded Light. Television talk show host which features authors. C.D. Grant, Publisher, Post Office Box 437, Bronx, New York 10467 Phone: (914) 282-5747 E-mail: blindbeggar1@juno.com Website: www.blindbeggarpress.org

Henry Grimes An author, Henry Grimes is a world-renowned jazz musician (playing acoustic bass and violin) and also a poet. His first published volume of poetry was printed in Cologne in 2007, and it is called "Signs Along the Road," and it includes a written introduction by guitarist Marc Ribot. Contact Mr. Henry Grimes, Buddy's Knife Jazz Edition, Teutoburgerstrasse 17, 50678 Cologne, Germany Phone: +49 221 48 48 242 E-mail: **musicmargaret@earthlink.net** Website: **www.henrygrimes.com**

Tania Guerrera Author of the book Thoughts and Transformations. The book contains poetry, art and essays all dealing with love, social issues, justice and spirituality from the point of view of an Afro-Puertorican and Native American (Arawak/Taino) woman. Tania Guerrera, 412 North Avenue, New Rochelle, New York 10801 E-mail: **theartist@taniaguerrera.com** Website: **www.taniaguerrera.com**

William Hairston Author, playwright and poet, William Hairston has had poems published in numerous anthologies and magazines. His books include: "The World of Carlos" (novel) "Sex and Conflict" (novel) "History of The National Capital Area Council/Boy Scouts of America" "Spaced Out" (space adventure) "Showdown At Sundown" (western novel)" Ira Frederick Aldridge" (The London Conflict) (Play, non-fiction). Contact Mr. William Hairston, 5501 Seminary Road, #511-S, Falls Church, Virginia 22041 Phone: (703) 845-1281 E-mail: **WilliamRHairston1@msn.com**

Evelyn D. Hall Self-published author, residing in, Atlanta, Georgia, Ms. Hall has published three books, Enter Eve's Poetic Paradise, Dontay's Poetic Playground and Dontay's Alphabet Book of Color. Evelyn D. Hall, Post Office Box 1775, Mableton, Georgia 30126 E-mail: **lilpoet2you@aol.com** Website: **www.publish.bluesky40.com**

Robyn Maria Hamlin Author and Screenwriter. Novels, "The Zone of Danger Test" is my breakout novel. I have 3 other working novels in progress. "Shades of Gray" and "Zone of Danger" are my only two registered screenplays to date. I have 4 other working screenplays in progress. Poetry, "The Red Flag," "Bread Crumbs," "The Teamplayer," "A Hand for ME," and "There Is A River" are a few of my poems that have been published to date. My writings have also been featured in both EBONY (October 2005) and ESSENCE (January 2006) magazines. Contact Ms. Robyn Maria Hamlin, 1900 Wesleyan Drive, #2807, Macon, Georgia 31210 Phone: (478) 476-8776 E-mail: **weeda5weeda@aol.com**

Leslie Harris Born and raised in Detroit, Michgan. Received B.S. from Michigan State University and J.D. from University of Detroit Mercy School of Law. Author of 18 manuscripts of poetry. Individual works have been publsihed in various magazines and ezines (Facets Magazine, FRESH! Literary Magazine, and others). Also a songwriter (in various genres). Member of the songwriting team known as Infectious Grooves. E-mail: **quality6287@aol.com**

Rochell D. (Ro Deezy) Hart Author of four published books, From The Ghettos To The Heavens (1999), A Black Girl's Song (Highbridge Press, NY 2001), Urban Journeys (2002) and the forthcoming Woke Up And Put My Crown On: The Project of 76 Voices. Rochell D. Hart, Post Office Box 20511, Portland, Oregon 97294 E-mail: **poetrybyro2@hotmail** Website: **www.cdbaby/rochelldhart**

Barbara Haskins Poet, public speaker and educator who has professionally interacted with many African-American luminaries; including Media Host Bob Law, Dr. Jawanza Kunjufu, and the Rev. Al Sharpton, among others. Ms. Haskins, credited for bringing the Kwanzaa holiday celebration to Queens, New York over 25 years ago, has been heralded by legions of cult fans as the 'Nikki Giovanni' of the New Millennium. LET A NEW WOMAN RISE is her first published poetry collection. Ms. Haskins (also known as Barbara Scott) is a public speaker and educator and her commitment to preserve African-American self esteem is apparent through her countless array of cumulative, civic and political citations. Barbara Haskins, 4465 PReSS, 610-A East Battlefield Road, Suite 279, Springfield, Missouri 65807 Phone: (866) 842-1042 Fax: (775) 257-1286 E-mail: press4465@yahoo.com Website: www.4465press.com

Linda Hayes Born Linda Diane Mayfield, this aspiring African American poetess grew up in the Red Hook housing projects, of Brooklyn, New York. She graduated from Kingsborough Community College with an Associate in Applied Science degree in Data Processing. Author of a self-published poetry chapbook, "Life Is A Roller Coaster." This book is a collection of poems depicting life's ups, downs twists and turns. She covers such topics as the joys of motherhood, the loss of a parent, abortion, college graduation, homelessness, 9/11 to name a few. Ms. Linda Hayes, 31 Palmetto Drive, New Castle, Delaware 19720 E-mail: ldmhayes@yahoo.com

Janet Marlene Henderson Adjunct English Composition Professor with the City Colleges of Chicago. She was born in Chicago and, as the daughter of a U.S. Marine grew up in Virginia, North Carolina, California, and Hawaii. She has lectured at Chicago State University and East-West University. A writer of romantic fiction, her first novel is LUNCH WITH CASSIE (2005). Her second novel, THE ASSASSIN WHO LOVED HER, will be published in 2007. She has written four other books, which are all based on the contemporary romantic relationships of young, successful African-American females. Ms. Henderson, who has also lived in Virgina, North Carolina, California, Georgia, Hawaii and Washington, D.C., lives on the Southside of Chicago. Ms. Janet M. Henderson, 7837 South Ada Street, Chicago, Illinois 60620 Phone: (773) 873-8298 E-mail: janhenderson_3@hotmail.com Website: www.janethenderson.net

Kenneth Henry Jr. Owner of Real Ink Publishing and has authored a poetry book entitled Tears That Grip A Whole Nation. Real Ink specializes in poetry, self help, and youth centered books. Kenneth Henry, Jr., Real Ink Publishing, Post Office Box 496, League City, Texas 77574 E-mail: realinkpub@yahoo.com

Akua Lezli Hope Award winning poet, fiction writer, journalist, and essayist, Akua has won a Creative Writing Fellowship from The National Endowment For The Arts, an Artists Fellowship from the New York Foundation for the Arts, and a Ragdale U.S. Africa Fellowship among other honors. Her collection, Embouchure, poems on jazz and other musics was published by ArtFarm Press in 1995, and won the Writer's Digest poetry book award. Her work appears in several anthologies including Sisterfire, an anthology of Black Womanist Fiction and Poetry, (HarperPerennial); Erotique, Noire, an anthology of Black Erotica (Doubleday/Anchor); and Confirmation, an anthology of Afrikan American Women Writers (Quill/Morrow); DARK MATTER, (the first!) anthology of African American Science Fiction (Time Warner Books, 2000); as well as numerous litetary magazines. Contact Ms. Akua Lezli Hope, Post Office Box 33, Corning, New York 14830 E-mail: akua@artfarm.com Website: www.artfarm.com

Renda Horne Best-selling author of "Seven Years in Egypt: Recognizing Your Setbacks as Set-Ups for Your comeback!" and highly sought-after conference speaker, Renda Horne is founder/overseer and president of Woman at the Wail Ministries, Renda Horne Ministries, and Wailing Enterprises. Contact Ms. Renda Horne, Post Office Box 401479, Redford, Michigan 48240 E-mail: **renda@rendahorne.com** Website: **www.rendahorne.com**

Terence E. Jackson Singer, playwright, poet, and novelist of the controversial book "Nigger's Heaven," a novel. Owns fine arts gallery. Terence E. Jackson, 690 Durant Place, North East, #2, Atlanta, Georgia 30308 Phone: (404) 873-1296 E-mail: **terenceejackson@uspacegallery.com** Website: **www.uspacegallery.com**

Samuel Jefferson Assistant Professor of Law, Professor Jefferson teaches Contracts and in the Community Development Clinic, University of the District of Columbia. He earned his Bachelor of Arts degree at Georgetown University, and a J.D. and an LL.M. at the Georgetown University Law Center. Upon graduation from law school, Professor Jefferson clerked at the U.S. District Court for the District of Columbia for the Honorable Deborah Robinson and then joined the firm, Anderson Kill Olick & Oshinsky, where his primary practice area was insurance coverage. In 1996, he continued the practice of law at Dickstein Shapiro Morin & Oshinsky where he represented various Fortune 500 companies in complex civil litigation and professional athletes and entertainers in numerous endeavors including formation of corporations, negotiating and drafting agreements, and intellectual property matters. As a teaching fellow at the Harrison Institute Legal Clinic at Georgetown University Law Center, he taught seminars and classes and supervised student teams in legal representation of clients for transactional matters related to the acquisition of multi-million dollar, multi-family housing projects. He founded Amistad, Inc., a publishing company for community based poets, authored two books of poetry, A...Z...Infinity and Crucifixion of My Soul, and has performed his works of poetry for audiences from California to New York. He also conducts seminars and workshops for the AYA Educational Institute throughout the United States for African-American men and women, focusing on empowerment and the examination of multicultural issues including racism, sexism, classism, and homophobia. After college, he played professional basketball with the Washington Wizards. Contact Mr. Samuel Jackson, University of the District of Columbia, 4200 Connecticut Avenue, North West, Washington DC 20008 Phone: (202) 274-7339 E-mail: **sjefferson@udc.edu** Website: **www.udc.edu**

Gary Johnson Both a writer and poet, Gary saw the need to create another, unique vehicle for emerging and established writers/artists of color. In 1977 he co-founded Blind Beggar Press. The title of the company comes from a poem written by Gary Johnson, Blind Beggar Blues, which speaks of a blind beggar who sees many things better than sighted people. Contact Mr. Gary Johnson, Publisher, Blind Beggar Press, Post Office Box 437, Bronx, New York 10467 Phone: (914) 282-5747 E-mail: **gary127@netzero.net** Website: **www.blindbeggarpress.org**

Vanessa Alexander Johnson Author of 'When Death Comes a Knockin', a self-help, inspirational book about loss and the grief process (unpublished). Also contributing author of the following anthologies: Down The Cereal Aisle (2003), Living by Faith (Obadiah Press, 2004), Celebrations Anthologies (2004). Vanessa Johnson, 303 Kennedy Street, Ama, Louisiana 70031 Phone: (504) 431-7360 E-mail: **vjohns1@bellsouth.net**

L. Dranae Jones Author and publisher of Provocative Poetry and Prose: Portraits of Black Love (2003) and four calendars of poetry and the chap book Trap'd by Damnyo (2004). L. Dranae Jones aka Sardonyx Jade is the owner and operator of Sardonyx Jade Publishing (SJP), operating out of Los Angeles, California. He is a California State University Dominguez Hills graduate with a Bachelor of Arts in Psychology. He has been published by Watermark Press, The International Library of Poetry, Poetry.com, Famous Poets Society, UK, Rolling Out Urban Style Weekly and Playgirl Magazine. L. Dranae Jones, Sardonyx Jade Publishing, 1401 North La Brea Avenue, Suite 137, Los Angeles, California Phone: (323) 898-7339 Fax: (213) 252-8471 E-mail: **ldjones@sardonyx-jade.com** Website: **www.sardonyx-jade.com**

Raenell Jones Published author of poetry book titled Healing Psalms. Second book will be released May 2009. Recited original poetry on television show titled Spending a Little Time With PoetryEducation: UCLA Screenwriting Professional Program Los Angeles, California (July 2007). Completed 2 Day Film School with Dov S-S Simens, New York, New York (April 2005). Completed Dave Trottier's Successful Spec Script 4 week course (September 2005). Recognition and Accomplishments: Reached semi-finalist position in the 2009 Organization of Screenwriters (OBS) Screenwriting Competition with a one hour pilot episode; MS. HALL OF FAME Script made top 15% of 2007 Don and Gee Nicholls Screenwriting competition; Teleplay placed in the quarterfinalist position for 2007 Scriptapalooza T.V. Contest; MS. HALL OF FAME Script made top 10 of 2007 Writers on the Storm Contest; Completed two dramatic readings for a teleplay and a screenplay with over 20 actors and actresses (February and December 2008); Actress in three church plays and in various skits. Two childrens books completed (seeking publisher). Completed Scripts: Three completed urban drama screenplays, two completed teleplays, two completed faith based/urban screenplay, four completed sitcoms, and two completed episodes of pilot drama series. One animation screenplay Holiday Movie of the Week (M.O.W). Raenell Jones, 1622 West 25th Street, #4, Los Angeles, California 90007 Phone: (310) 775-7244 E-mail: **rdjones08@yahoo.com**

Ty Granderson Jones Noted poet who has a spoken word band called Coloured Boyz featuring the famed legendary drummer of The Doors....John Densmore. Screenwriter with an MFA in Acting from UCSD in La Jolla, California. Ty Granderson Jones, Creole Celina Films, A division of Creative Quest, Inc., 8306 Wilshire Boulevard. Suite 432, Beverly Hills, California 90211 Phone: (323) 960-1035 E-mail: **tygrandjones@aol.com**

Joylynn M. Jossel A full-time multi-genre writer who, in addition to her debut title, Please Tell Me If The Grass Is Greener, has completed three diaries of poetry. Her first completed self-published novel, The Root of All Evil, St. Martin's Press picked up and re-released in June 2004. Joylynn M. Jossel, Post Office Box 298238, Columbus, Ohio 43229 Phone: (614) 284-7933 E-mail: **joylynnjossel@aol.com** Website: **www.joylynnjossel.com**

Chris Knight Author of two books of poetry and practical wisdom for everyday living. Her books entitled, Sister To Sister: Dimensions of a Woman and Sister To Brother: From My Heart to Yours, focuses on self empowerment and relationships with self and significant others. She is writing her first novel that should be completed in the fall. Her forthcoming CD entitled 4YoMind to be released in the spring. Contact Chris Knight, Post Office Box 245457, Brooklyn, New York 11224 E-mail: **Mindgear@Hotmail.com** Website: **www.4YoMind.com**

Melvin Lars 1975 graduate (BS/Health and English) Louisiana Tech University. Extended matriculation (MA) Texas Southern University 1983, Eastern Michigan University, Saginaw Valley State University, Centenary College (Administrative certification), and Youngstown State University. Principal; Woodrow Wilson High School, Youngstown, Ohio. Pastor/founder: Genesis Christian Life Ministries. Publications: Two books of Poetry; "Painted Images", "Reflections of Life." One Educational offering; "Dare To Be Positive/Slammin' Limitations". Honors: Golden Gloves/Heavyweight bosing champion (1975); All (MVSU) SWAC off. guard, NFL free-agent 1975. Greek affiliation: Kappa Alpha Psi Fraternity, Inc. Contact Mr. Melvin Lars, 2032 East Reserve Circle, Avon, Ohio 44011 Phone: (440) 934-8032 Fax: (440) 934-8033 E-mail: larschief@yahoo.com

Suzanne B. Lester Author of "Expressions from a Jar of Clay" which is her first published book of inspirational/religious poetry. The author currently resides in Athens, Georgia and is employed at Athens Technical College. She is an active member of Timothy Baptist Church under the leadership of the infamous Bishop Jerry F. Hutchins of Jerry F. Hutchins Ministries. In addition to publishing her first book, the author writes and sells specialty poetry. She is also a contributing writer to Reflect-A-Moment newsletter which is a web newsletter by Margie Epps and is also a kingdom poet of the site. Suzanne B. Lester, 151 Sweetgum Way, Athens, Georgia 30601 Phone: (706) 353-3738 E-mail: **poetrylady3@yahoo.com**

Cassie A. Levy Author and poet, Ms. Cassie A. Levy is a contributing author to "Delta Girls, Stories of Sisterhood." Her story is entitled "Where's the 1st Aid Kit?" She is contributing poet to "Violets, Inspirational Poems by Women of Delta Sigma Theta Sorority, Inc." (multiple poems).   Her poem entitled "Late at Night" accepted for publication by the American Poets Society, Poem entitled "Echo My Blessings" in recognition of Nikki Giovanni placed 1st runner-up in contest sponsored by the Writers of the Wood in Houston, Texas. Contact Ms. Cassie Levy, 4950 Sugar Grove #2105, Stafford, Texas 77477 Phone: (832) 465-4064 E-mail: **essence4thesoul@yahoo.com**

Pamela deLeon-Lewis A motivational speaker and poet, Ms. deLeon- Lewis, (a breast cancer survivor), has authored ' Smiling Thru the Tears- a Breast Cancer Survivor Odyssey, her first book of motivational and inspirational poetry that empowers the survivors of cancer. Pamela deleon-Lewis, Post Office Box 101041, Brooklyn, New York 11210 Phone: (917) 673-6350 E-mail: **pamela.deleonlewis@gmail.com**

Tracey Michae'l Lewis As a writer, Lewis' collection of poetry, Collapsed on the Wings of a Sigh: a Poetic Journey won 2002 Best Poetry Book by the SCBC Independent Publishers Awards. She is also the author of the new collection, Divine Nepotism. Dubbed as a young Nikki Giovanni, Divine Nepotism was recently endorsed by the legendary poet/writer. Lewis has completed work on several screenplays, and the critically acclaimed stage play, KHEPERA, which ran off-Broadway in 2002. Tracey Michae'l Lewis, 1845 West Superior, Apartment #1R, Chicago, Illinois 60622 E-mail: **traceylewis33@yahoo.com**

Craigal R. Lindo Author of Heart's Glory. Craigal R. Lindo, Heart Writer, LLC, 2551 North West 41st Avenue, Suite 405, Lauderhill, Florida 33313 E-mail: **Heartwriter14@aol.com** Website: **www.heartsglory.com**

Haki R. Madhubuti Writer, publisher, educator Haki R. Madhubuti is one of the world's bestselling authors. His poetry has been widely anthologized, Mr. Madhubuti has given readings and workshops at over 1,000 colleges, universities and community centers in Africa, Asia, South America, the Caribbean and the United States. He is founder of Third World Press. He has been a contributing editor of Black Scholar, Cololines, GRIO', and The Zora Neale Hurston Forum. He received the 1991 American Book Award and was named Author of the Year by the Illinois Association of Teachers of English in 1991. Contact Haki R. Madhubuti, Publisher, Third World Press, 7822 South Dobson Street, Chicago, Illinois 60619 Phone: (773) 651-0700 Fax: (773) 651-7286 E-mail: **twpress3@aol.com** Website: **www.thirdworldpressinc.com**

Maxine Malone A native Californian who now resides in Georgia, the author holds a doctoral degree in Special Education. She currently has poetic work published international and national. Askthlogical Views of the Tigress is her latest work. Maxine Malone, 175 Melrose Creek Drive, Stockbridge, Georgia Phone: (323) 422-0165 E-mail: **Suwynn@charter.net**

Michele Rene Matthews An essayist and poet Michele's work has been published in the Journal of Intergroup Relations and How We Got Over: Testimonies of Faith, Hope and Courage (Reyomi Publishing, June 2003). Her debut novel, Raymond's Daughters was released in September of 2004. Michele Rene Matthews, 5706 Earnhardt Street, Virginia Beach, Virginia 23464 Phone: (757) 420-9119 E-mail: **chele_rene@hotmail.com**

Karen McMeo Her poetry has appeared in ABAFAZI, the Simmons College Journal of Women of African Descent. She holds a Bachelor of Arts in English from the University of Massachusetts at Boston and a Master of Arts in English from Northeastern University. She has worked as a college English instructor, freelance writer, proofreader/copyeditor, public relations assistant, and as a staff reporter. She works as a manuscripts coordinator and is completing Holy Ghost Stories. Karen McMeo, Post Office Box 6382, Woodbridge, Virginia 22195 E-mail: **karenmcmeo@hotmail.com** Website: **www.perfectpathpublishing.com**

Renée McRae Author of the inspirational book of poetry entitled Truth In Rhyme, a textbook for NYC Board of Education. Keynote speaker, workshop facilitator and performance poet, her award-winning poetry has been published in nine anthologies of the National Library of Poetry, and is also displayed on poetry.com. Renee has been a featured guest on various television and radio programs sucha s HealthWatch (PBSTV) and The Hottest Poets, (WABC – New York). She is currently facilitating on-going workshops with New York City Board of Education and Mental Health Association of NYC, Inc. Ms. Renée McRae, Poetic Motivations, Post Office Box 230174, Hollis, New York 11423 Phone: (877) 814-9864 Fax: (253) 681-0464 Website: **www.reneemcrae.com**

Michelle Mellon Served as communications consultant for four years before completing her Master's in Liberal Studies and becoming a freelance writer and editor. She has had articles published in Imprint and Blue Planet Quarterly, poetry in journals and anthologies such as Hodgepodge and Seasons of the Heart, and was co-author of a book chapter on professional mentoring. Completed articles for the Encyclopedia of African American Literature. Ms. Michelle Mellon, 2416 Casa Way, Walnut Creek, California 94597 Phone: (925) 876-4121 Fax: (818) 474-7236 E-mail: **michelle@mpmellon.com** Website: **www.mpmellon.com**

Natalie Milton Writer/Poet. Natalie Milton, 320 Oak Park Square, College Park, Georgia 30349 Phone: (404) 761-0484 E-mail: **n1poem@bellsouth.net**

S. Renee Mitchell   M.B.A. Award-winning writer, playwright, spoken word recording artist, author, novelist, and empowerment speaker. Renee is a former award-winning newspaper columnist who was nominated twice for the prestigious Pulitzer Prize. She also is a powerful public speaker, who uses poetry and personal experiences to bring audiences to their feet, as well as touch their hearts. Renee, a survivor of domestic violence and sexual assault, experienced decades of low self-esteem and feelings of unworthiness. Her tireless and creative work to support other survivors of domestic violence resulted in her being selected as one of 2006's 21 Leaders of the 21st Century by New York City-based Women eNews, which bestowed Renee with the international Ida B. Wells Award for Bravery in Journalism. Renee also teaches writing workshops. Renee Mitchell Speaks LLC, 6835 South West Capitol Hill Road #34, Portland, Oregon 97219 Phone: (503) 278-8280 E-mail: **reneemitchellspeaks@yahoo.com** Website: **http://www.myppk.com/go/reneemitchellspeaks.aspx**

Tiffany Mitchell Also known as Wrythym, I write poetry and spoken word with song. Tiffany Mitchell, 177 Sycamore Drive, Apartnt110, Park Forest, Illinois 60466 Phone: (708) 748-1392 E-mail: **tmitchel214@msn.com**

Linda Everett Moye' Poet and author of four books of poetry, From A Delta's Heart, The Courage to Say It, Where Spirits Dance and Imagine This. She is also publisher, managing editor, and a contributing author of the collective work, Delta Girls Stories of Sisterhood. She is completing her first two novels for publication in 2005, The Pharaoh's Queen and The Pledge. Her work is included in the poetry anthology, Violets and the cookbook, Occasions to Savor. She has served as guest speaker at colleges, universities, churches, artistic and literary events. She was inducted into the San Antonio Women's Hall of Fame, 2001 in the Creative Arts category for her writing accomplishments. Linda Everett Moye', LEJ Poetic Expressions, Post Office Box 301973, San Antonio, Texas 78703 Phone: (210) 643-4365 Fax: (512) 482-8454 E-mail: **lindamoye@aol.com**   Website: **www.lindamoye.com**

Daphne Muse Writer, social commentator, and poet, Daphne has written more than 300 feature articles, essays, reviews and op-ed pieces for major newspapers, academic journals and on-line zines. Daphne Muse, 2429 East 23rd Street, Oakland, California 94601 Phone: (510) 436-4716 E-mail: **msmusewriter@gmail.com** Website: **www.oasisinthediaspora.com**

Ngoma Performance poet, multi-instrumentalist, singer/songwriter and paradigm shifter, for over 40 years. A former member of the Spirit House Movers and Players with Amiri Baraka and the Contemporary Freedom Song Duo, SERIOUS BIZNESS, Ngoma weaves poetry and song that raises contradictions and searches for a solution for a just and peaceful world. He was the Prop Slam winner of the 1997 National Poetry Slam Competition in Middletown, Connecticut and was published in African Voices Magazine, Long Shot Anthology, The Underwood Review, Signifyin' Harlem Review and 'Bum Rush The Page/Def Poetry Jam Anthology & Poems on the Road To Peace (Volumes 1, 2 &3, Yale Press). Ngoma, 1845 Adam Clayton Powell Boulevard, #3D, New York, New York Phone: (212) 663-2591 E-mail: **Ngomazworld@aol.com** Website: **www.Ngomazworld.com**

Frances Callaway Parks Author, poet, seminar leader, speaker, Ms. Parks is the author of several titles. Her latest is a book of inspirational poetry " From the Depths of Silence" released September 2004. Parks is a professor at Chicago State University and publishes under her own company, Victory Services Ink. Contact Frances Callaway Park, Victory Services Ink, 3473 King Drive #333, Chicago, Illinois Phone: (312) 326-2530 Fax: (312) 326-1047 E-mail: fcparks@sbcglobal.net Website: www.wordstransformimgworlds.com

Richard A. Parks Jr. A 27 year old poet/author who has self published two works, Someone Is Sleeping In My Head (2000) and Lost In A Mellow Rain. Someone was nominated for a Golden Pen Award for poetry collection of the year by the Black Writer's Alliance. His work has appeared on Timbooktu, Mental Satin, The Writeous, Poetry.com, and various newspapers and editorials throughout the southeast. Richard A. Parks Jr., Nusawf Inc., Post Office Box 23901, Alexandria, Virginia 22304 Fax: (703) 614-1663 E-mail: rip@richardparksjr.com Website: www.richardparksjr.com

Queen Esther Franks Phillips A licensed minister of the gospel of Jesus Christ, freelance writer, author, poet, motivational speaker, public administrator, and mother of three. Ms. Phillips is the founder of Majestic Publications, a Christian online writing ministry. Queen Esther Phillips, Post Office Box 980372, Houston, Texas 77098 Phone: (713) 866-7768 E-mail: gfphillips@gmail.com Website: www.queenphillips.books.officelive.com

Marcia Denrique Preudhomme Published a collection of poetry, Reflections of Realism, a collection of short fiction, Stranger Than Fiction, and completed a booklet of poems, The Heart of Truth. Received the Editor's Choice Award for Outstanding Achievement in Poetry from the International Library of Poetry, and has been selected for inclusion in the 59th Edition of Marquis Who's Who in America. Marcia Denrique Preudhomme, c/o Teresa R Martin, Esq., Law Offices of Teresa R Martin, P.C., 67 Wall Street, Suite #2211, New York, New York 10005 Phone: (212) 709-8224 E-mail: denriquebooks@aol.com Website: www.denrique.com

Stephanie M. Pruitt Voted 2004 Poet of the Year by SpokenVizions Magazine, Stephanie is the author of "I AM: A Poetic Journey Towards Self Definition" (2002), and she released her first spoken word CD entitled Choice. She co-hosts a social commentary radio talk show Stephanie M. Pruitt, 1708 21st Avenue South, Suite #149, Nashville, Tennessee 37212 Phone: (615) 545-8018 E-mail: SPruitt@StephaniePruitt.com Website: www.StephaniePruitt.com

Darren B. Rankins Poet and author of two books of poetry. Christian T-shirt ministry. Darren B. Rankins, 117 Winsford Court Murfreesboro, Tennessee 31730 Phone: (615) 898-0471 E-mail: Darren_Rankins@yahoo.com Website: www.purethoughts.net

F. B. Rasheed Graduated from Langston University in 1969, with a degree in Math Education. Taught ninth grade math classes at John F. Kennedy Jr. High School in Oklahoma City before being drafted into the US Army. Graduated from University of Oklahoma in 1972 with MRCPL. 1000's of poems and some short stories to credit with 2 self publish books of poems, "Some Sum Words" and "Read Qur'an the Message You Can Depend Upon.". Contact Mr. F. B. Rasheed, 1621 South West Pennsylvania Avenue, Lawton, Oklahoma 73501 Phone: (580) 678-4993 E-mail: fbrasheed1@aol.com

Pat McLean RaShine   A Philadelphia Pennsylvania poet and author, Ms. Pat Mclean-Rashine has two books, "HEALING HER HURTS: A collection of short stories that speaks to the soul of a woman," and "Ain't Gonna Bite My Tongue NO More. She is the recipient of several awards, including 1st place for the Sonia Sanchez/Audre Lorde Poetry Competition and second place for Judith Stark Creative Writing Competition at Community College of Philadelphia.   Pat presently co-facilitates poetry and creative writing workshops Temple University's Pan-African Studies Community Education Program (PASCEP) and at Drexel University, both of Philadelphia. She has appeared on several multi media programs, such as WUSL Power 99 FM, WHAT AM "Etches", Politics & Poetry, to name a few. Published in "BMa: The Sonia Sanchez Literary Review – Legends and Legacies." and, X-Magazine. Pat McLean RaShine, 632 Elkins Avenue, Philadelphia, Pennsylvania 19120 Phone: (215) 683-3620 E-mail: PMcPoet@aol.com

Darlene Mai Roberts   Poet/Author of Erotica Escapades. Contact Ms. Darlene Mai Roberts, 451 Robinson Drive, Dunleith Estates, Wilmington, Delaware 19801 Phone: (302) 573-5115 E-mail: ladydigsu2003@yahoo.com

Janeen Robichaud   Author of two erotic/romance books entitled "Candy" and "Candy2, The Sequel" and "They Killed Me." Janeen Robichaud, 7000 Donald Street, Millville, New Jersey 08332 E-mail: candyjaneen@aol.com Website: www.geocities.com/candyjaneen

Tina Denise Rodgers   Published poet Tina is a graduate from East Carolina University with a BSW in Social Work and trained CPS. She is a motivational speaker for African-American women and youth, and has published a book of poems Expressions of the Heart about real life situations. Tina Denise Rodgers, Post Office Box 1236, Williamston North Carolina, 27892 Phone: (252) 217-9806 E-mail: tdrjames@yahoo.com

Christopher Donshale Sims   Poet, spoken word artists and author of three chapbooks of poetry: Super Lyrical (2003), Knowledge Manifest: A Book of Life, Community and Culture (2006), and most recently, Barefoot On Wooden Floors (2006). Christopher Sims, 312 Adams Street, Rockford, Illinois 61107 E-mail: universoulove@yahoo.com

Ty Smith   Graduate Student at the University of Central Oklahoma. Member of the "IMPACT Movement" and Leads Campus Bible Study at the Nigh University Center. Ty has an Internet Radio Ministry called "Ty Speaks Life" which airs on KTLV. He has a self-published book of poetry and CD called "Kingdom Poetry."   In 2005, he opened up for Gospel artist Shirley Caesar in concert at the Mabee Center, Tulsa Oklahoma. Ty Smith, 1900 Kickingbird Road, Apt. 109 Edmond,Oklahoma 73034 Contact: (405) 412-5693 E-mail: kami7910@yahoo.com

Cheryl Samuel Stover   Author.   Owner of Academic Connections, a growing consulting business offering customized services to meet your organization's educational and training needs. She has three books, From the Inside Out: How to Transform Your School to Increase Student Achievement, Elementary Basic Skills Through Black History; and Walk Out of the Shadows: Poetry to Inspire and Encourage Youth in the 21st Century. This book was written to give our young people a sense of self-worth, hope, and faith. Dr. Cheryl Samuel Stover, 3516 John G. Richards Road, Post Office Box 153, Liberty Hill, South Carolina 29074 Phone: (803) 273-3772 E-mail: chrylstover@yahoo.com Website: www.wastelandpress.net

George Edward Tait   Born in Oakland and raised in Harlem, George graduated from Pace University in 1968 with a B.A. in English Language and Literature and a minor in French Language and Literature after being a member of the literary society and The Pace Press. From 1968-1972, he taught and tutored English at Queens College while conducting Creative Writing workshops. Defining music as the poetry of sound, Tait became a bandleader and from 1972 to 1975 spearheaded a group called Black Massical Music. He founded The Society of Afrikan Poets and produced a seven year series of weekly poetry readings entitled Black Words for a Wednesday Night. While teaching at Malcolm-King College (1981-1986), his first volume of poetry At Warwas published in 1983, the same year he was named The Poet Laureate of Afrikan Nationalism by leaders of the nationalist community. Several of Tait's poems and articles were published by the New York Amsterdam News. At Arms was published in 1992 in addition to his work being included in the landmark anthology Brotherman; The Odyssey of Black Men in America (1995). George Edward Tait, Post Office Box 1305, New York, New York 10035 E-mail: **georgeedwardtait@msn.com** Website: **www.georgeedwardtait.org**

Jarvis Talley Author of the debut book, No Candles. He began his literary journey as a spoken word artist and performer who has been highlighted at the Showtime at Apollo, BET, and venues across the nation. His work has been highlighted in Ebony, Consciousness and Noire Magazines and featured on many literary sites including, Trimaxx Publishers, The Writers Inn, and Black Men In America. He is writing his second book, 7 Troubles, "Journey to the Green Eyes Beneath the Fedora," slated for publication in 2007. Jarvis Talley, Post Office Box 1265, Austell, Georgia 30012 E-mail: **mrtalley@gmail.com** Website: **www.mrtalley.com**

Antoinette Oglesby Taylor Playwright/Writer of greeting cards, poems and short stories. I have 5 plays that have been stage read in Louisville, Kentucky. Antoinette Oglesby Taylor, 6411 Shirley Avenue, Prospect, Kentucky 40059 E-mail: **jtnursing@aol.com**

Saundra Lee Taylor I'm a young 55 year Black Female from the midwest. I've written some poety over the years, and one is published. My frist love is the theatre. I have written and directed 6 plays. (all Christian base). I believe in God and I trust that my future is a bright one. Saundra Lee Taylor, 1117 North 24th Street, Saint Joseph, Missouri 64506 Phone: (816) 244-7099 Fax: (816) 232-7435 E-mail: **still_i_rise2@yahoo.com**

Juanita Torrence-Thompson The authors 5th poetry book, New York and African Tapestries (Fly By Night Press) is Small Press Review "pick". As Editor/Publisher of non-profit Mobius, The Poetry Magazine since 2006, she has 2 acclaimed issues with award-winning poets: Rita Dove, Nikki Giovanni, Marge Piercy, Diane Wakoski, Robert Bly, Samuel Menashe, Colette Inez, Toi Derricotte, Daniela Gioseffi, Louis Reyes Rivera, Hal Sirowitz, & Mobius 25th anniversary gala. Juanita has read on TV & radio & widely at U.S. colleges, schools, libraries, stores and South Africa, Singapore & Switzerland. Featured speaker Nati Federation of State Poetry Societies convention San Antonio, AAUW, etc. Read at Queensboro President Helen Marshall events, Queens Theatre, Queens Botanical Garden, New Years Marathon Reading, New York Summer Festival, etc. Published in Europe, Canada, Australia, widely in U.S. journals. Poetry columns in New York and Massachusetts papers. 2nd prize spoken word. Juanita Torrence-Thompson, Post Office Box 671058, Flushing, New York 11367 E-mail: **poetrytown@earthlink.net** Website: **www.poetrytown.com**

Maxine E. Thompson Writer, poet and literary agent. Maxine E. Thompson, Black Butterfly Press, Post Office Box 25279, Philadelphia Pennsylvania, 19119 E-mail: maxtho@aol.com Website: www.maxinethompson.com

Wilbur Thornton Teacher, community worker, actor, instructor, and new author of the book, "The StoryTeller" Uncle Will Tip-Top-Tips, poems, short stories, tips, and fun!. Wilbur "Thorntize" Thornton, Andrew College, 413 College Street, Cuthbert, Georgia 39840 Phone: (229) 209-5218 E-mail: wilburthornton@andrewcollege.edu

Brenda M. Tillman A native of Hartford, Connecticut, the author who now resides in Atlanta, Georgia, shares her life experiences – real and imagined, through poetic expression, in her first book, Shades of Mandingo. She has been writing poetry since her preteen years. She has interviewed several jazz musicians and has been a contributing writer for former Atlanta magazine, Strictly Jazz. Those interviewed include pianist David Beniot, violinist Regina Carter, the late Art Porter, saxophonist, and vocalist Dianne Reeves. She has also written book reviews for Black Issues Book Review Magazine and contributed scriptural-based messages in religious booklets. Brenda M. Tillman, Jobrelika Enterprises International, LLC, Post Office Box 311223, Atlanta, Georgia 31131 Phone: (404) 556-7534 E-mail: shadesofmandingo@yahoo.com

toniwo Some of the authors creative work has been featured in Black & Single Magazine, Honey Magazine, an upcoming poem featured in Essence Magazine and several national anthologies. toniwo has also been featured on ArtistFirst radio show. toniwo, Blacklight Productions, 2410 South Kirkwood, Suite 136, Houston, Texas 77077 Phone: (713) 591-6610 Fax: (281) 870-1633 E-mail: toni@toniwo.com Website: www.toniwo.com

Kendal S. Turner Author and Poet, Kendal has written Broken: Yet Sustained By God and the book, Anatomy Of The Soul; revealing in more depth the struggles of her past, the redemptive power of Christ and the peace, prosperity and pleasures of Kingdom living. She has done radio interviews on 1140AM in Oklahoma. Kendal S. Turner, Post Office Box 32713, Oklahoma City, Oklahoma 73123 E-mail: contact@kendalsturner.com Website: www.kendalsturner.com

Vincent Tyler Poet. Tyler has performed at a variety of venues, including poetry sets, book clubs and book signings but it is the way he brings his writing to life during a performance that often first captures what becomes loyal readers. His well recognized piece, "Chocolate Cookies" is a story about a man who's life drastically changes after meeting the woman whom he believes to be his soulmate. Mr. Vincent Tyler, Rose Petals Publishing, Post Office Box 19071, Chicago, Illinois 60619 E-mail: chccookies@aol.com   Website: vtyler@rosepetalspublishing.com

Suzanne E. Uzzell Poet and author of two books of poetry, Words 2 Ignite The Soul, and the book Chosen Words, a book of poems. Suzanne E. Uzzell, 1806 Fox Boulevard, Honolulu, Hawaii 96818 Phone: (808) 206-9658 E-mail: suzanneuzzell@yahoo.com

Carmel S. Victor Author of award-winning novel: "Facing Our Skeletons" and Best Work of Poetry for 2005 "Every Day Again: Real Life through Poetry and Short Stories." Carmel S. Victor, Post Office Box 1132, Union, New Jersey 07083 E-mail: carmel@carmelsvictor.com Website: www.carmelsvictor.com

Frank X Walker   Author of four collections of poetry, Affrilachia, Black Box, Buffalo Dance and most recent When Winter Come. Also the editor of Eclipsing a Nappy New Mellinium and America! What's My Name: The Other 'Poets' Unfurl the Flag. Walker is the editor of PLUCK! The Journal of Affrilachian Arts and Culture, a founding member of the Affrilachian Poets and a Cave Canem fellow. Currently Writer In Resident at Northern Kentucky University. Frank X Walker, Northern Kentucky University, Department of Literature and Language, 207A Landrum Academic Building, Highland Heights, Kentucky 41099 E-mail: **affrilachia@aol.com**

Tonya M. Evans-Walls   Poet and author of Literary Law Guide for Authors: Copyright, Trademark, and Contracts in Plain Language, Seasons of Her and SHINE! Her short story, Not Tonight appears in a new anthology titled Proverbs for the People, published by Kensington. Tonya M. Evans-Walls, Esq., TME Law, 6703 Germantown Avenue, Suite 200, Philadelphia, Pennsylvania 19119 Phone: (215) 438-0468 Fax: (215) 438-0469 E-mail: **tme@tmelaw.net** Website: **www.tmelaw.net**

Jerry W. Ward, Jr. Professor of English at Dillard University, Jerry Washington Ward, Jr., is a poet, literary critic, and editor. His current projects include The Richard Wright Encyclopedia and Reading Race, Reading America, a collection of social and literary essays. Contact Jerry W. Ward, Jr., Department of English, Dillard University, 2601 Gentilly Boulevard, New Orleans, Louisiana 70122 E-mail: **jerryward31@hotmail.com**

Nagueyalti Warren Poet and editor living in Atlanta, Georgia, Ms. Nagueyalti Warren has published Lodestar and Other Night Lights, (New York: Mellen Press, 1992, a collection of poems); co-edited Southern Mothers: Fact and Fictions in Southern Women's Writing (Baton Rouge: Louisiana State University Press, 1999); Temba Tupu! (Walking Naked) Africana Women's Poetic Self-Protrait, (The Africa World Press, forthcoming). Contact Nagueyalti Warren, 7469 Asbury Drive, Lithonia, Georgia 30058 Phone: (404) 727-6040 E-mail: **nwarren@emory.edu**

Cecil Washington Author, Cecil writes science fiction, fantasy and horror, in addition to poetry. Some of his published books include Alien Erotica, A collection of short stories and verses, Walkware, A techno-thriller and Badlands: An Underground Science Fiction Novel. Education: graduated from Bowie State University in 1993 with a degree in Business Administration, and minors in Marketing, Music, Communications and Economics. Worked as a QA Test Analyst. Also founded Brothers Sci-Fi Magazine. Cecil Washington, 5701 Galloway Drive, Oxon Hill, Maryland 20745 E-mail: **cecilwashington@yahoo.com** Website: **www.cecilwashington.com**

K. C. Washington Novella, "Mourning Becomes Her" was published by the Harlem Writers Guild Press (2006). Over 10 of my articles were published as a contributing writer and editor for The Hill. Most recently, I worked as a freelancer providing proofreading, research, and writing services to clientele as diverse as Cover and Urban Latino Magazines. Published a chapbook of poetry through Ridgeway Press and have recorded a spoken word CD. Featured in The Nubian Gallery, a new anthology of African-American poetry. Bachelor of Arts in English, minor in Journalism. Four-year Ford Foundation Scholarship in Journalism, $24,000. Two-year Mellon Fellowship, $12,000. K. C. Washington, 237 Dekalb Avenue, Brooklyn, New York 11205 Phone: (718) 789-0443 E-mail: **kcwbrooklyn@juno.com** Website: **www.a-dark-lady.com**

Roberta Sonsaray White Poet, author, and motivational speaker, her first book entitled "Spiritual Metamorphosis" is a dialogue/poetry text. Her second book is forth coming and is a novel. Contact Ms. Sonsaray White, Emory UMC, 6100 Georgia Avenue North West, Washington, DC 20011 Phone: (202) 538-6238 E-mail: **SM4RSWhite@aol.com**

Hubert P. Williams, Jr. An anointed singer/songwriter/producer, that also writes poetry and inspirational messages to uplift the Name of the Lord. Currently serves as Chair, Cumberland County Coalition on Teen Pregnancy Prevention and Adolescent Parenting; Member of Coalition for Awareness, Resources, and Education of Substances, (C.A.R.E.S). Rev. Hubert P. Williams, Jr., Trinity Music Group, 2907 Kingfisher Drive, Fayetteville, North Carolina. Phone: (910) 977-7354 E-mail: **min.hpwilliams@yahoo.com**

Gloria Dulan-Wilson. Uses poetry to depict and convey information of importance and concern to African Americasn under her company "Poetic License(c)." Gloria Dulan-Wilson, 90 Church Street, Suite 3343, New York City, New York 10008 E-mail: **geemomadee@yahoo.com**

Larry Winfield Poet. Larry organized the protest poetry reading at the ' 96 Democratic Convention; hosted a weekly poetry and jazz show on pirate station Guerilla Love Radio as DJ Merlot; published the poetry books Rosedust, Erzulie and Wicker Park Sonata and the online/print zines Liquid Glyph and City Table Review; produced short films, and performed in Paris, Berlin, Frankfurt, New York, and with ensemble groups Brothers in Verse and his poetry band Brass Orchid. Produced the CD's, "Monkey King" and "Erzulie Freda." Hosts the Sundown Lounge podcast. Contact Mr. Larry Winfield, Post Office Box 812091, Los Angeles, California 90017 E-mail: **lwin@larrywinfield.com** Website: **www.larrywinfield.com**

Fredrick Woodard Visual artist and a published poet. Fredrick Woodard, 2905 Prairie du Chien Road North East, Iowa City, Iowa 52240 E-mail: **fredrick-woodard@uiowa.edu**

Olu Butterfly Woods Performance poet and author of The Revenge of Dandelions: a collection of poetry. Also, Director of Poetry for the People, Baltimore, Maryland. Olu Butterfly Woods, 6023 Greenspring Avenue, Baltimore, Maryland 21209 Phone: (410) 358-6484 E-mail: **contactus@blackoutstudios.com** Website: **www.blackoutstudios.com**

Edwin "Future" Wilson Jr. After graduating from Northern High School, Future attended the University of Michigan where he received his bachelor's degree in Mass Communications Media. He has become one of the most sought-after spoken word artists in the country. After only a few years writing and performing, he became the Redemption Poetry Slam Champion - Detroit Region, a nationwide poetry slam contest sponsored by FX Movies. He also was a showcased artist for the BET Pantene Total You Tour in Detroit and Washington, D.C. Future shared the stage with the talents of poet Nikki Giovanni, hip-hop pioneer MC Lyte, BET anchor Jacque Reid, and Grammy-winning gospel recording artist Yolanda Adams. Winner of the Erotic Poetry Slam at the University of Michigan; Winner of the Michigan Intrastate College Team Slam competition; Placed 9th overall in the 2005 IWPS (Individual World Poetry Slam) Worcester, Massachusetts; Winner of the 2005 Big Bang Poetry Slam competition, Toledo, Ohio. Mr. Edwin "Future" Wilson Jr., 726 Collingwood Dr., Davison, Michigan 48823 Phone: (810) 449-9897 E-mail: **futurethepoet@gmail.com** Website: **www.futurethepoet.com**

Frances Faye Ward-Worthy   Poet.   Published works: Broadside Press Anthology. Catfish Poets Society Anthology. Columnist: Power, Money, Influence Magazine. Graduated from the Art Institute of Atlanta. I've had classes at Cranbrook Institute (film & video); scriptwriting with Tim Jeffrey. I've been Producion Assistant on music videos, documentaries and TV productions. Headed the poetry committee of the Romance Writers, Houston chapter. Frances Faye Ward-Worthy, 242 Chalmers Detroit, Michigan 48215 E-mail: worth23karat@yahoo.com

Marvin X Author of the following: How To Recover From the Addiction to White Supremacy, (A Pan African 12 Step Model for a Mental Health Peer Group), Beyond Religion, toward Spirituality, essays on consciousness, (2007), Wish I Could Tell You The Truth, essays, (2005), Land of My Daughters, poems, (2005), and In the Crazy House Called America, essays, (2002). Contact Marvin X, Black Bird Press, Post Office Box 1317, Paradise, California 95967 E-mail: mrvnx@yahoo.com Website: www.marvinxwrites.blogspot.com

Sankofa Camille Yarbrough Author of the children's classic book "Cornrows;" Yarbrough was a member of the Katherine Dunham Dance Company for five years and taught Dunham Technique at Southern Illinois University; The Association for the Study of Classical African Civilizations (ASCAC); The New School For Social Research (The Journey of the Griots-Souls: Unsold); Kean College (Misuse of the African Image in the Media). Ms. Sankofa Camille Yarbrough, African American Traditions Workshop, 80 Saint Nicholas Avenue Suite 4G, New York, New York 10026 Phone: (212) 865-7460 E-mail: Yarbroughchosan@aol.com

Alecia Goodlow-Young Author, screenwriter, poet, columnist and a freelance writer, she write for a newspaper, a magazine, a union organization. Currently with The National Writer's Union / UAW. She is Co-chair of The National Diversity Committee, A Delegate at the Delegate's Assembly and a Southeast Michigan Steering Committee member. Alecia Goodlow-Young, 28490 Tavistock Trail, Southfield, Michigan 48034 Phone: (313) 796-7949 Fax: (313) 541-6638 E-mail: aleciawrites@sbcglobal.net

Derrell Young Author, minister, spoken word artist, his new book is Grace 2 Speak (December 2008). Many have said that YOUNG shares the look of Common and the sound of DMX, but he's the Soul of Spoken Word. YOUNG has released 3 CDs filled with the wholesome, pure, God centered poetry, while being featured on over 6 CDs lending support to other artists (Hip Hop and Soul). He's comprised with such diversity to rockout and minister with rock bands and then switches the tempo to flow with Holy Hip Hop, Soul Music, Praise Music/Comptemporary Christian Music, as well as his Spoken Worship. YOUNG is certainly a multifaceted, out-of-the-box minister that is able to raise the bar in any arena as he worships God wholeheartedly. He has shared the stage with Cynthia Jones and many others as far west as Tennessee, south as Georgia, and north as Philadelphia as he gears up for his next album release and moving WhoIsYOUNG Ministries to the next level. Derrell Young, WhoIsYOUNG, Post Office Box 39662, Greensboro, North Carolina 27438 Phone: (336) 255-4910 E-mail: booking@whoisyoung.com

Jackie Y. Young Author of the provocative poetry collection, "Love's Reparations: the Learning Curve between Heartache & Healing" (2006). Jackie Y. Young, 1st Stream Publishing, Post Office Box 26687, Richmond, Virginia 23261 E-mail: msjayy@jackieyoungwrites.com Website: www.jackieyoungwrites.com

Charles W. Cherry II, Esq.
Broadcaster * Publisher * Author * Attorney

A native of Daytona Beach, Florida, Media Mogul, Cherry W. Cherry II, Esq., is a former prosecutor as well as practicing trial attorney in his own firm in Fort Lauderdale, Florida. He is a 1978 honors graduate of Morehouse College, Atlanta Georgia. On December 18, 1982, he was the second African-American student to be simultaneously awarded both the juris Doctor and Master of Business Administration degrees from the University of Florida.

Charles Cherry has more than 25 years of media management experience when he began as the publisher of his family-owned weekly newspaper, the Daytona Times, a weekly community newspaper that recently celebrated its 25th anniversary. Cherry has served as the General Manager of WPUL-AM since 2000. He has also served as General Manager of WCSZ-AM from 1998 to 2000. He has been on the lecture circuit for over 15 years. His most recent publication is entitled <u>Excellence Without Excuse: The Black Student's Guide to Academic Excellence</u> (International Scholastic Press, 1994)

Currently, he is Vice President/General Counsel and principal shareholder of Tama Broadcasting, Inc., the largest privately Black owned media company in the State of Florida. Tama Broadcasting (Tama) was founded in 2001, by his father the late civil rights activist, Dr. Glen W. Cherry. Tama has holdings that include two newspapers and nine radio stations. Mr. Cherry resides in Plantation, Florida with his family.

Producers

Film, Song and Play

Abdul-Jalil al-Hakim President/CEO of Superstar Management world renowned for unprecedented services for Muhammed Ali, Brian Taylor, U.S. Rep. J.C. Watts, Warner Bros. Records, Deion Sanders, Delvin Williams, Giant Records, Kareem Abdul-Jabbar, M.C. Hammer, Capitol Records, Lyman Bostock, Evander Holyfield, Spencer Haywood, Cliff Robinson, Abbey Lincoln, EMI Records, Emanuel Stewart (Lennox Lewis, Prince Naseem Hamed, Oscar DeLa Hoya), Pebbles, John Carlos, Reggie White, Marvin Gaye, Mos Def, Martin Wyatt, and Leslie Allen. He has produced shows for Disney, ABC-TV and ESPN, events in Japan, Russia, Egypt, Romania, Paris, Europe, Brunei, U.S.; consulted BBDO Worldwide Advertising, Starter, Royal Family of Saudi Arabia, The ESPY'S, National Football League EXPERIENCE- Super Bowl, "90210", Black Entertainment Television (BET), Sega, Independant Film Producers (IFP), Screen Actors Guild (SAG), Producers Guild of America (PGA), and Broadcast Music Inc. (BMI), to name a few. Contact Mr. Abdul-Jalil al-Hakim, Superstar Management, 7633 Sunkist Drive, Oakland California 94605 E-mail: (510) 638-0808 Fax: (510) 638-8889 E-mail: jalil@superstarmanagement.com Website: www.superstarmanagement.com

ArtMattan Productions We distribute films that focus on the human experience of black people in Africa, the Caribbean, North and South America and Europe. All these films were shown during our annual African Diaspora Film Festival in New York. ArtMattan Productions, 535 Cathedral Parkway, Suite 14B, New York, New York 10025 Phone: (212) 864-1769 Fax: (212) 316-6020 E-mail: info@africanfilm.com Website: www.africanfilm.com

B.A.B.'s Filmworks and Theatrical Productions Founded in 2001. A community based theatrical group that produces plays to provide amateur actors with a venue to hone and sharpen their theatrical skills; as well as creating productions that are relative to our community life. The trio of B.A.B.'s, Dara Bragg, Alvertis Alexander and Koya Bragg brings a multitude of talents to the company: Director, Playwrights, Actors, Casting Directors, Poet, Model, Fashion Designer, Singers, Writers, Educator and so much more. B.A.B.'s productions range from comedy to drama, and everything in between. We continue to bring positive images to the forefront and educate as we entertain our audiences with a wide range of plays from comedy to drama for fundraisers and any other events. Alvertis Alexander, B.A.B.'s Filmworks and Theatrical Productions, Post Office Box 110162, Cambrai Heights, New York 11411 Phone: (718) 926-4939 E-mail: alvecouture@yahoo.com

Big Fish Productions, Inc Artists Management/Indielabel/Productions. We do any/everything from Artist Management to Director of Events. Nominated for an Audelco Recognition Award. James Carter, President. Carter Management, Big Fish Productions, Inc., Post Office Box 782. Bronx, New York 10462 Phone: (212) 860-3639 E-mail: jcarter891@aol.com Website: www.bigfishproductioninc.com

Troy Buckner Producer for the theatrical production, 'Tell Hell I Aint Comin', starring Tommy Ford from the Grammy nominated R & B Group, 'Az Yet' on the La Face Record label. She has managed and co-produced Gospel Renown Artist and Stella Award Winner, Kenny Smith and Vernessa Mitchell from the Motown's Grammy Award winning R & B Group, 'Hi-Energy.' Troy Buckner, Hy'tara Entertainment, Post Office Box 19049, Anaheim, California 92817 Phone: (714) 227-5000 E-mail: birdinflight@aol.com Website: www.abirdinflight.com

Jillian Bullock Award winning writer, director and producer. Credits include: "The Champion Inside", Writer, Producer, Actor, Fight Choreographer (A P in A Pod Productions); "Spirit", Writer, Director, Producer, Actor, Fight Choreographer (Jaguar Productions); "A Filmmaker's Personal Journey," Documentary, Writer, Director, Actor, Producer (Jaguar Productions, won the Mickey Michaux award). Also works as a freelance writer, a script doctor and a screenwriting judge. Jillian Bullock, Jaguar Productions, Inc., 311 South Park Way, Suite 308F, Broomall, Pennsylvania 19008 Phone: (484) 682-6932 E-mail: jaguarpro1161@aol.com

Celestial Music Studio Offers original productions for artist that need original music and lyric for their creative projects. Specializes in Voice Lessons, Piano, Drums, Saxophone, Bass, Guitar and Keyboard lessons. Teaches students to play by ear, sight read, music theory, improvisation, composition and memorization. Eddie Corley, Music Director. Contact Eddie Corley, Celestial Music Studio, 2218 22nd Avenue, Gulfport, Mississippi 39501 Phone: (228) 216-2558 E-mail: eddiecorley1@aol.com Website: www.celestialmusicproduction.com

The Charles Group, Inc. Accepts script submissions for possible production. Seeking feature length or short film scripts that are character driven with an Afro-American or Afro-Caribbean theme preferred. Must be able to be produced as a low budget project. The Charles Group, 478 North Highland, Suite 11, Atlanta, Georgia 30307 E-mail: cynthia_charles@yahoo.com

The Color Of Film Collaborative Non-profit organization that works to support media makers of color and others who have an interest in creating and developing new and diverse images of people of color in film, video and performing arts. Lisa Simmons, Executive Director. The Color of Film Collaborative, Post Office Box 191901, Roxbury, Massachusetts 02119 Phone: (617) 445-6051 E-mail: info@coloroffilm.com Website: coloroffilm.com

Courtesy Is Contagious Productions, Inc Record/film production company. Producer, Tico Wells, "Choir Boy", The Five Heartbeats. The company is available to produce and/or direct projects for film, TV, stage, or provide original music. Courtesy Is Contagious Productions, Inc., 11288 Ventura Boulevard, Suite 401, Studio City, California 91604 Phone: (818) 775-3871

Julie Dash Producer, Writer, Director, Ms. Julie Dash was born in New York City. She is currently a residence of Los Angeles, California. EDUCATION: 1985 M.F.A, Motion Picture and Television Production, UCLA; 1974 AFI, Producing and Writing Conservatory Fellow; 1973 B.A., City College of New York, Leonard Davis Center for the Performing Arts, David; Picker Film Institute; 1968 Studio Museum of Harlem, Film Workshop, NYC. ORIGINAL SCRIPTS: 2006 Departure and Arrival, Screenplay for Multimedia Event SF; Arts Festival; 2004 Digital Diva, Feature Screenplay. Ms. Julie Dash, Geechee, LLC, Post Office Box 48853, Los Angeles, California 90048 E-mail: jdash@mac.com Website: www.geechee.tv

Emtro Music Production Music production company specializing in Gospel music. Welcomes "ALL" songwriters to submit copy written material to be considered for future projects. Chief Financial Officer, Ms. Emily Sneed. The independent label astounded the music industry by placing eight songs in the Top 20 on Billbard's Hot Gospel Chart within two years – including Youth For Christ's Stellar-award winning smash, 'The Struggle is Over. Contact Emtro Music Production, 420 College Drive, Suite 205, Middleburgh, Florida 32068 Phone: (904) 213-1330 Fax: (213) 1331 E-mail: info@emtro.com Website: www.emtro.com

Face To Face, Inc. Company is headed by President/CEO and Multi-platinum Artist/Producer Fred Hammond whose writing style and production skills have created a demand for his services in both Gospel/Christian and Secular Music. He has worked with some of the industry's most sought after and influential talents from The Winans to James Cleveland, Stevie Wonder to Eric Clapton, American Idol Winner Ruben Studdard to Musiq Soulchild, Quincy Jones to Sean "Diddy" Combs, DreamWorks to ABC Films. Provides songwriting, music production, audio recording, engineering, mixing and mastering of musical content for records, commercials, audio soundtracks for film, television and theatre. Morris Townsend, Face To Face, Inc., 2812 Sonterra Drive, Cedar Hill, Texas 75104 Phone: (972) 293-2885 Fax: (972) 293-6866 E-mail: facetofacemgt@aol.com

Faith Filmworks, Inc. Independent motion picture production company. No unsolicited screenplays or extended treatments except through established agents or entertainment attorney. Individuals may submit a short pitch or synopsis no longer than half a page in length. Michael Swanson, Producer, Faith Filmworks, Inc., 859 Hollywood Way, Suite 255, Burbank, California 91505 E-mail: christine@faithfilmworks.com Website: www.faithfilmworks.com

Fat Boy Hits Music Group Publishing company. Arthur Douse, Vice President, writer, and HipHop artist. Fat Boy Hits Music Group, 1244 Herkamer, Brooklyn, New York 11233 Phone: (718) 216-5334 E-mail: celsiusbk@aol.com

Film Life, Inc. A film marketing and distribution company whose mission is to spearhead the commercial development of independent Black films. Mr. Jeff Friday, founder. Film Life, Inc., Post Office Box 688, New York, New York 10012 Phone: (212) 966-2411 Fax: (212) 966-2411 E-mail: info@thefilmlife.com Website: www.thefilmlife.com

First Lady Productions, Inc Producer. CEO Dr. Vera J. Goodman is a native of Jacksonville, Florida. She is the advisor, director, and lead vocalist for her husband, Recording Artist Bishop Dr. Jan D. Goodman, Sr., & The Voices of One Accord. Dr. Goodman is also a songwriter. She has produced and written songs for CD such as Cause He's Worthy & The Rock. Her second CD is entitled Santuary of Praise which was released in 2008. Contact Dr. Vera J. Goodman, First Lady Productions, Inc., 2971 Waller Street, Jacksonville, Florida 32254 Phone: (904) 425-0806 E-mail: firstladypro@aol.com Website: www.firstladyproductions.net

Kenneth Gamble Co-founder/Chairman, Gamble-Huff Music. Legends, Kenny Gamble and Leon Huff have been songwriting and producing partners for 30 years. Contact Chuck Gamble, 309 South Broad Street, Philadelphia, Pennsylvania 19107 Phone: (215) 985 0900 Phone: (215) 885-0924 E-mail: chuckgamblepir@aol.com Website: www.gamble-huffmusic.com

GODProjects Film Company producing multi-cultural bible based films. We are also a Live Multi-Cultural Comedy Troupe making folks laugh around the world. Gilda O. Davies, GodProjects, Post Office Box 4622, Orange, California 92863 Phone: (714) 322-0526 E-mail: GODProjects@gmail.com Website: www.SGODKS.org

Lou Gossett Jr. Producer/film, production company - motion picture/television. Produce movies, will review agent-submitted scripts, treatments. Producers, Lou Gossett Jr., and Dennis Considine. Contact Mr. Louis Gossett, Jr., Logo Entertainment, 301 North Canon Drive, Suite 300, Beverly Hills, California 90210 Phone: (310) 456-2147 E-mail: logo@louisgossett.com Website: www.louisgossett.com

Michael A. Grant Jr. Music producer. Contact Mr. Michael A. Grant, Jr., Imani Jordan Music, 5716 Malcolm Street, Philadelphia, Pennsylvania 19143 Phone: (215) 316-7269 E-mail: michaelgrant_2@msn.Com

Tim Greene Film, and song producer. Tim has written and produced over 17 national record releases with such acts as "Soft Touch." B.S. Degree in Business Management, with a communications minor, Shaw University. Contact Tim Greene Films, Post Office Box 20554, Philadelphia, Pennsylvania 19138 Phone: (213) 399-0600 E-mail: timgreene2009@yahoo.com Website: www.timgreenefilms.com

Eddie Gurren CEO/Owner of Golden Boy Music. Contact Mr. Eddie Gurren, Golden Boy Music, 16311 Askin Drive, Pine Mountain, California 93222 Phone: (661) 242-0125 E-mail: gbrmusic@frazmtn.com

Herman Hall Producer/promoter and booking agent. Herman Hall Communications, Inc, 1630 Nostrand Avenue, Brooklyn, New York 11226 Phone: (718) 941-1879 Fax: (718) 941-1886 E-mail: everybodys@msn.com Website: www.everybodysmag.com

Forest Hairston Songwriter/music producer, screenwriter and poet. Contact Mr. Forest Hairston, ForGen Productions, 3654 Barham Boulevard. Suite Q301, Los Angeles, California Phone: (323) 851-1225 E-mail: fgprod@forgen.com Website: www.forgen.com

Joseph Harrison Published songwriter. Demo production/multimedia packages using our original music. Contact Mr. Joseph Harrison, Post Office Box 2742, Prairie View, Texas 77446 E-mail: Joseph_Harrison@pvamu.edu Website: www.GrooveDepot.com

Hermit Arts A not for profit organization committed to producing new performance work co-founded by playwright, performer, director, and educator, Idris Goodman. Contact Mr. Idris Goodwin, Hermit Arts, 1721 West Huron, Apartment 2f, Chicago, Illinois 60622 E-mail: Idris@hermitsite.com Website: www.Idrisgoodwin.com

Hi-Tech Media Corp Having written and directed several screenplays, the company is currently involved in the promotion of their first full feature film release "The Evolution of Honey Girl. Ralph Johnson, President, Hi-Tech Media Corp., RR11, Box 11005, Stroudsburg, Pennsylvania 18360 E-mail: pj@htechmedia.com Website: www.htechmedia.com

Byron Hurt   An Award-winning documentary filmmaker and published writer. His film Hip-Hop: Beyond Beats and Rhymes was selected to appear in more than 50 film festivals worldwide and the Chicago Tribune named it "one of the best documentary films in 2007." Contact Mr. Byron Hurt, Akila Worksongs, Post Office Box 250553, Brooklyn, New York 11225 E-mail: lisadurden@bhurt.com Website: www.bhurt.com

I'm Ready Productions, Inc.   Professional touring production company. Contact Mr. Gary Guidry, Producer, I'm Ready Productions, Post Office Box 10254, Houston, Texas 77206 E-mail: info@imreadyproductions.com Website: www.imreadyproductions.com

Jamar F. FilmWorks   Multimedia company that is parent to FilmTrack Recordings, and The Entertainment Source (TES). Contact J.J.E.F., Post Office Box 2170, Atlanta, Georgia 30301 Phone: (678) 318-3607 E-mail: info@jjefholdings.com Website: www.jjefholdings.com

Rodney Jenkins   Musician, songwriter, producer, and savvy businessman, Dubbed "Hitman" by the music industry, Rodney is one of the most sought after pop, R&B and Gospel music producers in the industry. Grammy (s) Award winner, he has written, produced and co-wrote songs for such artists as N'Sync, Backstreet Boys, Destiny Child, to name a few. Rodney Jenkins, Dark Child, Inc. E-mail: info@darkchild.com Website: www.darkchild.com

Jacquie Jones   An award-winning writer, director and producer of documentary films, Jacquie is also Executive Director of the National Black Programming Consortium (NBPC). Jacquie Jones, NBPC, 68 East 131st Street, 7th Floor, Harlem, New York 10037 Phone: (212) 234-8200 Fax: (212) 234-7032 E-mail: jacquie@nbpc.tv Website: www.nbpc.tv

Ty Granderson Jones   Owns Creole Celina Films, and is currently in pursuit of producing several of his original screenplays including The Cool and Creepy (a finalist in the Sundance Feature Film Program), and the Pilot Presentation/Short of his edgy character study, Napoleonic. Ty G. Jones, Creative Quest, Inc./Creole Celina Films, 8306 Wilshire Boulevard., Suite 432, Beverly Hills, California 90211 Phone: (323) 960-1035 E-mail: tygrandjones@aol.com

Just Me Productions, Inc.   A company whose interest is in theater and film. JMPI produced the award winning short film "A Song for Jade." Contact Ms. Shari Lynn, Just Me Productions, Inc., 3748 Kinnear Avenue, Indianapolis, Indiana 46218 Phone: (317) 509-2210 E-mail: justmeproduction@aol.com

Darryl D. Lassiter   Composer, Writer, Producer-Director/Filmmaker. Darryl D'Wayne Lassiter, Post Office Box 50374, Atlanta, Georgia 30302 Phone: (770) 732-0484 Fax: (770) 819-9153 E-mail: darryl@ddlentertainment.net Website: www.ddlentertainment.net

Spike Lee   Film and movie producer. Spike Lee, Forty Acres & A Mule Filworks, Inc., 124 Dekalb Avenue, Brooklyn, New York 11217 Phone: (718) 624-3703 Fax: (718) 624-2008

L O H Productions   Modern music jingles and music production company. Founder, Michelle Hicks. L O H Productions, 420 Polk Avenue, Box 3, Cape Canaveral, Florida 32920 Phone: (321) 205-6555 E-mail: mhicks@lohproductions.com Website: www.lohproductions.com

Midastouch Productions International   Global production company specializing in total film & video production, project packaging, budgeting & marketing of documentaries, features, shorts, commercials & music videos. Credits include: Resurrection: From New York to New Zealand (2004 NZ documentary) and video projects in Paris (France - 1997 & 2005), Fiji Islands (2002), Barcelona (Spain - 2005) and Tokyo (Japan - 2005). Michael Deet, Executive Producer, Midastouch Productions International, 21604 Dumetz Road, Woodland Hills, California 91364 Phone: (818) 674-6490 E-mail: **midastouchintl@yahoo.com**

MoBetta Films Kevin Craig West is director, producer and professional union actor working in film, television, radio and stage. "Let's make a film," were the only words needed for his company, MoBetta Films, to spring into existence. Project Mo(u)rning, the inaugural project from MoBetta Films, was nominated one of the top five submissions to the San Francisco Black Independent Film Festival. Selected by IFP Rough Cut Lab, Lake Placid Film Forum and Urbanworld VIBE Film Festival is The Assassin, where Kevin served as an Actor, Cinematographer and Producer. Kevin is a member of The Barrow Group in New York City, Chair member of Upstate Independents and in addition to being a Voice Acting Teacher and Producer for Voice Coaches he also works as a Teacher/Artist with Symphony Space. Contact Mr. Kevin Craig Wests, MoBetta Films, Post Office Box 484, Troy, New York 12181 E-mail: **contact@kevincraigwest.com** Website: **www.kevincraigwest.com**

Multi-Provision Music, Inc. Gospel music recording company. International distribution through Infinity/Central South Distribution, Inc. Artist: Kenneth Wilson Chorale CD Project - "Lifestyles of Worship." Multi-Provision Music, Inc., Post Office Box 363, St. Clair, Michigan 48079 Phone: (810) 326 1609 E-mail: **multiprovisionmusic@yahoo.com**

National Association of Black Female Executives in Music & Entertainment, Inc. A 501 (c) (6) nonprofit professional organization led by volunteer entertainment executives, NABFEME was launched in February 1999 with a mission to raise the profile and elevate the awareness of Black women in music and entertainment. The organization's COO is Elektra Entertainment Vice President, Michelle Madison.   Contact NABFEME, Offices of Padell Nadell Fine Weinberger, 59 Maiden Lane, 27th Floor, New York, New York 10038 Phone: (212) 424-9568 E-mail: **johnnie_walker1@msn.com** Website: **www.nabfeme.org**

The National Black Programming Consortium   NBPC is committed to the presentation, funding, promotion, distribution and preservation of positive images of African Americans and the African Diaspora. NBPC accepts proposals for the production, post-production, distribution or acquisition phase of programs suitable for national public television broadcasts. Jacquie Jones, Contact NBPC, 68 East 131st Street, 7th Floor, Harlem, New York 10037 Phone: (212) 234-8200 Fax: (212) 234-7032 E-mail: **info@nbpc.tv** Website: **www.nbpc.tv**

Emma E. Pullen Writer/producer/director. Winner of the US International Film and Video Festival's "Certificate for Creative Excellence" for "Documentary, Current Events, Special Events", 1999. In theater, she was writer/producer/director on "Women Of The Bible," a play with Reverend Della Reese-Lett, 2000. She is associate producer of "Colors Straight Up" which was nominated for an Oscar for "Best Documentary Feature" in 1998. Emma E. Pullen, 1339 North Odgen Drive, Los Angeles, California 90046 E-mail: **eepblackseeds@sbcglobal.net**

Pemon Rami Since the 1960's, Pemon Rami has been involved in the development of television production, films, music concerts, documentaries, plays, and multimedia designs for theatres and medical institutions across the country. He co-founded, Mixed Media Productions in 1987, which produced film projects. He also served as Managing/Artistic Director for the Phoenix Black Theatre Troupe. He produced concerts in Los Angeles at the Marla Gibbs Crossroads Theatre featuring: Nancy Wilson, The Winans, Stevie Wonder and others. A former casting director, Rami provided talent for the highly acclaimed feature films and television movies; "Blues Brothers", Mahogany", " Cooley High", "Welcome to Success", "The Spook Who Sat By The Door", "One In A Million", and "Dummy" He has directed plays and over thirty theatrical productions nationally, including "Madame Lily" starring Gladys Knight and Dorian Harewood. Pemon Rami, CTO, Masequa Myers & Associates, 6100 South Dorchester Avenue, 1 West, Chicago, Illinois 60637 E-mail: pemon@sbcglobal.net Website: www.masequa.com

Red Wall Productions We are filmmakers. We write, direct and produce, high-quality, low-cost, digital, multimedia stories. Rosalyn Coleman Williams and Craig T. Williams, CEOs. Red Wall Productions, 400 West 43rd Street, New York, New York 10036 Phone: (646) 374-8403 E-mail: info@redwallproductions.com Website: www.redwallproductions.com

Gregory J. Reed, Esq. Author, agent, entertainment attorney, and play producer, Reed represents sports figures, entertainers, firms, and numerous persons from TV to Broadway, including Anita Baker, Wynston Marsalis, The Winans, and First Black Miss USA, Carole Gist and many other artists. He has produced such plays as the Pulitzer Prize winning production, *A Soldier's Play*, which was developed into a screenplay by Columbia Pictures as *A Soldier's Story*, awarded an Oscar. He has produced and represented the following Broadway plays: "Ain't Misbehavin"; "For Colored Girls Who Have Considered Suicide When the Rainbow Is Enuf"; "What The Wine Sellers Buy"; "The Wiz"; "Your Arms Too Short To Box With God"; and Rosa Parks "More Than a Bus Story." He also staged the largest tour entertainment tribute in the U.S. in honor of Dr. Martin Luther King Jr., with Emmy winner Al Eaton in *We Are The Dream*. Gregory J. Reed & Associates, 1201 Bagley, Detroit, Michigan 48226 Phone: (313) 961-3580 Fax: (313) 961-3582 E-mail: gjrassoc@aol.com Website: www.gjreedlaw.com

Simmons Lathan Media Group Russell Simmons and Stan Lathan, the production team responsible for the Tony-award winning Def Poetry Jam on Broadway, the Peabody-award winning Def Poetry series on HBO and the blockbuster Def Comedy Jam franchise, are looking for up and coming urban filmmakers to submit their completed work for consideration for acquisitions, distribution and our New Def Filmmakers Program. Contact Ms. Alexis Frank, Attn: Film Submission, Simmons Lathan Media Group, 521 Fifth Avenue, 28th Floor, New York, New York 10175 E-mail: alexis@simmonslathan.com Website: simmonslathan.com

SpokenVizions Entertainment Group, L.L.C. Floyd Boykin Jr., producer. Also publishes SpokenVizions Magazine. Contact SVEG, Post Office Box 373, Florissant, Missouri 63032 Phone: (314) 517-8764 E-mail: info@spokenvizions.com Website: www.spokenvizions.com

Third Coast Productions Production Services. Melvin Joseph Claverie, Producer/Director. Third Coast Productions, Post Office Box 51072, New Orleans, Louisiana 70150 Phone: (504) 915-1731 E-mail: themelman99@yahoo.com

C. Sade Turnipseed Professor and executive producer of: educational and literary concept developments for film, television, radio, live stage events and festivals. She is an international consultant for film festivals and literary performances. Her current projects include: FESPACO: Paul Robeson Award Initiative, Burkina Faso, Africa; FESPACO 2005 The Best of the Best, the documentary; Kissin' My Dust: A Collection of Love Notes; No More Space for Anything, But LOVE!; and, Saving Our Babies Anthology: By Writers of the 21st Century. C. Sade Turnipseed, Red Clay Publishing, Post Office Box 4221, Greenville, Mississippi 38704 Phone: (662) 773-2048 E-mail: **khafre@peoplepc.com** Website: **www.khafre.us**

Narada Michael Walden Musician, songwriter, composer and producer. Top 10 hits written and/or produced by this very talented musician and composer include *Songbird* (Kenny G); *Baby Come To Me* (Regina Belle); *Kisses In the Moonlight* (from the George Benson album, *While The City Sleeps*). Narada Michael Walden, Tarpan Studios, 1925 East Francisco Boulevard, Suite L, San Rafael, California 94901 Phone: (415) 485-1999 Fax: (415) 459-3234 E-mail: **inquiries@tarpanstudios.com** Website: **www.tarpanstudios.com**

Television & Radio

Magdalene Breaux Television host, producer and author Breaux's publishing services include technical writing, book production consulting for independent authors and TV production and editing. Magdalene Breaux, Post Office Box 67, Fairburn, Georgia 30213 Phone: (770) 842-4792 E-mail: **magbreaux@mindspring.com** Website: **www.familycurse.com**

Denver Entertainment Group A coalition of 15 companies from five countries - including the United Kingdom, Singapore and Japan - that includes all segments of media and entertainment production. DEG is linked directly to actors, musicians, composers, producers and business people - and even a chef host to the stars. Art Thomas, a co-founder of DEG. He is also vice president of program development and acquisitions for CoLours TV. He has a master's degree in International Marketing from Notre Dame de Namur University, International Certification from Metro State College. SoNew Productions, (sonew.tv) invited Thomas to the 2004 Cannes Film Festival to promote their documentary film, Earthlings. Afterwards he went to England to work on his first international collaboration wich ACF Productions, entitled, "The Passerby". Contact Mr. Art Thomas, Denver Entertainment Group c/o Main Man Films, LLC Post Office Box 3773 Englewood, Colorado 80155 Phone: (303) 331-0339 Fax: (303) 439-0315 E-mail: **info@mainmanfilms.com** Website: **www.mainmanfilms.com**

Future Network Productions Television, video and web design services. Darlene Lewis, FN, 400 West 153rd Street, Suite 2C, New York, New York 10031 Phone: (646) 548-9501 E-mail: **darlenereneelewis@yahoo.com** Website: **www.FutureNetworkProductions.com**

The National Black Programming Consortium (NBPC) Accepts proposals for the production, post-production, distribution or acquisition phase of programs suitable for national public television broadcasts. Ms. Jacquie Jones, Executive Director. Mable Haddock, Member and Founding Director. NBPC, 68 East 131st Street, 7th Floor, Harlem, New York 10037 Phone: (212) 234-8200 E-mail: **info@nbpc.tv** Website: **www.nbpc.tv**

Nelson Davis Television Productions (NDTP) Television program production and marketing. Nelson Davis, NDTP, 5800 Sunset Boulevard, Los Angeles, California 90028 Phone: (323) 460-5253 E-mail: info@makingittv.com Website: www.makingittv.com

NiteLite Productions A commerical production company, services include editorial/post production; theatrical/television pictures. Creates both broadcast television spots and theatrical trailers. NiteLite Productions, 10529 Valparaiso Street, Suite 2, Los Angeles, California 90034 Phone: (310) 839-0136 E-mail: harry@nitelite.org Website: www.nitelite.org

Dane Reid Media Media production company headed by childrens author Dane Reid provides voice services, creative advertising solutions, and interactive publishings. Company covers radio production, TV voice over, and childrens books and audiobooks. Mr. Dane Reid, Dane Reid Media, Post Office Box 640055, Atlanta, Georgia 30364 Phone: (404) 822-7107 E-mail: DR@DaneReidMedia.com Website: www.danereidmedia.com

Naomi Roberson Producer, director, and camera operator. Has produced and directed documentaries, award shows, public service announcements, and interviews for local television and the outlying areas. Dr. Naomi Roberson, Post Office Box 557533 Chicago, Illinois 60655 Phone: (773) 573-5805 Fax: (708) 596-0226 E-mail: username:nrshow@comcast.net

Star Planet Television Since 1986, full service television production facility that produces talk shows geared to the African American community. W. L. Lillard is Founder and CEO/Senior Executive Producer. Contact Star Planet Television Network, 8658 South Cottage Grove Avenue, Chicago, Illinois 60643 Phone: (773) 445-7788 Website: www.starplanettv.com

Quest Media Entertainment, Inc. Television production company, specializes in TV programs, commercials, corporate videos, and event production. Bill McCreary. Vice President, Quest Media Entertainment, Inc, 1000 Richmond Terrace, Staten Island, New York, 10301 Phone: (718) 727 3777 E-mail: questmedia@questmedia.net Website: www.questmedia.net

Video

Diasporic Communications A multi-media consulting firm specializing in video production consulting and electronic communications development. Deborah Ray-Sims, Diasporic Communications, 2932 Cinnamon Teal Circle, Elk Grove, California 95757 Phone: (916) 479-1161 E-mail: diasporic@comcast.net

Joseph Harrison Demo production/multimedia packages using our original music. Also a songwriter. Contact Mr. Joseph Harrison, Post Office Box 2742, Prairie View, Texas 77446 E-mail: Joseph_Harrison@pvamu.edu Website: www.GrooveDepot.com

Imaginative Media Concepts Full service multi-media music company specializing in unique and innovative ways to use visual as well as musical mediums. Anthony S. Murray, Creative Consultant, Imaginative Media Concepts, 56 Dobbs Ferry Road, White Plains, New York 10607 Phone: (914) 562-1774 E-mail: amurrayw@aol.com

KDB Productions A cutting edge audio services production founded by air personality and Gospel Light radio talk show host, KD Bowe. Contact KD Bowe, KDB Productions c/o KDYA, Gospel 1190 AM The Light, 3260 Blume Drive, Suite 520, Richmond, California 94806 Phone: (510) 222-4242 Fax: (510) 262-9054 E-mail: **kdbowe@kdbowemorningshow.com** Website: **www.gospel1190.net**

Midastouch Productions International A global production company specializing in total film & video production, project packaging, budgeting and marketing of documentaries, features, shorts, commercial and music videos. Credits include Hip-Hop Resurrection: From New York to New Zealand (2004 NZ documentary). Michael Deet, Executive Producer, Midustouch Productions International, 7957 Nita Avenue, West Hills, California 91304 Phone: (818) 888-6798 Fax: (818) 674-6490 E-mail: **midastouchintl@yahoo.com**

NiteLite Productions Commerical production company; broadcast television spots and theatrical trailers; editorial/post/production, promos, music videos and advertising commercials; theatrical/television pictures. Contact NiteLite Productions, 10529 Valparaiso Street, Suite 2, Los Angeles, California 90034 Phone: (310) 839-0707 Fax: (310) 839-0149 E-mail: **harry@nitelite.org** Website: **www.nitelite.org**

Ron Clowney Design Design company offers both traditional art services in addition to computer graphics design work in the areas of print and animation. We also design and construct websites. Mr. Ron Clowney Design, 5513 Adode Falls Road, Unit 10, San Diego, California 92120 Phone: (619) 501-5740

Leo D. Sullivan Animator, writer, publisher, director and producer of videos and books that present positive images for African American children and adults. Leo D. Sullivan, Vignette Multimedia, 1800 South Robertson Boulevard, #286, Los Angeles, California 90035 Phone: (323) 939-4174 E-mail: **lsullassoc@aol.com** Website: **www.afrokids.com**

Public Relations

Advanced Consulting & Marketing Services Company offers support to authors, artist, small businesses, women and nonprofit to establish or develop their businesses or personal life toward success. Contact Ms. Pamela Hudson, Advanced Consulting & Marketing Services, 20110 Trinity, Detroit, Michigan 48219 Phone: (313) 534-6343 Fax: (313) 345-9534 E-mail: pam@advancewithpam.org Website: www.advanwithpam.org

Black Gospel Promo, Inc. Worldwide leader in E-Marketing to the Gospel Consumer Market and African American Church. Veda Brown is President and has over twenty years experience in the business and entertainment industry. A graduate of Moore College of Art and Design with a Bachelor of Fine Arts, Ms. Brown has extensive additional training in Business Development, Music Management, and Project Management from the University of Arts and Temple University. She has worked for CGI Records, Vickie Winans, and Bajada Records and consulted for many Gospel Record labels and artist. Veda Brown, Black Gospel Promo, Inc., 45 East Cityline Avenue, #303, Bala Cynwyd, Pennsylvania 19004 Phone: (215) 883-1000 Fax: (267) 257-8136 E-mail: info@blackgospelpromo.com Website: www.blackgospelpromo.com

Crystal C. Brown CEO and President of Crystal Clear Communications, an award winning public relations and marketing firm in Houston, Texas. Currently we work with local and national clients in the following industries: Oil & Gas, Retail, Legal, Religion, and Entertainment. Provide services to several Fortune 100 companies and have been instrumental in the planning and execution of some the largest products launches in the U.S. Ms. Crystal C. Brown-Tatum, 2470 S. Dairy Ashford #252, Houston, Texas 77077 Phone: (832) 867-4660 Fax: (318) 309-0019 E-mail: cbrown5530@aol.com Website: www.crystalcommunicates.net

Capital Entertainment Bil Carpenter is CEO of Capital Entertainment, a small public relations company that has worked extensively with gospel artists such as Vickie Winans, Bishop T.D. Jakes, CeCe Winans, and Donald Lawrence & the Tri-City Singers, among many others. He has worked both as a music journalist and a record label publicist. Contact Mr. Bil Carpenter, Capital Entertainment, 217 Seaton Place North East, Washington, D.C. 20002 Phone: (202) 506 5051 E-mail: carpbil@aol.com Website: www.bilcarpenter.com

The Cherry Group A professional writing and public relations service. Contact The Cherry Group, Post Office Box 614, Jackson, Tennessee 38302 Phone: (731) 422-2524 Fax: (731) 422-2524 E-mail: thecherrygroup1@yahoo.com

Yasmin Coleman Literary publicist and promoter, book reviewer and founder of APOOO Books and BookClub, Coleman has over 20 years of marketing experiences and is a seasoned veteran at marketing, advertising, promotions, and publicity. Contact Yasmin Coleman, APOOO Books, 4426 Pinewood Court, Harrisburg, Pennsylvania 17112 E-mail: apooo4u@yahoo.com Website: www.apooobooks.com

Diasporic Communications The company provides consulting services for public relations campaigns, produces personal and corporate videos, and advises on communications technology services involving web site content management, and technology feasibility studies involving teleconferencing, distance learning and communications equipment procurement. President of Diasporic Communications, Deborah Ray-Sims is a veteran in the communications field where she has served as Television Producer, Writer, and Educator. Deborah Ray-Sims, Diasporic Communications, 2932 Cinnamon Teal Circle, Elk Grove, California 95757 Phone: (916) 479-1161 E-mail: diasporic@comcast.net

Diversity City Media Multicultural marketing, public relations, and retail firm. We produce BlackNews.com, BlackShopping.com, BlackStudents.com, and BlackPr.com, a newswire service which provides press release distribution to the Black media. Contact Diversity City Media, 225 West 3rd Street, Suite #203, Long Beach, California 90802 Phone: (866) 910-6277 E-mail: sales@diversitycity.com Website: www.blackpr.com

Down to Earth Public Relations Company is committed to delivering top media exposure for publishers, author's and motivational speaker's. Down to Earth Public Relations, c/o Earth O. Jallow, Post Office Box 83442, Columbus, Ohio 43203 Phone: (614) 284-7933 Fax: (614) 372-1755 E-mail: dwn2earthpr@juno.com

Yvette Hayward President of Y. Hayward Inc, a public relations company that has been a powerful resource in the literary field for over seven (7) years. She has represented well-known authors such as, Essence Best-selling authors, Lolita Files, Victoria Christopher Murray, five-time NAACP award recipient, David E. Talbert, New York Times Best-selling author, Wendy Williams, and LaJoyce Brookshire, author of Soul Food. Yvette is also the co-chair of Flowers & Hayward Publicity & Entertainment, Inc. F& H Publicity has worked with the preeminent publisher, Simon & Schuster, as well as Culture Plus Books Distributors, the leading distributors of African- American books in the country. Contact Ms. Yvette Hayward, African American Literary Awards Show, Inc., 1325 5th Avenue Suite 5M, New York, New York 10029 E-mail: yvette@literaryawardshow.com Website: www.literaryawardshow.com

Images & Ideas, Inc. PR firm. Karen Dumas is president. She is a columnist for The Michigan Chronicle and African-American Family Magazine, and also host of the radio show Sunday Afternoon heard weekly on 107.5 WGPR-FM. A respected local radio & television personality she formerly served as Director of Culture, City of Detroit, which included the Detroit Film Office and Eastern Market, and as Director of Community Relations for Mayor Kwame M. Kilpatrick. Karen Dumas, Images & Ideas, Inc., Post Office Box 14724, Detroit, Michigan 48214 Phone: (866) 330-4585 Fax: (313) 824-6987 karendumas2@aol.com Website: www.KarenDumas.com

Jusbee Jones Author, President and CEO of her own sports entertainment publicity firm, Jusbee Jones has worked with professional athletes for over fifteen years in the capacity of sports public relations and marketing. She also serves on the Board of Directors for several of her clients charitable organizations. Contributes to a monthly sports entertainment column. Contact Ms. Jusbee Jones, 15030 Ventura Boulevard, Suite 525, Sherman Oaks, California 91403 E-mail: JusbeeJones@aol.com Website: www.confessionsofthe12thman.com

Kensey & Kensey Communications A public relations firm with a specialty in media relations and event marketing in the arts & entertainment arena for both non-profit and for-profit organizations and corporations. Celebrating its 20th anniversary in 2010, founder/CEO Barbara Kensey has worked with numerous national figures. In addition, she is a publisher and writer who has written about numerous destinations for travel publications, including ebonyjet.com among numerous other types of writing. A charter member and former executive vice president of the Black Public Relations Society, she is a recipient of the Merit Award from the Publicity Club of Chicago and a Phenomenal Woman Award from Today's Black Woman Expo. Barbara Kensey, Kensey & Kensey Communications, 5212 South Dorchester Avenue, Chicago, Illinois 60615 Phone: (773) 288-8776 Fax: (312) 454-7454 E-mail: Kenseycomm@sbcglobal.net

Marc Curtis Little Public relations counselor coordinates publicity for authors, especially in Florida and Georgia. Mr. Little has been a public relations counselor since 1984 and has worked with Benilde Little, author of Good Hair, The Itch and Acting Out, all with Simon and Shuster. Contact Mr. Marc Curtis Little, 8070 Wakefield Avenue, Jacksonville, Florida 32208 Phone: (904) 924-0303 E-mail: marc@marcpr.com Website: www.marcpr.com

Mays Media Creates marketing materials including press releases, and e-mail flyers. Shetia Mays, Mays Media, 5456 Peachtree Industrial Boulevard, #457, Atlanta, Georgia 30341 Phone: (770) 256-8710 E-mail: smmays@maysmediainc.com Website: www.maysmediainc.com

Denise Meridith BS from Cornell University and a MPA from the University of Southern California, Ms. Meridith was the first female professional hired by the US Bureau of Land Management. She retired early in 2002 and has her own public and community relations firm. Since 1998, she has been a regular columnist with the Phoenix Business Journal and was a finalist in the 2004 National Association of Black Journalists' excellence awards. Contact Denise Meridith Consultants Inc, 5515 North 7th Street, Suite 5, Phoenix, Arizona 85014 Phone: (602) 763-9900 Fax: (602) 222-9072 E-mail: denisemeridithconsultants@cox.net

Ministry Marketing Solutions Inc. A Christian marketing firm. Provides target marketing to the African American Christian community. Markets inspiring promotions, products, people and publications. Pam Perry, PR coach, veteran publicist. Publisher's weekly called Pam Perry the "Christian Book PR Guru." Detroit Free Press called her a "Marketing Genius." Perry has placed clients on media such as TBN, Daystar, Harvest Show, The Tom Joyner Morning Show, Essence, Ebony and Black Enterprise Magazines, and countless others. She is also the author of Synergy Energy: How to Use the Power of Partnerships to Market Your Book, Grow Your Business and Brand Your Ministry. Contact Ms. Pam Perry, Ministry Marketing Solutions Inc., 33011 Tall Oaks, Farmington Hills, Michigan 48336 Phone: (248) 426-2300 E-mail: pamperry@ministrymarketingsolutions.com Website: ministrymarketingsolutions.com

Morgan Communications Full-service communications company. Founder, Shanté Morgan, has worked for over a decade as a reporter, writing for both newspapers and magazines, covering everything from Hollywood trends to presidential campaigns. She freelances as a copyeditor and proofreader and has worked as a college instructor teaching journalism. Contact Shanté Morgan, Morgan Communications, 1710 North Moorpark Road #163, Thousand Oaks, California 91360 Phone: (818) 677-9890 Fax: (818) 677-4909 E-mail: ShanteMorgan@aol.com

Multicultural Marketing Resources, Inc. (MMR) Established in 1994, is a public relations and marketing company representing minority and women owned businesses and specializing in promoting multicultural marketing & diversity news. We represent the nation's leading experts in marketing to Hispanic, Asian American, African American, and other multicultural consumers. President, Editor and Publisher, Ms. Lisa Skriloff. Multicultural Marketing Resources, 101 5th Avenue Suite 10B, New York, New York 10003 Phone: (212) 242-3351 Fax: (212) 691-5969 E-mail: lisa@multicultural.com Website: www.multicultural.com

National Black News Service A weekly compilation of the leading black news and information developments. The digital news service is distributed to over 1,000 newspapers and 40,000 individual subscribers.by President and CEO Robert S. Taylor currently Editor of the online digital newspaper. He also edits the Black History Journal, a free weekly email-distributed journal detailing with the most important Black historical events of each week. Taylor was born and raised in South Carolina. He received his BA from Howard University in Washington, D.C., and his Masters Degree in Mass Communications from Columbia University in New York City. Robert Taylor, National Black News Services, Taylor Media Services, 1517 T Street, South East, Washington, D.C. 20020 Phone: (202) 657-8872 E-mail: taylormediaservices@yahoo.com Website: www.freewebs.com/blacknewsjournal

PA Public Relations Company A public relations company headed by Mr. Phil Andrews, President & CEO. Andrews was the Vice President and Marketing Director of Haircut Hut franchise for over a decade. His new ebook is The Day I Decided to Become CEO. He is listed in Who's Who in Black America and International Who's Who. Also featured in a book by Mr. Robert H. Adams entitled, 15 Years of Minority Business Development. In 1995, he was presented the Nassau Council of Chamber of Commerce/Roosevelt Chamber of Commerce Small Business Person of the Year Award. Contact Mr. Phil Andrews, PA Public Relations Company, 158-13 72nd Avenue, Suite 5B, Fresh Meadows, New York 11365 Phone: (718) 380-2062 E-mail: phil.andrews@papublicrelations.com Website: www.papublicrelations.com

PowerFlow Media We offer cutting edge public relations and complete marketing solutions for emerging and established businesses. Events featuring PowerFlow Media clients, Descending Dove Productions (The Last Adam), author and journalist, Farai Chideya (NPR's News & Notes with Ed Gordon, PopandPolitics.com), ArtsTalk, Call To Womanhood, Heart & Soul Editorial Director Yanick Rice Lamb (Rise and Fly: Tall Tales and Mostly True Rules of Bid Whist). Ms. Joyce E. Davis, PowerFlow Media, 5157 Seashell Lane, Atlanta, Georgia 30349 Phone: (404) 209-9021 E-mail: jdavis@powerflowmedia.com Website: www.powerflowmedia.com

Right Hand Concepts Founder, Ms. Vonetta Booker-Brown has over eight years of experience as an administrative assistant, writer, editor, web designer and graphic artist. Her client roster includes CB Commercial, UBS Warburg, Pitney Bowes, Southern Connecticut State University, Weekly Reader Corporation, Essence Communications, Daymon Worldwide and PH Factor Productions. She is also an accomplished journalist and writer who has contributed to various publications including Stamford Advocate, Fairfield County Weekly, New Haven Register, MediaBistro.com, HealthQuest, Essence, Vibe, Honey and XXL. Vonetta Booker-Brown, Right Hand Concepts, 2020 Pennsylvania Avenue, North West, #341, Washington, DC 20006 E-mail: chiefelement@gmail.com Website: www.righthandconcepts.com

Shaw Biz Group, Inc. (Formerly Shaw Literary Group) Julia Shaw, President who has been a part of the literary arena for over fifteen years, involved in various roles relating to the sales, marketing, and publicity of African American books and authors. In addition to her consulting business, Shaw recently served as the Director of Sales & Marketing for Harlin Jacque Publications, a publisher of children's books and educational products and services (lindamichellebaron.com) and consulting publicist for Kimani Press a division of an international publishing company Harlequin Enterprises, Ltd. (kimanipress.com) launching the Young adult Imprint Kimani TRU (KimaniTRU.com). She is currently a consultant for The Center of Black Literature at Medgar Evers College (blacklitcenter.org) and as the Executive Director for the Cambria Heights Development Corporation (chdcqueens.org). Contact Shaw Business Group, LLC, 1204 Washington Avenue, Suite 401, Saint Louis, Missouri 63103 Phone: (917) 501-6780 E-mail: **info@shawbizgroupinc.com** Website: **www.shawbizgroupinc.com**

Terrie Williams Agency Founded by CEO Terrie Williams in 1988; management entertainment company and consultant: executive coaching, marketing and communications advice, public relations, individual and corporate counseling. Contact Ms. Terrie Williams Agency, 382 Central Park West, Suite 7R, New York, New York 10023 Phone: (212) 316-0305 Fax: (212) 749-8867 E-mail: **tmwms@terriewilliams.com** Website: **www.terriewilliams.com**

TimeZone International Vivian Scott Chew is the Founder and Principal of TimeZone International, a U.S. based international marketing and promotion company focusing on the global careers of urban artists. Vivian began her career as the first African American female membership representative for ASCAP (American Society of Composers, Authors and Publishers) and went on to hold senior positions at Polygram, and Epic/Sony Records. It was during her tenure at Sony that she introduced the world to the dancehall phenomenon by producing platinum albums and back to back Grammy's for Shabba Ranks. TimeZone has provided international marketing and promotion, touring and licensing/distribution opportunities for such artists as Diddy, Jay-Z, India.Arie, Jill Scott, Lil' Wayne, Toni Braxton and Brian McKnight. Contact Mrs. Vivian Chew, Chew Entertainment, 460 Queen Anne Road @1B, Teaneck, NJ 07666 Phone: (201) 928-1696 E-mail: **info@chewentertainment.com** Website: **www.chewentertainment.com**

Ed Bullins
Author * Playwright
Lecturer * Instructor

Ed Bullins is currently the Distinguished Artist-in-Residence at Northeastern University in Boston. He earned his MFA in playwriting from San Francisco State University in California. His teaching interests include playwriting, scriptwriting, Afro-American literature, Black History, acting, and directing, and African-American Cultural expressions, i.e. music, film, thought.

He is author of seven books, including <u>Five Plays By Ed Bullins</u>, <u>The Duplex</u>, <u>The Hungered One</u>, <u>Four Dynamite Plays</u>, <u>The Theme is Blackness</u>, and <u>The Reluctant Rapist</u>. His latest book is ED BULLINS: 12 Plays and Selected Writings (U of Michigan Press, 2006). He wrote and produced for the theatre several commission works, including *Rainin' Down Stairs* for the 1992 San Francisco Theatre Artaud, and has been editor for a number of theatre magazines and publications. He was producer of *Circles of Times,* Boston's Lyric Theatre in August 2003.

Among his awards and grants is three Obie Awards, four Rockefeller Foundation Playwriting Grants, two Guffenheim Playwriting Fellowships, an NEA Playwriting Grant, the AUDELCO Award, the New York Drama Critics Circle Award for Best American Play of 1974 -75, the National Black Theatre Festival Living Legend Award, and the OTTO Award in 2004.

Mr. Bullins is an active member of the ACT Roxbury Consortium. His professional affiliations include PEN American Center, The Dramatists Guild, WGAe, and the Modern Language Association.

Publishers

Africa World Press and The Red Sea Press Sister presses" based in Lawrenceville, New Jersey, and dedicated to the publication and distribution of books on the African World and fulfilling a great demand for "non-mainstream" academic texts, poetry, short stories and children's books. Africa World Press Inc., & The Red Sea Press Inc., 541 West Ingham Avenue, Suite B, Trenton, New Jersey 08638 Phone: (609) 695-3200 Fax: (609) 695-6466 E-mail: senaitkassahun@verizon.net Website: africanworld.com

African American Images Publishes and distributes books of an Africentric nature that promote self-esteem, collective values, liberation, and skill development. We have one of the largest black-owned bookstores in the country, with over 10,000 square feet of space and over 4,000 titles. Owner, President and Publisher, Dr. Jawanza Kunjufu. Contact African American Images, 1909 West 95th Street, Chicago, Illinois 60643 Phone: (312) 445-0322 E-mail: aarcher@africanamericanimages.com Website: www.africanamericanimages.com

Africana Homestead Legacy Publishers We welcome book proposals of scholarly work from all individuals. The work must document and analyze aspects of the lives of people of African descent throughout the diaspora. We have a special interest in these academic disciplines: African Studies; African American Studies; African Canadian Studies; Art; Anthropology; Biography; Caribbean and Latin American Studies; Communications; Conflict Studies; Culture; Literature and Fiction; Language; Law; Medicine; Music; Science; Sociology; Women's Studies. Will re-publish titles that are out of print. Africana Homestead Legacy Publishers, Post Office Box 2957, Cherry Hill, New Jersey 08034 Phone: (856) 662-9858 Fax: (856) 662-9516 E-mail: editors@ahlpub.com Website: www.ahlpub.com

Amani Publishing Publisher. Writing contests. Founder and Publisher, author, Ms. Barbara Joe-Williams. Amani Publishing, Post Office Box 12045, Tallahassee, Florida 32317 Phone: (850) 264-3341 E-mail: Amanipublishing@aol.com Website: www.amanipublishing.net

Amber Communications Group, Inc. Publisher is the recipient of several awards, including: the Chicago Black Book Fair and Conference Independent Publisher/Press Award, the 2003 BlackBoard Bestseller's African-American Publisher of the Year Award, the 2003 American Library Association Reluctant Reader Award, the 2004 Cape Verdean News Millennium Award for Excellence in Book Publishing and the 2004 1st YOUnity and Disilgold Soul Magazine. The Company continues to expand with Amber Books, its self-help imprint, Busta Books, its celebrity bio imprint; Colossus Books, the imprint for international personalities and topics; Ambrosia Books, the imprint for literature, fiction and non-fiction; Amber Books for in-general specialty books, and Amber/Wiley Books, its co-publishing/imprint with John Wiley & Sons, Inc. Tony Rose, Publisher. Amber Communications Group, Inc., 1334 East Chandler Boulevard, Suite 5-D67, Phoenix, Arizona 85048 Phone: (480) 460-1660 Fax: (480) 283-0991 amberbk@aol.com Website: www.amberbooks.com

August Press The company was founded in October 1992 in New Jersey by Wayne Dawkins, president and chief executive officer. August Press has published seven books, all trade paperbacks. Manuscript submissions must include a stamped, self-addressed envelope and a cover letter. Please allow six to eight weeks for a reply.   Contact Mr. Wayne Dawkins, August Press, Post Office Box 6693, Newport News, Virginia 23606 Phone: (757) 727-5437 wdawkins4bj@aol.com Website: www.augustpress.net

Better Day Publishing Founded by Naresha S. Perry. Better Day has provided quality child book publishing and illustration services in the Houston Metro area since April 2001. Also accepts finished adult and fictions manuscripts from many genres including science fiction, mystery, and adventure. Contact Ms. Naresha S. Perry, Better Day Publishing Company, 11152 Westheimer, #341, Houston, Texas 77042 Phone: (713) 548-4048 E-mail: contact@betterdaypublishing.com Website: www.betterdaypublishing.com

Black Classic Press Devoted to publishing obscure and significant works by and about people of African descent. We specialize in republishing works that are out of print. W. Paul Coates, Founder. Contact Editor, Black Classic Press, Post Office Box 13414, Baltimore, Maryland 21203 Phone: (410) 358-0980 Fax: (410) 358-0987 E-mail: bcp@charm.net Website: www.blackclassicbooks.com

Blind Beggar Press A publishing company owned and operated by People of Colour, and based in the Bronx in New York City, New York. It was founded in 1977 by Gary Johnson and C.D. Grant, both writers and poets who saw the need to create another, unique vehicle for emerging and established writers/artists of color. We have approximately 25 books in print. Blind Beggar Press, Post Office Box 437, Bronx, New York 10467 Phone: (914) 282-5747 E-mail: blindbeggar1@juno.com Website: www.blindbeggarpress.org

Books for Black Children, Inc. African American children's book publisher. Contact Books For Black Children, Inc., Post Office Box 13261, Reading, Pennsylvania 19612 E-mail: bbc-inc@att.net

Clarity Press, Inc. Publishes books on the human dimension of current issues; human rights and social justice. Send query letter first, with c.v., table of contents and synopsis. Contact Editor, Clarity Press, Inc., Suite 469, 3277 Roswell Road, North East, Atlanta, Georgia 30305 Phone: (877) 613-1495 Fax: (877) 613-7868 E-mail: clarity@islandnet.com Website: www.claritypress.com

Divine Truth Press Publisher of books and ebooks in a keeping-it-real Christian style. D. S. White Publisher. Contact D. S. White, Divine Truth Press, Post Office Box 145, Whitehall, Pennsylvania 18052 Fax: (530) 504-7094 E-mail: info@divinetruthpress.com Website: www.divinetruthpress.com

Disilgold Small Bronx press founded in 2001. Publishes new books and anthologies via various genres. Contact Ms. Heather Covington, Publisher, Disilgold, Post Office Box 652, Baychester Station, Bronx, New York 10469 Phone: (718) 547-0499 E-mail: desilgold@aol.com Website: www.disilgold.com

Dreams Publishing company Publishes books that promote faith, kindness, honesty, loyalty, and virtue that is well-written, persuasive, and interesting. We want authors that have a different kind of story to tell. We want Authors who want to be published in electronic and print media and who are willing to promote their books worldwide. Please inquire before sending a manuscript. Teresa Rhodes, Acquisition Director. Dreams Publishing Company, Post Office Box 4731, Rocky Mount, North Carolina 27803 Phone: (877) 209-5200 E-mail: Books@DreamsPublishing.com Website: www.dreamspublishing.com

Eschar Publications African-American book publisher. Contact Ms. Vivian Owens, Eschar Publications, Post Office Box 1194, Mount Dora, Florida 32756 Phone: (352) 455-3554 E-mail: escharpub@earthlink.net

First Scribe Books An independently-owned publishing company committed to bringing quality writings expressing the vast dimensions of the Black experience to the world. Contact Publisher, First Scribe Books, Post Office Box 62, Fort Lauderdale, Florida 33302 E-mail: Firstscribebooks@yahoo.com Website: www.firstscribebooks.com

4465 PReSS A new and popular, online publisher of multicultural fiction and non-fiction book titles. The focus of 4465 PReSS is to deploy and achieve the singular mission of multicentric-representational, publishing excellence. 4465 PReSS is a wholly owned subsidiary of barrendau LLC and 4465 Media. Contact Ms. Deidra Scott Wilson, Associate Publisher, 4465 PReSS, 610-A East Battlefield Road, Suite 279, Springfield, Missouri 65807 Phone: (866) 842-1042 Fax: (775) 257-1286 E-mail: press4465@yahoo.com Website: www.4465press.com

Genesis Press, Inc. America's largetst privately owned African-American book publisher. Founded in Columbus, Mississippi in 1993 by attorneys Wilbur and Dorothy Colom. We do accept unagented material and multiple submissions. When submitting, include a query letter, a 2-3 page (and no longer) synopsis of the entire manuscript, and the first three chapters. Acquisitions Editor, Genesis Press, Inc., Post Office Box 101, Columbus, Mississippi 39701 Phone: (662) 329-9927 Fax: (662) 329-9399 E-mail: customerservice@genesis-press.com Website: www.genesis-press.com

GrantHouse Publishers George C. Grant, Owner/CEO. Publishes and reprints original paperback and hard cover book, manuscript editing, cover design, etc. George C. Grant, PhD, GrantHouse Publishers, 2101 Green Leaf Trail, Jonesboro, Arkansas, 72401 Phone: (901) 218-3135 E-mail: granthousepub@aol.com Website: www.granthousepublishers.com

Greene Bark Press Inc. A children's book publishing company and distributor of educational toys and games. Mr. Thomas J. Greene, Publisher. Contact Greene Bark Press Inc, Post Office Box 1108, Bridgeport, Connecticut 06601 Phone: (610) 434-2802 Fax: (610) 434-2803 E-mail: greenebark@aol.com Website: www.greenebarkpress.com

Gumbs & Thomas Publishers, Inc. Specializing in Kwanzaa books, teachers' guides, cards, posters, children's books & travel guides. Gumbs & Thomas Publishers Inc., Post Office Box 381, New York, New York 10039 Phone: (212) 694-0602 E-mail: ragumb@aol.com

Just Us Books Independent publishing company specializing in books and learning materials for children and young people. Wade and Cheryl Willis Hudson, Publishers. Contact Mr. Willie Hudson, Just Us Books, 356 Glenwood Avenue, East Orange, New Jersey 07017 Phone: (973) 672-7701 E-mail: **justusbooks@mindspring.com** Website: **www.justusbooks.com**

Kings Crossing Publishing   Award-winning words by award-winning writers. Award-winning independent publishing company serving the LGBT writing community since 2001. Authors in the past have included award-winners, Penny Mickelbury and Robin G. White. Anthologized works have included Ami Mattison and Alix Olson to name a few.   The company publishes, fiction, non-fiction, self-help, poetry, and memoir. Manuscripts, partial manuscripts or synopsis may be mailed and should not exceed 50 pages in length.   King Crossing Publishing, Post Office Box 673121, Atlanta, Georgia 30006 Phone: (770) 640-9963 E-mail: **kingscrossingpub@aol.com** Website: **www.kingscrossingpublishing.com**

La Caille Nous Established October, 1995.   La Caille Nous will collaborate with individuals or institutions to publish works that may fall in or out of our specialty Guichard Cadet, La Caille Nous Publishing Company, 328 Flatbush Avenue, Suite 240, Brooklyn, New York 11238 Phone: (212) 726-1293 Fax: (212) 591-6465 E-mail: **inq@lcnpub.com** Website: **www.lcnpub.com**

Leon Jean Publications   Along with its imprint Rocky D Publishing publishes works in the Urban Fiction genre. Contact Leon Jean Publications, Post Office Box 85214, Westland, Michigan 48185 Phone: (734) 722-9219 E-mail: **leonjeanpublications_ljp@yahoo.com** Website: **www.leonjeanpublications.com**

Milligan Books Since its founding in 1990, Milligan Books has skyrocketed to become the fastest-growing Black female-owned publishing company in America. Has published more than 100 Black authors. Founder/Host of The Authors on Tour annual event. Rosie Milligan, founder, publisher. Publisher, Milligan Books, Inc., 1425 West Manchester Avenue, Suite C, Los Angeles, California 90047 Phone: (323) 750-3592 Fax: (323) 750-2886 E-mail: **DrRosie@aol.com** Website: **www.drrosie.com**

Mirror-Gibbs Publications Frank Jones is the CEO/publisher of Mirror-Gibbs Publications, a Black Oakland base small press-publishing house. Contact Mr. Frank A. Jones, Mirror-Gibbs Publication, Post Office Box 6573, Oakland, California 94603 Phone: (510) 409-9571 E-mail: **pinoquit@hotmail.com** Website: **www.gibbsmagazine.com**

Now U No Publishing Company Religious, inspirational and children's book publisher. Also offers copyright assistance, coverditorial design and manuscript editing services. Contact Ms. Tonya Bratton, Now U No Publishing Company, Post Office Box 9501, Cincinnati Ohio 45209 Phone: (513) 226-6450 E-mail: **tonya.bratton@nowuno-enterprises.com** Website: **www.nowunopublishingco.com**

Oasis Publishing Group Founded in 2006 by Oasis, author of Push Comes To Shove. Only publishes three books annually. Oasis Publishing Group, Post Office Box 19101, Cleveland, Ohio 44119 E-mail: **acquisitions@oasisnovels.com** Website: **www.oasisnovels.com**

Prioritybooks Publications Publisher. Also, supports youths and teens as they pursue writing careers. The owner and staff assists potential writers in finding a voice, consultant on book issues and help securing book signing facilities. Founder, Chief Executive Officer, Ms. Rose Jackson-Beavers. Prioritybooks Publication, Post Office Box 2535, Florissant, Missouri 63033 Phone: (314) 741-6789 E-mail: **rosbeav03@yahoo.com** Website: **www.prioritybooks.com**

Red Clay Publishing C. Sade Turnipseed, publisher. Red Clay Publishing, Post Office Box 4221, Greenville, Mississippi 38704 Phone: (662) 773-2048 E-mail: **khafre@peoplepc.com** Website: **www.khafre.us**

Strebor Books African American publishing company founded in 1999. Strebor has published over 60 authors, produced numerous best sellers and has recently become an official imprint of Simon and Schuster. Contact Publisher, Strebor Books International/Simon and Schuster, Post Office Box 6505, Largo, Maryland 20792 Phone: (301) 583-0616 Fax: (301) 583-0003 E-mail: **streborbooks@aol.com** Website: **www.streborbooks.com**

Third World Press Since 1967, the nation's oldest, continuously running Black-owned press that published books in all genres. Haki R. Madhubuti, Publisher, Third World Press, 7822 Dobson Street, Chicago, Illinois 60619 Phone: (312) 651-0700 Fax: (312) 651-7286 E-mail: **twpress3@aol.com** Website: **www.thirdworldpressinc.com**

Triple Crown Publications Publisher of urban fiction novels, since 2001. Ms. Vickie M. Stringer, Publisher. Contact Michael, Triple Crown Publications, P.O. Box 247378, Columbus, Ohio 43224 Phone: (614) 934-1233 E-mail: **admin@triplecrownpublications.com** Website: **www.triplecrownpublications.com**

Write The Vision, Inc. Christian publishing company committed to assisting writers to bring forth their creative visions and to prepare them for publication. Owner/operator Maurice M. Gray, Jr. Contact Write The Vision, Inc., Box 12926, Wilmington, Delaware 19850 Phone: (302) 778-2407 E-mail: **writevision2000@yahoo.com**

Roy Meriwether
*Composer * Pianist*

Roy Dennis Meriwether is a contemporary, classic composer. His music is rooted in a strong gospel tradition, infused with jazz, blues, and rock elements, all interwined with classical influences. His compositions range from jazz ballads to big band arrangements to folk operas (scored for vocal chorus, orchestra and dancers) to compositions orchestrated for an 85-piece orchestra. A 1973 NEA Jazz Composition Fellowship Grant allowed Meriwether to write a musical work tracing the 350 year history of the Black experience in America. The scope and breadth of the project resulted in the 21-piece suite, *Black Snow*, written and premiered for the United States Bicentennial Celebration in April 1976 with the Howard Roberts Chorale and the Dayton Contemporary Dance Guild.

Living in New York City since 1976, he is frequently called upon to compose specific works for special events, such as the 1989 NAUBA Salute To Women Conference in the Bahamas where he performed his latest piece, *A Tribute To You, My Lady*. *Live At the Four Queens* was recorded live at the Four Queens Hotel/Casino, Las Vegas, Nevada, by KULV radio in 1991 and released for syndication on APR Radio in October 1991. After the death of Mile Davis, Meriwether wrote *I Think of Miles*, released by Chum Fun/ASCAP. In progress is a love ballad written in Meriwether's contemporary classical jazz style titled, *"This One's On Me."*

Publishing Services

BCP Digital Printing   Print-On-Demand and document processing company. We are proud to be a family-run business committed to caring for our customers, employees and community. BCP Digital Printing, 3921 Vero Road, Suite F, Baltimore, Maryland 21227 Phone:(410) 242-6954 E-mail: **blackclassicpress@yahoo.com** Website: **www.bcpdigital.com**

Better Day Publishing The company has provided quality child book publishing and child book illustration services in the Houston Metro area since April, 2001. Offers creative solutions ranging from book design, editing services and production of web-based marketing materials. Better Day Publishing, 11152 Westheimer #341, Houston, TX. 77042 Phone: (713) 548-4048 E-mail: **contact@betterdaypublishing** Website: **www.betterdaypublishing.com**

Black Star Consulting Former Random House book editor, freelance writer, book editor and editorial consultant who has worked with book publishers, agents, new writers, and best selling authors. Carol A. Taylor, Black Star Consulting, 295 Clinton Avenue #E3, Brooklyn, New York 11205 E-mail: **carol@brownsugarbooks.com**   Website: **www.BrownSugarBooks.com**.

CB Publishing & Design A one-stop Printing, Publishing and Design business. We can provide you with all the assistance you need to get your manuscript produced and sold. CB Publishing & Design, PO Box 560431, Charlotte, North Carolina 28256 Phone: (704) 649-3585 E-mail: **info@cbpublishing-design.com** Website: **www.cbpublishing-design.com**

Patrick PJ Davis Marketing and Web Solutions for authors, entertainers and publishing companies. Contact Patrick PJ Davis, Post Office Box 420725, Houston, Texas 77242   Phone: (713) 866-6548 E-mail: **info@blackcottonworks.net** Website: **www.blackcottonworks.net**

Ronald Davis An award winning visual artist and graphic designer providing full artistic services: quality web backgrounds, book and CD covers, posters/fliers/handbills, brochures, fine art, etc. Contact Mr. Ronald Davis, Post Office Box 3861, Midway, Kentucky 40347 Phone: (859) 433-1503 E-mail: **upfromsumdirt@yahoo.com** Website: **www.mythiumlitmag.com**

Disilgold Book publisher. Founded in 2001. Publishes new books and anthologies via various genres. Also provides writers services: press releases, book marketing resources.   Heather Covington, Disilgold, Post Office Box 652, Baychester Station, Bronx, New York 10469 Phone: (718) 547-0499 E-mail: **disilgold@aol.com**   Website: **www.disilgold.com**

Docuversion Andrea Hinton, CEO of Docuversion, is dedicated to the advancement of African-American literature and the enhancement of reading experiences with well-edited books. Docuversion is a full-service editing firm that specializes in all genres, but with an emphasis on urban lit. Contact Ms. Andrea Hinton, Post Office Box 19101, Cleveland, Ohio 44119. Phone: (216) 633-2397 E-mail: **andrea@docuversion.com** Website: **www.docuversion.com**

Dreams Publishing Company If you are a nonfiction author you need to have some credentials and/or experience in the subject matter, we are accepting fiction and nonfiction manuscripts. Dreams Publishing Company, Post Office Box 4731, Rocky Mount, North Carolina 27803 E-mail: info@DreamsPublishing.com Website: www.dreamspublishing.com

Freeman Multimedia, Inc. Founded in 2004 by CEO, Jamain Freeman. Freeman Multimedia (FMI Design) is geared towards helping the small to large sized business model develop branding through facets of media including: website development, graphic design, video production and multimedia presence. Freeman Multimedia, Inc., 111 Lodestone Drive, Durham, North Carolina 27703 Phone: (919) 696-8066 E-mail: info@freemanmultimedia.com Website: www.freemanmultimedia.com

HDB Editorial Services Professional editorial services at affordable rates. HDB Editorial Services, Post Office Box 85214, Westland, Michigan 48185 Phone: (734) 578-0427 E-mail: hdbeditorialservices@yahoo.com

Jazzy Pen Communications Provides a wide range of editing services from basic proofreading to comprehensive content editing. Specializes in editing African American fiction. Jazzy Pen Communications, Post Office Box 838, Rancho Cucamonga, California 91729 Phone: (909) 484-7933 E-mail: editor@jazzypen.com Website: www.jazzypen.com

K & K Houston, LLC Book Publishing and Web Design & Internet Marketing Services. We handle the publishing of authors and writers in the areas of Poetry, Motivational, Inspirational, Self-Help and Romance. We handle all aspects of your publishing projects from book design & layout, typesetting, editing, printing, marketing and distribution. Kevin J Houston, K & K Houston, LLC, Post Office Box 1006, Lorton, Virginia 22199 Phone: (703) 878-1905 Fax: (877) 264-8835 E-mail: kkhouston@kkhouston.com Website: www.kkhouston.com

Images & Illuminations We specialize in web design and development: book design, logos, brochures, posters, invitations, catalogs and more. Ms. Cheryl Hanna, Director, Images & Illuminations, 214 Sixth Avenue, Suite 3B, Brooklyn, New York 11215 Phone: (718) 783-0131 E-mail: imagesandilluminations@earthlink.net Website: www.imagesandilluminations.com

Johnswriteme The company is available for professional proofreading, book, manuscript and copyediting. We also proof and edit web pages. Maricia D. C. Johns, President. Contact johnswriteme, Post Office Box 40261, Fort Worth, Texas 76140 Phone: (817) 366-9440 E-mail: johnswriteme@sbcglobal.net Website: www.johnswriteme.net

Loose Leaves Full service editing service for manuscripts, novels, poems and any literary work. Sharon Hudson, Loose Leaves Enterprises, Post Office Box 548, Tyrone, Georgia 30290 Phone: (770) 314-5932 E-mail: akaivyleaf@looseleaves.org Website: www.looseleaves.org

Lemrac Books We specialize in author consultations and assistance in writing/editing, printing, promoting, marketing, and distributing their books. Contact Ms. Carmel S. Victor, Lemrac Books, Post Office Box 1132, Union, New Jersey 07083 Phone: (908) 206-0828 E-mail: carmel@carmelsvictor.com   Website: www.carmelsvictor.com

Marion Designs Book Cover Designs. Several of Marion Designs book covers have made the Essence best seller list and are featured on Black Expressions. Contact Keith Saunders, Marion Designs, 225 Sunderland Way, Suite # U, Stockbridge, Georgia 30281 Phone: (678) 641-8689 E-mail: **mariondesigns@bellsouth.net** Website: **www.mariondesigns.com**

Mays Printing Company Founded in 1946, Mays has consistently met the challenge of delivering quality printing products to corporations, advertisement agencies, government agencies, educational institutions, publishers, packagers, small businesses in addition to personalized services for each individual customer. Mays Printing Company, 15800 Livernois Avenue, Detroit, Michigan 48238 Phone: (313) 861-1900 Fax: (313) 861-5660 E-mail: **contact@maysprinting.com** Website: **www.maysprinting.com**

Ministry Marketing Solutions Marketing consulting and public relations agency that targets the African American Christian market. Pam Perry, publicist. Ministry Marketing Solutions, 21442 Hamilton Avenue, Farmington Hills, Michigan 48336 Phone: (248) 426-2300 E-mail: **pamperry@ministrymarketingsolutions.com** Website: **ministrymarketingsolutions.com**

Daphne Muse Through her more than ten year old editorial service, she works with emerging and established writers; move them from Concept to Manuscript. Contact Ms. Daphne Muse, 2429 East 23rd Street, Oakland, California 94601 Phone: (510) 436-4716 Fax: (510) 261-6064 E-mail: **msmusewriter@gmail.com** Website: **www.oasisinthediaspora.com**

National Black News Service Digital news service is distributed to over 1,000 newspapers and 40,000 individual subscribers. Contact Robert Taylor, National Black News Services, Taylor Media Services, 1517 T Street, South East, Washington, D.C. 20020 Phone: (202) 657-8872 E-mail: **taylormediaservices@yahoo.com** Website: **www.freewebs.com/blacknewsjournal**

Novel Ideal Publishing & Editorial Services Company Full service editorial service offering copy editing, content editing and proofreading services. Electa Rome Parks, Novel Ideal Publishing & Editorial Services Company, 2274 Salem Road, Suite 106, PMB 173, Conyers, Georgia 30013 E-mail: **novelideal@aol.com** Website: **www.electaromeparks.com**

PageTurner.net The company provides author web site design, internet consulting services and website hosting. Contact Pageturner.net, Post Office Box 120, 2951 Marina Bay Drive, #130, League City, Texas 77573 Phone: (866) 875-1044 E-mail: **pwsquare@pageturner.net** Website: **pageturner.net**

Per-fect Words Publishing A professional typeset and book cover design services company: maunscript editing and distribution, and web design. Per-fect Words Publishing, Post Office. Box 170451, San Francisco, California 94117 Phone: (415) 252-0577 E-mail: **regina@per-fectwords.com** Website: **www.per-fectwords.com**

Prioritybooks Publications Assist potential writers in finding a voice; consultant on book issues and help securing book signing facilities. Chief Executive Officer, Rose Jackson-Beavers. Contact Prioritybooks Publication, Post Office Box 2535, Florissant, Missouri 63032 Phone: (314) 741-6789 E-mail: **rosbeav03@yahoo.com** Website: **www.prioritybooks.com**

PriorityONE Publications Since 2001. We endeavor to assist Christian writers in self-publishing. Christina Dixon, PriorityONE Publications, Post Office Box 725, Farmington, Michigan 48332 Phone: (800) 331-8841 E-mail: **cdixon@p1pubs.com**

Prism Pages Literary services and publishing company: copy writing, ghost writing, literary critiques. Ms. Lisette Peterson, Prism Pages, Post Office Box 7189, Hampton, Virginia 23666 Phone: (757) 218-8587 E-mail: **info@prismpages.com** Website: **www.prismpages.com**

Publishing Communications Provides publishing services for the publication of books, magazines, newsletters and various other publications. Publisher, Publishing Communications, Post Office Box 1023, Austell, Georgia 30168 E-mail: **publisher@publishingcomm.com**

Winona Rasheed Author, freelance writer and editor, and entrepreneur with her own online writing and editing business Dream Writers' Essentials. Winona writes children stories and has four published books. Winona Rasheed, Dream Writers Essentials, 2426 Otis Street, North East, Washington DC 20018 Phone: (202) 635-3588 E-mil: **rasheedwinona@yahoo.com** Website: **www.winonarasheed.com**

Same Page Promotions Sets up book signings and various venues for authors to meet their West Coast readers in small informal gatherings. Ms. Christine Battle-Ellington, Same Page Promotions, Post Office Box 3581, San Leandro, California 94578 Phone: (510) 632-1600 E-mail: **christine@samepagepromotions.com** Website: **www.samepagepromotions.com**

Sardonyx Jade Publishing SJP Provides editing and consulting services to new authors. Contact Sardonyx Jade Publishing, 1401 North La Brea Avenue, Suite 137, Los Angeles, California Phone: (323) 898-7339 Fax: (213) 252-8471 E-mail: **ldjones@sardonyx-jade.com** Website: **www.sardonyx-jade.com**

Nicole Tadgell Children's book illustration. Contact Ms. Nicole Tadgell, 14 Sampson Street, Spencer, Massachusetts 01562 Phone: (508) 885-7723 E-mail: **nic.art@verizon.net** Website: **www.nicoletadgell.com**

Martha "Marti" Tucker Ghost writer for three books. Writer, story editor. Contact Ms. Martha Tucker, 6605 Green Valley Circle, Culver City, California 90230 Phone: (310) 337-7008 E-mail: **writelink3@aol.com**

22nd Century Press Publishes multicultural literature and non-fiction emphasizing creative diversity in the tratioal model (approximately 6 books per year). Also assist in choosing the right services, technology, marketing methods, and all of the basics needed by self-published authors. Diane Williams, 12138 Central Avenue, 223, Mitchellville, Maryland 20721 Phone: (443) 483-4261 E-mail: **diane@22ndCenturyPress.com** Website: **www.22ndCenturyPress.com**

VIP Editing Editing Services. Specializes in fictional novels. We can assist with story and character development by offering suggestions for improvement or actually assisting with rewrites. Harriet Wilson, 30 Sta Les Cove, Suite 1, Jackson, Tennessee 38305 Phone: (731) 313-1820 E-mail: **vip_editing@yahoo.com** Website: **www.vip-editing.webs.com**

Write Page Literary Service, Inc. Business and creative writing firm. Write Page Literary Service, Inc., Post Office Box 38288, Atlanta, Georgia 30334 Phone: (404) 280-5029 Fax: (404) 656-0238 E-mail: **writepagemo@yahoo.com**

Write The Vision, Inc. Editing, proofreading and some publishing services for Christian authors. Contact Mr. Maurice Gray, Write The Vision, Inc., Post Office Box 12926, Wilmington, Delaware 19850 Phone: (302) 778-2407 E-mail: **writevision2000@yahoo.com**

Zhanes' Literary Service ZLS offers publicity services to authors. Kenyatta Ingram, publicist. Zhanes' Literary Service, Post Office Box 15381, Chesapeake, Virginia 23323 Phone: (757) 715-4720 E-mail: **zhanespublicity@hotmail.com** Website: **zhanespublicity.5u.com**

Rodney Saulsberry
Author * Actor * Voice Over Artist

Rodney Saulsberry's distinctive announcers voice is literally everywhere. One of the top voice-over talents in the country movie fans have heard Rodney's voice promoting some of their favorites: Tupac Resurrection, How Stella Got Her Groove Back, Diary of a Mad Black Woman, Friday After Next, Drumline, Undercover Brother, The Best Man, Dumb & Dumberer, Finding Forrester, Soul Food, Hardball, Crooklyn, Bamboozled, Clockers, and many more. Black Enterprise Magazine called Saulsberry: "The voice of choice for behind-the-scenes-narration." Saulsberry first set foot on west coast soil when he came to town with a national touring company of Your Arms Too Short To Box With God after a successful Broadway run. The musical was an instant hit in the Los Angeles area and led to an illustrious television acting career for Rodney that included guest starring roles on Taxi, Mash, Gimme a Break, 227, Hill Street Blues and Dr. Quinn Medicine Woman. He also enjoyed series regular status on the soap opera, Capitol and a recurring role on The Young and the Restless. He has been a voiceover commercial pitchman for Zatarain's, Twix, Toyota Camry, ALPO, Honda Accord, Lincoln LS, Verizon, White Castle, 7UP, Burger King, SBC, and Nestle Crunch. He can also be heard reading Books on Tape, as well as narrating E! Entertainments, True Hollywood Story, about Motown R&B singer, Marvin Gaye. In the summer of 2006 he announced promos for the ABC hit Dancing With The Stars. His voice promoted the ABC critically acclaimed Charlie Brown Christmas Special in 2007, announced the 34th NAACP Image Awards and the Essence Awards specials on FOX Television, the Grammy Awards and the Country Music Awards for CBS.

Rodney Saulsberry is the voice of Joe Robbie Robertson on the hit cartoon series Spider-Man and James Rhodey Rhodes in the new animated feature film, The Invincible Iron Man, Chyron in the Animatrix, Ufwapo on Ahh...Real Monsters, Willy on Xyber 9, and has guest starred on many other Saturday morning cartoons that include Rugrats, Duckman, Static Shock and Minoriteam. Rodney lent his melodious baritone singing voice to a jubilant ensemble of background singers on a spirited recording of Hakuna Matata on The Lion King soundtrack. He continued his animation musical journey singing on two numbers from The Prince of Egypt soundtrack, When You Believe and Playing With The Big Boys. As a soloist, Mr. Saulsberry has recorded two rhythm and blues albums that have produced two Billboard charting singles, I Wonder and Look Whatcha Done Now.

He recently released his first book, <u>You Can Bank on Your Voice: Your Guide to a Successful Career in Voice-Overs</u>. His second book is <u>Step Up to the Mic: A Positive Approach to Succeeding in Voice-Overs</u>. Mr. Saulsberry currently resides in Agoura, California.

Radio Stations

American Urban Radio Networks (AURN) The Nation's largest and only African-American owned network radio company in the United States providing programming to more than 300 affiliated stations. Contact AURN, 432 Park Avenue, South, 14th Floor, New York, New York 10016 Phone: (212) 883-2100 Fax: (212) 297-2571 Website: www.aurn.com

Chicago Public Radio Home of numerous Black talk radio programs. Vanessa Harris, Public Relations, CPR, Navy Pier, 848 East Grand Avenue, Chicago, Illinois 60611 Phone: (312) 948-4600 E-mail: Vanessa@vocalo.org Website: www.wbez.org

Inner City Broadcasting Steve Patterson, VP/Market Manager. ICBC Broadcast Holdings, Inc.1900 Pineview Drive, Columbia, South Carolina 29209 Phone: (803) 227-4624 Fax: (803) 695-8605 E-mail: spatterson@innercitysc.com Website: www.innercitysc.com

Inspiration 1390 Interviews artists, authors. Effie Rolfe, Program Director, 1390-AM, 233 North Michigan Avenue, Suite 2800, Chicago, Illinois 60601 Phone: (312) 540-2000 E-mail: effierolse@clearchannel.com Website: www.Inspiration1390.com

KBFB-FM The Beat 97.9 FM Mainstream/Urban; on-air personalities. Station Manager, Gary Spurgeon. KBFB-FM, Radio-One, 13331 Preston Rd., Suite 1180, Dallas, Texas 75240 Phone: (972) 331-5400 E-mail: jwilliams@radio-one.com Website: www.thebeatdfw.com

KBLX-FM Contemporary music. Kevin Brown, Program Director. KBLX-FM, 55 Hawthorne Street, Suite 900, San Francisco, California 94105 Phone: (415) 284-1029 Fax: (415) 764-1029 E-mail: kbrown@kblx.com Website: www.kblx.com

KDYA-AM Gospel 1190-AM The Light. Clifford Brown, Jr., Program Director. KDYA, 3260 Blume Drive, Suite 520, Richmond, California 94806 Phone: (510) 222-4242 Fax: (510) 262-9054 E-mail: brownradio@comcast.net Website: www.gospel1190.net

KDIA-AM 1640-AM. Operations Manager, Clifford Brown Jr. KDIA, 3260 Blume Drive, Suite 520, Richmond, California 94806 Phone: (510) 222-4242 Fax: (510) 262-9054 E-mail: brownradio@comcast.net Website: www.gospel1190.net

KJLH 102.3 FM Urban Contemporary. Aundrae Russell, Program Director. Contact Greg Johnson, KJLH, 161 North La Brea Avenue, Inglewood, California 90301 Phone: (310) 330-2200 Fax: (310) 330-5555 E-mail: aundrae@kjlhradio.com Website: www.kjlhradio.com

KZWA 104.9 FM Coverage area includes Southwest Louisiana and Southeast Texas. Faye Blackwell, Owner. KZWA, 305 Enterprise Boulevard, Lake Charles, Louisiana 70601 Phone: (337) 491-9955 E-mail: FBBkzwa@aol.com

Sheridan Gospel Network Gospel music; targets African-American Adults 25-54. Sheridan is the majority owner and manager of American Urban Radio Networks (AURN). AURN provides news, sports, information, and entertainment programming to over 400 affiliates across the country. Contact Michael Gamble, Director, Sheridan Gospel Network, 2424 Old Rex Morrow Road, Ellenwood, Georgia 30294 Phone: (404) 361-1570 E-mail: **mgamble@sgnthelight.com** Website: **www.sgnthelight.com**

WAJZ-FM Hip hop and R&B. Contact Program Manager, Albany Broadcasting, 6 Johnson Road, Latham, New York 12110 Phone: (518) 786-6600   Fax: (518) 786-6696   E-mail: **Tanch@jamz963.com** Website: **www.jamz963.com**

WCHB 1200 AM News Talk. Hosts and producers, Mildred Gaddis and Angelo Henderson. WCHB, 3250 Franklin, Detroit, Michigan 48207 Phone: (313) 259-2000 Fax: (313) 259-7011 Website: **www.WCHBNewsDetroit.com**

WCLK-FM Jazz 91.9-FM. Aaron Cohen, Programming Director. Contact WCLK-FM, Clark Atlanta University, 111 James P. Brawley Drive, South West, Atlanta, Georgia 30314 Phone: (404) 880-8273 Fax: (404) 880-8869 E-mail: **wclkfm@cau.edu** Website: **www.wclk.com**

WDBZ 1230-AM The Buzz Reach the urban Cincinnati Metro market; news and headlines. Contact Mr. Jeri Tolliver, Program Director. WDBZ-AM, 1 Centennial Plaza, Suite 200, 705 Central Avenue, Cincinnati, Ohio 45202 Phone: (513) 749-1230 Fax: (513) 948-1985 E-mail: **jtolliver@radio-one.com** Website: **www.thebuzzcincy.com**

WEUP-AM/FM Hip Hop and R & B. Contact Hundley Batts, Sales Coordinator, WEUP Radio Station, Post Office Box 11398, Huntsville, Alabama 35814 Phone: (256) 837-9387 Fax: (256) 837-9404 E-mail: **hundley@103wcup.com** Website: **www.103weup.com**

WFDU-FM 89.1 Community owned radio station. Fairleigh Dickinson University. Contact WFDU, 114 Shepard Avenue, Teaneck, New Jersey 07666 Phone: (201) 692-2806 E-mail: **GospelVibrations@aol.com** Website: **www.wfdu.fm**

WFLM 104.7 The Flame Hot Talk morning show addresses local and national issues. Joseph Jenkins, Operations Director. WFLM, 6803 S. Federal Highway, Port SaintLucie, Florida 34952 Phone: (772) 460-9356 E-mail: **jumpinjoe@wflm.cc** Website: **www.1047theflame.com**

WFVS AM/FM Student operated radio studio. Shirley Ellis, Radio Manager. Contact WFVS AM/FM, Fort Valley State University, 1005 State University Drive, Fort Valley, Georgia 31030 Phone: (478) 825-6911 E-mail: **elliss@fvsu.edu** Website: **www.fvsu.edu**

WFXM-FM Chris Murray, Owner, President. Claudel Price, General Manager. Chrisopher Murray, 6174 Highway 57, Macon, Georgia 31217 Phone: (478) 745-3301 Fax: (478) 742-2293 E-mail: **clmurray@aol.com** Website: **www.mypower1071.com**

WGFT General Manager, Skip Bednarczysk. WGFT, 401 North Blaine, Youngstown, Ohio 44505 Phone: (330) 744-5115 E-mail: **skip@ytownradio.com** Website: **www.1330wgft.com**

WHIY 1600-AM Oldies and blues. Contact Hundley Batts, Sales Coordinator, WEUP Radio Station, Post Office Box 11398, Huntsville, Alabama 35814 Phone: (256) 837-9387 Fax: (256) 837-9404 E-mail: **hundley@103wcup.com** Website: **www.whiyam.com**

WHUR-FM 96.3 Howard University radio. Adult Contemporary. Home of the Audrey Chapman Show, Saturdays, 8 a.m., call in, author interviews, guests. Jim Watkins, General Manager, WHUR_FM, Howard University, 529 Bryant Street North West, Washington, DC 20059 Phone: (202) 806-3500 E-mail: **jwatkins@whur.com** Website: **www.whur.com**

WJAM-FM Adult, Urban Contemporary. Also has a Gospel talk show hosted by Dr. Feelgood. Interviews authors. Scott Communications, Inc., 273 Persimmon Tree Road., Selma, Alabama 36701 Phone: (334) 875-9360 Fax: (334) 875-1340

WJMI FM Hip-Hop, R& B, Urban. Contact Kevin Webb, General Manager. Contact WJMI, Inner City Broadcast, 731 S. Pear Orchard Road, Ridgeland, Mississippi 39157 Phone: (601) 957-1300 Fax: (601) 956-0516 E-mail: **kwebb1234@aol.com** Website: **www.wkxi.com**

WJYD-FM Joy 106.3. Christian radio. Program Director, Dawn Mosby. WJYD-FM, 350 East 1st Avenue, Suite 100, Columbus Ohio 43201 Phone: (614) 487-1444 E-mail: **dmosby@radio-one.com** Website: **www.mycolumbusjoy.com**

WKYS 93.9FM KISS. Urban. Hip-Hop. Program Director, Ron Thompson. WKYS, 5900 Princess Garden Parkway, 8th Floor, Lanham, Maryland 20706 Phone: (301) 306-1111 E-mail: **rthompson@radio-one.com** Website: **www.radio-one.com**

WKXI-AM Kevin Webb, General Manager. Contact Inner City Broadcast, 731 S. Pear Orchard Road, Ridgeland, Mississippi 39157 Phone: (601) 957-1300 Fax: (601) 956-0516 E-mail: **kwebb1234@aol.com** Website: **www.wkxi.com**

WLDB B93.3 FM. Bill Hurwitz, General Manager. Milwaukee Radio Alliance. WLDB, N72 W12922 Goodhope Road, Menomonee, Wisconsin 53051 Phone: (414) 771-1021 Fax: (414) 444-3036 E-mail: **bhurwiez@milwaukeeradio.com** Website: **www.milwaukeeradio.com**

WLUM 102.1 FM. Bill Hurwitz, General Manager. Milwaukee Radio Alliance. WLUM, N72 W12922 Goodhope Road, Menomonee, Wisconsin 53051 Phone: (414) 771-1021 Fax: (414) 444-3036 E-mail: **bhurwiez@milwaukeeradio.com** Website: **www.milwaukeeradio.com**

WMCS-AM 1290AM. Expanded talk format. Committed to the Milwaukee urban community where we focus on issues and concerns pertinent to the community. Willie Davis, owner. Tyrene Jackson, Program Director. Contact WMCS-AM, 4222 West Capitol Drive, Milwaukee, Wisconsin 53216 Phone: (414) 444-1290 Fax: (414) 444-1409 E-mail: **tj@1290wmcs.com** Website: **www.1290wmcs.com**

WMMJ-FM 102.3 FM Urban Contemporary. Adult R & B. Program Director, Jamillah Muhammad. WMMJ-FM, 5900 Princess Garden Parkway, 8th Floor, Lanham, Maryland 20706 Phone: (301) 306-1111 E-mail: **jam@radio-one.com** Website: **www.radio-one.com**

WOAD 105.9AM FM Praise Early Morning Praise with host Percy Davis. Inner City Broadcast, 731 South Pear Orchard Road, Suite 27, Ridgeland, Mississippi 39157 Phone: (601) 957-1300 Fax: (601) 956-0516 E-mail: kwebb1234@aol.com Website: www.woad.com

WPRS Contempory. Program Director, Ron Thompson. Contact WPRS, 5900 Princess Garden Parkway, 8th Fl, Lanham, Maryland 20706 Phone: (301) 306-1111 E-mail: rthompson@radio-one.com Website: www.radio-one.com

WPZZ 104.7 FM Gospel programming. Contact Ms. Linda Forem, General Manager, 2809 Emerywood Parkway, #300, Richmond, Virginia 23294 Phone: (804) 672-9299 Fax: (804) 672-9314 E-mail: lforem@radio-one.com Website: www.praiserichmond.com

WQNC-FM 92.7 Urban AC. Home of Fly Ty's weekly variety showcase highlights some of the wackiest, funniest talented people in Charlotte. Debbie Kwei Cook, General Manager, WQNC, 8809 Lenox Pointe Drive, Suite A, Charlotte, North Carolina 28273 Phone: (704) 548-7800 Fax: (704) 548-7810 E-mail: djacobs@radio-one.com Website: www.My927Charlotte.com

WQOK K97.5-FM Hip Hop and R&B. Program Director, Shena J. Contact WQOK-FM, 8001-101 Creedmoor Road, Raleigh, North Carolina 27613 Phone: (919) 848.9736 E-mail: Shenaj@radio-one.com Website: www.k975.com

WRSU-FM Student-operated radio station. Produces the call-in radio talk show African New Dawn with host, Alvin Fair and guests on Sundays at 8 p.m. Contact Program Director, Rebecca Grant, WRSU-FM, Rutgers Univerisy, 126 College Avenue, New Brunswick New Jersey 08903 Phone: (732) 932-7800 Fax: (732) 932-1768 E-mail: pd@wrsu.org Website: www.wrsu.org

WTLC 106.7 FM Urban AC. Complete up to date news weekdays and Sunday with host, Terri D. Chuck Williams, General Manager. WTLC, 21 East Saint Joseph Street, Indianapolis, Indiana 46204 Phone: (317) 266-9600 Fax: (317) 328-3860 E-mail: tdledsinger@radio-one.com Website: www.TLCNapTown.com

WTPS 1240 AM Linda Forem, General Manager, 2809 Emerywood Parkway, #300, Richmond, Virginia 23294 Phone: (804) 672-9299 Fax: (804) 672-9314 E-mail: lforem@radio-one.com Website: www.UrbanPetersburg.com

WVAZ-FM Music; entertainment personalities. Derrick Brown, Program Director. WVAZ-FM, 233 North Michigan Avenue, Suite 2800, Chicago, Illinois 60601 Phone: (312) 540-2000 E-mail: dbrowni@clearchannel.com Website: www.wvaz.com

WVON 1690AM For over 45 years, WVON has been the drum major for the African-American community of Chicago, and provides an interactive forum for Chicago's African-American community. Anita Vaughn, Program Director. WVON 1450AM, 3350 South Kedzie, Chicago, Illinois 60623 Phone: (773) 247-6200 E-mail: anita@wvon.com Website: www.wvon.com

WZAK 93.1 FM R&B. Contact WZAK, 2510 St. Clair Avenue NE, Cleveland, Ohio 44114 Phone: (216) 579-1111 E-mail: 931wzak@gmail.com Website: www.WZAKCleveland.com

Radio Talk Shows

Africa & World Beat   Nationally syndicated news/talk program.   On air Host, Arthur "DJ Lovey" Mahlangu. WEAA 88.9 FM, 1700 East Cold Spring Lane, Baltimore, Maryland 21251 Phone: (443) 885-3564 Fax: (443) 885-8206 E-mail: info@weaa.org Website: www.weaa.org

African Diaspora Today   Hosted by Dr. Carol L. Adams, the show airs every Sunday, from 3pm to 5pm on Chicago radio station WVON am 1690, and live on the web at wvon.com. Dr. Carol L. Adams, WVON 1450AM, 3350 South Kedzie, Chicago, Illinois 60623 Phone: (773) 247-6200 E-mail: africandiasporatoday@wvon.com Website: www.wvon.com

The Warren Ballentine Show   Host, Warren Ballentine is an attorney, and his nationally syndicated show is heard Monday thru Friday. Warren Ballentine, WDBZ-AM, 1 Centennial Plaza, Suite 200, 705 Central Avenue, Cincinnati, Ohio 45202 Phone: (513) 749-1230 Fax: (513) 948-1985 E-mail: warrenballentine@radio-one.com Website: www.1230thebuzz.com

The Doug Banks Show   Adult conversation. Interviews. Host, Doug Banks. Doug has received numerous radio awards. AURN, 432 Park Avenue, South, 14th Floor, New York, New York 10016 Phone: (212) 883-2100 Fax: (212) 297-2571 Website: www.aurn.com

Bay View Public affairs program. Interviews artists and authors. Host Nikki Thomas. KBLX-FM, 55 Hawthorne Street, Suite 900, San Francisco, California 94105 Phone: (415) 284-1029 Fax: (415) 764-1029 E-mail: info@kblx.com Website: www.kblx.com

Black Radio Is Back Syndicated radio show with DJ Fusion aka Mary Nichols and Jon Judah. Features a variety of music as well as various news issues and guests. Mary Nichols, FuseBox Radio/BlackRadioIsBack.com, Post Office Box2465, Waldorf, Maryland 20604 Phone: (347) 252 4032 E-mail: djfusion5@Yahoo.com Website: www.blackradioisback.com

KD Bowe Morning Show Host, KD Bowe. Contact KDYA, Gospel 1190 AM The Light, 3260 Blume Drive, Suite 520, Richmond, California 94806 Phone: (510) 222-4242   E-mail: KDBoweMorningShow@sgnthelight.com Website: www.sgnthelight.com

The Kevin Brown Morning Show Call in talk show at WOL 1450 and WOL-B 1010 hosted by Kevin Brown. Contact Mr. Kevin Brown, KBLX-FM, Post Office Box 76854, Washington, DC 20013 Phone: (800) 450-7876 E-mail: kbrown@kblx.com Website: www.kblx.com

The Michael Eric Dyson Show News/talk show hosted by New York Award-winning author, scholar and social commentator, Dr. Michael Eric Dyson. Show airs Monday through Friday in eighteen markets. Contact Rachel Irving, Public Relations Coordinator, WEAA 88.9 FM, 1700 East Cold Spring Lane, Baltimore, Maryland 21251 Phone: (443) 885-3564 Fax: (443) 885-8206 E-mail: staff@dysonshow.org Website: www.dysonshow.org

Jackie Campbell   Air personality. Originally from Detroit, Jackie has worked for WTVS-TV 56 and WDIV-TV 4 in Detroit, Michigan and WDTN-TV 2 in Dayton, Ohio. Jackie Campbell, KDYA, Gospel 1190 AM The Light, 3260 Blume Drive, Suite 520, Richmond, California 94806 Phone: (510) 222-4242 Fax: (510) 262-9054 E-mail: jcampbell@sgnthelight.com Website: www.sgnthelight.com

The Monique Caradine Show   Fridays 9 - 11am. As a media professional for 15 years, Monique Caradine has worked in every aspect of the business—including television, advertising, public relations and radio. Known as Mo in the Midday, she discussed a wide range of issues. She has also interviewed such notables as Tavis Smiley, Patti LaBelle, Maya Angelou, Magic Johnson, Queen Latifah, Les Brown and many more. Mo in the Midday was twice named Best Midday Talk Show in Chicago. Contact Ms. Monique Caradine, WVON 1450AM, 3350 South Kedzie, Chicago, Illinois 60623 Phone: (773) 247-6200 E-mail: media@momentum-media.tv Website: www.moniquecaradine.com

Caribbeanwomentoday   A community affairs program produced by CaribVoice Radio-Aubry Padmore, and hosted by Dr. Anita Davis-DeFoe, the author of A Woman's Guide to Soulful Living: Seven Keys to Life and Work Successl Tropical Escapes Follow Her Lead: Leadership Lessons For Women As They Journey From the Backroom to the Boardroom. Anita Davis DeFoe, 47474 Hollywood Boulevard, Suite 303, Hollywood, Florida 33021 Phone: (954) 213-4093 E-mail: dradefoe@gmail.com Website: www.dranitadavisdefoe.com

Conscious Rasta Report   Daily talk radio show hosted by Keidi Obi Awadu on LIBRadio.com and LIBtv.com. He is author of 18 published books. Keidi Obi Awadu, Black Star Media, 6243 South La Tijera Boulevard, Los Angeles, California 90056 Phone: (323) 902-2919   E-mail: info@libradio.net Website: www.LIBRadio.com

The Daily Drum   A news and interview program covering local politics by reporter, host, Harold T. Fisher. Fisher is author of Two Weeks Until the Rest of My Life. Contact Mr. Harold T. Fisher, Howard University, WHUR-FM, 529 Bryant Street North West, Washington, DC 20059 Phone: (202) 806-3500 E-mail: haroldtfisher@gmail.com Website: www.whur.com

Diasporic Music   Call in talk show. Interviews authors, etc. Producer, host, Norman "Otis" Redmond. Located on the Ryerson University campus CKLN is the first campus community radio station in Toronto. Diasporic Music, CKLN, Post Office Box 6777, Station A, Toronto, Canada, MSW 1X5 Phone: (416) 979-5251 E-mail: norman@ckln.fm Website: www.ckln.fm

DJ WIZ   Show airs 7pm – 12pm. Chris Murray, Owner, President. Claudel Price, General Manager. Contact Chrisopher Murray, 6174 Highway 57, Macon, Georgia 31217 Phone: (478) 745-3301 Fax: (478) 742-2293 E-mail: djwiz@aol.com Website: www.mypower1071.com

From A Different Prospective   News magazine show. Shows Third World topics include African music, aids in Africa, sanctions, the Grenada revolutions, news and information. Interviews authors. Producer, host, Norman "Otis" Redmond. Otis Redmond, From A Different Prospective, Post Office Box 6777, Station A, Toronto, Canada, MSW 1X5 Phone: (416) 408-2817 E-mail: norman@ckln.fm Website: www.ckln.fm

Frontpage 102.3-FM radio talk show hosted by Dominique, covers topics affecting African Americans locally, nationally and internationally. Interviews authors and artists. Carl Nelson, Frontpage, KJLH, 161 North La Brea Avenue, Inglewood, California 90301 Phone: (310) 330-2200 Fax: (310) 330-5555 E-mail: fp@kjlhradio.com Website: www.kjlhradio.com

Global Beat Experience Host, Gary Byrd. WBAI, 120 Wall Street, 10th Floor, New York, New York 10005 Phone: (212) 209-2800 E-mail: editor@wbai.org   Website: www.wbai.org

Gospel 1190 The Light Show features Bible trivia, entertainment news, African American history, and gospel music! Jackie Campbell is host. Contact KDYA Gospel 1190 AM The Light, 3260 Blume Drive, Suite 520, Richmond, California 94806 Phone: (510) 222-4242 Fax: (510) 262-9054 E-mail: jcampbell@sgnthelight.com Website: www.sgnthelight.com

The Gospel Express   Host Morgan Dukes. Show airs Weekdays 7:00am - 12:00pm. Morgan Dukes, SGN The Light, 2424 Old Rex Morrow Road, Ellenwood, Georgia 30294 Phone: (404) 361-1570 E-mail: mdukes@sgnthelight.com Website: www.sgnthelight.com

The John Hannah Morning Show Mostly music driven, contests, comedy. Gospel Radio 1390-AM, 233 North Michigan Avenue, Suite 2800, Chicago, Illinois 60601 Phone: (312) 540-2000 E-mail: ChurchNews@gospel1390.com Website: www.gospel1390.com

Earl Ingram Talk Radio host. Interviews authors. Earl Ingram, 1290 WMCS, 4222 West Capitol Drive, Suite 1290, Milwaukee, Wisconsin 53216 Phone: (414) 444-1290 Fax: (414) 444-1409 E-mail: earl@1290wmcs.com Website: www.1290wmcs.com

Insight Hosted by Harold T. Fisher. Howard University radio. Adult Contemporary. WHUR-FM 96.3, Howard University, 529 Bryant Street North West, Washington, DC 20059 Phone: (202) 806-3500 E-mail: haroldtfisher@gmail.com Website: www.whur.com

IT'S RELATIONAL Nationally Syndicated Radio Show which airs Wednesdays at 8amCST or 9amEST on rejoice-now.com.   Host, Dr. Sabrina D. Black, L.L.P.C., C.A.C.-1. Dr. Sabrina D. Black, Abundant Life Counseling Center, 20700 Civic Center Drive #170, Southfield, Michigan 48076 Phone: (313) 201-6286 E-mail: jadebooks@aol.com Website: www.sabrinablack.com

The Santita Jackson Show   Airs Monday - Friday 9am – Noon. Santita brings her worldly perspective on current events and contemporary issues from behind-the-scenes to behind-the-mic. Santita Jackson, WVON, 1690AM, 1000 East 87th Street, Chicago, Illinois 60619 Phone: (773) 247-6200 E-mail: santita@wvon.com Website: www.wvon.com

Jammin for Jesus Show airs on 96.3 Fm and 1340am. Host, Carl Moore aka Dr. Feel Good. Contact Scott Alexander, Owner/Producer. Scott Communications, Post Office Box 1150, Selma, Alabama 36702 Phone: (334) 875-9360 Fax: (334) 875-1340

The Joy Ride Home Sonya Blakey, Host. WGRB, 233 North Michigan Avenue, Suite 2700 Chicago, Illinois 60601 Phone: (312) 540-2000 E-mail: sonyablakey@clearchannel.com Website: www.gospel1390.com

Just About Books Talk Show Internet radio talk show with a worldwide audience. Features authors, book reviews, book clubs, and literary events for African American book lovers." Executive Producer and Host, Cheryl Robinson. Cheryl Robinson, Just About Books Talk Show, 1282 Smallwood Drive, West, Suite 116, Waldorf, Maryland 20603 Phone: (301) 643-2077 E-mail: JustAboutBooks@yahoo.com Website: www.JustAboutBookTalkShow.com

The Cliff Kelley Show Monday through Friday 3pm - 7pm. Cliff Kelley has distinguished himself as a popular talk show host who brings a wealth of knowledge on local, national and international affairs to WVON's vast listening audience. Cliff Kelley, WVON 1450AM, 3350 South Kedzie, Chicago, Illinois 60623 Phone: (773) 247-6200 E-mail: Michael@wvon.com Website: www.wvon.com

Tales Knight 6 a.m. - 10 a.m. daily. Trivia. Chris Murray, Owner, President. Contact Tales Knight, 6174 Highway 57, Macon, Georgia 31217 Phone: (478) 745-3301 Fax: (478) 742-2293 E-mail: gotales@gmail.com Website: www.mypower1071.com

Ladies First Radio talk show airs Mondays 7pm/ET Sirius 146/XM 167, hosted by Ms. Blanche Williams-Corey, author. Interview authors. Contact Ms. Blanche Williams-Corey, Greatness by Design, LLC, 5900 Princess Garden Parkway, 8th Floor, Lanham, Maryland 20706 Phone: (202) 497-4564 E-mail: blanche@blanchewilliams.com Website: www.greatnessbydesign.com

LA Speaks Out Weekly interactive talk show of current topics affecting the African American community in Los Angeles, hosted by Jacquie Stephens, News and Public Affairs Director. KJLH Radio, 161 North La Brea Avenue, Inglewood, California 90301 Phone: (310) 330-2200 Fax: (310) 330-5555 E-mail: jacquie@kjlhradio.com Website: www.kjlhradio.com

Love Lust & Lies Syndicated drive time radio talk show hosted by best selling author, Michael Baisden. Michael is author and publisher of three highly successful provocative books including Never Satisfied, The Maintenance Man, and God's Gift to Women. Pamela Yvette Exum, Business Manager, 1844 North Nob Hill Road, #610, Plantation, Florida 33322 Phone: (877) 622-3269 E-mail: hotnews@minglecity.com Website: www.michaelbaisden.com

The Marshalen Martin Show Host, Marshalen Martin. A professional radio broadcaster Marshlen has also worked at KEST in San Francisco, and KJAM in Pittsburg. Marshalen Martin, KDYA, Gospel 1190, 3260 Blume Drive, Suite 520, Richmond, California 94806 Phone: (510) 222-4242 E-mail: marshalenmartin@gospel1190.net Website: www.gospel1190.net

The Matt McGill Show Talk show airs Monday through Friday 6am - 9am. Producer: Anita Rochelle Vaughn, WVON 1450AM, 3350 South Kedzie, Chicago, Illinois 60623 Phone: (773) 247-6200 E-mail: perri@wvon.com Website: www.wvon.com

The Anthony McCarthy Show Live Interviews with host, Anthony McCarthy. The show airs weekly from 9 a.m. to 10 a.m. on WEAA 88.9 FM features national issues and top newsmakers. Anthony McCarthy, WEAA-FM 89.9, 1700 East Coldspring Lane, Benjamin Banneker Building, Room 401, Baltimore, Maryland 21251 Phone: (443) 885-3564 Fax: (443) 885-8206 E-mail: anthony@anthonymccarthy.com Website: www.weaa.org

Memphis Real Talk Show WJMB Internet Radio show hosted by owner and founder, Jennings Bernard, since 1985. Contact WJMB, Bernard Broadcasting Company, 5316 Cottonwood Road, Memphis, Tennessee 38118 Phone: (877) 825-5014 E-mail: OnAir@memphisrealtalk.com Website: www.memphisrealtalk.com

Moment Creole WLIB 1190 Host, Stanley Barbot. Information topics directly related to the French Caribbean speaking community. WLIB 1190, I.C.B.C. Broadcast Holdings, Inc., New York, New York E-mail: momentcreole@wlib.com Website: www.wlib.com

Money Matters Host, Alfred Edmonds is an award-winning reporter and editor. Shows offers advice on investments, taxes, retirement and estate planning. Show airs Monday - Friday. Alfred Edmonds, AURN, 432 Park Avenue, South, 14th Floor, New York, New York 10016 Phone: (212) 883-2100 Fax: (212) 297-2571 Website: www.aurn.com

The Kendall Moore Show Friday 7 p.m. - 10pm - Saturday 5 p.m. – 6 p.m. Host, Kendall D. Moore. Contact WVON 1450AM, 3350 South Kedzie, Chicago, Illinois 60623 Phone: (773) 247-6200 E-mail: kendall@wvon.com Website: www.wvon.com

The Salim Muwakkil Show Host, Salim Muwakkil is a Senior Editor of In These Times, and an op-ed columnist for the Chicago Tribune. Currently a Crime and Communities Media Fellow of the Open Society Institute. Salim Muwakkil, WVON 1450AM, 3350 South Kedzie, Chicago, Illinois 60623 Phone: (773) 247-6200 E-mail: salim4x@aol.com Website: www.wvon.com

Neek Words Of Wisdom, all the latest gossip...tune in each weekday Monday thru Friday, 2 p.m. - 6 p.m. General Manager: Steve Patterson, WHXT 103.9 FM, 1900 Pineview Drive Columbia, South Carolina 29209 Phone: (803) 695-8600 Fax: (803) 695-8605 E-mail: neek@hot1039fm.com Website: www.hot1039fm.com

The New Voice of Praise Covers national and local Gospel music. Host, Kimberly. Call in during show hours. Interviews authors. Kimberly, WCLM 1450 AM, 3165 Hull Street, Richmond, Virginia 23224 Phone: (804) 231-7685 Website: www.wclmradio.com

NewsWorld This Morning   Show hosted by Kim Lampkins, Morning News Anchor on American Urban Radio Networks, is a broadcast veteran of 24 years. Kim is a multi-faceted professional, who moves with ease from news to music to production aspects of radio programming. Graduate of Clarion University in Clarion, Pennsylvania. Kim Lampkins, AURN, 432 Park Avenue, South, 14th Floor, New York, New York 10016 Phone: (212) 883-2100 Fax: (212) 297-2571 Website: www.aurn.com

Off The Shelf Internet Radio program hosted by author, Denise Turney. Contact Off The Shelf, Chistell Publishing, 2500 Knights Road, Suite 19-01, Bensalem, Pennsylvania 19020 E-mail: soulfar@aol.com Website: www.blogtalkradio.com/denise-turney

On the Beat Weekday Mornings. Host, Curtis Wright. Rhonda Bellamy, news Director, 980-AM WAAV, 3233 Burnt Mill Road #4, Wilmington, North Carolina 28403 Phone: (910) 763-9977 Fax: (910) 762-0456 E-mail: rhonda@980waav.com Website: www.980waav.com

Phil Nelson On air personality. Contact Mr. Phil Nelson, Howard University, WHUR-FM, 529 Bryant Street North West, Washington, DC 20059 Phone: (202) 806-3500 E-mail: pnelson@whur.com Website: www.whur.com

The Russ Parr Show Top rated nationally syndicated Morning Show. Russ Parr, host. Russ is an author, scriptwriter and film producres. Interviews authors locally. Russ Parr, WFXM-FM, Roberts Communications, Inc., Route 6, Box 735, Highway 57, Macon, Georgia Phone: (478) 745-3301 Fax: (478) 742-2293 E-mail: robertsrci@aol.com   Website: www.uptoparr.com

The Poets Corner Internet talk show. Host, Jamalo White. Contact Bernard Broadcasting Company, 5316 Cottonwood Road, Memphis, Tennessee 38118 Phone: (877) 825-5014 E-mail: OnAir@memphisrealtalk.com Website: www.memphisrealtalk.com

Positively People Talk show hosted by Bailey Coleman. Interviews. WKKV-FM V100, 12100 West Howard Avenue, Greenfield, Wisconsin 53228 Phone: (414) 321-1007 Fax: (414) 799-8100 E-mail: baileycoleman@clearchannel.com Website: www.v100.com

The Praise Party Show Show airs weekdays 12:00pm - 4:00pm. Born in Chicago, IL and raised in Memphis, TN, Host, Ace Alexander. Contact Gospel 1190 AM The Light, 3260 Blume Drive, Suite 520, Richmond, California 94806 Phone: (510) 222-4242 Fax: (510) 262-9054 E-mail: acealexander@thepraiseparty.com Website: www.sgnthelight.com

Pulse Of The City Hosted by Robert S. Interviews authors and artists. 1140 WJNZ has a unique niche in the minds of Grand Rapids' consumers. We balance the hottest Hits and Oldies R&B with a distinctly community-minded presentation. Contact Robert S., 1140 WJNZ-AM, Goodrich Radio Group, 1919 Eastern Avenue, S.E., Grand Rapids, Michigan 49507 Phone: (616) 475-4299 E-mail: mjs@wjnz.com Website: www.wjnz.com

Real Talk w/K.J. A live internet broadcast show hosted by author, Kalico Jones at the website artistfirst.com. The weekly internet radio broadcast features the hottest unsigned acts in the world. Kalico Jones, Artistfirst World Radio, 1062 Parkside Drive, Alliance, Ohio 44601 Phone: (862) 202-1866 E-mail: kalicojones@yahoo.com Website: www.artistfirst.com

The Relationship Fitness Show Co-host Cheryl Martin, and relationship fitness coach Johnny Parker provide practical insight to singles and married couples for building and nurturing strong, lasting relationships. Cheryl is the author of 1st Class Single: Rules for Dating and Waiting God's Way. She also writes a column, "Successfully Single," in Gospel Today. Cheryl Martin, Post Office Box 15285, Chevy Chase, Maryland 20825 Phone: (301) 907-8215 E-mail: info@cherylmartin.org Website: www.cherylmartin.org

Reynolds Rap Show hosted by author and award winning journalist, Dr. Barbara A. Reynolds, received her BA in journalism from The Ohio State University, her Masters Degree from Howard University School of Divinity in 1991, and her doctorate in Ministry from the United Theological Seminary in Dayton, Ohio in 1998. Contact Dr. Barbara A. Reynolds, 4806 Saint Barnabas Road, Suite 598, Temple Hills, Maryland 20757 Phone: (301) 899-1341 E-mail: reynew@aol.com Website: www.reynoldsnews.com

Richmond is Talking Radio talk show hosted by author, Gloria Taylor Edwards. Interviews authors. A mystery writer/women's issues and an inspirational speaker, Ms. Taylor is the author of The Proclamation, 1992; Stories From Ancient Africa,1995; Death Will Pay The Debt, 2000; and, Sins Of The Parents, 2004. Contact Ms. Gloria Taylor Edwards, VFTD, Post Office Box 27504, Richmond, Virginia 23261 Phone: (804) 323-6441 E-mail: vftdgte@aol.com

Effie Rolfe Midday Host from 10 a.m. to 2 p.m. at radio station Inspiration1390. Effie gives you: Super Size Your Thinking at 10:10 a.m., Signs of The Time at 10:43 a.m., Job File Mon/Fri at 11:10 a.m. and Bible Trivia at 11:42 a.m. She is author of the newly released book, The (K)Nots Prayer Journal--Finding Your Passion by Eliminating the nots in life. Motivational Speaker, at churches, schools, graduations, anniversary, non-for profits, etc. Effie Rolfe, 233 North Michigan Avenue, #2700, Chicago, Illinois 60601 Phone: (312) 540-2396 E-mail: EffieRolfe@clearchannel.com Website: www.supersizeyourthinking.com

The Saturday Vibe Show airs 10 p.m.-2 a. m. every weekend with host, DJ Orion. WNOU-FM, 21 East St. Joseph Street, Indianapolis, Indiana 46204 Phone: (317) 266-9600 Fax: (317) 261-4664 E-mail: anturner@radio-one.com Website: www.radionowindy.com

The Al Sharpton Show A daily talk show hosted by community leader, politician, minister and advocate, the Reverand Al Sharpton one of America 's most-renowned civil rights leaders. Contact Rev. Al Sharpton, 52 East 125th Street, New York, New York 10035 Phone: (212) 690-3070 E-mail: revalmedia@yahoo.com Website: www.nationalactionetwork.net

The Bev Smith Show Essence Award Winner and Host, Bev Smith delivers critical information and entertainment news. Her show features the latest news makers. Bev Smith, The Bev Smith Show, 960 Penn Avenue, #200, Pittsburgh, Pennsylvania 15222 Phone: (412) 456-4007 E-mail: contact@thebevsmithshow.com Website: www.thebevsmithshow.com

Kim McLaughlin-Smith Mid-day radio air personality at WBNE 93.7. Show interviews artists and authors. Contact Ms. Kim McLaughlin, WBNE 93.7, Sea-Communications Media, 122 Cinema Drive, Wilmington, North Carolina 28403 Phone: (910) 772-6300 Fax: (910) 772-6337 E-mail: radiobutter@hotmail.com Website: www.1037thebone.com

Spotlight Host, Carla Rowser Canty at WQTQ 89.9 FM. Poets, authors and musicians are encouraged to showcase their work. Canty is the author of Author of Diary of A Blackgurl. Carla Rowser Canty, Post Office Box 843, Hartford, Connecticut 06143 Phone: (860) 983-3257 E-mail: BlackGurrl@aol.com Website: www.wqtqfm.com/wqtq

Soulfully Speaking On CaribVoice Radio and Akeru Radio. Host, Dr. Anita Davis-DeFoe, The Defoe Group, Post Office Box 451973, Sunrise, Florida 33345 Phone: (954) 816-9462 E-mail: dranitadavisdefoe@hotmail.com Website: www.dranitadavisdefoe.com

Soopa Dave Weekdays 3-7pm. Soopa Dave features the Word of The Day. Interviews authors and artists. Claudel Price, General Manager. Contact Soopa Dave, 6174 Highway 57, Macon, Georgia 31217 Phone: (478) 745-3301 Fax: (478) 742-2293 E-mail: soopaone@gmail.com Website: www.mypower1071.com

Sunday Afternoon   Weekly radio show on 107.5 WGPR-FM hosted by author, radio & television personality, Karen Dumas. Contact Images & Ideas, Inc., Post Office Box 14724, Detroit, Michigan 48214 Phone: (866) 330-4585 E-mail: karendumas2@aol.com Website: www.KarenDumas.com

Nicole "Swingin" Sweeney Midday Jazz Swing with Nicole 'Swinging' Sweeney, weekdays from 10:00 AM until 2:00 PM for an eclectic mix of mainstream Jazz fused with familiar tunes, standards, vocals and, Atlanta based Jazz artists. Midday Jazz Swing with Nicole 'Swinging' Sweeney, weekdays from 10:00 AM until 2:00 PM. Contact Mr. Aaron Cohen, Programming Director, WCLK-FM, Jazz 91.9-FM, Clark Atlanta University, 111 James P. Brawley Drive, South West, Atlanta, Georgia 30314 Phone: (404) 880-8273 Fax: (404) 880-8869 E-mail: kayceecole@gmail.com Website: www.wclk.com

The Talus on Demand Morning Show Airs Monday thru Friday 6 a.m. – 10 a.m "The realist news" on the 10 (the only live & local morning Show). Claudel Price, General Manager, 107.1, 6174 Highway 57, Macon, Georgia 31217 Phone: (478) 745-3301 Fax: (478) 742-2293 E-mail: soopaone@gmail.com Website: www.mypower1071.com

The Tavis Smiley Show Tavis Smiley, Host. Weekly radio show of news and newsmakers in expanded conversations. Show is distributed by Public Radio International (PRI). The Tavis Smiley Show, The Smiley Group, 3870 Crenshaw Boulevard, Suite 391, Los Angeles, California 90008 E-mail: tavis@tavistalks.com Website: www.tavistalks.com

Tell Me More Daily NPR news and talk show, weekdays, afternoon news and talk show. Highlights significance of cultural inclusion, fused with sharp debates between show host and contributors, topics to include politics, faith, lifestyle, politics, arts and family. Michel Martin, Host. NPR, 635 Massachusetts Avenue, NW, Washington DC 20001 Phone: (202) 513-3232 Fax: (202) 513-3329 E-mail: mecommentary@npr.org Website: www.npr.org

Thinking It Through Host, Dr. Carlos E. Russell and his nightly guests. Carlos E. Russell, WLIB 1190, I.C.B.C. Broadcast Holdings, Inc., New York, New York Phone: (212) 889-1190 Fax: (212) 447-5193 E-mail: think@wlib.com Website: www.wlib.com

The Ticktin Law Firm's Legal Advice Radio Show Airs every Monday from 11:30 a.m. - 12:30 p.m. The show is hosted by Franklin Nickins, Jumpin Joe, and attorneys from the firm. Joseph Jenkins, Operations Director. WIRA, 6803 S. Federal Highway, Port SaintLucie, Florida 34952 Phone: (772) 460-9356 E-mail: jumpinjoe@wflm.cc Website: www.wira1400am.com

Today's Black Woman A Nationally syndicated radio talk show reaching over 1.000,000 women weekly. Founder/host, Jennifer Kreitt. The Today's Black Woman Corporation, Post Office Box 440981, Kennesaw, Georgia 30160 Phone: (678) 569-2407 Fax: (678) 354-4334 E-mail: zakarmagazine@gmail.com Website: www.todaysblackwomanradio.com

Tone E. Fly Show Morning show host, Tone E. Fly. Interviews guests. Contact KTTB-FM, Blue Chip Broadcasting, 5300 Edina Industrial Boulevard, Edina, Minnesota 55439 Phone: (952) 842-7200 Fax: (952) 842-1048 E-mail: tfly@963now.com Website: www.963.com

The Tree of Life Show Internet radio show airs on BlakeRadio.com, Channel 5. Kanya Vashon McGhee, Host, 1701 M. L. King Drive SW, Atlanta, Georgia 30314 Phone: (404) 753-5700 E-mail: drkanya@GMail.com Website: www.naturalusa.com/ads/treeoflife.html

The Urban Business Roundtable (UBR) Show promotes engaging dialogue and debate about the impact of business and economic trends on the African-American community. All-star line-up to create a hub for entrepreneurs that helps them navigate, survive, and thrive in the current economy. Host, Alfred Edmond Jr., WVON 1450AM, 3350 South Kedzie, Chicago, Illinois 60623 Phone: (773) 247-6200 E-mail: Monique@wvon.com Website: www.wvon.com

Voices from the Drum (VFTD) Radio talk show hosted by mystery writer and author, Gloria Taylor Edwards. Gloria Taylor Ediwards, VFTD, Post Office Box 27504, Richmond, Virginia 23261 Phone: (804) 323-6441 E-mail: vftdgte@aol.com

Eric Von Talk Radio host. Contact Mr. Eric Von, 1290 WMCS, 4222 West Capitol Drive, Suite 1290, Milwaukee, Wisconsin 53216 Phone: (414) 444-1290 Fax: (414) 444-1409 E-mail: evontalk@1290wmcs.com Website: www.1290wmcs.com

The Lincoln Ware Show Talk show discusses local and national issues, hot topics and opinions. Interviews authors. Host, Lincoln Ware. Contact WDBZ-AM, 1 Centennial Plaza, Suite 200, 705 Central Avenue, Cincinnati, Ohio 45202 Phone: (513) 749-1230 Fax: (513) 948-1985 E-mail: lware@radio-one.com Website: www.1230thebuzz.com

WEUP Talk Show airs daily 5-6 p.m. Host by David Person. Hundley Batts, Sales Coordinator, WEUP Radio Station, Post Office Box 11398, Huntsville, Alabama 35814 Phone: (256) 837-9387 Fax: (256) 837-9404 E-mail: weuptalk@aol.com Website: www.103weup.com

What's Going On? Community affairs program serving the greater San Francisco Bay Area. Interviews artists and authors. Host, Ms. Nikki Thomas. KBLX-FM, 55 Hawthorne Street, Suite 900, San Francisco, California 94105 Phone: (415) 284-1029 Fax: (415) 764-1029 E-mail: nthomas@kblx.com Website: www.kblx.com

Yolanda Joe
Author * Journalist

Yolanda Joe is a native of Chicago, Illinois. She is an author, and a former producer and writer for CBS News, Chicago where she currently resides. A prolific mystery writer she has authored eight best selling books: <u>Falling Leaves of Ivy</u> (Longmeadow Press, 1992), <u>He Say, She Say</u> (Doubleday, 1997), <u>Bebe's By Golly Wow</u>, (Doubleday, 1998), <u>This Just In</u> (One World/Ballantine, 2001), <u>Details at Ten: A Georgia Barnett Mystery</u> (Pocket, 2002), <u>Hit Time</u> (Simon & Schuster, 2002), <u>The Hatwearer's Lesson</u> (Dutton, 2003), and <u>My Fine Lady</u> (Dutton, 2004). Her new book Video Cowboys: A Georgia Barnett Mystery will be released by Simon & Schuster in June, 2005.

Yolanda earned her B.A. in English literature from Yale University; and her M.A. in Journalism from Columbia University.

Theatres

African Continuum Theatre Company (ACTCO)   Since 1989.   ActCo is a professional theater company whose mission is to illuminate the human condition through producing and presenting professional theatrical productions.   ACTco productions reflect an aesthetic rooted in the African and American-American experience. Contact African Continuum Theatre Company, 3523 12th Street, North East, 2nd Floor, Washington, DC 20017 Phone: (202) 529-5763 E-mail: info@africancontinuumtheatre.com Website: www.africancontinuumtheatre.com

Alliance Theatre Company   Now in its fourth decade, the Alliance Theatre has achieved recognition as one of the country's leading theatres, having premiered such works as Pearl Cleage's, Blues for an Alabama Sky; Elton John and Tim Rice's, Elaborate Lives: The Legend of Aida (in partnership with Disney Theatricals); Sandra Deer's, So Long on Lonely Street, and Alfred Uhry's, The Last Night of Ballyhoo. Artistic Director Susan V. Booth.   The Alliance Theatre Company, 1280 Peachtree Street, North East, Atlanta, Georgia 30309 Phone: (404) 733-4600 E-mail: info@alliancetheatre.org Website: www.alliancetheatre.org

Black Ensemble Theater Corporation   Organization seeks to produce entertaining, educational and enlightening African American theater of excellence that reaches an interracial audience. Jackie Taylor, founder, producer, executive director. Black Ensemble Theater Corporation, 4520 North Beacon Street, Chicago, Illinois 60640 Phone: (773) 769-4451 Fax: (773) 769-4533 E-mail: BlackEnsemble@aol.com   Website: www.blackensembletheater.org

Black Spectrum Theatre Company   Lawrence Evans, Director. Contact Black Spectrum Theatre Company, 119-07 Merrick Boulevard, Jamaica, New York 11434 Phone: (718) 723-1800 E-mail: BlackTheatre@yahoogroups.com Website: www.blackspectrum.com

Bronx Renaissance Community Theater   Bevin Sinclair Turnbull, Executive Director. Bevin Sinclair Turnbull, Bronx Renaissance Community Theater, 1170 East 225th Street, Bronx, New York 10466 Phone: (718) 405-1553 Fax: (718) 231-5681 E-mail: bjazz7@aol.com

Castillo Theatre   Established in 1984. Privately funded from the beginning, it has gained recognition as a leading voice in the world of avant-garde and political theatre, creating works that are both topical and entertaining. Castillo hosts the annual Otto Rene Castillo Awards and its annual theatrical seasons feature improvisational comedy and plays. Castillo Theatre, 543 West 42nd Street, New York, New York 10036 Phone: (212) 941-9400 E-mail: castillo@allstars.org. Websites: www.castillo.org, www.allstars.org

Cincinnati Black Theatre Company   Offers theatrical productions, performance and children's theatre, educational programs and community outreach in all aspects of theatre arts. Contact Cincinnati Black Theatre Company, 5919 Hamilton Avenue, Cincinnati, Ohio 45224 Phone: (513) 241-6060 Fax: (513) 241-6671 E-mail: cbtcsherman@hotmail.com

Dramastage-Qumran Recovery Theater Melvin Ishmael Johnson, Director. Dramastage-Qumran Recovery Theater, 1335 North La Brea, #2179, Hollywood, California 90028 Phone: (323) 850-4436 E-mail: bymel2004@yahoo.com Website: www.dramastage-qumran.org

Frank Silvera Writers' Workshop Foundation, Inc. A nonprofit theatre arts organization and playwright development program. founded by playwright/director Garland Lee Thompson, Sr., along with actor/director Morgan Freeman, director/actress Billie Allen and journalist Clayton Riley. Frank Silvera Writers Workshop Foundations, Inc., Post Office Box 1791, Manhattanville Station, New York, New York 10027 Phone: (212) 281-8832 E-mail: playrite@earthlink.net Website: www.fsww.org

Karamu House Terrence Spivey, Artistic Director.   Contact Karamu House, 2355 East 89th, Cleveland, Ohio 44106 Phone: (216) 795-7077 Website: www.karamu.com

New Federal Theatre Specializes in minority dramas by presenting plays to the culturally diverse greater New York area and supports emerging writers by bringing their work to full scale productions; hires directors, actors, designers and playwrights. Woodie King Jr., Director. New Federal Theatre, 292 Henry Street, New York, New York 10002 Phone: (212) 353-1176 Fax: (212) 353-1088 E-mail: info@newfederaltheatre.org   Website: www.newfederaltheatre.org

North Carolina Black Repertory Company (NCBRC) Host of the National Black Theatre Festival. A large number of workshops and seminars are available at the National Black Theatre Festival. NCBRC, 610 Coliseum Drive, Winston-Salem, North Carolina 27106 Phone: (336) 723-2266 Fax: (336) 723-2223 E-mail: llhamlin@bellsouth.net Website: www.nbtf.org

Orisha Tales Repertory Radio Theatre Company The theatre company and it's author/producer, produces and writes dance dramas based on the Yoruba tradition in the Old World and the Diaspora. Founder, David D. Wright. Orisha Tales Repertory Radio Theatre Company, 133 East 96th Street, Brooklyn, New York 11212 Phone: (718) 735-8905 E-mail: orisatalesradio@aol.com   Website: www.orishatalesrepertoryradiotheatrecompany.org

Pin Points Theatre Company Since 1980, Pin Points Theatre's productions have toured stages in thirty-seven states and nine countries. Ersky Freeman, Pin Points Theatre Company, 4353 Dubois Place, South East, Washington, DC 20019 Phone: (202) 582-0002 E-mail: pinpoints@aol.com Website: www.pinpoints.org

TV News Reporters

Roslyn Anderson Weekend Anchor/Reporter. Prior to joining WLBT in 1993 Roslyn was a weather anchor/reporter with WTOK-TV in Meridian, Mississippi. During her 3 and a half years at the Meridian station she received awards from the Mississipppi Associated Press for Best Spot News Story and Best Newscast for her role as 10 p.m. Weathercaster. Contact Ms. Roslyn Anderson, WLBT-TV3, Post Box 1712, Jackson, Mississippi 39215 Phone: (601) 948-3333 E-mail: roslyn@wlbt.net Website: www.wlbt.net

Howard Ballou In addition to his anchoring at WLBT, he is currently a general assignment reporter and has served as producer and executive producer for the station. Mr. Ballou has been in the broadcast journalism profession for more than 20 years. He has won several awards of excellence in his field, including United Press International's "Best Documentary" category for a report he did on Tennessee Drunk Driving Legislation. He is former Regional Director for the Society of Professional Journalists. Howard Ballous, WLBT-TV3, Post Box 1712, Jackson, Mississippi 39215 Phone: (601) 948-3333 E-mail: howard@wlbt.net Website: www.wlbt.net

Audrey Barnes A frequent substitute anchor, Audrey Barnes joined WUSA 9 as a general assignment reporter in May of 2003. Audrey is a graduate of the University of Maryland College Park and has a degree in Broadcast Journalism. She also has a Master's degree from the Medill School of Journalism at Northwestern University. Prior to coming to WUSA 9, Audrey worked at two other Washington stations. She also spent three years as morning anchor for WBAL-TV in Baltimore and has also been a reporter and anchor for television stations in Salisbury, Maryland; Jacksonville, Florida; and Charlotte, North Carolina. Ms. Audrey Barnes, WUSA-TV (Channel 9, CBS) 4100 Wisconsin Avenue, North West, Washington, DC 20016 Phone: (202) 895-5999 E-mail: abarnes@wusa9.com Website: www.wusa9.com

Kara Brooks Joined the FOX 59 News Team in March, 2005. Kara came to FOX 59 from WPSD in Paducah, Kentucky where she anchored the weekend evening news. She was also the Education and General Assignment Reporter for the station. Kara's career began in Michigan's cold Upper Peninsula at WLUC in Marquette, Michigan. In Michigan, she wore many hats. Kara produced, reported, edited, and shot her own news stories. Kara has earned several Kentucky Associated Press Awards. She also won a fellowship to the Casey Journalism Center for Children and Families. Kara Brooks,WXIN-TV, 6910 Network Place, Indianapolis, Indiana 46278 Phone: (317) 632-5900 E-mail: kbrooks@tribune.com Website: www.fox59.com

Anissa Centers Before coming to KLTV Anissa anchored the news at WSB-TV in Atlanta, Georgia and prior to that she was the primary evening news anchor at WALA-TV in Mobile, Alabama. A native East Texan, Anissa has done live reporting for CNN and interviewed former President George W. Bush and First Lady Laura Bush. Contact Ms. Anissa Centers, KLTV, 105 West Ferguson, Tyler, Texas 75702 Phone: (903) 597-5588 E-mail: acenters@kltv.com Website: www.kltv.com

Linda Coles   Executive Producer of Another View, NJN's award-winning public affairs program serving New Jersey's diverse African-American community, Linda has more than 20 years experience in the broadcasting industry. Her work has received numerous regional Emmy nominations from the Philadelphia Chapter of the National Academy of Television Arts and Sciences. A graduate of Rutgers University, she serves as president of the the Garden State Association of Black Journalists. Linda Coles, New Jersey Network, 25 South Stockton Street, Trenton, New Jersey 08625   Phone: (609) 777-5030   E-mail: lcoles@njn.org   Website: www.njn.org

Gina Ford   Native of Washington, DC, Gina grew up on Capitol Hill. She comes from a family of reporters, and went to the University of Kansas where she earned her undergraduate degree in broadcast journalism. She was a reporter and anchor for KUJH-TV in Lawrence, Kansas for two and a half years. Over the years, she knew that news was her calling, so interned at WJLA-TV in Washington, DC, KAKE-TV in Wichita, Kansas, and Fox News Channel, to get an inside look. Gina loves to travel abroad and so far has visited Brazil, Africa, France, Germany, Hong Kong, Canada and Mexico. She hopes one day, her love for journalism will allow her to work abroad. Gina Ford, KSEE 24, 5035 East McKinley Avenue, Fresno, California 93727 Phone: (559) 454-2424 E-mail: gford@week.com Website: www.ksee24.com

Ralph Gaston   Sports Reporter. A former collegiate football and baseball player, he got his start in journalism as a sportswriter for the Montgomery County Sentinel in Rockville, Maryland. After attending the School of Journalism at Cal-Berkeley, he switched from print to broadcast, landing a job at WBOY in Clarksburg, West Virginia as a sports anchor/reporter. Mr. Ralph Gastibm KSEE 24, 5035 East McKinley Avenue, Fresno, California 93727 Phone: (559) 454-2424 E-mail: ralphg@ksee.com Website: www.ksee24.com

Chauncy Glover   News Reporter. Chauncy studied Broadcast Journalism and Theatre at Troy University. He has won several awards for his work, including Associate Press recognition for a story that exposed several pharmacies in Columbus, caught violating HIPPA laws. He has a degree in Public Relations. Chauncy Glover, Action News Jacksonville, 11700 Central Parkway #2, Jacksonville, Florida 32224 Phone: (904) 996-0400 E-mail: cglover@actionnewsjax.com Website: www.actionnewsjax.com

Shelton Green   A News Reporter, since 1995, Shelton came to KVUE from Dallas where he worked on the assignment desk at KTVT-Channel 11. Contact Mr. Shelton Green, KVUE News, 3201 Steck Avenue, Austin, Texas 78757 Phone: (512) 459-2086 E-mail: Sgreen@kvue.com Website: www.kvue.com

JC Hayward   Anchors WUSA 9 News. In 30 years at WUSA 9, JC has consistently been rated one of the top news people in Washington broadcast journalism. In 1976, she won a local Emmy Award in the Best Newscaster category. In 1994, she won a local Emmy Award for her interview with Riddick Bowe. In June 1995, she was awarded the prestigious Board of Governors Award, a local Emmy given for "truly outstanding achievement and unique accomplishment of some duration and durability." JC Hayward, WUSA-TV (Channel 9, CBS) 4100 Wisconsin Avenue, North West, Washington, DC 20016 Phone: (202) 895-5999 E-mail: jhayward@wusa9.com Website: www.wusa9.com

Jerry Henry General Assignment Reporter. Since 1987, Jerry has been a part of the NJN News Team, where he has been reporting on New Jersey's sports scene. In 1993 he won the Associated Press First Place Award for sports reporting. Jerry has also hosted the NJN public affairs show, Another View, for which he won two Mid-Atlantic "Emmy" awards. Mr. Jerry Henry, NJN News, 50 Park Place, Newark, New Jersey 07102 Phone: (609-652) 8385 Fax: (609) 652-1629 E-mail: jhenry@njn.org Website: www.njn.org

Denise Jackson A native of Peoria, Denise attended Richwoods High and went on to Bradley University, graduating in 1986 with a bachelor's degree in journalism. Denise has been with WEEK since 1999, and is currently a reporter, as well as News 25 Weekend co-anchor. Previously, Denise was a news anchor for WWNY-TV, Watertown, New York. Denise serves on the board of directors of the Tri-County Urban League and the YMCA Invest in Youth Campaign 2000, and is active in her church. Ms. Denise Jackson, WEEK-TV, 2907 Springfield Road, East Peoria, Illinois 61611 Phone: (309) 698-2525 Fax: (309) 698-2070 E-mail: djackson@week.com Website: www.week.com

Rick Jackson CBS 42 Morning Reporter, Rick previously worked for the NBC and Fox affiliates as a general assignment reporter. He is a graduate of Auburn University. Rick Jackson, WIAT-TV CBS 42, 2075 Golden Crest Drive, Birmingham, Alabama 35209 Phone: (205) 322-4200 Fax: (205) 320-2713 E-mail: newsrelease@cbs42.com Website: www.cbs42.com

Sherri Jackson Weekday Anchor for CBS 42 News at 5, 6 & 10 o'clock, Sherri is a veteran journalist who prior to coming to CBS 42 in 1998, worked for WGXA-TV in Macon, Georgia, WSAV-TV in Savannah Georgia, and WSAZ-TV in Charleston and Huntington West Virginia. Education: Graduate of Morehead State University in Morehead, Kentucky. She currently serves as Vice President of Broadcast for the Birmingham Association of Black Journalists. Sherri Jackson, WIAT-TV CBS 42, 2075 Golden Crest Drive, Birmingham, Alabama 35209 Phone: (205) 322-4200 Fax: (205) 320-2713 Website: www.cbs42.com

Rob Jay Currently works in both radio and television. He is the morning show host on WYJS 105.9 F.M. and he also does freelance reporting for Major Black College Sports on the MBC network, sideline reporting for Jackson State Football radio broadcast, and fill in play by play announcer for Jackson State basketball. Rob appeared in the movie A Time to Kill where his role was reporter. Rob came to WLBT in 1991 as a reporter/photographer and had worked his way up to sports director by 1996. Rob Jay, WLBT-TV3, Post Box 1712, Jackson, Mississippi 39215 Phone: (601) 948-3333 E-mail: robj@wlbt.net Website: www.wlbt.net

Bruce Johnson Working on special assignment for WUSA 9, Johnson has covered stories in Rome, Moscow, Paris, Stockholm, Budapest, Bangkok, Tokyo, Dakar and Haiti. Bruce is recognized in Washington as an expert on city government and politics for his Mayoral and City Council coverage. He has been a reporter/anchor for 9NEWS NOW since February of 1976. He began his career at WCPO-TV in Cincinnati, Ohio. He has an undergraduate degree in Political Science from Northern Kentucky State University and a Master's degree in Public Affairs (MPA) from the University of Cincinnati. Bruce Johnson, WUSA-TV (Channel 9, CBS) 4100 Wisconsin Avenue, North West, Washington, DC 20016 Phone: (202) 895-5999 E-mail: bjohnson@wusa9.com Website: www.wusa9.com

David Kenney Began working at WLBT as a general assignment report in December of 1996. Since then he has covered all types of stories around the state, from Presidential visits, the shootings at Pearl High School, to Hurricane George on the Mississippi Gulf coast, tornadoes in Madison County and the city of Newton. David is from Minneapolis Minnesota. He graduated from the University of Wisconsin River Falls. Since 2002, David has been a member of the Craft Committee at the Career Development Center. David often does classroom visits, working with students in the Television Production department on video editing, reporting and anchoring. David Kenney, WLBT-TV3, Post Box 1712, Jackson, Mississippi 39215 Phone: (601) 948-3333 E-mail: david@wlbt.net Website: www.wlbt.net

Dawn Lopez Co-anchor of CBS47 News at 5:00 p.m., 5:30 p.m. and 11 p.m., Dawn is an alumni of Wolfson High School and the University of North Florida. After graduation, she moved to Columbus, Georgia to do general assignment reporting at ABC affiliate WTVM-9. Her next move was to WGHP-TV, in High Point, North Carolina, where she anchored the investigative & consumer team at FOX-8 News. She is actively involved in community work making speaking engagements with local schools and organizations. Dawn Lopez, Action News Jacksonville, 11700 Central Parkway #2, Jacksonville, Florida 32224 Phone: (904) 996-0400 E-mail: dlopez@actionnewsjax.com Website: www.actionnewsjax.com

Beverly Mahone A veteran journalist with more than 25 years of experience in radio and television. In May 2006, Ms. Mahone published her first non-fiction book entitled: "Whatever! A Baby Boomer's Journey Into Middle Age." The book resulted from a journal Ms. Mahone was writing about her menopausal experiences and other challenging life issues, aging, hot flashes, mood swings, depression, middle age spread, stressed out, divorce, second chances, new opportunities, transformation. Also a motivational speaker she owns a media coaching and consulting business. Listen to Beverly Live on Thursdays at 1 p.m. on 103.5 FM WCOM Radio in North Carolina. Beverly Mahone, Post Office Box 11037, Durham, North Carolina 27703 Phone: (301) 356-6280 E-mail: Beverly@talk2bev.com Website: www.beverlymahone.com

Michelle Marsh General assignment reporter, since 2009. Formerly an investigative reporter and anchor at CBS 6 in Albany, New York, Michelle graduated Magna Cum Laude from the Syracuse University Newhouse School of Public Communications with a B.S. in Broadcast Journalism. Contact Ms. Michelle Marsh, CBS Atlanta, 425 14th Street NW, Atlanta, Georgia 30318 Phone: (404) 325-4646 Fax: (404) 327-3004 E-mail: michelle.marsh@cbsatlanta.com Website: www.cbsatlanta.com

Derek McGinty Weekday anchor for 9NEWS NOW at 7 pm, and weeknight co-anchor for 9NEWS NOW at 11pm. From March 2001 to June 2003, he was co-anchor of ABC NEWS' overnight broadcast, World News Now, and anchor of World News This Morning. Additionally, Derek was a correspondent for "HBO's Real Sports" for 4 years. Until recently, he was the host of "Eye On Washington", a politically-based roundtable talk show produced at WUSA 9's studios that provided analysis and perspective on top stories from our Nation's Capital. At WETA, he had a similar role for the station's Emmy-nominated "Here and Now," a weekly half-hour local program focusing on issues, events, and people in metropolitan Washington, DC. Derek McGinty, WUSA-TV, 4100 Wisconsin Avenue, North West, Washington, DC 20016 Phone: (202) 895-5999 E-mail: dmcginty@wusa9.com Website: www.wusa9.com

Edward Moody Weekend Anchor/Reporter. Edward was an Anchor/Reporter at 13WHAM-TV in Rochester New York and a Morning Anchor in Duluth, Minnesota before that. He was born and raised in Kansas City, Missouri. He graduated from the University of Missouri-Kansas City with a Degree in Communication Studies. He has covered everything from a mass school shooting in northern Minnesota to the disappearance of IU student Lauren Spierer. Edward Moody, WXIN-TV, 6910 Network Place, Indianapolis, Indiana 46278 Phone: (317) 632-5900 E-mail: emoody@fox59.com Website: www.fox59.com

Garry Moore A Chicago native, Gary is a news anchor and senior producer of News 25 Today. He grauduated from Bradley University, with a Masters and a Bachelors Degree In Liberal Studies and Broadcast Production/Management respectively. Prior to his television career he started his reporting career as a reporter and eventual news director for WXCL-AM in Peoria. He is a writer and producer of several successful theatre arts productions, including Black to the Future, Dancing My Sisters Back Home, and The Ghosts of Haiti. As an adjunct professor Gary taught Black Music at Illinois State University and has conducted numerous hand drumming classes throughout the area. Gary Moore, WEEK-TV, 2907 Springfield Road, East Peoria, Illinois 61611 Phone: (309) 698-2525 E-mail: gmoore@week.com Website: www.week.com

Christine Nelson Co-anchor of WBTV News This Morning and WBTV News at Noon. Before coming to WBTV Christine was an anchor for WABG-TV where she became a Delta favorite most recently being named 2004 Television Personality of the Year by newspaper readers. In 2001, she broke the story on the construction halt of a plant being built in the Delta. It led to a protest by hundreds of residents and her coverage of the story placed in the "Best General News" category in the Mississippi Associated Press Awards. Christine is a graduate of the University of Georgia. Christine Nelson, WBTV Television, 1 Julian Price Place, Charlotte, North Carolina 28208 Phone: (704) 374-3500 E-mail: cnelson@wbtv.com Website: www.wbtv.com

Katina Rankin A native of Magee, Mississippi Katina is WLBT's weekday morning anchor. She received her bachelor's degree in mass communications from Alcorn State University and her master's degree in broadcast journalism from Jackson State University. While attending ASU, Katina began her journalism career as an intern at WLBT. After six years on the air in Mississippi, Katina's career led her to Raleigh-Durham, North Carolina, where she co-anchored the main newscast at Eyewitness News. During her journalism career, Katina has covered everything from the Mississippi murder trials of Byron De La Beckwith and Sam Bowers to the Space Shuttle Columbia disaster in Texas. Katina has also taught writing classes at Jackson State University. And she has been featured on the Oprah Winfrey Show. Katina Rankin, WLBT-TV3, Post Box 1712, Jackson, Mississippi 39215 Phone: (601) 948-3333 E-mail: krankin@wlbt.net Website: www.wlbt.net

Dee Registre Reporter. Before joining Action News, Dee was a general assignment reporter at WALB in Albany, Georgia. She was a writer at WSVN and also contributed to the community pages of the Miami Herald. She also interned in WPLG's news department and WFOR's sports department. She received her M.A. in Television Broadcast Journalism from the University of Miami and her B.A. from Florida State University. Dee Registre, Action News Jacksonville, 11700 Central Parkway #2, Jacksonville, Florida 32224 Phone: (904) 996-0400 E-mail: dregistre@actionnewsjax.com Website: www.actionnewsjax.com

Andrea Roane Has been with WUSA 9 since 1981, and currently anchors 9 NEWS NOW from 5-7 a.m. and 9-10 a.m. Andrea was selected as a distinguished annual honoree by the ASAE & The Center for Association Leadership's Greater Washington Network, which recognized Andrea's outstanding work within the community and the region as a "leader and trailblazer deserving of recognition." During her career, she has covered a wealth of hard news stories, from politics, the arts, education and sports to women's health issues. She has interviewed newsmakers, entertainers, and politicians including Archbishop Desmond Tutu, Hillary Rodham Clinton, former Defense Secretary William Cohen, David Rockefeller, Michael J. Fox, Danny Glover, Magic Johnson and author Mary Higgins Clarke. She covered the 1996 Republican and Democratic conventions and the 1988 GOP convention. Awards: 2004 Lombardi Symbol of Caring Award 2004 Innovators in Advocacy Award- GW MFA Mobile Mammography Program 2002 Women of Distinction Award - Northern Seaboard Region and Greater Washington Area Chapter Hadassah, among others. She earned a Bachelor of Arts degree in Speech Education and a Master of Arts degree in Drama and Communications from Louisiana State University in New Orleans, now the University of New Orleans. Andrea Roane, WUSA-TV (Channel 9, CBS) 4100 Wisconsin Avenue, North West, Washington, DC 20016 Phone: (202) 895-5999 E-mail: aroane@wusa9.com Website: www.wusa9.com

Ronda Robinson Award-winning Investigative News Reporter. In 2001 and 2002 Rhonda received Associated Press Awards for her coverage of the Tom Blanton and Bob Cherry murder trials, for the 16th Street Baptist Church bombing. Rhonda's consumer news as part of the 5pm and 6pm newscasts earned her an Associated Press Award in 2003 and an Emmy nomination in 2004. Received the National Association of Black Journalist Best Investigative Reporting Award in 2005. Ronda Robinson, WBRC-TV, 1720 Valleyview Drive, Birmingham, Alabama 35209 Phone: (205) 583-8413 E-mail: rrobinson@wbrc.com Website: www.wbrc.com

Regina Russo Weekend News Anchor. Since joining Fox19 in 1996 Regina has anchored First Look, 19 in the Morning, and now the weekends of the 10 o'clock news. She explores current events through Fox19's half hour program Cincinnati Maaters. Graduate of Perdue University. Contact Regina Russo, WXIX-TV, 635 West Seventh Street, Cincinnati, Ohio 45203 Phone: (513) 421-0119 Fax: (513) 421-3022 E-mail: rrusso@fox19.com Website: www.fox19.com

LaKecia Shockley News Reporter. Before coming to KLTV, LaKecia was the noon anchor, producer, and medical reporter for WDAY-TV in Oak Hill, West Virginia. LaKecia graduated from Western Kentucky University where she majored in Broadcast Journalism. LeKecia Shockley, KLTV-7, 105 West Ferguson, Tyler, Texas 75702 Phone: (903) 597-5588 Fax: (903) 753-7111 E-mail: lshockley@kltv.com Website: www.kltv.com

Mark Spain Co-anchor of CBS47 News at 6 p.m. and FOX30 News at 10 p.m. He has worked in the Jacksonville television market since 2000 and joined CBS47 & FOX30 in August 2007. Mark's journey in the news business actually began as a paper carrier for The Cleveland Press and then The Plain Dealer. He is an award winning journalist with a BA in Communications from Cleveland State University. In college, he earned 100% of his college expenses and made the Dean's list. Contact Mr. Mark Spain, Action News Jacksonville, 11700 Central Parkway #2, Jacksonville, Florida 32224 Phone: (904) 996-0400 E-mail: mspain@Actionnewsjax.com Website: www.actionnewsjax.com

Fanchon Stinger Evening news co-anchor for Fox 59 News in Indianapolis. She currently anchors the 4pm and 10 pm newscasts. Before joining Fox 59 News, Stinger was a news anchor and reporter for 11 years in Detroit, Michigan where she was born and raised. She co-anchored FOX 2 News Morning weekdays. Stinger was an investigative reporter in the FOX 2 Problem Solver unit and the editor of "Gen Next Honor Roll," a special news feature that profiles outstanding young people. Fanchon Stinger has won eleven Emmy awards from the National Academy of Television Arts and Sciences: The Associated Press-Michigan named Stinger Best Reporter in 2000. She also was the Society of Professional Journalists finalist for Young Journalist of the Year 2002; The United States Department of Health and Human Services awarded Stinger its highest honor, the Inspector General's Integrity Award. Education: Graduated from the University of Michigan with honors, completing a dual Bachelor's degree in English and communications. Fanchon Stinger, WXIN-TV, 6910 Network Place, Indianapolis, Indiana 46278 Phone: (317) 632-5900 E-mail: **fstinger@fox59.com** Website: **www.fox59.com**

Kent St. John General Assignment Reporter, Backup Anchor. A lifelong resident of New Jersey and veteran newsman, St. John is chief of the NJN News South Jersey bureau. His dedication to his work has earned an Emmy Award nomination. St. John is a key member of the NJN News team which earned the 1996 Mid-Atlantic Emmy Award for best news program from the Philadelphia chapter of the National Academy of Television Arts and Sciences. He also worked as the New Jersey Bureau Chief and editorial columnist for the Philadelphia Sunday Press. He worked on the air at WWSJ-AM in Camden, WMBV-FM in Vineland; and NBS Radio in Philadelphia. He is a graduate of Rutgers University, New Brunswick. Mr. Kent St. John, NJN News, 50 Park Place, Newark, New Jersey 07102 Phone: (609) 652- 8385 Fax: (609) 652-1629 E-mail: **kstjohn@njn.org** Website: **www.njn.net**

Maggie Wade A native of Crystal Springs, Mississippi, Maggie Wade works as weekend weather anchor, news reporter, coordinator and producer of children's programming, and now serves as 4, 4:30, 5, and 10 p.m. news co-anchor and covers stories on education, children's issues and anything else that might pop up. She has received more than 500 awards, including being recognized by the United States Congress in September, 2001, for her work on Wednesday's Child, a segment featuring foster children in the state in need of permanent homes. Maggie is an adjunct professor at Belhaven College in Jackson. Maggie Wade, WLBT-TV3, Post Box 1712, Jackson, Mississippi 39215 Phone: (601) 948-3333 E-mail: **maggie@wlbt.net** Website: **www.wlbt.net**

Bernard Watson CBS Atlanta reporter since December, 2009. An Emory University Graduate, Bernard started his journalist career as a reporter at the Atlanta Journal Constitution. While working for the AJC, he also hosted a TV talk show in Smyrna, Georgia. A year later, Bernard was hired as a Video Journalist by CNN. Then he decided to go back to school and he earned a Masters Degree in Journalism from Northwestern University. An award-winning journalist, Bernard has worked as a reporter /anchor at TV stations in Charlottesville, Virginia, Las Vegas, Nevada, Phoenix Arizona, Atlanta, Memphis, Tennessee and Cincinnati, Ohio. Bernard is a member of Kappa Alpha Psi Fraternity, Inc., as well as the National Association of Black Journalists. Bernard Watson, CBS Atlanta, 425 14th Street NW, Atlanta, Georgia 30318 Phone: (404) 325-4646 Fax: (404) 327-3004 E-mail: **Bernard.Watson@cbsatlanta.com** Website: **www.cbsatlanta.com**

Tiffany Westry A reporter at CBS 42 since 2009, and native of Mobile, Alabama, Tiffany attended the University of Montevallo where she received a bachelor's degree in Mass Communication. Tiffany Westry, WIAT-TV CBS 42, 2075 Golden Crest Drive, Birmingham, Alabama 35209 Phone: (205) 322-4200 Fax: (205) 320-2713 Website: **www.cbs42.com**

Derrick Wilkerson General assignment news reporter for Fox 59 News, Derrick earned a degree from the University of Evansville in Radio/TV Communications. Before joining Fox 59 he worked for WTVW TV and WFIE TV in Evansville, Indiana. He also worked for WHP-TV in Harrisburg, Pennsylvania. He has helped Fox 59 News win two Emmy Awards for news magazine shows. He has received several awards from the Society of Professional Journalists. In 2008, his report on "Hot Kids" earned 1st place from the Indiana Chapter of the Society of Professional Journalists. His crime reports have been recognized by the Indiana Judges Association. He has also received the President's Award from Indiana Black Expo and an education reporter award from the Indianapolis Education Association. He is also cofounder of a nonprofit youth sports education organization called Pike Junior Red Devils Inc., where he is the General Manager and defensive backs coach for the Junior Red Devils football team. Derrick Wilkerson, WXIN-TV, 6910 Network Place, Indianapolis, Indiana 46278 Phone: (317) 687-6555 E-mail: **dwilkerson@tribune.com** Website: **www.fox59.com**

JaQuitta Williams Joined CBS Atlanta News in July 2010 as an anchor and reporter. She anchors the 4 p.m. and 6 p.m. newscasts. Before joining CBS Atlanta News, she spent four years as an anchor and reporter at WSB-TV. JaQuitta came to Atlanta after serving as a morning anchor and reporter at KSHB-TV/NBC Action News in Kansas City, Missouri. JaQuitta's career in TV news spans nearly 20 years and has included anchoring, reporting, producing and writing. JaQuitta has been featured on CNN Newsroom with Kyra Phillips, and CNN's "Your Bottom Line," hosted by Gerri Willis, along with CNN Newsroom with Fredricka Whitfield. In addition to her extensive experience in television news, JaQuitta co-hosted Magic 107.5's radio show called "Women's Wednesday" and was an actress and singer in Director Robert Townsend's "Musical Theatre of Hope" which aired on the Gospel Music Channel in 2009. Jaquitta Williams, CBS Atlanta, 425 14th Street NW, Atlanta, Georgia 30318 Phone: (404) 325-4646 Fax: (404) 327-3004 E-mail: **jaquitta.williams@cbsatlanta.com** Website: **www.cbsatlanta.com**

Paul Williams Double graduate from Jackson State University, where he received his first degree in Mass Communications with a minor in Biology/Chemistry, which he earned in 1989. His second degree was earned in Meteorology with a minor in Physics/Advanced Math. He earned the American Meteorological Society Television Seal of Approval while working with an NBC affiliate in St. Louis, Missouri. During his previous working tour at WLBT, Paul was part of the award-winning 30-minute special, "Without Warning," a report on the tornadoes that pounded Rankin County. The program won several awards and nominations for special projects and spot news which occurred in November, 1992. In 1993, Paul left WLBT for a larger market opportunity in St. Louis, at KSDK-TV and was recruited by WTIC-TV in Hartford, Connecticut, to serve as their Chief Meteorologist for the award winning FOX affiliate. Paul also serves as the chief meteorologist for Oldies 105.9 FM radio station, WOAD AM gospel station, WSSI Country, WKXI (KIXIE 107) and 99Jams FM. Contact Mr. Paul Williams, WLBT-TV3, Post Box 1712, Jackson, Mississippi 39215 Phone: (601) 948-3333 E-mail: **paul@wlbt.net** Website: **www.wlbt.net**

TV Talk Shows

America's Black Forum Created twenty-eight years ago ABF presents insightful and balanced debate on current and critical issues with top newsmakers from around the world. Tavis Smiley, host. Contact Ms. Nikki Webber, Director of Talent, TVOne, 1010 Wayne Avenue, 10th Floor, Silver Spring, Maryland 20910 Phone: (301) 755-0400 E-mail: nwebber@tv-one.tv Website: www.tv-one.tv

Black Accent on LA "For Members Only" TV The longest running locally produced African-American TV program in LA, 31 years running. Tom Reed, Host/Executive Producer. Black Accent on LA, Post Office Box 27487, Los Angeles, California 90027 Phone: (818) 894-8880

Black Enterprise Business Report Nationally Syndicated Business & Personal Finance TV Series hosted by Caroline Clarke. The show highlights success secrets of movers and shakers, from the most powerful Blacks in Corporate America to CEOs of the nation's largest Black-owned businesses. It is the only syndicated television program providing viewers with relevant and up-to-date information about the minority business world, with a focus on financial and personal empowerment. Show airs weekly, on Saturday in most markets. Nationally syndicated, reaching over 91% of African American households in 103 markets. Half-hour program, shot on-location around the country using a magazine style approach. Mr. Don Jackson, Central City Productions, Inc., 212 E. Ohio, Suite 300, Chicago, Illinois 60611 Phone: (312) 654-1100 Fax: (312) 654-0368 E-mail: info@ccptv.com Website: www.ccptv.com

Caribbeanwomentoday A segment on Caribbean Weekly; an informational and community affairs program produced by the Duke of Earle Media Group (Florida/Jamaica) and hosted by Dr. Anita Davis-DeFoe, author of A Woman's Guide to Soulful Living and resident advice guru for She-Caribbean, a St. Lucian magazine that is sold in 20 islands, New York, Atlanta, South Florida, Ghana, London, Germany and Italy. Contact Dr. Anita Davis-Defoe, The Defoe Group, Post Office Box 451973, Sunrise, Florida 33345 Phone: (954) 816-9462 E-mail: dranitadavisdefoe@hotmail.com Website: www.dranitadavisdefoe.com

Colours TV Multicultural television network production of Black Star Communications (BSC), an African American owned, non-profit corporation formed for civic, charitable, and educational purposes. Ms. Tracy Jenkins Winchester, President. Art Thomas, Vice President. Contact Colours TV, 200 Quebec Street, Building 600, Suite 209, Denver, Colorado 80230 Phone: (303) 326-0088 Fax: (303) 326-0087 E-Mail: info@colourstv.org Website: www.colourstv.org

Delta Renaissance The cultural arts show of the Mississippi Delta. Weekly talk show hosted by author, C. Sade Turnipseed focusing on Mississippi artists and historic preservation efforts underway throughout the region. Contact Ms. C. Sade Turnipseed, KHAFRE, Inc., Post Office Box 4221, Greenville, Mississippi 38704 Phone: (662) 773-2048 Fax: (662) 887-2900 E-mail: DeltaRenaissance@aol.com Website: www.deltarenaissance.com

Distortion 2 Static (D2S) The D2S crew makes it a point to interview both the best in Bay Area Hip Hop, as well as out-of-town artists visiting the Bay on KOFY TV Channel 13. Host, Mac Mall, aka "the Mac-nificent." Distortion 2 Static, 570 Beale Street Suite 204, San Francisco, California 94107 E-mail: **holla@distortion2static.com** Website: **www.distortion2static.com**

Express Yourself Literary Café Cable TV show hosted by Dr. Rosie Milligan, founder and director of "Black Writers on Tour." Contact Dr. Rosie, Milligan Books, 1425 West Manchester Avenue, Suite C, Los Angeles, California 90047 Phone: (323) 750-3592 Fax: (323) 750-2886 E-mail: **DrRosie@aol.com** Website: **www.drrosie.com**

In the Corner TV show features the hottest music videos and celebrity interviews in Atlanta. Carleen Brown, station manager. CAU-TV, Clark Atlanta University, 111 James P. Brawley Drive, South West, Atlanta, Georgia 30314 Phone: (404) 880-6230 Website: **www.cautv.com**

Making It! Minority Success Stories A weekly television program that focuses on minority entrepreneurs hosted by award winning journalist Nelson Davis. Contact Nelson Davis, Making It!, 5800 Sunset Boulevard, Los Angeles, California 90028 Phone: (323) 460-5253 E-mail: **info@makingittv.com** Website: **www.makingittv.com**

News 25 Today Central Illinois' first and highest rated morning news show. Interviews guest. Garry Moore. Gary Moore, WEEK-TV, 2907 Springfield Road, East Peoria, Illinois 61611 Phone: (309) 698-2525 E-mail: **gmoore@week.com** Website: **www.week.com**

Our World with Black Enterprise A weekly lifestyle program that features compelling and exclusive headline interviews, groundbreaking discussions, celebrity profiles, and commentary on the issues affecting today's African American community hosted by Dr. Marc Lamont Hill. Weekly, Sundays, in most markets. Half-hour program with informative headline interviews, groundbreaking discussions, and celebrity profiles filmed in the studio and on-locations across the country. Nationally syndicated, reaching 94% of Black households in 127 markets, on 156 stations, with a 1.7 Rating for Black Households. Mr. Don Jackson, Central City Productions, Inc., 212 E. Ohio, Suite 300, Chicago, Illinois 60611 Phone: (312) 654-1100 Fax: (312) 654-0368 E-mail: **info@ccptv.com** Website: **www.ccptv.com**

Perspective A weekly news affairs program hosted by Monique Caradine. Show airs Sundays on FOX affiliate WPWR My50Chicago.com. Monique is also host of her own radio show that airs on WVON 1450AM in Chicagok, Illinos. She has been featured in the Chicago Tribune, the Chicago Sun-Times, The Chicago Defender, N'DIGO and a variety of other local and national media outlets. These days, Monique loves producing top quality television and radio programs and providing media coaching to high-achieving women executives and entrepreneurs around the world. Contact Ms. Monique Caradine, WVON 1450AM, 3350 South Kedzie, Chicago, Illinois 60623 Phone: (708) 720-4252 Fax: (708) 283-6376 E-mail: **media@momentum-media.tv** Website: **www.wvon.com**

Platinum Plus TV Hip Hop driven talk show featuring local young up and coming artists due to air on FOX 54 network in October. Platinum Plus Productions, 301 Converse Court Columbus, Georgia 31907 Phone: (706) 687-4581

Poetree-N-Motion Community events, book reviews, and guests. Host, Dee Freeman. Airs in Lansing, Michigan on Comcast Cable Channel 16, and East Lansing, Michigan, Channel 30 WELM. Dee Freeman, 1127 Alexandria Drive, Lansing, Michigan 48917 Phone: (517) 321-3122 Fax: (517) 321-3122 E-mail: deekfreeman@yahoo.com Website: www.deepoette.com

Sayword An entertainment television show hosted by Carla Rowser Canty. Poets, musicians, public speakers, authors, etc., are encouraged to showcase. Contact Ms. Carla Rowser Canty, A Blackgurl Production, Post Office Box 843, Hartford, Connecticut 06143 Phone: (860) 983-3257 E-mail: BlackGurrl@aol.com Website: www.wqtqfm.com/wqtq

Straight Talk Hosted by President and CEO, W. L. Lillard. Show airs on channel 25. Star Planet Television Network, 8658 South Cottage Grove Avenue, Chicago, Illinois 60619 Phone: (773) 483-7788 E-mail: tianna@starplanettv.com Website: www.starplanettv.com

Tell Me More Host, Michel Martin. National Public Radio (NPR), 635 Massachuetts Avenue, North West, Washington DC 2001   Phone: 202) 513-3232 Fax: (202) 513-3329 Website: www.npr.org

Tony Brown's Journal The longest running show on PBS, hosted by Tony Brown.   Guests. Tony Brown Productions, 2214 Frederick Douglass Boulevard, Suite 124, New York, New York 10026 Phone: (212) 694-4800 E-mail: mail@tbol.net Website: www.tonybrown.com

TV One on One Host, Cathy Hughes interviews the most influential African American from business leaders, to entertainment gurus to spectacular athletes. Contact Nikki Webber, Director of Talent, TVOne, 1010 Wayne Avenue, 10th Floor, Silver Spring, Maryland 20910 Phone: (301) 755-0400 E-mail: nwebber@tv-one.tv Website: www.tv-one.tv

UDC Books African American writers and books. Cheryl Lewis Hawkins, host. UDCBooks, Cable TV 19, University of the District of Columbia, 4200 Connecticut Avenue, North West, Building 41, Room 203, Washington, DC 20008 Phone: (202) 274-5300 Fax: (202) 274-5999 E-mail: chawkins@udc.edu Website: www.udc.edu

Wordz in Motion TV Literary and Entertainment TV on WHPR TV 33 and Comcast Cable 20 and 71. Contact Dynasty Publications Inc, Post Office Box 35274, Detroit, Michigan 48235 Phone: (248) 763-2254 E-mail: metrodetroitliterarycollective@mllbnetwork.com Website: www.dynastypublications.net

Wright Place™ TV Show Dr. Letitia S. Wright, D.C, host. The only business lifestyle show for women, seen on Southern California Network Television KVMD. Dr. Letitia S. Wright, The Wright Place™ TV Show, 8300 Utica Avenue, 3rd Floor, Rancho Cucamonga, California 91730 E-mail: info@wrightplacetv.com Website: www.wrightplacetv.com

The Writer's Network Cable television program celebrating 27 years. Mr. C.D. Grant, host. Show interviews contemporary writers, publishers, artists, and musicians. Contact The Writer's Network, Post Office Box 437, Bronx, New York 10467 Phone: (914) 282-5747 E-mail: blindbeggar1@juno.com Website: www.blindbeggarpress.org

James Tatum
Composer * Musician

Award winning pianist, composer, educator and director of the James Tatum Trio Plus, James Tatum is one of America's leading jazz musicians. His remarkable virtuosity and musicianship have placed him among the most outstanding keyboard artists of this generation. Tatum is a former Detroit School's High School Fine Arts Department Head and has been honored by the Black Jazz Music Caucus of the National Association of Jazz Educators for his outstanding contributions to jazz in education. Named Musician of the Year by the State of Michigan in 1990, he has been recognized by the Michigan Senate and the U.S. House of Representatives for his efforts to make jazz a national American treasure. He has been awarded keys to several cities throughout the United States. His Trio Plus is a regular performer at the Detroit Montreaux Jazz Festival.

In 1987, Tatum and a coalition of concerned educators and civic leaders founded the James Tatum Foundation For the Arts, Inc., a non-profit organization dedicated to serving the needs of artistic youth. The Foundation awards scholarships to deserving talented youth to assist their arts studies beyond high school. The Foundation's primary fundraiser is the presentation of music from Tatum's original composition, *The Contemporary Jazz Mass*, performed annually at Detroit Orchestra Hall, Detroit, Michigan.

James Tatum also presents a unique lecture program designed to enhance music appreciation in the educational setting with special emphasis on jazz music, one of America's richest forms of cultural heritage. His jazz lecture seminar/performance covers such topics as *Jaxx-What Is It?, The History of Jazz, Jazz Artists and Their Styles, and Listening To Jazz Throughout Its History.* The series is designed to encourage audience participation throughout the lecture and appeals to audiences in K-12 and university and adult level.

Voice-Over Artists

KD Bowe Known nation wide for his comedic, witty, and sometimes controversial radio show, KD's rich baritone voice has been used on hundreds of commercials, and as the signature voice for radio and TV stations both nationally and abroad. He's been featured on several artists' recording projects and has even recorded his own single that gained national airplay. A recipient of the 1998 Trailblazer Award for excellence in the arena of mass media. KD Bowe, KDYA, Gospel 1190 AM The Light, 3260 Blume Drive, Suite 520, Richmond, California 94806 Phone: (510) 222-4242 Fax: (510) 262-9054 E-mail: kdbowe@kdbowemorningshow.com Website: www.gospel1190.net

Jackie Campbell Air personality, originally from Detroit, Jackie Campbell graduated from Wayne State University with a degree specializing in Radio and Television. She does voice-overs, and can be heard on several public TV affiliates and various radio stations across the United States. Contact Ms. Jackie Campbell, KDYA, Gospel 1190 AM The Light, 3260 Blume Drive, Suite 520, Richmond, California 94806 Phone: (510) 222-4242 Fax: (510) 262-9054 E-mail: jcampbell@sgnthelight.com Website: www.gospel1190.net

Vivi Monroe Congress Author of The Bankrupt Spirit Principles for Turning Setbacks into Comebacks, and the newly released, Manna for Mamma: Wisdom for Women in the Wilderness, she hold a Bachelor of Arts in Human Relations, a Master of Theological Studies and a Doctor of Ministry degree in Christan Counseling. Creatively couples her formal training in psychology, dance, voice-over and modeling. Vivi Monroe Congress, Post Office Box 540741, Grand Prairie, Texas 75054 E-mail: littlelightprod@aol.com Website: http://www.myspace.com/drvivi

Vanessa Cooper A well known broadcaster on WBAI since November of 1997, Vanessa, "V'luv" as she's affectionately referred to is best known as a Voice-Over Artist, Jazz Disc Jockey, Radio and TV Talk Show host. She attended Syracuse University. Contact Ms. Vanessa Cooper, WBAI, 120 Wall Street, 10th Floor, New York, New York 10005 Phone: (212) 209-2913 E-mail: TheRadioGoddess@gmail.com Website: www.wbai.org

Dane Reid Professional voice talent and author known nationally and internationally for his voice over work which can be heard on radio, television, Internet, corporate videos and more. Owns a media production company that covers radio production, TV voice over, children's books and audio books. Dane Reid Media, Post Office Box 640055, Atlanta, Georgia 30364 Phone: (404) 822-7107 E-mail: DR@DaneReidMedia.com Website: www.KidsReid.com

Mary T. Sala A Master of Fine Arts with over 20 years experience teaching on the university level, Mary is a Certified Voice, Speech and Movement trainer, professional actor, VO artist, voice, speech and awareness coach, poet, author, wife and working mom. Mary T. Sala, Living at Flashpoint, 735 Los Angeles Avenue, Monrovia, California 91016 Phone: (818) 618-5921 Fax: (626) 599-8337 E-mail: marytsala@yahoo.com Website: www.atflashpoint247.com

Rodney Saulsberry This Detroit native and University of Michigan Graduates' distinctive announcers voice is literally everywhere. His voice promoted the ABC critically acclaimed Charlie Brown Christmas Special in 2007, announced the 34th NAACP Image Awards and the Essence Awards specials on FOX Television, the Grammy Awards and the Country Music Awards for CBS. He is the voice of Joe Robbie Robertson on the hit cartoon series Spider-Man and James Rhodey Rhodes in the new animated feature film, The Invincible Iron Man. Rodney Saulsberry, Post Office Box 1735, Agoura Hills, California 91376 Phone: (818) 207-2682 E-mail: rodtalks@aol.com Website: www.rodneysaulsberry.com

Troy Smauldon Voice-over artist. Experience: actor, voice-over artist for Christian based-theme, films, ect. Contact Mr. Troy Smauldon, 44201 Bayview Avenue, # 41206, Clinton Township, Michigan 48038 Phone: (586) 260-8915 E-mail: troyboywonder@msn.com

TKO Productions Specializes in voiceovers and copywriting. Originated by former female production director, T.K. Jones. Contact TKO Productions, 2637 G Suffolk Avenue, High Point, North Carolina 27265 Phone: (843) 437-6009 E-mail: info@tko-productions.com Website: www.tko-productions.com

Voice Addict Productions, LLC Voice-over imaging and commercial/promo production company: promos, commericials, trailers, and narrations. Contact Mr. Kevin Genus, Voice Addict Productions, 5670 Wilshire Boulevard, Los Angeles, California 90036 Phone: (732) 452-0320 E-mail: studio@kevingenus.com Website: www.kevingenus.com

Kevin Craig West Director, producer and actor working in film, television, radio and stage and also a member of The Barrow Group in NYC, Chair member of Upstate Independents and in addition to being a Voice Acting Teacher and Producer for Voice Coaches, he also works as a Teacher/Artist with Symphony Space. Kevin West, MoBetta Films, Post Office Box 484, Troy, New York 12181 E-mail: contact@kevincraigwest.com Website: www.kevincraigwest.com

Web Designers

Artic Designs, Inc. Web design and hosting company. Contact Mr. Arthur Huntley, Artic Designs, Inc., Post Office Box 44191, Atlanta, Georgia 30336 Phone: (404) 213-4991 E-mail: info@articdesigns.com Website: www.articdesigns.com

Association of African American Web Designers Directory An index of black professional web developers located throughout the United States: graphic designers, programmers, writers, system administrators, marketers, e-commerce, and other web professionals. AAWDD, Post Office Box 146, Malone, New York 12953 Website: www.africanamericanwebdesigners.com

Ronald Davis An award winning visual artist and graphic designer providing full artistic services for those needing quality web backgrounds, book and CD covers. Contact Mr. Ronald Davis, Upfromsumdirt, Post Office Box 3861, Midway, Kentucky 40347 Phone: (859) 433-1503 E-mail: upfromsumdirt@yahoo.com Website: www.mythiumlitmag.com

Designs4U Web design and development, hosting. Ms. Kinya McDowell, Owner, Designs4U, Chicago, Illinois 60649 Phone: (312) 699-9277 Website: www.designs4u.net

Designing Vision A Christian based professional graphic and web design services company. Contact Designing Vision, 904 Kostner Avenue, Matteson, Illinois 60443 Phone: (708) 747-9733 E-mail: info@designingvision.com Website: www.designingvision.com

Freeman Multimedia, Inc. Founded in 2004 by CEO, Jamain Freeman. Geared towards helping the small to large sized business model develop branding through facets of media including: website development, graphic design, video production and multimedia presence. Freeman Multimedia, Inc., 111 Lodestone Drive, Durham, North Carolina 27703 Phone: (919) 696-8066 E-mail: info@freemanmultimedia.com Website: www.freemanmultimedia.com

Fruitful Works, Inc. Dedicated to providing professional high-quality web services to small businesses, gospel recording artists, and Christian churches at a reasonable cost. FruitfulWorks, Inc., Historic Masonic Temple, 500 Temple Avenue Suite #600M, Detroit, Michigan 48201 Phone: (313) 833-3555 E-mail: editor@detroitgospel.com Website: www.fruitfulworks.com

Future Network Productions Television, video and web design services. Lewis, FNP, 400 West 153rd Street, Suite 2C, New York, New York 10031 Phone: (646) 548-9501 E-mail: darlenereneelewis@yahoo.com Website: www.FutureNetworkProductions.com

Images & Illuminations Offers extensive print design services including design, editing, writing, illustration and photography, book design, logos, brochures, and posters. Images & Illuminations, 214 Sixth Avenue, Suite 3B, Brooklyn, New York 11215 Phone: (718) 783-0131 E-mail: info@imagesandilluminations.com Website: www.imagesandilluminations.com

Overjoy Creations Web Design   Web development since, 2003.   Founded by Michelle Hammonds. Company dedicated to helping individuals and businesses create a presence on the web. Overjoy Creations Web Design, Post Office Box 711117, Houston, Texas 77271 Phone: 713-723-2188 E-mail: info@overjoycreations.com Website: www.overjoycreations.com

PageTurner.net   Provides web site design, internet consulting services and website hosting. Ms. Pamela Walker-Williams, Pageturner.net, Post Office Box 120, 2951 Marina Bay Drive, #130, League City, Texas 77573 Phone: (866) 875-1044 E-mail: pwsquare@pageturner.net Website: www.pageturner.net

Patrick PJ Davis   Marketing and web solutions for authors, entertainers and publishing companies. Contact Patrick PJ Davis, Post Office Box 420725, Houston, Texas 77242   Phone: (713) 866-6548 E-mail: info@blackcottonworks.net Website: www.blackcottonworks.net

Derek Payne   Creative Art Director, graphic designer, website designer. He established DPI Graphic Design along with his older brother, also a graphic designer. Derek Payne, Trendsetters to Trendsetters Magazine, 3007 Panola Road, Suite 283C, Lithonia, Georgia 30038 Phone: (404) 437-4311 E-mail: dpi@trendtotrendmag.com Website: www.trendtotrendmag.com

Right Hand Concepts   Web designer. Founder, Vonetta Booker-Brown creates press releases, bios and media kits for artists and small businesses. Contact Ms. Vonetta Booker-Brown, Right Hand Concepts, 2020 Pennsylvania Avenue, North West, #341, Washington, DC 20006 E-mail: chiefelement@gmail.com Website: www.righthandconcepts.com

Ron Clowney Design   Founder, Ron Clowney offers both traditional art services in addition to computer graphics design work in the areas of print and animation.   Ron Clowney Design, 5513 Adode Falls Road, Unit 10, San Diego, California 92120 Phone: (619) 501-5740

Shilo Web Design   Monique Boea is the principal developer for Shilo and has over 8 years experience in designing Web sites for clients across the country. Contact Mr. Lee Thomas, President. Shilo Web Design, 619 East College Avenue, Suite C3, Decatur, Georgia 30030 E-mail: info@shilowebdesign.net Website: www.shilowebdesign.net

Web Sites

Reader's Sites:

African American Literature Book Club	www.aalbc.com
A Place of Our Own (APOOO)	www.apooobooks.com
Black Book Plus	www.blackbookplus.com
The Black Library	www.theblacklibrary.com
Black Expressions	www.blackexpressions.com
Book Remarks	www.book-remarks.com
CushCity	www.cushcity.com
Escapade Book Club	www.escapadebookclub.com
The G.R.I.T.S. Reading Group	www.thegrits.com
Hueman Bookstore On-line	www.huemanbookstore.com
R.A.W. Sistaz Reading Group	www.Rawsistaz.com
The Romer Review	www.theromerreview.com
Thumperscorner.com	www.thumperscorner.com

Romance Sites:

Heartrate Reviews	www.heartratereviews.com
Romance in Color	www.romanceincolor.com
The Romance Reader's Connection	www.theromancereadersconnection.com

Writer's Sites:

BAPWD	www.bapwd.com
Black Film	www.blackfilm.com
Black Press Foundation	www.blackpress.org
Black Talent News	www.blackwriters.org
Black Writer's Alliance	www.blacktalentnews.com
The Hurston/Wright Foundation	www.hurstonwright.org
Motown Writers Network	www.motownwriters.wordpress.com
Top Cat Live	www.topcatlive.com

Web Groups: (@Yahoo.com)

African American Female Playwrights

African American Media Club

African American Women in Cinema

Black Ink

Black Theatre Productions

Blaque Magic Readers Book Club

Books Club 4 Boys

Brown Bag Entertainment

Ebony Book Luvers

Ebony Readers

Gather The Fire

Inside Urban Hollywood

BDPA Bookclub

Black Filmmakers

Black Filmakers and Crew

Black Film Talent

The Making Of A Bestseller

Mixed Minds Book Club

Pentouch News

RAWSISTAZ Review

Readers Cafe

Romance Announce

Romance Noire Book Club

SistatoSista Literary Reading Group

Index

Index

Profiles